T0322424

Praise for *A Desperate Business*

A Desperate Business is a brilliant piece of investigative journalism and a true crime masterpiece. Farquhar's book is forensically researched, his storytelling propulsive and gripping. In his re-examination of the case, he tries to provide answers to lingering questions, chiefly: where was Muriel McKay's body hidden? This might be a 50-year-old landmark case, but the themes still resonate today: a police force struggling to crack the case, a salivating Press and a female victim cruelly used as a pawn in a tawdry circulation war.

Jeremy Craddock,
author of *The Jigsaw Murders*

This is utterly gripping from the first page, and the complex and delicate subject matter is handled deftly and sensitively. It is an extraordinary feat of research too, but what is perhaps most impressive is how the book straddles the genres of true crime and social history. As well as shining new light on what remains a compelling mystery (and one which seemed destined to remain in the shadows), Simon Farquhar evokes a Britain that is distinctly familiar even as it rapidly slips into the rear-view mirror. *A Desperate Business* is the sort of book that I read with delight combined with a tinge of envy at how good it is.

Daniel Smith,
author of *The Peer and the Gangster*

It was a case I had wondered about researching myself with a view to writing a book, but I'm very glad that I didn't, because Simon Farquhar was clearly the person for the task. The case itself is unremittingly harrowing, complex and frustrating, not least because the much-loved Muriel McKay remains unfound. Nonetheless, Simon succeeds brilliantly (and with real empathy for all concerned) in setting the story in its historical, social and emotional context, with the victim and her family always at the heart of his writing. I hope one day he will be called upon to write a new epilogue, when Muriel McKay is laid to rest, but until then for anyone interested in the case and in that period of British history too, which is brought vividly to life, *A Desperate Business* is an absolute must-read.

Carol Ann Lee,
bestselling author of *The Murders at White House Farm*

A Desperate
Business

A Desperate Business

Business

The Murder of Muriel McKay

Simon Farquhar

With special thanks to the McKay family for the use of photographs.

Every effort has been made to identify copyright holders and obtain their permission for the use of copyright material. If any omissions have occurred, please get in touch with the publisher for corrections to be made in future reprints and editions.

First published 2022

The History Press
97 St George's Place, Cheltenham,
Gloucestershire, GL50 3QB
www.thehistorypress.co.uk

British Library Cataloguing in Publication Data.
A catalogue record for this book is available from the British Library.

ISBN 978 0 7509 9723 2

Typesetting and origination by The History Press
Printed and bound in Great Britain by TJ Books Limited, Padstow, Cornwall.

Trees for Life

For my Mum

and in memory of
Muriel Frieda McKay

CONTENTS

PREFACE

My introduction to this dreadful story came through my father, a dedicated police officer, a fine detective and a very great man. When I was a teenager, he became newsworthy for having secured a conviction for murder without a body being found, in an appalling case of a teenage girl who had been abused and ultimately murdered by her stepfather. While securing a conviction for murder without a body was not unique, it was unusual, and it naturally evoked memories of the tragedy of Muriel McKay, which had taken place sixteen years earlier. I was inspired to ask him about it, and he told me the brief facts of a case which remains both heartbreaking and mystifying.

Sometime later, I read the concise account of the case in Gordon Honeycombe's *Murders of the Black Museum*. Who can say why one story will possess or obsess a person, but even today I can still see, beyond this sea of research, those early images that my mind created of this case: the dark, wintry countryside on the Hertfordshire–Essex border (an area that I knew well and close to where I grew up); that spartan farmhouse; the isolated telephone boxes from which those dreadful calls were made, some eerily cold, some brutally hot-tempered; and, above all, the image of an adored woman, reading the newspaper on a December evening, the warmth of the fire inside, the promise of snow outside, whose life was turned in an instant from comfort to horror.

In the decades since first becoming acquainted with the case, it continually tugged at me that while Nizamodeen Hosein was still alive, while many of those involved in the case were still alive, there was surely some hope of finding some answers. Half a century on, it felt, at the very least, a duty to history to capture what I could. I imagined someone twenty years in the future questioning why no one had revisited the case while there were still living witnesses and a living perpetrator, as crime historians now wish had been done in other cases that continue to perplex, from the Rillington Place murders to the mystery of Jack the Ripper.

The opportunity finally presented itself when my comissioning editor, Mark Beynon, requested a follow-up to my book, *A Dangerous Place: The Story of the Railway Murders*. Since no book had been written on the McKay case for forty years – the ones that had been were all long out of print – and the case was now being mostly misrepresented in documentaries, magazines and blogs revelling in gruesome theories and showing scant regard for facts, I suggested a new study, only to find that another book had just been commissioned on the subject. That book was subsequently abandoned due to a lack of new information, but I too felt that it would be hard to justify a new book that merely regurgitated the established facts and assumptions.

However, when some of the long-closed police files were opened, the wealth of previously unpublished information held within them cast a powerful new light on the origins of the crime. This convinced me that there was a new story here that should be told. I also traced the current whereabouts of Nizamodeen Hosein, although it never felt a very real possibility that I would one day be able to put my questions to him.

I was extremely wary of approaching the McKay family, since they had made no public appearances in connection with the case since 1970 and I had no clue as to whether they were still searching for answers or had managed to lock their tragedy away. I decided that I would not pester them with my questions unless I could offer some answers to theirs.

There have been challenges along the way, not least the closure of archives and libraries during the coronavirus pandemic, and the navigation of the arcane world of Freedom of Information Act (FOI) requests. When Britain entered its first lockdown, with my research well under way, I decided to use that time while the National Archives were closed to visitors to submit a request for access to those files which remain closed until 2062. The request was refused, but to my horror, it also resulted in a decision to reclose all open files on the case. Although I had already had considerable use of them, it would have wrecked any hopes of this book being a comprehensive one.

Challenging the decision was a process that took months, and was mostly conducted by email, since I was told that the FOI assessors 'were not taking telephone enquiries during the pandemic'. Finally, with certain necessary redactions, I was granted access to the material that I needed, but the whole affair, and the current obstructions and contradictions that the McKay family are facing in their quest to have the remaining files on the case reopened, have left me firmly of the belief that while the principles of the FOI are commendable, on a practical level it is in desperate need of revision.

A puzzle set by fools can be harder to crack than one set by a genius. At the end of a three-year journey, during which time the case has also been revisited by the police and the world's media, I hope that this account – a personal journey through a dreadful history – offers new information, new insights and even, perhaps, a solution.

Throughout the text, generally only primary documents are quoted without caution. Nothing claimed by the Hosein brothers (including Adam) should be considered trustworthy by itself. I regret having to use the brothers' first names throughout, something necessitated by them sharing a surname but which inevitably risks softening the presentation of them.

This book travels back to a distant and very different Britain, populated by pubs that no longer survive and no longer could survive, pubs where farmers struck lunchtime cattle deals. It was a quaint age populated by people with occupations that also no longer survive, from buttonhole makers to bread roundsmen, but it was also a pre-#MeToo era of relentless sexual harassment, a dimension to the story that has not been previously explored.

Both Arthur and Nizamodeen Hosein have used racial prejudice as a smokescreen for their guilt, to elicit sympathy or to apportion blame. However, while race relations in Britain were in a sorrowful state at this time, they have little relevance to this story. I have found barely any evidence, among the statements of the residents of Stocking Pelham or the tailors of the East End, that racism was a factor of any significance to the murder of Muriel McKay.

This is not complacency, but a simple refusal to allow convicted murderers to control a narrative and to exploit one of society's most serious problems to their own advantage. The only consistent and wilful racism I could find in this story came from Arthur Hosein, whose clear antisemitism climaxed with his outrageous attack on the trial judge.

While modern Britain continues to struggle to combat racism, it has become sterner at monitoring the language that it uses. The past is often inconvenient, frequently embarrassing and sometimes shameful, but we cannot change it and we cannot destroy it. We can only try to understand it. Therefore, where necessary, the language of those times has been retained. While we may wince at the mislabelling of Indo-Trinidadians as 'Pakistani' and at the use of the term 'coloured' today (it was used readily by people of colour at this time), I hope that the reluctance to replace these terms retains historical accuracy without causing contemporary offence.

I have strived to keep Muriel McKay at the centre of this account. When combing the files, I discovered a bundle of postcards that were collected by the police to provide handwriting comparisons with the letters that were written by Muriel during her captivity. These postcards had been sent to her housekeeper, Mrs Nightingale, over a twelve-year period, the last one dating from just a few weeks before Muriel's abduction. While picture postcards will never be the most profound expression of a personality, they do provide a kind and sensitive impression of Muriel McKay, and quoting from them has allowed me to begin each chapter with her voice.

Above all others, my sincere thanks go to the McKay family, for their hospitality and warmth, and for placing their trust in me. I am also most grateful to The History Press, particularly my commissioning editor, Mark Beynon, for his devotion to this project from its very beginnings.

So many people gave up their time to assist in my research, and I extend my deepest thanks to Walter Whyte, Roger Street, Peter Rimmer, Des Hiller, Paul Dockley, Brian Roberts, Peter Miller, Roy Herridge, Paul Bickley, Ewan and Nicky Gilmour, Chloe Baveystock, Aubrey Rose, Professor Patricia Wiltshire, Freida Hosein, Yasmin Strube, Sharly Hughes, Martin Rosenbaum, Jeff Edwards, Norie Miles, Matthew Gayle, Clive Stafford Smith, Jill Murray, Tom Mangold, Leela Ramdeen, Dr Dominic Watt, Don Jordan, David Cowler, William Stevens, David and Marion Ryan, Colin Parker, Tom May, Michelle Bowden and Holly Kennings of the Solicitors Regulation Authority, Sarah Nithsdale of HMP Wakefield, Abigail Leckebusch of the West Yorkshire Archive Service, Hertfordshire Archives and Local Studies Library, the Law Society, the Metropolitan Police, the Metropolitan Police History Society, the General Register Office, the office of Manor Park Cemetery and Crematorium, the staff of the British Library, especially Nicola Beech, the staff of the National Archives and Freedom of Information, Equity, Merton Heritage and Local Studies Centre, George Hardwick of Clacton Local History Society, Clacton Library, Andrew Frost of John Frost Newspapers, Luke O'Shea of the BBC Photo Library, Nicholas Mays of the News UK Archive, Hertfordshire Coroner Service, Andrew Wood of the

Telecommunications Heritage Group, Austin Graham of the Grosvenor Victoria Casino, Park View Care Home, and Lindsay Ould and the staff of the Museum of Croydon.

On a personal note, I thank Naomi Harvey, Andrew Conway, Mark Nickol, Nick Kirby, Keith Skinner, Lindsay Siviter, Ian Greaves, Chris Croucher, Sue Scott, David Wigram, Alex Paltos, Joey Langer, Tinamaria Fairbrass, Julie Peacock, Natalie Froome and Jules Porter, and finally, Suzy Robinson, Sarah David and Debra Sergeant for their unfailing enthusiasm and support.

Simon Farquhar
London
September 2022

A NOTE ON MONEY

Money – and the love of it – is a key ingredient of this story. The preposterousness of the £1 million ransom demanded by the Hoseins, compared with the everyday cost of living in 1969, may not be immediately apparent today, when far greater sums are regularly won on the National Lottery. At necessary points in the narrative, I have noted the amounts translated into today's money, taking into account that money has inflated at 1,554 per cent in Britain since 1969.[1]

The Bank of England's inflation calculator translates £1 million in 1969 as £17.5 million in 2022. However, this is an oversimplification of the amount in real terms. Attitudes to money, spending habits and the valuation of different items have changed in many ways over the last half-century. Food, clothes, appliances and holidays are more affordable today, while wages for men have remained reasonably steady and the costs of alcohol, housing and live entertainment have increased dramatically.

The average full-time (male) worker was paid £30 a week in 1969, an annual wage of £1,560, which is £24,050 in today's money, compared with the average full-time wage today of £31,834. However, the average house price was £4,312, a mere £71,333 in today's money, whereas the average house price today is £215,910. Conversely, a loaf of bread was three times more expensive then than it is today, most working-class people could not afford to holiday abroad and renting a colour television from Radio Rentals cost £1 a week, which amounts to £865 a year in today's terms.

What is perhaps most important to remember is that there was a much clearer financial divide in economic terms in Britain in 1969. Many items that were seen as luxuries then are affordable treats today, and there were far fewer opportunities then for extensive credit. People were more inclined to live within their means. Most people were paid in cash, and bank accounts were far from being essential.

Living above one's means in 1969 was a far more transgressive activity than it is considered today.

1

HOME

The first evening we had a dinner party out on the terrace for twelve (David's birthday). It was a lovely mild evening, no jackets needed. Dancing on the terrace until 2am.

Muriel McKay, Calader, Mallorca, 9 September 1969.

Christmas descends again, a season of enchantment and disillusion, anticipation and mourning, prettiness and sadness. I am standing outside St Mary House, on Arthur Road in Wimbledon village. It is approaching six o'clock in the evening. Across London, white winter sunshine is handing over to the night shift of headlights and fairy lights. It is almost precisely half a century since this fine, cherished house, in this safe and stately realm, which was then home to the McKay family, became a scene of atrocity and despair.

On 29 December 1969, sometime between 5.30 p.m. and 7.45 p.m., between driving her housekeeper home and her husband returning from work, Muriel Frieda McKay had her home invaded and her life devastated. She was never seen again. We will never know for certain the precise details of what happened that evening, nor the precise details of the torturous events which followed.

Christmas delivers prettiness and sadness, and so too, for the last fifty years, have the few photographs that the world has seen of Muriel McKay. Once images of happiness, they are now images of anguish. Happy photographs from carefree, happy times, like the carefree, happy words on picture postcards, develop a poignancy and a pathos when the lives that they remain souvenirs of are no more.

Like so many of the victims of extraordinary or infamous crimes, this blameless woman is remembered for her death and not for her life. Her name has been remembered more than that of many victims, since to a country that became obsessed with the story, she was a missing person, and the first victim of kidnapping-for-ransom in Britain since the Middle Ages, long before she was declared a victim of murder and her killers identified. Her name and her image endure because of the continuing, perplexing question of what exactly happened to her, and where her body may lie, and her story remains one of the most tragic and outlandish mysteries of modern criminal history.

Some months later, on a bright afternoon, I am making a return visit to Arthur Road, where the charming owners of St Mary House today have allowed me to visit the scene of modern Britain's first-ever kidnapping. As I walk up the hill to the village and away from the hurry-scurry of the station and the shops, life becomes noticeably quieter and more expensive. Two girls, meeting outside a pub for the first time since lockdown, joking that they are both still alive, greet each other with noisy delight, brimming with life and unmindful of the vicious tragedy that began nearby and which, for the McKay family, continues to this day.

Wimbledon village today is as charming as it was half a century ago, but considerably more costly. The shops that Muriel visited on her last afternoon of normality have long since regenerated, but still that attractive blend of locality and quality exists when one wanders the parade of butchers, boutiques and bistros. One is also struck by the diversity of the neighbourhood. This is a very different Britain to the one that so embittered Arthur Hosein – a Britain still far from perfect, a Britain not so naive and not so happy, but perhaps a Britain progressing.

After two years of studying newsreels, police files and press coverage, walking up the drive of St Mary House stirs a strange trepidation and déjà vu. It is always odd surveying a scene that one has been used to seeing on film. Unlike the world around it, the house has changed little since the days when it was immortalised in forensic photographs and tabloid splashes. The welcoming red-brick neo-Georgian home is set 10 yards back from the road and given partial privacy by a fence and hedgerow, though from the pavement one can clearly see the front porchway, as Mrs Mona Lillian could when she walked past on 29 December 1969 at 6 p.m. and saw a dark saloon parked in the drive while, inside, history was being made and lives destroyed.[1]

Inside, it is a happy, placid place, its owners blessed with good taste without ostentation. Pausing in the porchway, I wonder again just what did happen on that dreadful evening so long ago. Alick McKay arrived home to find that, uncharacteristically, the chain was off the porch door and the inner door had been forced open. A tangled band of Elastoplast lay on the hall table, and on the bureau immediately to the right of the door lay a brutal, rusted chopper, the telephone was upturned on the floor, its cord ripped from the wall and the smashed dial robbed of the paper disc containing the number, Wimbledon 01-946-2656.

Although where the story ended remains a mystery, how it began will also forever be uncertain. Why was the chain not on the outer door, when Muriel was always so particular about keeping it on when she was alone in the house? Peter Rimmer, one of the few surviving CID officers who worked on the case, reflects, 'This was always the great question. How did they get her away from the house and how did they gain entry?'[2]

The inner door had been forced by bodily pressure. Had Muriel refused to open it, or had she opened it and then panicked and tried to close it again? Was one of her kidnappers holding the Elastoplast, ready to silence her, only for it to self-adhere in the ensuing struggle? Just why was the chain off the outer door?

Despite its grim antecedents, this hallway hosts no ghosts today. This is still a happy home, the lemon colours outshining the sweet pastel shades that the McKays chose. Structurally it is virtually unchanged, and the mood of the place makes it obvious why the McKays adored this house and why they lived here for a dozen contented years, its bright spell not even broken when they were the victims of a burglary in September 1969.

The hallway opens on to the square living room, immediately recognisable as the scene of the television appeals in which Alick, flanked by his family, exhaustedly pleaded for his wife's abductors to contact him. Off the living room is the snug, the room where Muriel settled by the fire with a cup of tea, the evening newspaper and Carl, her beloved 7-year-old dachshund, in her last moments of comfort and joy. How someone can be nestled in the safety of their own home and then seconds later be snatched away and plunged into darkness remains, for me, the most persistent horror of this story. Yet today, again, this is a room with no sorrow, no echo of tragedy.

The kitchen – where Muriel sat having coffee with her housekeeper, Mrs Nightingale, just hours before her abduction, where the McKay daughters,

Dianne and Jennifer, catered for the constant police presence in the weeks following the kidnapping, and where Detective Sergeant Walter Whyte listened
in on the telephone extension early the following morning and transcribed
the first of the sinister calls from a man calling himself 'M3' – looks out on to
the wide, grassy garden, which was then tended to by Leslie Galashan every
Saturday and Sunday morning, for whom Muriel had made a warming cup
of tea the previous day. Off the kitchen, past a back staircase which would
once have led to the staff quarters, is the only corner of the house to have
undergone any structural alteration, with what was once the garage now converted into an extra room. The windows are barred, not because of the house's
history but because of another burglary some years ago, not that even these
would have saved Muriel's life.

I am curious as to whether potential buyers of a house with an unhappy
history are told about it before purchasing, and in this instance, they certainly
were not. Ewen Gilmour, the current owner, says:

> My wife and I bought the house in 1985 from the Baveystocks, who in turn
> had bought it from Alick McKay. A few months after moving in, a neigh-
> bour happened to ask if what had happened here bothered us at all. That was
> how we found out. I was pretty aware of the story, which was huge when I
> was at school, but as we didn't come from Wimbledon, for us it was history
> rather than anything personal. That said, memories in Wimbledon fifteen
> years on were still fairly fresh, and taxi drivers taking me home would often
> say: 'Is that *the* house?'[3]

Returning to the hall, we ascend the main staircase, down which the contents
of Muriel's handbag were once scattered, and at the end of the landing, I discover the master bedroom. The layout is identical to that in the crime scene
photographs, in which one also notices a Sunday colour supplement and a
handsome edition of *Shaw's Prefaces*, as well as a drawer left open, from which
Muriel's jewellery was snatched. Suddenly and overwhelmingly, for the first
time in this peaceful place, I feel the anticipated sense of intrusion and fear.

The impression of those cruel strangers invading this private space and wrest-
ing treasured jewellery from the drawer is a vivid one. But there is another, even
more persistent mood for one who stands here reliving this story. For it was in
this room, one cold January morning, that Detective Chief Superintendent Bill
Smith sat with a broken Alick McKay and told him that he would probably

never see his wife again, putting his arm around him as he cried. Two eminent men of an uncrying generation, one weeping, one comforting him.

On 4 December 1969, Alick McKay came out of a reluctant retirement, at the personal invitation of Rupert Murdoch, to begin working at Murdoch's newly acquired *News of the World* newspaper. The McKays saw ahead of them a Christmas with their children and grandchildren and a prosperous new year. Within three months, however, Alick McKay was gone from St Mary House, living alone in a small central London flat, his family fractured by tragedy and surrounded everywhere by the absence of his wife.

Although Muriel's death has been endlessly speculated on, hardly anything of the person she was or the life she lived has ever been set down. Even Norman Lucas's respectable account of the story, published a few months after the case was over, opened with a biography of Muriel's husband rather than of Muriel herself. However, while Muriel McKay devoted her life to being a wife and mother and did not have a professional career by which to record her achievements, that is no reason to allow her presence to drift from the centre of any account of her tragedy. She should be remembered for her life as much as for her death.

Graced with a kindly beauty, Muriel came into the world as Muriel Frieda Searcy. She was born into an Australian family with long-standing legal and seafaring connections on 4 February 1914, the youngest child of Charles and Freida Searcy, and was raised with her brother and three sisters in Durham Terrace, in the suburb of Cheltenham, Adelaide. Her father, an executive in the motor industry, was one of fourteen children born to Arthur Searcy, President of the Public Service, Deputy Commissioner of Taxes and Stamps, Controller of Harbours and President of the Marine Board of South Australia, after whom Searcy Bay in the Eyre Peninsula was named. Arthur's father, William, had been Chief Inspector of Police in South Australia and alongside his maritime achievements, Arthur was also a Justice of the Peace. Muriel inherited from her grandfather a talent for photography; to this day, William's vast archive of nearly 20,000 photographs, along with twenty volumes of reminiscences and 3 metres of scrapbooks, the Searcy Collection, can be viewed in the State Library of South Australia. His granddaughter was also a talented artist; when she was 12, Muriel passed Grade II Freehand Drawing at the South Australian School of Arts and Crafts.[4]

The Searcys' neighbours were a family named McKay, the children attending Sunday school with Muriel. Through them, she was introduced to their cousin, Alick. Like Muriel, he was tall, dark and handsome, and although five years her senior, and state educated, unlike her, their shared times at church and club dances led to love. In the forty years between their first meeting in 1929 and Muriel's disappearance in 1969, the couple were never apart.

When she was 14, Muriel was admired in the local press as a bridesmaid at the wedding of her sister, Doreen. She wore pink floral taffeta and georgette, early Victorian style, and carried a bouquet in lavender shades. She and her sister Helen wore tulle caps, trimmed with coloured sequins. The church was decorated by the congregation, among whom were Alick and his parents.[5]

She was remarked upon again two years later, dancing to a blues band at Kalleema Dance Club at the Maris Palais in Semaphore.[6] Statuesque, green-eyed and winsome, she was later described by her husband as 'the quietest, most charitable person'[7] and by her daughter, Dianne, as 'so gentle, so kind, lovely and hospitable, she could never see the bad in anyone'.[8] Family friend Lady Jodi Cudlipp, wife of Hugh Cudlipp, journalist and Chairman of the Mirror Group, called her 'a lovely woman. She was always a friendly, charming, good-looking, nice lady.'[9]

Upon leaving school, Muriel worked as a stenographer. Although she was offered an art scholarship, she opted for the expected role of wife and mother, though she never neglected her talents. As well as a number of tapestries, the product of her love for needlework, the house at Wimbledon was plentifully decorated with her paintings, both watercolours and still lifes in oils, and with her photography. On the day of her abduction, she told Mrs Nightingale that she had just enrolled in a new painting class. That night, when Alick arrived home, amid the puzzling wreckage, he found a smashed flashbulb in the porch, which had probably come from his wife's handbag, part of her photography kit.

Muriel became engaged to Alick when she was 18 and they married when she was 21 on 15 June 1935, at St Peter's Church, Glenelg.[10] Their first child, Jennifer Louise, was born two years later, followed by Dianne Muriel in 1940 and Ian Alexander in 1942.

Meanwhile, Alick's career was gathering pace. The fourth son of Captain George Hugh McKay and Agnes Fotheringham Miller, he was born at their home on Tapley Hill Road, near Port Adelaide, on 5 August 1909. His father was a master mariner for the Coast Steamship Company, later master of HMAS *Warrawee*. His expert handling of that ship on one occasion prompted passengers to write to the Coast Steamship Company, commending 'the skilful manner in which he handled the steamer and turned it around in the raging storm'.[11] Like the Searcy family, whom they had a long association with, the McKays were impressive members of the community, respected for generations of nautical expertise and for being key players in the development of coastal trade in the region.

Alick and his siblings, however, would ultimately excel in the corporate world, with interests in timber, tobacco and newspapers. Alick was educated first at Alberton School, then at 16 spent a year at Thebarton Technical School. Like his younger brother, Ralph, he was actually planning a career in dentistry, but his traineeship was cut short when his employer and tutor was killed in a road accident. This was a matter of months after the Wall Street Crash, the Great Depression swiftly spreading to Australia, where unemployment reached 30 per cent within two years.

Alick quickly found work in sales promotion for General Motors and briefly as a seaman. In 1932, while in Edithburgh aboard the *Warrawee*, his father collapsed and died. His body was brought home in the vessel which he had captained for fourteen years. Perhaps it was the loss of his father or his engagement to Muriel that ended his attempt at a maritime career, for soon after, Alick entered the world of newspapers.

His first post was as an advertising salesman for the *News*, an Adelaide daily owned by the News Limited group, his department managed by Muriel's brother, Arthur. The *News* was owned by Sir Keith Murdoch, whose recent knighthood was reward for his campaign against the Labor Prime Minister James Scullin, at the start of the Depression, and for his championing of Joseph Lyons and his newly formed breakaway party, the United Australia Party.

Although never on the editorial side of the industry, newspapers were where Alick excelled. By the end of the 1930s, he was a manager of the News Limited Group in Melbourne. His role expanded into managing Queensland Newspapers in Sydney until, after nearly two decades working for Sir Keith Murdoch, in 1951 he left the News Limited Group to become advertising director of the Melbourne *Argus*, four years later being appointed its general manager.

Rising production costs and fierce competition had led to the paper being acquired by Britain's Mirror Group in 1949, and a year into Alick's time there it became the first newspaper in the world to print colour photographs – a huge feat technologically but one which allowed it to burn brightly for only a short time; the colour printers were expensive and temperamental and occasionally led to the paper not being distributed until late in the morning. In January 1957, the *Argus* admitted defeat.

However, Alick's achievements there had impressed the board. They offered him the role of advertising director for the Mirror Group, which he accepted. A few months later, shortly after the death of Muriel's mother, Frieda,[*] the rest of the family arrived in London. 'My father had gone on ahead of us,' says Dianne, 'leaving my mother to sell the house and organise the move, as well as to get teenagers who were very happy in their lives to emigrate, and bless her, she did it all by herself, she was wonderful.'[12]

Muriel ingeniously devised a gentle strategy for acclimatising the children to the relocation, getting out a map of the world and creating a trip to excite them. The multi-stop flight from Australia alone was a considerable task in those days, but after arriving in San Francisco, she took them on a train down to Chicago, then to Montreal to visit friends, down the Hudson Valley to New York, and finally sailing on the *Queen Elizabeth* to Southampton, where Alick was waiting for them.

The emotional, geographical and educational upheaval was enormous, Jennifer having to leave Melbourne University without graduating and Dianne and Ian having to leave their schools mid-term, 14-year-old Ian moving from the illustrious Geelong Grammar School, where he boarded, first to lessons with a private tutor in London and then to an equivalent boarding school in England, with Dianne ultimately completing her education in Switzerland.

The following year, Alick joined the Mirror Group's board of directors, and the McKays moved from their first home in Campden Hill into St Mary House, at that time only a twenty-minute drive from Fleet Street. It is a horrid irony that Arthur Road bore the name not only of Muriel's beloved grandfather, from whom she inherited her artistic talents, and that of her brother, but of one of the men who destroyed her existence.

The *Daily Mirror* was in quite remarkable health at this time, reigned over by the megalomaniac Cecil Harmsworth King and his editor, Hugh Cudlipp, the youngest editor on Fleet Street, who helped to make it the biggest selling daily in the world. In 1963, King controlled over 300 publications, including periodicals, consumer and trade magazines, national newspapers and books, and grouped them all together as the International Publishing Company. He appointed Alick McKay as a director.

---

[*] Muriel's father died in 1964.

Alick was by now recognised as one of the most industrious and ebullient executives in Fleet Street. Jennifer McKay speaks adoringly of her father but also with a sense of marvel:

> He wasn't interested in money, although of course they had a nice life. He was just very good at his job. I remember once watching him at a reception, and he worked the room like the Queen Mother. He did not miss a single person and devoted a bit of his time to each of them, something so skilful and yet it seemed effortless.[13]

He was made a Commander of the Order of the British Empire in the 1965 Birthday Honours for his voluntary work chairing the Victoria Promotion Committee, a charity generating tourism and investment in that state. He was by now also a chairman of the Advertising Association, along with several other charitable and corporate bodies. In 1967, sales of the *Daily Mirror* peaked at over 5 million copies per day. The same year, he suffered a heart attack.

He had in fact already suffered a mild heart attack the previous year. While he had not inherited his father's devotion to the sea, he had clearly inherited his weak heart, and his health was worsened when, on a boat trip to Australia to recuperate, he fell against a bollard, an injury which developed into another thrombosis. Conscious of his father's sudden death, after thirty-seven years, having risen from hard-working salesman to decorated and celebrated executive, he made plans for his retirement from the IPC.

By now, the couple were alone at St Mary House and already grandparents to two boys and a girl. After joining the rest of the family in London and working at an advertising agency, Jennifer had moved to Sussex with her husband, Ian Burgess, a property developer and horse breeder. Living nearby were Dianne and her husband, David Dyer, a director of Wilkinson Sword, while Ian was in Melbourne, working in the marketing department of the Hamlyn Publishing Group, which had opened an Australian operation in 1964, shortly after being acquired by the IPC.

'They were a lovely family, very decent people,' says former Detective Sergeant Walter Whyte, 'despite whatever assumptions people might have made at that time about Australian newspaper folk.' Jennifer told me:

> My mother would talk to anyone. In those days, it was not uncommon for people to fly separately, and whenever my mother was on a flight by herself,

when you met her at the airport there was always some man carrying her bag for her, who had engaged her in conversation on the plane, and whom she would have kept at arm's length but yet completely charmed.[14]

A 'courageous man' was how *News of the World* editor Stafford Somerfield described Alick.[15]

Margery Nightingale, the McKays' housekeeper for twelve years and the last person to see Muriel before her abduction, had been widowed in 1964, after which the McKays had suggested that she move in with them, though she chose to stay at her home a mile away. She found Muriel a peaceable person, good at defusing her husband's occasional crotchetiness. Alick 'used to say, "I don't like this" or "I don't think so and so is right", but Mrs McKay did not answer him back or get into arguments'.[16]

A local police constable who would befriend the McKays after their burglary considered Alick 'a very straightforward man. He would never use four words where one would do. I suppose you could say he was a typical forthright Australian.'[17] He found Muriel to be:

> ... one of the nicest people I have ever met. A very personable woman, very pleasant. There was no side to her at all. Although she was a person who was obviously used to the good things in life, she was completely natural. She was a family woman in every sense of the word, I would say.[18]

Aubrey Rose, later a defence solicitor in the case, remembered Alick as 'a very fine man, a decent fellow. That was my impression of the whole family in fact.'[19] In an old-fashioned division of labour, while Alick was the breadwinner, Muriel was a great deal more besides being the homemaker. As well as her creative talents, she was on the committee of the local Wives' Fellowship and involved in charitable work to assist unmarried mothers by helping to establish a local nursery to provide childcare and allow them to work.[20]

The opinions of those close to Muriel which were gathered in the days immediately following her disappearance are particularly important in correcting some of the misrepresentations of her in previous accounts of the case, particularly claims that she was in fragile health or dependent on medication. Her GP, Dr Tadeus Markowicz, also a family friend, described her as a 'very young, lively woman, who used to occupy herself with painting and the household', had 'a very great enthusiasm for life', and was 'very stable and strong minded'.[21] Mentally and physically she was a 'very strong and stable woman', though one likely to be 'slightly more affected by shock than the average woman of her age'.[22]

Her dressmaker, Ellen Richards, considered her 'a level-headed woman, who was very much involved with her home and family, and I feel that her husband was the foremost thought in her mind, apart from her children, whom she was very close to'.[23] In the confusion of her disappearance, Dianne stated firmly that 'my mother adored her grandchildren. My father and mother were a very happy couple and I have never known any serious arguments between them. Mother was happy and looking forward to going to the Savoy with very close family and friends on New Year's Eve.'[24] In his first statement to the police, the day after her abduction, Alick declared, 'We have had a very happy life ... we have never been parted and my wife loved her home and family.'[25]

Two misfortunes which had befallen the family would prove to be of great significance to the investigation. The first was in 1963 when, during one of Britain's fiercest winters of the century, Muriel came downstairs early one morning to find that the family's two dachshund dogs had died of asphyxiation from a faulty boiler. As a result of this, the McKays were extremely scrupulous about dangers in the home, Muriel always putting a guard in front of the fire when leaving a room for more than a few minutes and sitting up into the night if necessary until a fire had burned out.

The second significant event was that the McKays were victims of a burglary on 30 September 1969. Muriel 'was most upset and that kept on for days after',[26] although the doctor later insisted that it was 'no more than any other woman would be in the circumstances'.[27]

One of a spate of similar break-ins in the neighbourhood at the time, the thieves gained entry via the back door and took £3,000 worth of silver, the television set and the radiogram, though no jewellery. At the trial, Alick said that Muriel 'always had a feeling that this was something they might come back for'.[28] It was kept in the top drawer of a chest in her bedroom, but from then on, whenever the couple were out for the evening, she would carry it with her in a small silk bag. 'It was not of great value, but it was of value to her.'

Six days after the burglary, Dr Markowicz treated her for suspected influenza and joint pain, but after a further day in bed, she was refreshed by the birthday of one of her grandchildren and drove down to Sussex to see him. It was a measure of the McKays' love of St Mary House that the burglary did not induce in them any thoughts of moving. Its only lasting and understandable legacy was a mild sense of paranoia. On several occasions Muriel told Mrs Nightingale that she thought the house was being watched, so 'when we went out, we always looked up and down Arthur Road, but we never saw anything suspicious'.[29] Mrs Nightingale was told to keep the chain on the outer door when she was alone in the house, and Alick told Muriel to keep it on in the evenings until he was home. Alick very rarely carried a front door key, so from now on he would use a prearranged ring, of three short rings and a long ring, before she would open the door.

She was also occasionally being pestered by nuisance calls, as were several other local women. One had been receiving numerous calls from two years, which had recently gone from heavy breathing to 'seductive' talk.[30]

Despite having made a good recovery from his heart attack, Alick retired on 2 October 1969. He and Muriel made plans for more regular visits back to their home country, with one planned for the spring of 1970, since they had not seen Ian for nearly two years. But while they were making retirement plans, a revolution was underway in the British press which would have gigantic, irreversible effects on British politics and society, and on the McKay family.

Rupert Murdoch, son of Alick's first boss in the industry, and the crown prince of a family who had remained close friends of the McKays for decades, had arrived in England and immediately evoked outrage with his purchases of the *Sun* and the *News of the World*, the relaunch of the latter spearheaded by the publication of the confessions of Christine Keeler.

The night after Alick's retirement, Murdoch was invited to defend himself on London Weekend Television's *Frost on Friday* programme.* Pilloried by a match-fit David Frost, he now needed friends that he could rely on. A few days later, he bumped into Alick McKay.

He invited the man whom his father had held in such high regard to join him at the *News of the World*. The terms were extremely generous and the appointment, as deputy chairman, would in no way interfere with the McKays' plans for more frequent visits back to Australia, the first of which they had now begun to arrange, Muriel having even made an appointment for the necessary vaccinations for a trip that she would never make.

Muriel's dressmaker later said that Muriel had been delighted about Alick's appointment and had told her that 'Mr Murdoch had no intention of overworking her husband and would allow him as many holidays as he

---

*   No recording is known to exist of this edition.

wished'.[31] Alick was only required to stand in when Murdoch was out of the country.

It was an offer that Alick McKay could not refuse, and he started in the role on Monday, 4 December. For the McKays, it would have brought prosperity and ultimately delivered them a long and happy retirement, but for a devastating twist of fate which destroyed their happy and industrious lives.

Lady Cudlipp remembered, when Muriel disappeared, being tasked by the police with finding a photograph of her to be used on missing person posters and appeals. They wanted one in which she was not smiling, but Lady Cudlipp simply could not find a single photograph where Muriel was not either smiling or laughing. 'She was that sort of woman, she was always happy, always smiling.'[32] Eventually, a picture was selected which caught her just half-smiling. It is that uncharacteristic image that has remained history's representation of her for far too long.

2

PAPER TIGERS

We (the ladies!) are now going to look at the Rembrandt exhibition and walk around the city, which is charming with its canals.

Muriel McKay, Amsterdam, 14 November 1969.

In the half-century since the tragedy, different presentations of this story have selected different central characters and, erroneously, on several occasions that character has been the press. An exaggerated causal connection between the crime and the Murdoch empire persists, most recently presented in James Graham's play, *Ink*, in which the *Sun* and the *News of the World* conceitedly decide at the outset that this case is really all about them, that it is a crime against them, an attack on their operation, on what they stand for and on what they are doing to Britain (or in their mind, *for* Britain). In truth, the men who abducted Muriel McKay were not remotely interested in tabloid newspapers and did not even read them.

The reality is that the crime had nothing to do with the tabloid press, though the tabloid press had a great deal to do with the investigation. For, not only were the police dealing with a new kind of crime, they were dealing with a new type of journalism. The role of certain newspapers in the story was obstructive and, ultimately, destructive. They did not inspire the crime, but they did influence its outcome.

It is therefore important to set the stage, to understand how these newspapers operated at the time and how they were perceived, and why the McKay kidnapping sharpened the teeth of every tabloid in Britain, scornful of a story so close to home, to which the newest and most threatening paper on Fleet

Street had enviable access. The term 'tabloid' is not specific to the red tops, but included, at that time, the *Daily Sketch*, the *Evening Standard*, the *Daily Mirror*, the *Daily Mail* and the *Daily Express*. The *Sun* and the *News of the World* were not the villains of the piece; although they were granted access which was, with hindsight, a serious if understandable error of judgement by Alick McKay, on this occasion they conducted themselves a good deal better than did their rivals.

The red-top tabloid press as we know it is now in terminal decline. Ongoing costs from the phone-hacking scandal[*] and declining sales saw the *Sun* report a pre-tax loss of £202 million in June 2020.[1] The *News of the World*'s successor, the *Sun on Sunday*, has an average circulation of 1.16 million copies a week at the time of writing. Unlike the early days of Rupert Murdoch's ownership of the paper, when it boasted weekly sales of over 6 million, today titillation and disinformation can be found freely and more readily online. Soon it will be possible to forget the enormity of the influence that these publications once had on British society.

Walking down Fleet Street on a Friday afternoon today, a once-exciting street is now a sorrowful place, faintly echoing its past. Like the police force, it once ran on adrenaline and alcohol, and like police officers, some journalists in those days looked for the truth, others for anything that was believable. The once bustling wine bar El Vinos is now a quiet place, and the Wig and Pen pub, where the lawyers rubbed shoulders with the libellers, is boarded up. The only traces of the street's journalistic past are at No. 186, the fictional home of Sweeney Todd, in reality still the offices of Scottish publishers DC Thomson.[**] Slowly flaking away from the walls are painted banners for the long-forgotten *People's Journal*, and three publications that still just survive in Scotland: the *Dundee Courier*, the *Sunday Post* and the genteel, anachronistic *People's Friend*.

Tabloid newspapers in Britain massively pre-date the arrival of the red tops. They were tools forged for an aggressive and enlightened moral crusade by

---

[*] The *Sun* and *News of the World* archives, held at a secret location in north London and accessible only by invitation, remained closed to visitors at the time of writing. In an email on 18 November 2021, I was told that was due to 'civil claims litigation involving the newspaper regarding voicemail interception which have been ongoing since 2011'.

[**] The last journalists left Fleet Street when the London editorial office of DC Thomson closed in 2016, with only advertising staff remaining.

the combative but compassionate W.T. Stead,* who arrived in London in 1880 after ten years editing the *Darlington Northern Echo* to become assistant editor of the *Pall Mall Gazette*, taking full editorial control three years later.

The *Pall Mall Gazette* was a young and promising evening paper which, forty years later, would be absorbed into the *Evening Standard*. Tellingly, Stead's appointment was a piece of puppetry by Gladstone, who recognised that a liberal presence on a gentleman's newspaper would help to popularise his stony image, which was suffering beside his colourful rival, Disraeli. Stead took up the appointment with zeal.

Eschewing the paper's original Conservatism, he pioneered a more accessible presentation style, with copy broken up by illustrations and photographs, a look initially known as 'the new journalism'. By the 1890s, it had been christened 'the tabloid style'. Superseding the constant columns of punishingly close print, Stead enlivened his pages with crossheads, catchpenny headlines and pictures.

But the phrase 'tabloid' quickly came to refer as much to an attitude as to a layout, as Stead's muscular Christianity, social conscience and quest to expose injustice provoked alarm, outrage and anger. Stead wanted to 'rouse the nation' by purifying the heart with 'pity and horror', through 'that personal style, that trick of bright colloquial language … and that determination to arrest, amuse or startle'.[2] Although he was helping to mainstream a commercial formula that had existed since the 1840s 'in half-penny Sunday newspapers, such as the *News of the World*, *Reynolds' Newspaper* and *Lloyd's Weekly Newspaper*',[3] by foregrounding sex and crime, Stead was presenting these themes to higher social classes, and for higher motives.

Stead's incredible investigative journalism included an exposure of the horrors of child prostitution, an undercover operation which led to him serving three months' imprisonment, but also led to the age of consent being raised from 13 to 16. He also conducted a fearless campaign through the *Pall Mall Gazette* protesting the innocence of Israel Lipski, who had been sentenced to death for murdering his fiancée, the jury having taken just eight minutes to decide a guilty verdict. Stead's crusade was effective enough to see the execution delayed for a week while a reprieve was considered but, despite Stead's

---

*   Stead who, by coincidence, lived just yards from the future home of the McKays in Wimbledon, was twice nominated for the Nobel Peace Prize. A casualty of the *Titanic* disaster, reportedly he was last seen helping women and children into the lifeboats.

genuine concerns about scant evidence and possible antisemitic prejudices, Lipski ultimately confessed his crime to a rabbi and was hanged.

Three enduring characteristics of the new journalism are identifiable from these campaigns. The first was the demonstrable impact that the tabloids now had on public opinion and on the government. Secondly, the Lipski case was the creation of what was dubbed 'trial by journalism'.[4] Thirdly, it showed that the tabloid is a merciless beast, never forgiving anyone whom it wrongs, for Stead's persistent target throughout the Lipski campaign was Police Commissioner Sir Charles Warren, and Lipski's ultimate confession, vindicating the actions of Warren and his police force, only resulted in Stead from then on attacking Warren at every opportunity. In a hint of the tabloids a century later, Stead's treatment of Warren proved that the new journalism was as zealous and effective at destroying reputations as it was at creating them.

Five years into Stead's time at the *Pall Mall Gazette*, the press and the public were electrified by the Jack the Ripper killings. Stead denounced the 'vulgar sensationalism'[5] of the detailed reports in the *Times*, but like many other social reformers of the day, most notably George Bernard Shaw, he quickly realised that the crimes had value. To the social reformer, that value was in highlighting poverty, cruelty and neglect in society; to the wily newspaper editor, there was an undeniable commercial value too.

The ability to influence political and legal affairs, trial by journalism, fearless (and sometimes lawless) investigative journalism, aggressive morality and the use of crime as a commodity were now established characteristics of the tabloid press. But whereas Stead's influences were very much for the good of society, the tabloid press a century later, while using the same currency, had less lofty ambitions. The mentality and the look of them was now developing, but Stead's prose, although shamelessly emotive, was ornate and lacked immediacy. He described a letter written by a child to the drunken mother who had 'sold her into nameless infamy' as 'plentifully garlanded with kisses'.[6] It was not until fifty years later that the language of tabloid journalism was revolutionised.

The *Daily Mirror*, initially a paper run by and aimed at women, had launched in 1903, and after a slow start had gained momentum, thanks to its pictorial style. However, by the 1930s, it was becoming a casualty of the circulation war, being trounced by the *Daily Herald* and *Daily Express*. It reinvented itself spectacularly as a working-class, left-wing paper. Taking its visual lead from

American tabloids such as the *New York Daily News*, its new, direct, colloquial prose style was the voice of its editor, Harry Guy Bartholomew, a sparsely educated and self-made man, who had joined the newspaper as a cartoonist thirty years earlier. The *Daily Mirror* quickly realised the value of sensationalism, sauciness (the comic strip 'Jane') and sympathy with the reader who felt emasculated or disenfranchised.

In 1949, responding to calls for a Press Council, new editor Silvester Bolam defiantly proclaimed in a front-page editorial:

> The *Mirror* is a sensational newspaper. We make no apology for that. We believe in the sensational presentation of news and views ... We shall go on being sensational to the best of our ability ... Sensationalism means the vivid and dramatic presentation of events so as to give them a forceful impact on the mind of the reader. It means big headlines, vigorous writing, simplification into familiar everyday language, and the wide use of illustration by cartoon and photograph ... Every great problem facing us ... will only be understood by the ordinary man busy with his daily tasks if he is hit hard and hit often with the facts. Sensational treatment is the answer, whatever the 'sober' and 'superior' readers of some other journals may prefer.[7]

Bolam had just completed a three-month jail sentence for contempt of court over the paper's reporting of the trial of John George Haigh, the 'acid bath' murderer.

What is striking about the editorial is how much of it is shared in tone and attitude with the tabloids that were to come, most notably in its suspicion of supposedly 'superior' people and its boast of speaking to the 'ordinary man', though the *Sun* of course would go further, claiming to be speaking not just to him, but *for* him.

While never aspiring to W.T. Stead's level of benevolence, the *Daily Mirror* had more of a social conscience than the *Sun* and the *News of the World* could ever pretend to possess, but in its reinvention as a popular and populist newspaper in the 1930s with a fiercely unpretentious voice, it gave the modern tabloid its final key ingredient. By now, three-quarters of the adults in Britain read one of the eight daily national newspapers. All that was left was for the permissive age to begin.

Founded with the motto 'Our motto is the truth, our practice is fearless advocacy of the truth', the *News of the World* was the cheapest of newspapers, in price and in taste. A lowbrow, top-selling title of tittle-tattle and giggles, vicars and tarts, that tutted at its own smut, it was scurrilous, salacious and vastly successful from its first edition, on 1 October 1843. By the 1950s, it was selling up to 8 million copies a week.

After 150 years, when it was closed in the wake of the phone-hacking scandal, it was still the biggest-selling Sunday newspaper in the English-speaking world, with weekly sales of 7.4 million. Sir William Emsley Carr, whose family had owned the newspaper since 1891, addressed a hint of a decline in sales in 1960 by appointing as editor Stafford Somerfield, a wily warhorse who had been with the paper since 1945, pursuing 'salacious Puritanism with missionary zeal'.[8]

By now, cinema and independent television were creating a gallery of new celebrities, whose antics kept the *News of the World* merrily lucrative throughout the 1960s. Then, one morning in September 1968, Sir William Carr took Somerfield for a drink in the long bar of the Falstaff, the *News of the World*'s preferred pub, and revealed that just under a third of the shares in the paper were being liquidated but he couldn't afford them. Usually, such a large number of shares would command a discount, but times were changing, and gentlemen's rules were becoming unfashionable. Rothschild, the merchant bankers, took command of a situation which soon became what Somerfield would later describe as the bloodiest takeover battle in the history of Fleet Street, and one which 'ended an era and made Rupert Murdoch the boss of a thriving newspaper empire'.[9]

Robert Maxwell, then a Labour MP for Buckingham and owner of the Pergamon Press publishing house, already a sinister and fanatically litigious figure, put in an enormous bid for the *News of the World* organisation. The Carr family were outraged at the prospect of a Czechoslovakian socialist taking control, and Somerfield penned a leader to that effect, which was widely panned as xenophobic, in which he explained why 'it would not be a good thing for Mr Maxwell, formerly Jan Ludwig Hoch, to gain control of this newspaper which, I know, has your respect, loyalty and affection – a newspaper which I know is as British as roast beef and Yorkshire pudding'. He concluded that the *News of the World* was 'a British newspaper, run by British people. Let's keep it that way'.[10]

By 1968, Rupert Murdoch had not only inherited his father's newspaper empire but broadened it with television acquisitions. His interests now saturated every state in Australia, making him wealthy enough to set his sights on expanding into Britain and making it his new base of operations. He had been covertly buying shares in the *Daily Mirror* for several years, hoping in vain for a chance to gain control of it, but now the crisis at the *News of the World* presented a better opportunity.

Although he was hardly the establishmentarian figure that the Carr family would have preferred, to them he was preferable to Maxwell, the swarthy émigré with question marks hovering around his finances. 'I could smell that the establishment wouldn't let Maxwell in,' he would later comment.[11] Carr was satisfied that Murdoch had honour, if not nobility, but it was felt, in Somerfield's words, that he needed 'a little polishing, and maybe that was true, for he proved as hard as a diamond'.[12]

By the autumn of 1969, Murdoch had his sights set on another acquisition. In the week, a left-leaning working class was now being catered for by the *Daily Mirror*, but the effects of the 1941 Education Act and an emerging educated working class had suggested another gap in the market. The *Daily Telegraph*, *Times* and *Guardian* rose from 9 per cent to 12 per cent of total sales between 1958 and 1963. It was predicted that class barriers would continue to 'lose their clarity and become more confused'.[13] And so in 1964 the International Publishing Corporation, which had inherited unwanted 'old TUC carthorse',[14] the *Daily Herald* for just £75,000,* dispensed with its 'cloth cap Socialist image'[15] and regenerated it into the *Sun*.

Originally a broadsheet with bright ambitions, the *Sun* had a five-year future guaranteed at birth, to appease the unions. With a healthy slab of market research in its DNA, it would be 'The Paper Born of the Age We Live In',[16] inspired by a well-meaning but wrong-footed piece of futurology, *The Newspaper Reading Public of Tomorrow*, by sociologist Dr Mark Abrams. Setting out the case for this idyllic newspaper, Abrams envisioned a future Britain in which 'women enjoy a much higher status than ever before', a Britain 'no longer divided into Empire and a limbo of foreigners who were either wicked because they might harm Britain or contemptible because they were incapable of harming us'.[17] It was a touching and hopelessly optimistic forecast.

Unfortunately, the new polyocracy hadn't played ball, the gap in the market being rather narrower than predicted, and by the end of the *Sun*'s five-year trial period in 1969, the naive young paper had cost the International Publishing Corporation £12 million. The unions demanded that the IPC either continue

---

*   £1.5 million in today's money.

to publish the paper or auction it as a going concern. Terrified of what damage defying the unions could do to his *Daily Mirror*, IPC Chairman Cecil Harmsworth King put the paper on the market. Rupert Murdoch, 'who suffered few illusions about the effects of education on a mass market', [18] saw his opportunity.

Maxwell made a bid for the *Sun*, but Murdoch fended him off, acquiring the *Sun* for a song and changing everything but the name, the one thing that wasn't the product of market research but had in fact been a flash of inspiration when Mirror Group Chairman Hugh Cudlipp had glanced at a pub sign. The *News of the World* presses, which stood unused for six days of the week, would print the paper. Its politics, for now, would remain socialistic, but its soul would be flagrantly capitalist – Murdoch and his chosen editor, the arrogant but skilful Larry Lamb, sharing a vision of what Roy Greenslade would later describe as 'a tabloid in which entertainment would supersede information', which pushed at 'the barriers of taste and convention'. [19] The new paper would be about sex, sport and sensation.

The *News of the World* started to promote the new *Sun* with front-page adverts claiming that 'the new Sun will be YOUR kind of newspaper'. [20] The countdown continued the following week, claiming that the *Sun* would 'be run by the youngest, brightest team in daily journalism' and would cost 5p, adding, rather bafflingly, that this was 'the same price as an ordinary daily newspaper'. [21] Two days before the first edition, Murdoch told readers that the new *Sun* would be 'a paper that CARES. The paper that cares – passionately – about truth, beauty and justice.' [22]

With one day to go, the *News of the World*'s full-page teaser promised sex, via a serialisation of Jacqueline Susann's pulp novel *The Love Machine* ('dare YOU read it?') and sport, via a column by George Best. The first edition covered its own launch with a picture of Murdoch's 25-year-old wife, Anna, activating the printing presses. The strikingly beautiful daughter of Latvian migrants, she had been married to the magnate for two years, and the television profiles of Murdoch that had begun to appear had naturally devoted attention to her, since she was a powerful and engaging screen presence.

However, those expecting the promised sensation were to be disappointed. The first edition of the new *Sun* was an anti-climax; in fact, it was rather a dull affair. The paper launched on a slow news day, the front-page splashes being a brouhaha about horse doping and a rumour about a woman who was possibly dating Prince Charles. The *Sun* needed a major scoop.

Meanwhile, the *News of the World* did have a scoop: it announced that it would be serialising the confessions of Christine Keeler. In truth, it was hardly a scoop at all, since the story was already 6 years old. All the same, it was a useful splash, sharing with the paper's regenerative Diana Dors exposé, a decade earlier, a potent blend of sex and guns, and it was also a chance for Murdoch to goad the establishment.

But whatever Rupert Murdoch thought he knew about the British establishment in the autumn of 1969, he badly underestimated the furious reaction to his enterprise. To them, this was no scoop, but simply muck-raking. 'The Establishment are mad about it,' the *News of the World* proclaimed,[23] but in truth he was being attacked on a much broader scale. The rest of the press scorned him, and the Press Council censured the paper for 'a disservice both to the public welfare and to the press'.[24] Murdoch was said to have boasted that 'people can sneer as much as they like, but I'll take the 150,000 extra copies that we're going to sell', and empowered his readers by placing under a front-page banner that read, 'Keeler – YOUR right to decide – vote now', a form welcoming their replies to the rather weighted question: 'Should you be allowed to read the Christine Keeler story?'

He confidently accepted the invitation to appear on London Weekend Television's live *Frost on Friday* programme, a current affairs interrogation show whose host was at the peak of his powers, hugely popular and fearless in his questioning. The show's producer, Clive Irving, had co-authored the first book about the Profumo affair, *Scandal '63*, and was unconvinced by the *News of the World*'s promises that theirs would be a revelatory account. A planned appearance by Keeler on the Frost programme was cancelled. Such was the Independent Television Authority's wrath that it also banned all advertisements for the *News of the World*, even those without mention of the memoirs, until the serialisation was over.

Murdoch explained that he judged the story to be in the public interest 'as a cautionary tale to politicians',[25] but as the interview progressed, Frost 'really got his velvet-coated knife into Murdoch',[26] and the confidence before Frost and the studio audience of a man introduced as a millionaire 'seemed to wobble'.

That fateful appearance, broadcast at 10.30 p.m. on Friday, 3 October 1969, was an event with vivid consequences. As the large sums of money paid for the *Sun* and the *News of the World* were openly discussed, and mention was made that Murdoch had married for a second time two years ago, it cemented his credo as the outsider rallying against an assumed establishment and confirmed his belief that, as an upstart from the colonies, he would never be accepted into British society.

In the glow of the television screen in the chilly living room of a dilapidated farmhouse in Hertfordshire, Arthur Hosein, with his wife and brother, sat watching Murdoch openly discussing his wife and his wealth. In Arthur's diseased mind, the deranged plan for modern Britain's first ever kidnapping-for-ransom began to form.

3

DESPERATION

O, the town of Rothenberg is just out of this world, an artist's dream.
Muriel McKay, Rothenberg, 1969.

Several years after the murder of Muriel McKay, inexact waxworks of the Hosein brothers were unveiled for the public to peer at in the Chamber of Horrors at Madame Tussauds. They stood in a cell, alongside effigies of Donald Neilson, who had supposedly been inspired by their crime to kidnap and murder 17-year-old Lesley Whittle five years later, and Graham Young,* the 'teacup poisoner'.[1]

In the last half-century, police photographs of the Hoseins taken shortly after their arrest have become familiar images in encyclopaedias of true crime – Arthur looking unabashed, Nizamodeen insolent. Yet their personalities have been grossly oversimplified, their wickedness belittled in superficial accounts of the case. Arthur has been presented as a ludicrous, even comic figure, a deluded dandy, an aspirational bungler, and Nizamodeen as his spineless stooge. The reality is more complex.

The Hoseins may have been spectacularly incompetent criminals, but they were also violent, merciless, malevolent men whose evil persisted long after

---

★   Graham Young (1947–90) was sent to Broadmoor Hospital at 14, after poisoning his father, sister and several schoolfriends. He was released nine years later, promising to kill 'one person for every year I've spent in this place'. He found work in a factory, where he poisoned several of his colleagues, two of whom died. The case led to major reforms of mental health services and also led to the Poisons Act 1972, limiting the availability of toxic substances.

their arrest and imprisonment, with their refusal to allow Muriel McKay's family the closure of an explanation for her death and the opportunity for her to have a dignified burial. What has never been told in any detail is the story of their journey from a devout upbringing in Trinidad to life imprisonment in Britain. Finally, with the release of hundreds of pages of documents that have never been made public before, one can present a clearer picture of the appalling, predatory personality of Arthur Hosein and that of his shiftless, volatile younger brother Nizamodeen, and the devastating impact that they had on those with whom they came into contact.

Arthur's motivation for the crime has traditionally been explained as one of vaulting ambition: the desire of a man with expensive tastes and dwindling funds to become wealthy, a despised immigrant who saw £1 million as his way to enter the British aristocracy. But this narrative is an impersonal one, a socio-political construct.

It is certainly true that Arthur was a greedy man and an aspirational one, but such a banal explanation implies entirely materialistic reasons for his crime and completely ignores his rapacious personality and aggressive, pernicious history. Would this man, if born wealthy, have been law abiding? If the Hoseins had not watched that interview with Rupert Murdoch, the chain of events that mistakenly led them to Muriel McKay would never have begun, but it is hard to believe that a different dreadful crime would not have still been inevitable when one chronicles Arthur's descent from industrious tailor to hard-drinking predator.

No word defines Arthur more fittingly than rapacious. The awful irony is that he was perfectly capable of making a good living with the skills that he had. He was a fine tailor (some went so far as to call him 'excellent') but it was not enough and it would never be enough. He was impatient for wealth and status, but clearly it was not sufficient just to do as well or even better than others. He had to do better than everyone. No matter how wealthy he could have become, he was always going to offend, because of his attitudes towards his fellow man, and his attitude towards women. It is wrong to express these crimes purely in a material sense because it was in Arthur's nature to be not progressing but transgressing.

It is interesting that while he spoke a lot about money, and even candidly about wanting to be a millionaire, he never revealed any ambitions that £1 million would fulfil for him. Never once did he say that he yearned for anything except to be a millionaire. How exactly would he have been able to explain or disguise his sudden wealth, and what would it have bought him except for a life in clover? Sex and money are the commonest motives for crime. But Arthur's behaviours also suggest someone who, if he wanted something, took it; his behaviours were not so much motivational as pathological, and he showed an increasing recklessness and clumsiness – instinctual behaviour over careful planning.

The Hoseins came from Dow village, an Indian community in the California neighbourhood of Trinidad. A British colony from 1889, the island was not granted self-governance until 1958, nor independence until 1962. Aubrey Rose, later Nizamodeen Hosein's solicitor, has had a long, professional relationship with the Caribbean and explains that 'compared with the beautiful neighbouring island of Tobago, Trinidad had a lot more industry than the rest of the Caribbean, the sugar cane, the oil and the huge tar lake, but also a very diverse ethnic make-up'.[2] As well as the two major ethnicities, Afro-Trinidadian and Indo-Trinidadian, 'there was also a Portuguese and Spanish population, and Chinese, and tensions between the different groups'. A BBC report in 1971 described the island as mixing 'extreme sophistication with almost peasant simplicity'.[3]

Arthur Hosein (some records show a middle name of Mohammed) was born on 18 August 1936, the second of six children. Their home in Railway Road was a concrete, tin-roofed, one-storey building. Arthur's father, Shaffi, who was 55 at the time of his arrest, was a tailor and also an Imam of the local mosque. Arthur's mother, Shafirian, was houseproud, devout and respectable; Arthur would later describe her as having 'a heart of gold' and as being, like his father, very 'strict and straight'.[4] The couple worked side by side in the house, Shaffi as a tailor and Shafirian as a seamstress. Shaffi was active in politics as well as religion, a member of the now defunct Democratic Labour Party, then the major opposition party and the traditional voice of the island's Indian community. He spent three years serving on the local council, and the slogan 'VOTE DLP' was still scrawled on the front wall of the house when a BBC film crew visited in 1970.

Arthur's daughter, Freida, told me that while Arthur's mother was 'a lovely grandma, really nice, I liked to sit with her', she only remembered her grandfather as 'a very tall man. I had to show respect in front of him. I don't know why but I just couldn't feel warmth towards him.'[5]

'I got to know the father quite well when he came over after they were arrested,' remembers Aubrey Rose:

He and I became quite friendly. He was a well behaved, polite, gentle sort of man, dignified, not very bright but a nice man. Knowing that I was Jewish, he said to me, 'Mr Rose, I have the Koran here and the commentaries, and I will teach you,' so he and I sat down together, and he used to teach me what parts of it meant. He was very quiet and modest, totally unlike Arthur in that sense, and totally perplexed. He never believed that his sons could be involved in such an affair. But hardly anything was ever said about their mother.[6]

All the children were given 'a strict religious training', according to the eldest, Charles, 'and as young children were all much attached to our parents and the church. We can all read the Koran and we fully understand the teachings of the Moslem religion.'[7]

Arthur attended the Esperanza Presbyterian School, which to this day bears above its doors the motto 'knowledge is power'. His teacher, David Beharry, reflected later that Arthur 'had an ambition which showed very markedly. He always wanted to be somebody.'[8] Although Beharry detected a certain boastfulness in him, he tried to teach him that humility would serve him better. He would give all leaving boys advice on how to conduct themselves in interviews and in dealings with the opposite sex, and on a return visit in 1967, Arthur greatly impressed him, telling him that he was working day and night and that 'with the help of his wife, he was doing remarkably well',[9] something which at the time was perfectly true.

According to his father, Arthur was not only fiercely ambitious but fiercely acquisitive and fuelled by people telling him that a boy with his potential should look beyond Trinidad. His oldest brother, Charles, called him 'the adventurous type, he wanted to see the world, and to see the world you must have money. He was hard-working but his drives for adventure and for money were deeply interconnected.'[10]

After a stint at Scott's Commercial College in San Fernando, where he studied typing, shorthand and book-keeping, Arthur abandoned his education, later making the suspicious claim that he 'deliberately failed exams because he did not want to go to college'.[11] He worked in a restaurant in the Port of Spain, and spent six months as a bus conductor, but according to Charles, 'Trinidad was too slow for him. Arthur had been adventurous, even from a little boy. He wanted to see the world. He was never like the other boys of the village. He always wanted to make himself somebody … he loved the limelight.'[12]

At 19, armed with a flair for tailoring, which he had learned from his father, he decided, like so many men of his generation, to seek his fortune in England.

Arthur sailed on SS *Hilary*, which docked at Liverpool on 19 October 1955. The passenger lists give his occupation as 'salesman' and his lodgings as 4 Downside Crescent, in Maida Vale,[13] with a fellow passenger, Irwin Malsingh, but he spent most of his first year in Birmingham, working as a dispatch receiving clerk for Alba Television in Oxley at £7 per week, then as a fuel tester with ICI for £14 a week.* Returning to London, he found lodgings and tailoring work in the East End, living at 80 Cricketfield Road, Hackney, and becoming self-employed in November 1956, with a workshop on the first floor of 16 Mare Street.

For all its folklore and heritage, the East End has always been a place of shifting sands, a place where new communities and new eras begin. Yet even today, with its vastly diverse populace, costly properties, street art and chic subculture, traces of the East End that Arthur Hosein established himself within have survived in the dwindling but determined tailoring businesses dotted amid the health food shops, craft beer bars and takeaways. In marked contrast, 16 Mare Street has been restored to its Georgian glory and is now wholly residential, while opposite stands the shell of the once-crowded Rose and Crown pub, and beside it, with a strange aptness, the macabre Viktor Wynd Museum of Curiosities, Fine Art and Unnatural History.

However it might have looked from a distance, the Britain which Arthur Hosein arrived in was far from welcoming. Britain was changing, but for some it was changing too fast. A new generation was impatient for startling social reforms, while an older generation felt embattled and disorientated. Those who came to England full of hopes and dreams were given no assistance in integrating, nor were those they lived among given any education or guidance to ease the massive societal changes taking place. Within a few years, immigrants were having to contend not only with Rachman's winklers and Enoch Powell's disciples but with colour bars even in Labour clubs, and the infamous Smethwick election of 1964, won by apartheid-advocating Conservative Peter Griffiths on the slogan 'if you want a n——— for a neighbour, vote Labour'.

History is often most acutely captured at a local level, and even some of the headlines in the *Wimbledon News and Advertiser* of the time invoke consternation today at the readiness of some to exploit and weaponise contemporary insecurity and confusion. A local carpenter complained to the race relations

---

* £122 and £244 today.

board after he saw a local firm advertise for a stoker, a job which 'would suit a West Indian Jamaican of strong physique'.[14] The man claimed that this was discriminating against white men. A 21-year-old young Conservative, David Pole, waded in, saying, 'I think England should be for the English,' and preaching that 'Scots, Irish and Welsh as well as the coloured immigrants should be sent back to their own countries'. He called the Race Relations Bill* 'iniquitous' and said, 'because I don't choose to have a coloured man in my own property, I can be prosecuted for it. It infringes on my civil liberty.'

Colonialism has bitter legacies. An ingrained sense of superiority on one side, which views the relinquishment of empire as a sign of decline, faces mistrust and resentment from the other, whose aspiration is viewed as impertinence. Many immigrants felt that hard work and a low profile was the safest course of action in this new, hostile environment, and while there is no doubt that Arthur Hosein excelled at the former, the latter was alien to his nature.

An incessant liar, Arthur told everyone around him that his father held a position of great eminence back in Trinidad and was fabulously wealthy. He overestimated his own wealth and accomplishments and displayed a pathological need to impress and outdo those around him. He was also prone to irrational grudges, some of which were self-destructive, damaging his livelihood and the social standing that he obsessed over. Despite Harold Wilson's fearless denunciation of Peter Griffiths' racist campaign at Smethwick, his Selective Employment Tax enraged Arthur to the point that, three years later, he was still singing calypsos lampooning Wilson to his fellow drinkers.

A psychiatrist who examined Arthur while he was awaiting trial noted:

> He went into quite complex explanations as to his views on politics, those who were against him, what he would like to do in the future in politics, the Indians being used as scapegoats for the British in this country, class distinction ... many of his utterances had a flavour of persecutory ideas.

He considered Arthur to be a 'barrack-room lawyer' and 'a man who thought highly of himself'.[15] Robert Cullen, who drove Arthur briefly in 1968 after he had been given a temporary driving ban, said:

---

*   The 1965 and 1968 Acts banned racial discrimination in public places and made promoting racial hatred a crime, aiming to ensure that the second-generation immigrants 'who have been born here' and were 'going through our schools' would get 'the jobs for which they are qualified and the houses they can afford' (*Commons Hansard*, 9 July 1968, col. 466). The Act was the target of Enoch Powell's 'rivers of blood' speech.

Hosein was a peculiar man. He detested Englishmen and has said as much to me. He was always bragging about his wealth and tried to do everything in a big way. He spent heavily and on occasions he drank heavily. He seemed to have an inferiority complex about being coloured. He was always trying to impress everyone. I left him because I got fed up with the job.[16]

Arthur was a desperate man: desperate to be liked, desperate to be admired, desperate to be wealthy, desperate to impress and desperate to dominate those around him.

There is clear evidence in him of, at the very least, marked personality disorder, although perhaps in his everyday behaviour this was more at a bizarre or antisocial level than a clinical level. He was prone to mood swings and claimed that when tense or angry he suffered physical symptoms, such as stomach pains. Shortly after his arrival in London, he developed what would appear to have been an acute hysterical state and was admitted to Homerton Hospital at Hackney Wick, where he remained for two weeks, until he discharged himself. 'Arthur was clearly mentally ill,' says Aubrey Rose. 'There was a visible history of it, though it was never once referred to at his trial. His behaviour was peculiar, he was a most unusual personality.'[17]

There are also clear elements of narcissistic personality disorder in his exaggerated sense of self-importance, which is coupled with a notable lack of empathy for others, and in his sense of entitlement to more privileges and consideration than those around him. Narcissists are frequently flamboyant, feeding off attention, and tend to vainly, even absurdly, overestimate their abilities and achievements. Most tellingly, they 'constantly want to be seen with the right people but have few, if any, friends',[18] while being riddled with self-doubt, extremely sensitive to criticism and desperate for compliments and admiration. The excitable, frantic nature of his need to impress and his incessant sexual predation, yet the seemingly casual execution of his eventual crime, reveal him to have been a highly dangerous man.

Downstairs from Arthur's workshop in Mare Street was a ladies' hairdressers, Elsa's Continental Hair Fashions, run by Elisabeth Gregory, née Fischer. The daughter of a hotelier, and raised in Hiltrup, Germany, Elsa had come to England after meeting her first husband, a soldier, when she was 19, with whom she had a daughter, Monica, in 1948. He was 'a right cockney and it didn't work out'.[19] Flaxen-haired and decent, she was ten years older than Arthur. It took three years for her to get a divorce and marry him, by which time she was pregnant with their first child, and by which time Arthur had served his ignominious spell in the army.

He was called for National Service in July 1959. After a dismal performance in the entrance tests, he was admitted to the Royal Pioneer Corps and stationed in north Wales. The army shared the psychiatrists' later view of him as a 'barrack-room lawyer', but beneath his inflated ego and bombast, clear evidence of mental disturbance became apparent; while 'he complains of persistent enuresis … he has been seen to deliberately urinate on his bed'.[20]

After less than three months he deserted and was absent without leave for six months. Elsa had suffered an accident and he had been refused compassionate leave. Apparently, at a court martial in Wrexham, his commanding officer judged him to be 'immeasurably the worst soldier it has been my misfortune to have under me … that is, when he wasn't either absent or in detention'.[21]

He was sentenced to six months' detention at a military prison in Aldershot for what the judge tellingly called 'a very stupid offence'. On his way to the cells, he is supposed to have said, 'Watch how you go with me. I'll be worth a million one day.' Another conviction followed when he escaped from custody.

He married Elsa on 18 May 1960 and their daughter, Freida, was born in September. A son, Sarajudeen, was born the following year. Arthur ended his inglorious time in the army at Berechurch Hall Camp in Colchester, Essex, a corrective training centre. After fourteen months' service, he was discharged on medical grounds in September 1960, having been diagnosed as having a 'psychopathic personality', though this diagnosis was disputed in psychiatric assessments prepared for his trial for murder.[22] Back in civvy street, he told anyone who would listen that he had in fact been an officer in the Royal Electrical and Mechanical Engineers.

His next youngest brother, Adam, had arrived in England earlier that year and lodged with Elsa at Mare Street. When Arthur came home and resumed his tailoring business, Adam assisted him for a couple of months, but 'got fed up with the hours'[23] and joined the RAF on 10 October 1960, serving as a senior aircraftman until he too was medically discharged in April 1964.* Adam did not return to Arthur 'because we were different personalities and just did not get on together'.[24] Instead, he moved into a flat in Streatham and married in August 1964, living in Norwood and Richmond before moving

---

*   The reason for this is unknown.

to Thornton Heath and setting up as an insurance broker. Over the next few years, he and Arthur saw little of one another.

Less than two years into his marriage, Arthur had an affair with 18-year-old Farida Cellini,* whose family he had known back in Trinidad. She was a student nurse at Great Ormond Street Hospital and the affair culminated in her having a child by him, Michael. Elsa told the police after Arthur's arrest, 'you must remember that he is a Mohammedan, but I hope he hasn't got any more lives'.[25] She believed that Farida returned to Trinidad after the affair. In truth, although the child was there, she remained in London, and in the years that followed the birth, Arthur would make repeated, aggressive demands for custody. Freida Hosein remembers, 'At one point she actually came to Mum asking for help, because she was so scared of Arthur, and Mum being Mum took her in.'[26]

Arthur wrote home regularly, telling the family of his success and affluence in England. Unfortunately, now that he was making a living, he was also becoming a fanatical spendthrift. He joined a gambling club** and trained a couple of greyhounds which he raced at various tracks around London. He was a heavy drinker and smoker, had his hair cut as often as once a week, owned a range of natty suits and was recklessly generous with fellow drinkers.

The tailors and finishers he worked with had mixed feelings about him. One, William White, said, 'He was nothing more than a con merchant and told a lot of lies',[27] while others found him jolly and amusing. What is indisputable is his prowess and, for a time, his industriousness. By 1965, he had done well enough to lease new premises above Toby Reuben, a watchmaker and jeweller, at 134 Kingsland High Street, and made a home in the suburbs, heading to the traditional destination for successful east Londoners, Essex.

Arthur and Elsa's Chipping Ongar home, 5 Longfields, was a new, semi-detached house on a typically tidy and tranquil low-rise estate. But despite joining the local table tennis club and being disconcertingly generous in the local pubs, he did not feel welcome. Elsie Footitt, manageress of the Cock Tavern on the High Street, said he 'was always generous with his money but did not appear to have any special friends'.[28] Leonard Welham, the landlord of the Red Lion, said that he 'rather pushed his personality on everyone'. After being a regular for three months, 'I think he dropped away from our premises

---

*   Named Bertha Cellini at the trial.
**   This may have been the Victoria Sporting Club on Edgware Road. See Chapter 19.

because no one really made friends with him even though he appeared to try and buy his friendship'.[29]

His ethnicity, which was probably unique in the district at that time, would have meant that he had an uphill struggle for acceptance even without his bumptiousness and braggadocio. Yet he was determined to be accepted in England, and in June 1967, he applied for British citizenship, and for his passport, which the Passport Office were in possession of, to be returned to him 'with great urgency, as I am preparing to go abroad for a holiday at the end of July'.[30] Even if his boasting impressed few people in Ongar, he was eager to make a triumphant return to his homeland and bathe in some glory.

He visited Trinidad in July 1967, a visit which saw him impress not only his old schoolteacher but his father, with Arthur telling him that he would soon be paying for the whole family to move to England. However, the trip ended in humiliation when his British passport was seized by the High Commission, who believed it to be false. He was detained in Trinidad for several weeks, losing business, and even though he was awarded £170 compensation after suing the authorities, the incident left him with a bitter view of British officialdom.

His business continued to flourish when he returned, but in May 1968 he made the strange decision to move deeper into rural England. Exactly why is a question that has never been raised before. He may well have felt shunned and rejected by Ongar; it is telling that after he left, he kept in touch with hardly anyone he met there. It has been suggested that the experience regarding his passport was a catalyst for his retreating to Rooks Farm, but the move is more likely to have been to find space to make room for his expansive personality and lofty behaviour.

Moving twice as far away from the East End as he had been in Ongar was a folly, Arthur overreaching himself not only financially but in a business sense, since it was counterproductive to be spending considerable money on petrol and time on the road when he needed to be working and saving. Perhaps somewhere in the back of his mind something of his crime was already formulating and, for reasons that he had not yet identified, he felt a need to back away to somewhere covert and isolated. That move to the country, suspiciously unsound in a business sense – was it not because, in some dark corner of his mind, there was a strange sense that he should retreat to a remote, secretive location, somewhere that might be suitable for some yet unshaped, transgressive operation?

Rooks Farm consists of two seventeenth-century cottages converted into one house with outbuildings, standing in 12 acres of uncultivated land on the rural border of Essex and Hertfordshire. Surveyed today, one is immediately struck not only by how the site has transformed from a scruffy, sinister hideaway into a smart and salubrious country estate, complete with swimming pool, but by just how hidden away it remains. It lies suspiciously out of sight, at least a third of a mile back from the road, down a narrow, snaking, unmarked lane at the end of the village of Stocking Pelham. We are just a mile over the border with Essex here, a place where two pretty counties meet, but, like many borderlands, something of a wilderness. The undulating landscape stretches desert-like into the distance, the wanderer dwarfed beneath the vast skies.

'There is something creepy in the flat eastern counties,' wrote G.K. Chesterton, adding, 'Travelling in the great level lands has a curiously still and lonely quality'.[31] This is a land of cantering and hunting, awash with sunshine in the bright months but in winter, a countryside not so much open as empty. For all its English gorgeousness, its restored thatched cottages and polished pubs and the gentle grandeur of its churches, it is a secretive enclave, a strange realm, out of reasonable reach of railways and even bus routes. To live here today, one needs money and mobility.

Although nowhere is truly far from London today, one must stress that in 1968, this was very much rural England, a quiet parish of simple ways, with colourful names for its places and its people. While today one can still find on a map Barleycroft End, Cradle End, Tinkers Hill and Rookery Wood, and the curiously sinister Nasty, Maggots End, No Man's Grove and Cut-Throat Lane, bucolic surnames such as Scattergood, Clutterbuck and Wellbeloved are dying out. It is a measure of how, until recently, it was an unchanging place, that nearly all the surnames recorded in the 1851 census were still known in surrounding villages in 1974.[32] In 1968, Stocking Pelham had just fifty-eight houses and a population of 140, to which a new and unknown name was now added: Hosein.

'If the Londoner really wants rural quiet, he can get it almost at his door … in the smaller villages … in spite of the nearness of London, can be found remaining traits of local character and peculiarities of idiom'[33] was how one writer put it less than twenty years before the Hoseins arrived in Stocking Pelham. Half a century ago, this was a very different community – rustic, unfussy, populated by those who worked on the land.

Peter Miller, a Hertfordshire policeman at the time, says:

This was then a very rural county, and with Rooks Farm you really were right out in the sticks. A lot of people were living a very isolated, primitive existence in those parts. One of the first cases I dealt with was of a local girl who had been abused by her father, and that wasn't the only case of incest in the area. I was a Yorkshire lad who had just moved down here and I was shocked at how prevalent that was.[34]

Rooks Farm was sold to Arthur for £14,100, of which £9,000 was a mortgage requiring repayments of £18 per week.* From this point on, he had a continuous overdraft and steadily mounting though not ruinous debts. According to Elsa, 'when business was good, Arthur could do up to 100 pairs of trousers a week... he does at least thirty a week and clears £3 on each pair. That is after the finishers have been paid and the cost of petrol,'[35] which was £10 per week.

In direct contravention of Muslim law, he decided to keep pigs as well as chickens and cattle, the outbuildings becoming three piggeries and the sheds housing meat tables. Adjoining the back door of the farmhouse was a tumble-down shed where two extremely aggressive Alsatian guard dogs, Rex and Reggie, were kept chained up, with a sign warning of them erected on the entrance lane. This was now not just Arthur's castle, but his fortress.

Inside the four-bedroomed farmhouse, he splashed out on a pine-walled bathroom and installed a gilt and cream semi-circular bar in the living room. Yet, despite this extravagance, photographs of the interior of the house show it to be generally shabby and stark, particularly the upstairs rooms, suggesting that he had little inclination to indulge his wife and children as he indulged himself. A downstairs room at the front was converted into a tailoring workshop, through the window of which he could look out and be master of all he surveyed, which by autumn, included a brand-new dark-blue Volvo 144 saloon. Yet it wasn't enough.

On the opposite side of the fields to Rooks Farm was a thatched cottage, Bennills, occupied by local journalist Audrey Strube and her children. Her daughter, Yasmin, who was 15 at the time of the crime, recalls:

The cottage is probably worth a million today, but back then, we moved to it so that my mum could afford to send my two brothers to the Perse school in Cambridge. She paid £1,000 for it. There was no shop in the village, it

---

* £174,138, £111,152 and £222 today.

49

was a very quiet area, just a bus into Bishop's Stortford on a Saturday, and the ding-a-ling of the fish-and-chip van on a Tuesday night.

When the Hoseins moved in they wanted to be everybody's friend. He wanted to be lord of the manor. I don't think there was any feeling against them, I am sure that people didn't want to have much to do with them, but we did. I remember them coming often for a glass of something or a cup of tea and sitting in our sitting room. I don't know if we ever fed them, but I remember socialising with them. I thought that they were quite interesting really. I don't know that I'd ever met a person of colour before. I went to a girls' grammar school in Bishop's Stortford where every pupil was white. I am sure that in the village they were just accepted. Well, we accepted them but then maybe we were a bit unusual.[36]

A short walk from Rooks Farm was the Cock public house, long since gone, gutted by fire in 2008. On his first visit, Arthur announced that he would be starting a business at the farm, and 'spoke of having a big party at his place, but nothing ever came of it'.[37] On another occasion, he gestured to the man he was with* and said, 'You would not think that my friend was a millionaire, would you?' He never drank in the public bar, only the saloon.

Landlord Robert Bunkall's first impression of him was that he was 'very smartly dressed' and 'gave the impression that he was very prosperous'.[38] On one occasion, Arthur told landlady Joyce Bunkall that his wife had told him that he was a bit of a snob and that he should try to mix with people more:

He never mixed much with the local people at all, other than when he wanted a few odd jobs done … He always tried to give the impression that he had plenty of money although I never took too much notice and thought that he was really very conceited and a bit of a ladies' man.

He also let everybody know that he was a devoted member of the Liberal Party** and 'was thinking of standing for the local council'.[39]

After several months, he stopped going to the Cock. There must have been a strong reason, since it was not only within walking distance of his house but, from the recollections of local people, a very pleasant hostelry.

---

*   This was probably Arthur Rosenthal, a fellow tailor.
**   At this time led by Jeremy Thorpe, later to stand trial for conspiracy to murder.

A shocking story, related in the *Daily Mirror* after his conviction, told of how on one occasion, he was offered a drink and, asking for his usual whisky, 'he stuck his chest out as if to say he had at last been accepted. As the drink was passed to Hosein, three people spat in it. Not because Hosein was coloured, but because he was such an arrogant bastard.'[40] There is no disputing that Arthur's social persona was pushy and antagonistic, but it was clearly tolerated even less from an immigrant upstart than it would have been from a white man.

Arthur took to drinking in other nearby pubs, particularly the Black Horse at Brent Pelham and the Raven at Berden, where over Easter 1969 he met actor Griff Davies,* first when he was with three other actors, future movie star Jon Finch,** Michael Forrest and Beth Owen. 'There was a little actors' colony up there at that time,' says Jill Murray, who lived at neighbouring village Furneaux Pelham. 'Griff was a lovely man, who kept whippets, though Jon Finch was rather aloof.'[41] The group saw Arthur sitting alone in the public bar and, said Finch, 'feeling sorry for him, we let him join our company'.[42]

Arthur invited them all for a meal at the farm, where they went on a number of occasions, and Finch also occasionally drove some cloth to the East End for him after the driver he had employed during his ban quit. Elsa thought them 'a fast crowd'[43] but Arthur liked being seen with them and boasting that he also knew the most famous of the local actors, Rita Tushingham.

Griff Davies was an impish, colourful local character, known to be something of a womaniser. He found Arthur to be an 'effusive' man whose habit was 'to boast about his money and show off with it'.[44] On one occasion, Davies lunched at Rooks Farm when Elsa and the children were away, after which Arthur showed him the cine film of his trip back to Trinidad to see his family, but, curiously, played backwards because apparently, 'sometimes I like to see life backwards'.[45]

Frederick Butler, landlord of the Raven in Berden, said, 'Arthur was friendly to myself and other customers, and usually held any conversation by expounding on various topics and his own experiences in Trinidad.'[46] Yet there was a curious contrast between Arthur's gregariousness and the fierce privacy surrounding life at Rooks Farm. The Hoseins' nearest neighbour, Ernest

---

*   Michael Griffiths Davies was a member of Joan Littlewood's Theatre Workshop and a prolific supporting actor on television in the 1960s. Last TV credit: 1984.

** Jon Finch (1942–2012): unsmiling and adept British actor and former member of the SAS Reserve Regiment, who had a run of leading roles in movies of the 1970s. Famously publicity-shunning, he turned down the role of James Bond in 1973.

Woollard, a caretaker and handyman who lived at Old Rectory Cottage, at the end of the lane which leads to the farm, said that the Hoseins 'kept themselves to themselves, never encouraging visitors',[47] he and his wife talking to the children when they were going to and from school but having little interaction with Arthur. Another local said, 'He was a man who was always trying to impress people. He even offered to let us build a bungalow on his farm. We didn't know them at all well when this offer was made, and this seemed strange.'[48] William Baker, who ran a drinking club just off the Edgware Road which Arthur frequented, said, 'he would try to use big words but always got them in the wrong places.'[49]

Arthur was also an inveterate liar, but like all habitual liars, he lied even when the truth would have served him better. Rather than taking pride in his self-made success as a tailor, he would tell people that he was a designer for major fashion companies; when buying potatoes from a local farmer, he mentioned 'that he had been a solicitor and had been disbarred for helping his own people'.[50]

At the Star in Standon one evening, where he 'bought a large number of drinks for other persons in the bar',[51] the landlady told Elsa that the village needed a hairdresser, and that the Old Windmill, a vacant premises on the high street, was up for auction. Arthur decided that half of it could be a restaurant and announced that it would be a good business and that he 'would have two persons bidding for him'. He befriended the Westlakes, proprietors of a transport café at High Cross, a key location later in the story, introducing himself as a barrister. He invited them to the farm with a promise that he could serve them Indian curries. 'He was almost insistent that we should go.'[52] He then began calling at the café late in the afternoon on his journeys back from London, repeating the invitation.

Despite his wearying materialism and constant boasts, Arthur seems to have been generally accepted by most of the residents of east Hertfordshire. 'A handsome man, always immaculately dressed and always buying drinks, even for complete strangers' was how one regular in the Black Horse described him, although 'invariably when he bought a drink money matters would crop up. People got fed up with it.'[53] Landlady Mary Dodge said he was 'full of life, perky, a little bit of a dandy. With his eyes sparkling, he looked like a Babycham advert.'[54]

However, his thirst for alcohol was becoming ferocious. Elsa would later tell the Old Bailey that she would never ask him when he would be home, and that 'if he wants to go and have a drink, that is up to him. He works hard enough for it.'[55]

After making trousers, he would deliver them to finishers in London, who he employed on a casual basis for meagre wages, but his business was beginning to plateau. At least two of his clients, Maurice Herman and Morris Sunshine, dispensed with his services soon after his move out of London because 'his deliveries became so irregular'.[56] He advertised locally for a boy machinist apprentice in June 1968, planning to set up a clothing factory in the barn, but he was refused planning permission, something he again saw as a persecutory decision.

However, his colossal scotch intake – the night before his arrest he appears to have drunk somewhere in the region of ten double whiskies with ginger ale in the Raven, which he said was not unusual – was affecting not only his work but his marriage. His exuberance could switch in a moment to violence and he repeatedly beat Elsa, something that she went to great lengths to conceal from those around her. Their daughter, Freida, who cannot even bring herself to mention Arthur's name, says:

> I can never call him 'Dad' either, or 'my father'. He was never a father to me. He thought he was a king, he gave lots of parties, with Mum doing all the cooking, and could be quite charming, but in truth he was a monster. He would never touch us children but if we ever did anything to make him mad, Mum would get beaten. We had to get under the table in that kitchen and watch him beating her up.[57]

His treatment of other women is also deeply disturbing.

During the summer of 1968, he advertised for a woman to do some stitching work. Elsie Brown, a divorced woman who lived in nearby Furneaux Pelham, expressed an interest, and Arthur visited her that evening. They talked about him employing her and 'about coloured people being accepted by white people',[58] and he arranged to collect her the following morning. He arrived an hour late, and 'on the way out to the car he ran his hand down my back and over my buttocks'. When she was getting out of the car at Rooks Farm, 'he put his hand between my legs'. He did this twice more on their way into the house, before introducing her to Elsa and showing her through to the workroom.

The following day, he groped her again on the journey to the farm, so when they arrived, she hurried in by herself. In the kitchen, an argument broke out between Arthur and Elsa when he demanded a meal, picking up a carving knife and banging it on the table. Later in the afternoon, when Elsa went out to feed the pigs, Arthur told Mrs Brown that he would show her the bedroom, but she refused. He then asked her to stay late and keep his wife company, as he had to take some suits to Ongar. She agreed, but later in the evening noticed that the suits were still in the workroom. Arthur returned at 10 p.m. and took her home, 'again touching me as I got into and out of the car'.

She was molested again on the third day on her journey to the farm, and that afternoon told Elsa that she was leaving, saying that she had found a job nearer to her home. 'This was false, but I wanted to get away from Arthur.' She then told Arthur that she was leaving but that she would work until 5 p.m. Arthur was enraged and dismissed her, leaving her to walk home by herself. 'My impression was that Elsa was terrified of Arthur Hosein and that Arthur fancied himself as a woman's man.'

At the beginning of 1969, Elsa invited a Mr and Mrs Jackson to the farm for a fondue evening. Jackson managed the Kingsland branch of Ravel, the shoe shop, and had first got to know Arthur when he inquired about extending his workshop next door, subsequently attending a party at the house in Ongar while it was up for sale. They visited Rooks Farm in the middle of January, and sat up talking and drinking until 4 a.m., but when they went to bed, Mrs Jackson told her husband that Arthur had made her 'feel embarrassed'.[59] When they had been alone in the lounge, 'he said something to the effect that he had a good life and fancied her; this type of talk was used again at another occasion and once at the table he rubbed or tried to rub his legs against hers'.

Driving back the following morning, they decided to have nothing further to do with the Hoseins, but the next day Arthur telephoned while Mr Jackson was at work. His wife told Arthur that she had told her husband what had happened and that he was disgusted. Arthur replied that she 'shouldn't have done so as she had spoiled a beautiful friendship'. Mrs Jackson hung up on him, and they never saw or heard from the Hoseins again.

Although Elsa found few opportunities for hairdressing in the village, one of her clients was Eileen Green, to whose husband Arthur offered a job driving for him after a temporary ban:

> I became very good friends with her, but not with Arthur. On one occasion when he gave me a lift to Rooks Farm, he stopped the car and said, 'Come and see the pigs'. When we went into the pig house he said, 'I know you

fancy me'. He put his arms around me and I told him not to be so silly, I was old enough to be his mother.

Apparently, 'it was common gossip in the village that he was a womaniser. I certainly gave him no encouragement.'[60]

By now Arthur had also clocked up three motoring offences, and in June 1969 he cancelled his life insurance policies, the company also cancelling his car policies after he failed to declare his traffic convictions.[61] They had offered him revised terms, but he refused them, probably a sign of his outrage at being challenged as much as it was a sign of growing financial problems. Shortly after this, he loaned the uninsured Volvo to Jon Finch, who ran it into a ditch, causing £160 of damage.

At this point, Arthur's 14-year-old sister, Hafeeza Jaan Hosein, was also living at Rooks Farm and babysitting the children, but her life was not a happy one. 'She used to come on the school bus with us, although she didn't go to my school,' said Yasmin Strube. 'She had a very hard time. I remember particularly the boys being nasty to her.' Although Freida told me she did not remember experiencing any prejudice herself, Sharly Hughes, who also grew up in the area, recalled, 'There had never been anyone of colour living there and there has hardly been anyone since, and I think they suffered because of it.'[62]

By now, another member of the Hosein family had also arrived in England. Nizamodeen Hosein was born on 1 July 1948, the youngest of the brothers and the only one to be given a Muslim name. Aubrey Rose recalls on their first meeting being struck by the extraordinary difference between the brothers:

> Arthur was like a panther, in the way that he prowled and watched. Physically, I could see that Arthur shared some characteristics with his father. Nizamodeen, however, looked different, sounded different, and had an entirely different attitude. There was a slightly Chinese look about him, and I began to suspect that he might have had a different father. And of course, there was a Chinese population in Trinidad.[63]

Rose also remembers that 'he looked ill, so drawn', possibly a lasting legacy of rheumatic fever, which hospitalised him for six months when he was 16.

Nizamodeen attended the Excelsior High School in Couva until he was 17. After failing the London General Certificate of Education exam at O-level and receiving a beating from his father, he attempted suicide by taking twenty-four sleeping tablets at once. He was in hospital for several days, later claiming that he had been suffering from 'nervous tension'[64] and 'accidentally took an overdose while attempting to obtain relief, having found that the severe punishment from his father had left him feeling depressed, fed up and angry'.[65] He would also later say that he had a great hostility towards his father because of his strictness but, like Arthur, was affectionate about his mother.

After leaving school, he spent nearly a year out of work before taking a part-time job with Caroni County Council as a timekeeper. Joseph Belfon, a Trinidad and Tobago Police superintendent, considered him 'the troublesome one' of a family who were otherwise considered decent and respectable.

On 3 January 1968, he appeared before Couva Magistrates' Court on a charge of malicious wounding, having stabbed his eldest brother, Charles, in the abdomen, something he later claimed was an accident, his brother having collared him from behind while he was peeling fruit. Although the offence was proved, due to it being a first offence and in consideration of the circumstances of the offence, the relationship of the parties involved and the representations made on his behalf, the court did not register a conviction and discharged him. Shortly after this, he sustained minor head injuries in a road traffic accident which rendered him unconscious for four hours.

On 14 May 1969, he was back before Mr Holder, the local magistrate, this time on a charge of assault and battery of his father, whom he had enraged by coming home drunk and breaking some glasses. This time, he was fined $150 to keep the peace, and ordered to enter into a recognizance with his mother as surety, and to report fortnightly to a probation officer for the next three years, over which his sentence was suspended.[66] Instead, six days later he arrived in England on a chartered flight, with a five-month visitor permit which did not entitle him to paid employment.

Apparently, no one knew that he was coming to England. On arrival, he telephoned Adam, who collected him and with whom he stayed initially.[67] During his time at 2 Leander Road, Thornton Heath, Adam said that he 'tried to get Nizam to educate himself in order to establish himself in a secure job, but he was not interested'.[68] A distant relative, Shauffie Ali, a science student, befriended him over the summer, usually 'playing cards, watching television, or lifting weights. He was very talkative, and we used to talk about Trinidad and the state of affairs. While he was living with Adam, he was a labourer, working for Wimpey, I think.'[69]

Rahim Mohammed, a progress clerk for Pye Records, and his family, also distant relatives of the Hoseins, were living in nearby Norbury. Nizam told Rahim that he wanted to remain in England, but Rahim felt that he was 'unstable, because although he talked of settling in this country, he seemed to lose interest in his work very quickly'.[70] At the end of June, while Rahim's wife was in hospital, Nizam asked whether Dolly, a student nurse he had known back in Trinidad and who was now living in Yorkshire, could stay at their house, Adam having refused. He agreed, and Dolly stayed for a week, but when she left, Rahim learned that Nizam had twice slept with her in the house, which 'annoyed me because I have a teenage daughter'.[71] When confronted about it, Nizam simply denied that it had ever happened, a characteristic reaction to any accusation, trivial or weighty.

At a party at Adam's house, Nizam also met Liley Mohammed. She too had come to London from Trinidad and was now working as a nurse at the Whittington Hospital in Holloway. She was living in Hornsey with her two brothers and sister-in-law. She was the sister of Arthur's former mistress, Farida, although the two appear not to have had a great deal of interaction or affection for each other. Liley will become a crucial character in the story, but for now, it is worth acknowledging that she was nearly 30, so almost a decade older than Nizam, and had a husband back in Trinidad who was refusing to divorce her. She also had three children aged 11, 7 and 5, also in Trinidad and being looked after by her mother.

Nizam had asked Adam to make some arrangements for him to go to college, but on the day of his enrolment, he announced that he wanted to join the RAF instead. Adam tried to dissuade him, later explaining that because of 'the prejudice that occurs in the Air Force towards coloured persons, I thought it best for him not to join'.[72] Shauffie Ali said, 'Nizam came to me very distressed. He said he had quarrelled with Adam about joining the forces and wanted £1 to visit Arthur.'

Nizam then further angered Rahim, whom he had asked to be a referee for his application. Since Rahim knew nothing of his background, he was unable to answer all the required questions, but he then found that Nizam had given his address as his home address, without permission, presumably because of Adam's disapproval of the application. Soon after this, Adam came home from work to find that Nizam had gone. He had telephoned Arthur, who had driven down to collect him.

The pair returned some days later, while Adam was out, to collect Nizam's things, and he moved into Rooks Farm. On 25 September, he applied for an extension to his passport, because 'I have decided to join the Royal Air Force',[73] and although it was extended until 10 January, his RAF application came to nothing. He was interviewed at Northolt, but apparently turned up scruffy and unkempt, asking the wing commander for a cigarette, and when told he was not suitable, 'became unpleasant and accused the panel of colour prejudice'.[74]

In return for pocket money and cigarettes, Nizam's role at the farm was as Arthur's gofer and driver (though he had no licence to drive in Britain) and Elsa's helper in looking after the animals. Arthur had no skill or interest in farming and left everything to Elsa, who was the real farmer. 'Under Hitler I had to work for a year on a farm and I've always liked it,' she would later say.[75]

Harold Prime, the local licensing officer for Hertfordshire County Council, visited the farm regularly to inspect the livestock, usually dealing with Elsa, who:

> … kept all the books and as far as I know tended and fed the stock and did all the cleaning out and dealing over the livestock. Arthur used to come out sometimes to talk, but he didn't seem to have much to do with the farm side. The younger brother did, but he didn't know much about it. They were all rather unbusinesslike as far as buying and selling stock and would buy at very high prices.[76]

Intriguingly, Alfred Bardwell, a local market gardener and smallholder, judged Arthur 'a timid sort of person. When my son and I went there to castrate some pigs he ran out of the farm at the first sight of blood and didn't come back until we had finished'. He was 'always well dressed, very smart, and at no time did he get his hands dirty'.[77]

In contrast to Arthur's smartness, the scruffy Nizam quickly became known for his bizarre habit of wearing a crash helmet. He told Joyce Bunkall that he 'loved working with animals and liked them better than people. He was quite a pleasant chap and was always very polite when he came to the pub', but 'he had on this crash helmet affair which he always wore, even if he was just walking about, as well as when he was driving'.[78] He told one villager, who thought that he looked rather sinister, that 'he worked for a Trinidad security company'.[79] Tom Pateman, whose parents had a dairy farm 10 miles away at High Cross, says, 'They were friends with my mum and dad, and Arthur would come in for a cup of tea, but the younger brother would never come into the house, he'd have that crash helmet on and just walked up and down, which was a bit weird.'[80]

Freida describes life at the farm at this time as:

… horrible. Once Arthur drove away, it was lovely there, it was like being free again in your own home. Mum was smiling and laughing with us, Nizam as well, I loved him and used to play with him. But then, as soon as we heard Arthur come back up the lane, our freedom was gone. We were escaping everywhere in that house just not to see him, because you never knew what mood he would be in.

Frederick Butler, landlord of the Raven, said that compared with Arthur, who was 'always conspicuous by talking in a loud voice or singing to the radio' when in the pub, Nizam 'was quiet and did not join in'.[81] 'He seemed a very different personality to the older one,' says Yasmin Strube. 'They looked so different and had different builds. He was shy and quiet.' Yasmin's mother, Audrey, told the police later that when she first encountered Nizam, 'I realised that this boy may be lonely as a stranger in the village and asked him down to my house for coffee with my son'.[82] Yasmin adds, 'He did actually ask me out when my mum was befriending them, and we might have gone for a drink at the Cock. I was only 15, but underage drinking seemed to be accepted in those days.'[83]

Sharly Hughes remembers an unpleasant encounter that was typical of the brothers' increasingly fanatical guarding of Rooks Farm:

I lived half a mile across fields, and one of my circuits on the horse was right around the farm. One day the dogs got out and chased us, getting nastier and nastier. It was very frightening. The two brothers came out, both extremely bad-tempered and shouting at me, not wanting me anywhere near the place. It was all a bit strange. Ever since then I've had a fear of Alsatians.[84]

By the autumn, problems were mounting for the Hoseins. Arthur was spending more time spending money than earning it, and, according to Elsa, they had 'been caught and cheated over the animals'.[85] Although he continued to throw money at strangers in pubs, Arthur was truculent and dishonourable in his business affairs, constantly making enemies. He had the drive tarmacked by 'a group of gypsy-type people' but refused to pay them, criticising the quality of their work. He argued with 'a huge man, very tall and very broad', making Nizam 'afraid of retaliation' from him.[86] His failure to pay national insurance and income tax, on top of his other commitments, saw his debts now exceed £1,000.*

In contrast, his brother Adam was now earning 'about £4,000** a year'.[87] Arthur was a man on the way down, who had overreached himself and whose taste for the good life was now an insatiable greed. He was also a man becoming frighteningly reckless, predatory and violent.

Then, on the night of Friday, 3 October 1969, he and Nizam watched David Frost interviewing Rupert Murdoch. The same day, the local paper, the *Herts and Essex Observer*, advertised an auction of the contents of the Old Rectory at Stocking Pelham, which would be held on Wednesday, 15 October 1969 at 11 a.m. Among the items listed was a 'fine 12-bore hammer shotgun by Purdey's'.[88] They were spotted at the auction by a villager who noticed that Nizam was wearing dark glasses.[89] As well as a few items of furniture, the brothers made the winning bid for the shotgun.

A local farmer, Leonard Smith, drove their purchases back to Rooks Farm. When unloading the furniture, he set down on the ground his spare wheel and a rusty hedging billhook. When he got home, he realised that he had left the spare wheel and the billhook behind. The following morning, he telephoned Arthur, who called back twenty minutes later to say that Nizam had found the spare wheel but that there was no sign of the billhook. Both the billhook and the shotgun are now in a display cabinet at the Crime Museum, New Scotland Yard.

The Hoseins had selected their target, and they had drawn their weapons. To kidnap Anna Murdoch, all that remained was to find out where she lived.

---

*   £11,733 today.

**   £47,000 today.

4

ADVENT

A most pleasant trip, lovely country with the leaves on the trees, wonderful col-
ours. Hope you are all well and happy.

Muriel McKay, Munich, 10 November 1969.

Dreams were dying for Arthur as the leaves fell at Rooks Farm. Autumn brought with it bailiffs, who were now chasing him even over sums as low as £10, which he either could not or would not pay. Perhaps because of the mounting debts, on 13 October he made his wife the registered owner of the Volvo.

As the days darkened and the nights lengthened, the Hoseins began to make plans for Christmas, ordering two turkeys from George Cuda, a farmer at Sleepy Hollow, near Berden. However, shortly after this, Nizam suggested that Elsa go to Germany for two weeks with the children at Christmas and leave him to look after the animals. (This must have been agreed by the end of October, as Leonard Smith remembered it being mentioned when he dined at Rooks Farm a couple of weeks after the auction.)

Arthur now readily waved about and wielded his shotgun. He bragged about the £140 purchase to a neighbour, Herbert Mardell, whom he had previously pestered to sell him a gun. Mardell had repeatedly refused because Arthur had no licence or certificate. Examining the weapon, Mardell was unimpressed: 'It had two sets of barrels, one set wouldn't even match the stock and the other had a dent in, and in my opinion wouldn't have been worth more than £30.'[1] Nevertheless, the weapon allowed Arthur to indulge in his megalomania.

On 5 November the hounds of the Puckeridge Hunt, led by Captain Charles Barclay, crossed Arthur's field and scattered some chickens. Arthur and a helmeted Nizam shouted abuse and waved a stick. Arthur, according to Barclay, was 'in a violent temper and threatening to sue me for destruction of property and all kinds of damage'.[2] Outraged, Arthur telephoned the local police and even telephoned Scotland Yard before Barclay decided to visit the farm and make peace with him.

Something of a squireling, 50-year-old Charles Barclay lived at nearby Pelham Hall. His family had been masters of the Puckeridge Hunt since 1896. Educated at Eton and Cambridge, the aristocratic landowner, who hunted up to four times a week,[3] would have been, to Arthur, a symbol of an England that both intimidated and inspired him.[*]

Approaching Rooks Farm, even this old warhorse was 'a bit nervous, as the dogs were extremely savage'.[4] Arthur was in a temper, alleging that the hunt was responsible for 'killing at least forty chickens, that the calves were dying of shock and his wife had slipped a disc'.[5] Unable to provide proof of any of this when pressed, Arthur calmed, and 'after a sticky start, we got on very well. We repaired to the Black Horse and drank quite a lot of whisky',[6] although not before Arthur had taken the opportunity to show him all over the house.

Barclay was therefore utterly confused when, two days later, he received a solicitor's letter reiterating all the allegations. He countered this with one from his own solicitor, denying everything, and a personal letter to Arthur suggesting that they should be good neighbours. As a result, Arthur visited Barclay at Pelham Hall one evening with Elsa, throughout which 'he was in a most expansive mood and talked about his farm and tailoring interests'.[7] Barclay felt that he was 'more inclined to sharp practice than legitimate business'. He also sensed from what he had seen of the condition of the animals and the farm that Arthur was in financial difficulties.

Arthur followed up the visit with a letter, expressing his 'worthy thanks to you for your sincerity' and proclaiming that 'I am convinced after all you are a gentleman'.[8] Although he could not ride a horse, he applied to join the Puckeridge Hunt and asked Barclay to help Nizam obtain a work permit. Barclay was happy to oblige and wrote to the National Farmers' Union, only to be told that although they would usually be happy to assist, they had to refuse on this occasion because the pugnacious Arthur Hosein was currently involved in a dispute with another of their members.

---

[*]   Barclay was later High Sheriff of Hertfordshire.

Arthur had also asked Leonard Smith if he could guarantee Nizam employment in agriculture, with Smith agreeing to employ him on a part-time basis, although nothing ever came of this. Arthur and Elsa took Smith to the Home Office to make the arrangements, Arthur promising him £20 for his trouble, which was never honoured. Instead, all Smith got was a Chinese meal on the drive home from London, with Arthur having to borrow £1 from him to pay the bill.

Those who suspected from the state of the farm and the livestock that Arthur had financial troubles had it confirmed when his name appeared in newspapers for the first time on 21 November. The *Herts and Essex Observer* reported that he had been fined £5, with £1 costs, by Bishop's Stortford Magistrates. The court heard that he had been visited and his insurance card inspected in May but had said at the time that he couldn't pay because he did not have his cheque book. After ignoring two letters, he admitted the offence in writing and said that he would pay the sum owed, which was £49 15s 4d*, as soon as he had the money.[9] This public humiliation and indignity must have embittered him but, stultified by whisky and high-tar cigarettes, and increasingly petulant, the experience did little to restore his work ethic.

He called on Abraham Eckhardt, a Finchley tailor, asking for work. He gave Arthur a small order, but reluctantly, 'because he was so erratic in calling'.[10] At the start of December, one long-standing client, Steve Kutner, criticised his work. Arthur was incensed, said that he would not work for him anymore and refused to deliver the last four pairs of trousers that were outstanding. Kutner repeatedly rang the farm and Elsa covered for Arthur, claiming that he was sick and in hospital, although when Kutner asked which one, so that he could send him a get-well card, she 'appeared flustered and told me to send it to the farm address'.[11]

While any plans that he may have been turning over in his mind for the kidnapping must still have been fuzzy at this point, they gathered pace once the brothers had established that they would be alone at the farm from 13 December, when Elsa and the children would be sailing for Germany, until New Year. (She planned to spend a week with each of her two brothers and her sister.) Immediately she left the farm, another set of frustrated, desperate crimes began, which surely were the final spur that led him and Nizam to Wimbledon.

---

*   About £580 in 2022.

Relations with the neighbouring Strube family had been harmonious until now, although in early December, after the fanbelt had broken on the Hoseins' second car, a Morris Minor, Nizam had called Audrey for help when Arthur and Elsa had run out of petrol and were stranded at Clay Chimneys, about a mile and a half from Stocking Pelham. She drove Arthur to a petrol station and chatted with Elsa in the back of the Volvo while they waited, but then 'he pressed £1 on me. I felt rather embarrassed.'[12]

A few days before Elsa was due to leave for Germany, Arthur and Nizam called on Audrey, asking for her son's help to fix the spring in the double-barrelled shotgun. Arthur then asked what Yasmin was doing on the Saturday night as he needed a babysitter. She tried to make an excuse. In her statement to the police in 1970, she said, 'I don't know why, but I was determined I would not go alone as I never like being in a house on my own.'[13] Arthur said that he would pay her and that there would be plenty of food in the house, and although she did not actually say she would go, he 'seemed to take it for granted that I would'.

She arranged for a friend from school to accompany her, but as the girls arrived at Rooks Farm, they were puzzled to see that the whole family were leaving, including the children, who it seemed were accompanying Elsa to Germany. Deciding that perhaps they were really required simply to house-sit rather than babysit, they were told to expect the brothers back by 9 p.m., Arthur kissing her on the mouth before he left. Uneasy, and finding the house cold and, despite what Arthur had said, with barely anything to eat or drink, only the remains of a curry that the family had eaten before leaving and a tin of spaghetti rings, they watched television and 'stayed as close to the fire as we could'. Looking back at the incident today, Yasmin says, 'There is no way that I would let two 15-year-olds be alone with that huge Alsatian roaming around.'[14]

At about 9 p.m., Nizam called from the Raven, saying that they were out with Rita Tushingham, and asked whether they were all right to stay for another hour or so. In fact, the brothers did not return until 11.30 p.m. Also, despite what they had told the girls, Elsa and the children travelled to Germany by boat rather than plane, so rather than having taken her to the airport, they had probably only driven her to Liverpool Street Station, less than an hour's drive away.

When Audrey arrived home at 11.15 p.m., she was concerned that her daughter was not there. She telephoned Rooks Farm and as she and Yasmin were speaking, the Hoseins' car drew up outside. Yasmin's original statement continued:

They had been drinking, but were not drunk, although Arthur was the more under the influence of the two. They had brought with them about a dozen bottles of Guinness, some vodka, and some lime.

Arthur pressed vodkas on them both, which Nizam then kept topping up. Then Arthur walked over to her friend and said, 'Come and see the other room':

She said that she did not want to go, but Arthur took hold of her arm and said, 'Come on.' She later told me that they had got as far as the bathroom when Arthur wanted to kiss her, and she emptied her glass over him.

Audrey arrived at this point and, full of apology for the lateness of the hour, Arthur pressed a bottle of Guinness on her. She was concealing her anger as he insisted on showing her around the house, which 'they were obviously very proud of, though I thought it was rather sparsely furnished'.[15] Arthur gave Yasmin £1 and her friend 10s. As they tried to leave, 'Nizam came after us to the car still trying to press another drink on Mother'.[16] Today, she recalls that 'they both tried to grope us. We just grabbed each other's hands and ran out of the door. We were glad that we were out of the house. We must have thought it was a bit strange. I probably didn't tell my mother what had happened.'[17]

The brothers invited Audrey and her daughter to spend Christmas Eve with them at the farm, but they declined. Even though Arthur had no choice but to pay them, with their mother present, his usual spitefulness at being challenged showed in the petty insult of giving Yasmin's friend less money. It would not be the last time that the Strubes witnessed his unpleasant personality.

Three days later, Wilfred Hunt, a valuation clerk from Dane End, a hamlet about 10 miles from Stocking Pelham, called at Rooks Farm. Arthur made him coffee, boasting of recently having cocktails with Captain Barclay and that he was a designer who had employed 'a hundred people in London at one time'.[18] Arthur invited Hunt and his wife for a drink at the farm that evening, but when Hunt got home and told his wife, she felt that 'the way my husband spoke, I got the opinion that this man must have money, and as we are not too well off, I was not really interested in getting involved. In view of this we decided not to go.'[19]

The following evening, the couple were having a drink at the Plough in Great Munden when their daughter telephoned the pub to say that the Hoseins were at the house demanding to know why they hadn't visited the previous evening. Mr Hunt told her to send them up to the Plough, where Mr Hunt blamed the fog for them not visiting the previous evening. Arthur was quite jovial, claiming that they had been passing through on their way home from London. Although Mrs Hunt 'could not imagine how they could have been passing through Dane End, they were quite friendly, and I didn't think any more of it'. When the Plough closed at 10.30 p.m., Arthur splashed out on whisky, beer and Skol liqueurs, and insisted that they all go back to the farm, with landlord Gerald Carrington* accompanying them, for a meal which Mrs Hunt was expected to make.

On arrival at the farm, Carrington noticed the shotgun on the sideboard. Arthur told them that he had just bought it 'but thought that he had paid too much for it'. They were served drinks, but not only was there nothing to eat, the Aga was not working. Nizam was sent out to kill and behead a chicken, which Mr Hunt had to pluck, and his wife then used it to make a curry.

Arthur prattled about his outgoings and invented stories about elevated people that he had worked for, though he could not remember their names when asked. He said that he knew a local actor who was having an affair, criticised a famous actress that he had met as 'ugly', and said that he knew John Bloom** and fancied his wife, Anne, and that his own wife had wanted to divorce him five years ago (presumably after the affair with Farida).

Mrs Hunt was learning German and said that she would be interested to meet Elsa. After the meal, Arthur asked if she would like Nizam to show her the calves, 'and like a fool, I said that I would'. As she braved the two Alsatians outside the back door, she realised that Arthur was behind her, not Nizam:

> Out in the barn he grabbed me, and I pulled his hair and kicked his leg and he let go of me and told me to behave myself. I marched out and told him that I had not come there to be messed about by him and went to go back

---

* Carrington was a professional organ builder who had bought the pub as a retirement cottage, only to succumb to local pleas to keep it open as a public house. Wonderfully, he installed in the lounge bar an organ rescued from the Gaumont Cinema in Finchley and held weekly concerts featuring guest organists. The pub was featured in a British Movietone film of the time, but sadly is now long gone.

** John Bloom (1931–2019) was a British entrepreneur who made his fortune in the 'washing-machine wars' of the early 1960s. In 1962 he had an affair with 18-year-old Christine Holford, who was killed a few weeks later by her husband, club owner Harvey Holford. In October 1969, Bloom pleaded guilty to two charges under the Companies Act and was fined £30,000.

to the house but had to wait for him to calm the dogs before I could get by. I said nothing to my husband about his grabbing hold of me but said that it was about time we went. I purposely never said anything to my husband then because on the sideboard there was a shotgun and I was frightened, but I told him on the way home.

★★★

Hazrah Mohammed, a second cousin of the Hoseins who had attended school with Nizam, first met Arthur on his trip to Trinidad in 1967, when she told him that she had applied to train as a nurse in England. Just before midnight on 18 December, he and Nizam arrived at the North Middlesex Hospital's nurses' home in Silver Street, Edmonton, asking for her, again using the excuse that they were passing on their way home. They invited her to the farm, but she insisted on taking her friend, Margaret, who had only been in England for seven days. Margaret sat in the back of the Volvo with Nizam and realised that she was 'sitting on something hard and uncomfortable. It was covered in brown paper, and I somehow formed the opinion that it was a shotgun.'[20]

The four arrived back at Rooks Farm at 1.30 a.m. Margaret refused alcohol and was told by Arthur that 'things were different in London to back home, and that I would have to change my ways'. He also said that he didn't mind if she slept with Nizam. 'I became terribly embarrassed and apprehensive'[21] and went to bed. Nizam suggested that they sleep together, so she put her pyjamas on over her clothes and wedged the vacuum cleaner against the bedroom door.

Hazrah shared a bed with Arthur. 'He did touch me, but sexual intercourse did not take place.'[22] She nodded off but was awoken by a distressed Margaret complaining that Nizam had entered her room on the excuse of looking for his pyjamas. She was afraid of spending the night by herself and asked if Arthur could sleep in the other room so that she and Hazrah could share the double bed, but Arthur refused, growling that the other room was cold and that he would not give up his bed for anyone.

★★★

By now, the brothers had been trying without success to find out where Rupert Murdoch lived. If Arthur had possessed any interest in Murdoch beyond his millions, this would have been an easier task, since the BBC *24 Hours* profile put out at the time of the Keeler affair had not only shown the outside of his house and said that it was 'in a fashionable square near Hyde Park' but had displayed the frighteningly vulnerable spectacle of Anna walking their 1-year-old daughter Elisabeth in the gardens opposite. The street was also named casually in various newspaper reports about the mogul. Despite this, the address of 73 Sussex Gardens, W2, remained unknown to the Hoseins.

They resorted to driving to the *News of the World* offices in Bouverie Street, outside of which they noticed what was surely Murdoch's Rolls-Royce. Having noted down the registration number, ULO 18F, on Friday, 19 December, after dropping the nurses back at the hospital, they drove to the GLC Vehicle Registration Department at County Hall. Little did they know that as they were driving across London, the Murdochs were flying across the Indian Ocean on their way back to Australia, where they would be spending Christmas. Murdoch had left Alick McKay as acting chairman, and since the new Mercedes that Alick had been given with the job was currently in for repair, fatally, in his absence, Murdoch had given him use of the company Rolls-Royce.

Arthur sent Nizam into County Hall with a story that he had been in a minor accident with the Rolls-Royce and wanted to trace its owner. Nizam was issued with a form which he filled in with a false name, Sharif Mustafa (actually a school friend in Trinidad), and a false address, 175 Norbury Crescent, the home of his relatives, Rahim Mohammed and his family. The form was passed to Maureen Callanan, a 17-year-old clerical officer, who told him that the car was the property of the *News of the World*. Nizam then told her that the car perhaps belonged to the managing director and that he had already been on the telephone to the newspaper 'but had been unable to get on to anyone of importance. This man kept on and on about having previously rung the *News of the World* and had got no satisfaction from them.'[23] Despite his protests, he was told that there was nothing more they could tell him and he left. The only obvious way that remained of discovering the Murdochs' address, it seemed, would be simply to follow the car.

Over the weekend, an unexplained incident occurred 8 miles from Stocking Pelham, at Hatchetts Farm, Old Hall Green. Wilfred Lane, a 69-year-old farmer, was attacked in his home by two men 'who appeared to be of Indian origin',[24] one of whom was aged 30–40 years and 'in need of a shave'.[25] Lane had been drinking in the Horse and Groom nearby, and shortly after returning home, had answered the door to two men who kicked him and hit him with a blunt instrument.

There was no attempt at robbery, even though Lane had £175 in his wallet which he had just drawn from the pub's Christmas savings club. He was taken to hospital, where he was treated for a fractured ankle and given twelve stitches in his head.

Arthur had recently paid Lane £55 for a pony for his daughter, but the animal was wild, biting him on the leg and tearing his clothing, so he decided that it was not safe for the children. Having not paid for it, it was agreed that he could simply return it, but before he could do so, it had bolted. When the police learned of this, the Hoseins, as the only local people fitting the description, became suspects.

At 9 a.m. the following morning, Alick McKay's first day as acting chairman, William Nunn, the Murdochs' chauffeur, arrived at St Mary House to drive him to Bouverie Street in the car which would take him to and from work for the rest of the week and which would propel the family into tragedy.

Alick's journey home from work that evening must have been the one that was tailed by the Hoseins. It was eleven weeks since they had watched Murdoch on *Frost on Friday*. They now had what they thought was his address. They also had only two weeks left before Elsa and the children returned from Germany.

The following morning, Arthur left the Volvo at the Hailey garage in Hoddesdon and ordered a taxi back to Rooks Farm. He talked incessantly about how he did not get on with the locals and had nothing to do with them. The driver 'formed the impression that he was very agitated. From the time he got in the car he wanted a drink and appeared to want to talk to someone.'[26]

When they finally found a pub that was open, Arthur drank two double whiskies and fell into conversation with a man that he wanted to buy a field from. After half an hour, he asked the driver to stay longer with him, but he had another booking.

On Christmas Eve, Nizam telephoned Liley, asking her to come over for Christmas to cook for them. It was the first time she had heard from him since he'd left London, but she was unable to go as she was on night shifts over Christmas. The brothers went to the Raven in the afternoon, collected their two turkeys from George Cuda, and returned to the pub in the evening.

On Christmas Day, Nizam called Liley again. She was cross as she had just gone to bed after her night shift and put the phone down on him. He then telephoned her ward on Christmas night while she was on duty and she again told him that she didn't want to come. He passed her on to Arthur and finally she gave in and agreed to come and cook for them.

The brothers arrived at the Whittington Hospital to collect her at first light on Boxing Day. She noticed that Arthur was growing a beard. Back at the farm, she went to bed for a few hours. Outside, the Puckeridge Hunt rode by,[27] Captain Barclay this time having telephoned Arthur first to ask his permission.

Liley watched television with the brothers in the afternoon, then at 6 p.m. she went upstairs to have a bath and get ready for going to work, as her shift started at 9 p.m. Arthur told her that rather than her uniform, to put her dress on so that they could go to the pub first, insisting that they would have just one drink, but she refused. While she was taking her bath, Arthur entered with a drink for her. She scolded him, and he laughed as he left.

She appeared downstairs, dressed and hurrying them up, since the journey back to town would take about an hour. The three got into the Volvo, but at the end of the drive, rather than turning left for London, Arthur turned right and drove to the Black Horse at Brent Pelham.

They were still there at 8 p.m., and after two drinks, Liley was urging them to leave. Arthur insisted on staying for another drink, then another. Liley was cross and Nizam, who had said very little, tried to persuade him. She telephoned the hospital to warn them that she would be late and returned to find Arthur and Nizam arguing. Arthur suggested that Nizam drive her, to which Liley responded, 'You are unfair, you know he hasn't a licence to drive in England.'[28]

The argument continued as they went out to the car. They drove off, Liley assuming that they were now headed for London, only for Arthur to drive them back to the farm. Nizam suggested that she stay the night. When she refused, Arthur grabbed her arm and pulled her out of the vehicle. Liley twisted her ankle as she stumbled.

Indoors, she noticed her foot swelling up and started to cry. She refused Nizam's offer again to stay there for the night, so he picked up the telephone to call a minicab. Arthur then knocked the telephone out of his hand and the brothers fought. Arthur threw Nizam out of the back door and then locked it, before returning to a petrified Liley:

Arthur then got hold of me by the arm, he tried to drag me up the stairs, the ones by the bar. He hit me by the ear, a slap on my face. He was shouting and carrying on, he frightened me, I was crying. I went with him to his bedroom because I was frightened. He said after pushing me into his bedroom, 'Will you come to bed with me.' He closed the door, stood by it, wouldn't let me pass, took all his clothes off, then pushed me on to the bed. I bit him, I think it was on his chest, and on his lip when he tried to kiss me. We struggled, he tried to put his hand under my clothes. Then he said, 'Oh, you are cold.' He left me.

She sat on the floor, terrified, hearing the dogs barking outside. Once Arthur was asleep, she crept downstairs and found Nizam in the living room, having quietly climbed back in through a window. He had been to the police, and had telephoned Liley's brother, Junade, to see whether he could collect her. This upset Liley further, as she knew that her family would be angry about her associating with the brothers.

They sat by the fire. Arthur appeared at 3 a.m. and told them to go to bed and he would take her back to London in the morning. 'I saw Nizam was afraid of his brother. Nizam and I went to the same bed, he didn't touch me or suggest anything.'[29] She told Nizam that she was thinking of moving to Canada and he said that he would consider coming with her, although there was no chance of them marrying for the moment as her husband back in Trinidad was refusing to divorce her.[30]

The following morning, after Nizam had fed the animals, they took Liley back to London, where her ankle injury kept her off work for a couple of days. On their way back to Stocking Pelham, they called at the Smiths at Bourne Farm in Widford. Leonard Smith was at the Jolly Waggoners in Much Hadham, doing a deal with a man over a cow, but Mrs Smith made them something to eat, as Arthur grumbled that all they'd had for Christmas was two legs from a turkey. She noticed that 'neither man looked as though he'd had a shave, and Arthur had a growth of beard around his jaw line'.[31] He told her that he intended growing a beard.

The next day, Sunday, 28 December, began with a visit to Rooks Farm by two plain-clothes police officers investigating the assault on Wilfred Lane. As well as the Hoseins obviously fitting the vague description of the attackers, Arthur's disagreement with him over the pony had now come to light. Arthur antagonistically denied everything, and he and Nizam alibied each other. 'This is terrible for you to think that I did this,' Arthur told them. 'We are very peaceful-living people and would not hurt anyone.'[32]

Nizam also denied any knowledge of the incident, saying that he didn't leave the farm very often, since 'I have no transport and my brother won't let me drive his car'. He also denied having been in trouble with the police before.

When the police asked after Elsa, Arthur told them she was expected back at 'the beginning of January'.[33]

Lane himself had denied that the Hoseins were his attackers but the police were mistrustful of this since he was suspiciously uncooperative on every aspect of the inquiry. Lane was 'a broken-down farmer'[34] and heavy drinker with a number of criminal associates to whom he rented outbuildings, and a man who clearly did not welcome the attention of the police.

At 9.30 p.m. that night, the eve of the kidnapping of Muriel McKay, the brothers visited the Plough at Great Munden. An uncharacteristically sociable Nizam got into a conversation about motor cars with another customer, Malcolm Reid, and gave him his name and telephone number, saying that he was interested in buying a van.[35] He also invited the barman, John Bailey, to visit the farm sometime.

Arthur, meanwhile, was in high spirits, singing a calypso about Harold Wilson and claiming that he knew John Bloom and his wife, and that the High Commissioner of Jamaica had been invited to the farm at Christmas but had not turned up. 'Someone in the bar said that Arthur would be having dinner with the Queen next, and this caused a laugh.'[36]

Mrs Hunt was working in the pub that evening and purposely stayed behind the bar in view of what had happened at the farm. However, during the evening Arthur followed her into the kitchen:

He asked me if I had told my husband and when I said that I had, he said that I was silly because we could have had a good time. I called Gerald and Wilf to get him out which they did, and my husband then stayed with me.[37]

Back in the bar, she heard Arthur tell the clientele that he was going to a dinner party with the Murdochs. The name meant nothing to Mrs Hunt until something else that he said made her remember the *Frost on Friday* television programme. It also struck her because she and her husband were trying to sell their house and emigrate to Australia.

The brothers left the pub after midnight. Arthur 'was not clean-shaven. The younger man had long hair and was scruffy.'[38]

The following morning, Monday, 29 December, PC Richard Felton called at Rooks Farm regarding Nizam's complaint on Boxing Day night. Nizam told him that 'there is no bother, we are all right now'.[39] He asked to speak to Arthur but was told that he was out. There was no sign of the Volvo. It was the last anyone saw of either brother until five hours later, when they were spotted in Wimbledon.

Just before Muriel was kidnapped, Nizam approached Ernest Woollard at the Old Rectory about borrowing a hacksaw and blades, claiming that he wanted to saw through some piping. He kept the hacksaw for about a week, 'but when he returned it the blade was worn out, the teeth had gone'.[40] It had been used to saw down both barrels of the shotgun.

5

TRESPASSES

Have lunch daily by the pool – saves dressing. Enjoying this lazy life.
Muriel McKay, Las Palmas, Canary Islands, 23 October 1963.

Christmas began for the McKays when Alick arrived home on the afternoon of Christmas Eve. Mrs Nightingale had just finished her chores, and Alick asked William Nunn to drive her home in the Rolls-Royce. The McKays waved her off. She said that they were 'in a happy mood and we had been laughing together'.[1] Two days earlier, Muriel had paid what would be her last visit to her dressmaker, to whom she gave Christmas gifts of Guerlain talcum powder and hand soap, which had been bought and wrapped at Harrods.

The McKays spent Christmas in Sussex with their daughters. They arrived at Dianne's at midnight on Christmas Eve and sat talking by the fire until 2 a.m. The next day, they had Christmas lunch there, then left at 5 p.m. to stay with Jennifer and her husband, Ian Burgess, their 3-year-old son and Ian's 9-year-old son by his first marriage.

The pressure of Alick's new appointment had put him in a somewhat grumpy mood, and although Muriel was a little quiet, David Dyer felt that this was probably the aftermath of Christmas and having had a late night. Muriel spent most of the visit playing with her grandchildren.

They returned to St Mary House on Boxing Day, relieved that they had not been burgled again on their first overnight stay away since the break-in. The following day, Dr Markowicz joined them for lunch. He found Muriel to be 'her usual happy self'.[2]

Monday, 29 December began for the McKays with the delivery of all the day's national newspapers, Alick always keeping a close eye on the competition. The young *Sun* that day, staunchly opposed to capital punishment – an editorial position unimaginable a couple of decades later – reflected on the abolition of the death penalty and on evidence that after twelve years 'a prisoner begins to deteriorate psychologically and the chances of ultimate reform decline steeply', questioning whether society has the right to condemn people to life imprisonment, which it considered 'a fate worse than death'.[3]

Alick was collected by William Nunn at 9.30 a.m. The forecast warned of a maximum temperature of freezing and light snow flurries. Sunset in London was 4.59 p.m.

After collecting Mrs Nightingale, Muriel prepared a steak and kidney pudding for the evening meal. She made coffee for their elevenses, over which they 'spoke about Christmas generally and about the nude lady* in the Sunday papers'.[4] Muriel told Mrs Nightingale how thrilled she was to be embarking on a new painting class in Putney. 'She was really looking forward to this and was in a happy mood, her ordinary self.'[5]

At noon, Muriel went shopping in Wimbledon village, where she bought a new dress and matching coat for 59 guineas, leaving them at the shop for alteration. She called at the butcher and the cobbler, where she was frustrated to find that the shoes that she had planned to wear to the Savoy on New Year's Eve were still not ready. She returned home at 1.30 p.m. with oddments from Sainsbury's, had a coffee and a bun for her lunch, then telephoned Dianne, discussing the happy Christmas that they had shared and how relieved she had been to return home and find that the house had not been burgled again. She also told Dianne that she 'had bought a super dress in the village' and ended the last conversation they would ever have by saying that although it was expensive, she would enjoy wearing it 'for many years'.[6]

She then got ready for a dental appointment, leaving the house at 2.40 p.m. Mrs Nightingale put the chain on the door as instructed. There were no callers or telephone calls while she was alone in the house. Muriel drove to Upper Wimpole Street for her 3.30 p.m. appointment, where she had a scale and polish and one filling and the dentist took some X-rays.

---

* This was probably a reference to the previous day's *News of the World*, which devoted half of its front page to a picture of a naked girl clinging to a man dressed as Father Christmas, both astride a motorbike – a surprisingly explicit image considering that the Murdoch press was still eleven months away from presenting its first page-three girl.

While she was away, at some point between 3 p.m. and 4.30 p.m., June Maxwell Robinson, who lived almost opposite the McKays, noticed 'a coloured man, between 20 and 30' with a dark moustache and white polo-neck sweater, standing on the other side of Arthur Road, beside a grit bin. She thought he was carrying a broom or shovel and that he was dressed too smartly to be working on the road.[7]

At 4.40 p.m., Mr Alfred Anderson was driving along Parkside, which borders Wimbledon Common, heading towards Putney. His progress was hindered by a mud-splattered dark-blue Volvo saloon in front of him, which was travelling at about 15mph. Noting that it was a recent model and having an interest in Volvo cars, he wondered 'what sort of owner it had to let it get in such a state'.[8] He overtook the vehicle, noticing as he did that its two occupants were deep in conversation.*

Ten minutes later, he was driving back towards Wimbledon and found himself again behind the car, which this time was travelling at about 30mph. It turned off into Church Road, which leads to Arthur Road. The driver was:

> … about thirty, tanned Arab type, five foot ten, medium build. I cannot be sure, but he may have had a close untidy beard. He was dressed in a brown pullover. In the front passenger seat was another person, a head shorter than the driver. The only thing I can mention about this person was that it could have been a woman and that she was wearing some kind of headwear, which resembled something like a handkerchief.

At 4.50 p.m., Mrs Nightingale, having finished her housework, switched the television on to watch *Blue Peter*, first catching the end of a reading of Wimbledon Common-set story 'The Wombles' on *Jackanory*. Muriel returned at about 5 p.m. and said that she was ready to take her home.

Mrs Nightingale washed up her cup and saucer and put it away, Muriel saying that she would have her tea when she got back. Leaving the television on, she put the guard in front of what was, at this point, quite a small fire.

They left the house, noticing nothing unusual, and drove to Mrs Nightingale's home in Haydons Park Road, stopping at Leopold Road on the way, where Mrs Nightingale went into the newsagent to buy them each an *Evening News*.

---

*   Unfortunately, Anderson did not report the sighting to the police until 6 February.

The weather was bitter, and Muriel remarked that she wished she had not had her coat taken up so much as it made her legs cold.

The pair then proceeded to Haydons Park Road, where Muriel said that she would collect Mrs Nightingale at 1.45 p.m. the following day before her doctor's appointment. She waited for Mrs Nightingale to open her front door and go safely inside before driving off.

Muriel was wearing a green two-piece costume and flat, patent-leather, cream-coloured shoes with a black-and-white checked coat. It was now between 5.15 and 5.30 p.m. As the judges at the Court of Appeal would say in their account of the case, sixteen months later, Mrs Nightingale was 'the last person to see that benighted lady alive'.[9]

At about 5.45 p.m., a physics lecturer, Jaunsz Zarzycki, was driving home and noticed 'two Indian gentlemen walking along Arthur Road near the junction with Home Park Road, towards St Mary House. I say Indian, but of Asiatic origin.'[10] The two men were on the opposite side of the road from St Mary House, but he did not notice any other vehicles parked in that part of the road. One was 'about thirty/thirty-five and had something around his eyes, possibly dark spectacles. Both men had on a light tweed overcoat or something similar. Neither was wearing a hat.'[11]

At 5.50 p.m., George List, a retired engineer, was walking up Arthur Road and saw a car parked about 50 yards back from St Mary House. Although small cars were often parked there, this one was much larger, 'a dark coloured car … either a Ford Zephyr or a Vauxhall'.[12] Its lights weren't on, though he couldn't say whether it was occupied. It was parked completely on the pavement, facing towards St Mary House, and he had to squeeze to get past it.

Muriel garaged her car and stepped into her home for the final time. She poured a cup of tea, stoked up the fire and settled in the snug, with Carl at her feet, to read the evening paper, never imagining that she would be on its front page this time tomorrow. In the last moments of her life as she knew it, she would have read of a London bank robbery, the mistletoe wedding of actors Millicent Martin and Norman Eshley, of hospitals facing a surge in admissions due to a flu epidemic, and of approaching snow and cruel weather.

At 6 p.m., Mona Lillian, a company director who lived at 43 Arthur Road, passed St Mary House and noticed that the outside light and all the downstairs lights were on, and the curtains open. 'The front door was closed, but there was a dark-coloured saloon car parked in the drive. I did not see any people in or around the house.'[13]

Jack Harvey, a lecturer, who lived at Well House, almost exactly opposite Arthur Road, was working on the van in his drive until 6.15 p.m. He saw and heard nothing unusual.[14]

After lunching at the Savoy with *Sun* editor Larry Lamb, Alick attended a meeting at the *News of the World* offices that ended at 7 p.m. The Rolls returned him to St Mary House at 7.45 p.m. He stood for a moment talking to William Nunn, then walked to the front door as the driver reversed out. As he approached the house, he noticed several sheets of newspaper scattered on the ground outside the porch. He screwed them up and dropped them on the edge of the garden, then rang the bell with his usual ring. When Muriel did not appear, he tried the handle and found, to his puzzlement, that the porch door was unchained. 'This was very unusual as my wife always put the safety chain on when she was indoors alone.'[15]

The porchway light was on, and, although it was closed, as he pushed on the inner door it swung open to reveal a frightening scene within the house. Muriel's handbag was at the foot of the stairs and her high-heeled shoes, wallet and car keys were scattered down the bottom few steps. The hall chair, which would normally be by the window, had been knocked into the centre of the hall. On the right-hand side of the inner door, on the writing table, lay a rusty chopper. On the chair beside it was a length of brown bailing twine.

On the floor was the upturned telephone. The plastic shield in the centre of the dial had been smashed out and the paper disc displaying the number was missing. On the floor by the telephone was a pair of Muriel's spectacles. Also on the floor were several more sheets of the previous day's edition of the *People* newspaper.

Alick ran into the snug, the door of which was closed, and saw the dachshund whimpering in front of the fire, which was 'built up and glowing brightly'.[16] There was no fireguard in front of it. The television set and the reading lamp were on, and on the arm of the easy chair was a copy of the *Evening News*.

Alick then ran into the kitchen, which leads off that room, where he saw nothing except a cup and saucer, which appeared to have been recently used, and the black-and-white checked coat that Muriel had been wearing earlier that day, left over a work surface, which was unusual.

Thinking that intruders might still be in the house, he grabbed the chopper before running upstairs, dashing from room to room, calling his wife's name. He found nothing upstairs except, in her bedroom, the drawer in which she left her jewellery was open and the jewellery gone. He searched all the downstairs rooms again, the garden, greenhouse and outbuildings, and the garage, where he found both his wife's Capri and his Princess undisturbed.

Returning to the hall, he noticed that on the table opposite the front door was a 1ft length of white Elastoplast and its backing strip. The Elastoplast had stuck itself together, so appeared to be only half its actual width. Inspection of the crime scene photographs reveals there was also a second and much shorter piece which looks like it was intended as a gag. He picked up the telephone but found it was dead. He then tried several neighbours, eventually finding Mr Vladimir Khoroche at No. 27 was home. From there, he called the police.

PC Stafford at New Scotland Yard took the call, which he logged as 'burglary unusual circ', and addressed it to the CID wireless car in the area, but not getting any answer, he rerouted it to the uniform car, which responded. He noted that 'Mr McKay gave me all this information quite clearly without any signs of distress'.[17]

Returning to the house, although there was no sign of forced entry on the outer door, Alick now noticed that the inner door had clearly been forced, as the hasp was loose and the tongue of the Yale was bent. The paintwork around the staple side of the lock was cracked and there were flakes of white paint at the foot of the door jamb. He also noticed broken flash bulbs on the floor of the porch, which had probably come from Muriel's handbag.

A few minutes later, the duty officer arrived, Inspector William Anderson, and Alick accompanied him on his search of the house and outbuildings. Anderson noted all the same details, and that 'the coal fire was well stoked up with all the cinders glowing red, as if it had been made up an hour previously'.[18] Assuming that Mona Lillian's later statement about seeing the saloon in the drive at 6 p.m. was accurate (and it should be noted that she said 'when I passed at 6 p.m.' without ambiguity, suggesting that was a regular occurrence), the fire cannot have been made up any less than two hours earlier. However, the McKays used smokeless fuel, which burns more slowly than standard coal, and which could explain this puzzling detail.

It was established that about £600 worth of jewellery was missing, consisting of four rings (including Muriel's wedding ring), three pearl necklaces, a three-row choker, four brooches, three bracelets and a Longines wristlet watch. Since no other drawers had been disturbed, Muriel presumably had told the intruders where to find her jewellery. It is a measure of the Hoseins' rapaciousness that even though at any moment during the operation Alick could have returned home, the Rolls-Royce turning into the drive and blocking the

Hoseins' escape, they still took the time to steal it, even though they were expecting to be millionaires within forty-eight hours.

Alick knew that his wife could not have left of her own accord, since 'she would never leave the dog in front of an unguarded fire',[19] but Anderson's first impression was somewhat sceptical. In his report, he felt that while 'there had been a break-in and that the woman had left the house, without a struggle, because she had been threatened', he added:

> The reception room was like a stage setting the way the clues had been left in position. The main evidence against the woman going of her own free will was the forced open door. The remainder of the scene could have been set up by the missing woman before she left.[20]

Nevertheless, Anderson summoned the assistance of four Panda drivers, two dog handlers and dogs, CID and the Scenes of Crime Officer.

Detective Sergeant Graham Birch was the first CID officer to arrive, at 9 p.m. 'Mr McKay let me in and just said, "My wife's gone". That's all he said at that stage.'[21] Looking at the items dribbled down the staircase, 'it struck me almost immediately as being like the set-up for an Agatha Christie play'. Birch's impression was that 'it was a set-up. The stuff was strewn on the stairs and Mr McKay was so calm.'

The suspicion that this could be some sort of bizarre stunt by the tabloid press shows how the *News of the World* and the recently rerisen *Sun* were being viewed in the light of the takeover and the Keeler affair. Jeff Edwards, a seasoned and revered crime reporter, who worked occasional Saturday shifts in the 1970s and 1980s as one of its 'staff casuals', remembered that among reporters, 'There was a definite *News of the World* culture. They embraced it. If I had been there when Muriel McKay was kidnapped, one of my thoughts would have been, "this might be an inside job".'[22] Such suspicions were only exacerbated for Birch when 'Mr Lamb, the editor of the *Sun*, arrived with his photographer. Presumably Mr McKay had telephoned him.'[23]

Birch's comments have not aged well; nor have his words, a year after the crime, that the situation was akin to dealing with a woman who makes a complaint of rape, where 'you have her medically examined and then interrogate her to try to break her story down'.[24] Rather than being calm, Alick was obviously bewildered, stupefied even. However, it must be remembered that most murders are committed by someone known to the victim, and when a wife vanishes, the husband will usually be the first suspect that the police must eliminate. John Plimmer, reviewing the investigation two decades later, wrote, 'To maintain an objective view, it is necessary to eliminate all possibilities before or while investigating the crime itself.'[25]

The uncomfortable presence of Larry Lamb certainly got relations between Alick McKay and the police off to a bad start, with Birch refusing the *Sun* photographer entry to the house. But those initial concerns seem to have been short-lived. Despite this, they have been grossly exaggerated and have coloured accounts of the case ever since.

Any doubts about whether a crime had been committed were swept away within a few hours, and Alick was even quoted in the press as early as the following morning saying, 'The police think she was kidnapped. There's no doubt in my mind what happened to her.'[26]

Mrs Nightingale was brought back to St Mary House by the police, where she stayed the night, helping to build a picture of Muriel's movements that day. A police photographer was sent for, although some items, such as Muriel's handbag and the hall chair, had already been moved by the time he arrived. Detective Chief Inspector Brine of the Fingerprint Bureau at New Scotland Yard examined the house for prints, and at 10 p.m., Inspector Anderson returned to Wimbledon Police Station to brief the night-duty relief to search all open spaces and parked vehicles. He then informed Chief Superintendent Newell and the press bureau.

At 10.15 p.m., Alick telephoned his daughters. There was no answer from Jennifer, but he got through to Dianne, telling her husband, David Dyer, '"We've just had another burglary". He then paused and in a breaking voice said, "and mother's not here".' Dyer felt 'he sounded very upset and at one stage, he broke down'.[27]

Despite Alick saying that there was nothing they could do, the Dyers immediately drove to Arthur Road, arriving at 11.15 p.m. On arrival, Dianne searched her mother's clothes and discovered that her black and fawn reversible overcoat, green woollen two-piece jersey suit and driving shoes were missing. No suitcases were missing, and twenty-seven of her latest prescription of thirty Indocin tablets, which she took for arthritic pain, were still in the house.

By now, the story was making its way along Fleet Street. Apparently, a *Daily Express* reporter had contacted the *News of the World* editor, Stafford Somerfield, trying to glean more information, and although Somerfield knew nothing about Muriel's disappearance, he immediately telephoned Arthur

Road, where Alick confided to him that he was frustrated at the attitude of the police so far. Somerfield knew the McKays well enough to have no doubt that Muriel would not have disappeared voluntarily, so rang the home of Deputy Assistant Commissioner John du Rose,* advising him that the story would be presented very seriously by the morning's papers.[28]

★★★

At about 8 p.m., Liley had made a call to Rooks Farm, with another at 9.30 p.m. Both times there was no answer. She was looking forward to the Monday film on ITV, so she tried once more just before it started. This time Arthur answered and said that Nizam was not there. They had a brief conversation, and she asked for Nizam to call her back. The time was 10.30 p.m.

Rahim Mohammed and his family, the Hoseins' relations in south London, were also settling down to watch the film, the hokum adventure *Action of the Tiger*, at their home at 175 Norbury Crescent. During the first commercial break, Rahim's wife, Zaneefa, went to make some tea, and as she did, the doorbell rang. It was 11.03 p.m. She thought it was rather late for a caller, her husband having already gone to bed.

The caller was Nizam, claiming that he'd gone for a drive because he was bored at home, and that he had looked them up because when he drove past Adam's a few minutes earlier he saw that he had visitors. He said that he had left Arthur at the farm. He refused a drink but 'seemed his normal self and he was laughing and joking as usual'.[29] He had little to say, but told Zaneefa's nephew, Shauffie, that he had been shooting rabbits that day and, bizarrely, handed him an unused shotgun cartridge.

He stayed for just ten minutes before driving off in the blue Volvo, saying that he was going to call on Adam, whose house was less than a mile away. Zaneefa told her husband the following morning that 'Nizam had called and that there had been no real reason for his visit, which was unexpected'. Although he had visited the family weekly when he was living three

---

* John du Rose, known as 'Big Bad John' and 'Four-Day Johnnie' because of his reputation for making arrests so speedily, had been in charge of the unsolved 'Nudes in the Thames' murders of the early 1960s and was a senior figure in the conviction of the Kray twins. He retired in 1970 and published an autobiography, *Murder Was My Business*, in 1973.

streets away with Adam, he had not contacted any of them since moving to Rooks Farm.

Nizam drove back to Adam, who was still entertaining his visitor, Victor Clufermi Pinheiro, a civil engineer and business associate. Upon his arrival, Pinheiro heard Adam ask Nizam what he wanted. Nizam 'answered him in West Indian, and the brothers talked together in that language for two or three minutes'.[30] (They were possibly speaking in Arabic; Elsa later told the police that Arthur only spoke English and 'a little Arabic'.)[31] Nizam said little else, leaving the house at around midnight, the same time as Pinheiro.

The first press report of the case was on the 1 a.m. news on BBC Radio 1:

> Police in the London area have started a massive hunt for the wife of the deputy chairman of the *News of the World*, who was found to be missing from her house in Wimbledon this evening. The house had been ransacked and some jewellery had also been taken although other valuables appeared untouched.[32]

Driving from Adam's house in Thornton Heath back towards Stocking Pelham, the northbound A11 out of London darkens as it emerges from the city and passes through Epping Forest. The road opens out again briefly at Bell Common, where streetlamps return. On one side of the road lies the common, and opposite, set back from the road, is a motel. By a lay-by stands a telephone box.

Less than a mile away, at the Epping telephone exchange in Crows Road, 24-year-old operator Terence Underwood was alone, working the night shift, when the night bell rang and a green light flashed. He plugged in a cord and heard a pay tone, then a voice said, 'Can you get me 946-2656?' The caller, who spoke 'in a deep American drawl which to me sounded like he might be a Negro'[33] and who 'kept saying "man"', said that the number was not connecting. Underwood plugged into the lines to London, dialled the number, and told the caller to have his sixpence ready. He had no sixpence, only a shilling, another example of the Hoseins' hopeless lack of planning and foresight.

The telephone at Arthur Road was answered almost immediately by David Dyer, who was told to hold the line. Underwood joined the two calls together, told the caller to go ahead and removed his headset. The caller said to tell Mr McKay that this was 'the M3. Tell him it's the Mafia.' Underwood noticed that the conversation was unusually loud and, thinking that there was some disagreement over a wrong number, he listened in to the call to check. At this point, he received a test call from the Cambridge exchange but, concerned, he returned to the call once that was dealt with.

Meanwhile, at Arthur Road, Alick had taken the call in the sitting room. By now, all calls to the house were being monitored by Detective Sergeant Walter Whyte of New Malden CID, who had arrived at 11 p.m. to relieve Birch and was now listening in on the kitchen extension, pencil and paper at the ready. After verifying that he was talking to Mr McKay, the voice said, 'This is Mafia Group 3. We are from America. Mafia M3. We have your wife.'

Alick, incredulous, repeated back, 'You have my wife?'

The caller replied, 'You will need a million pounds by Wednesday.'

Alick protested that he hadn't 'a million pounds or anything like it' but the caller simply told him, 'You had better get it, you have friends, get it from them.' He added, 'We tried to get Rupert Murdoch's wife. We couldn't get her, so we took yours instead.'

Impatient with Alick's confusion, the caller then said, 'I haven't much time, don't waste it. You have a million pounds by Wednesday night, or we will kill her. Do you understand?'

Alick then asked what he would have to do, to which he was told, 'All you have to do is wait for the contact. We will contact you on Wednesday, just have the money. You will get your instructions. Have the money or you won't have a wife.'

The caller hung up, but the line was still open, and a few moments later Whyte heard Underwood asking if the call was finished and informing him that it had come from a public call box just outside Epping. Many years later, Terence Underwood reflected that, at first, he had thought that the call was a friend joking, but very quickly realised that it was something far more sinister. He would remain haunted by the fact that he had been so chilled by what he had heard that he did not think to alert the police immediately when he realised that 'there was an evil person on the other end. He really did sound evil. Why didn't I get the police round there when he was on the phone, would it have saved her life?'[34]

Underwood's failure to alert the police was put down partly to sheer fear, but it was also discovered that he had a conviction from when he was 13 years old at Stratford Juvenile Court for housebreaking and stealing jewellery, for which he served three months in a detention centre.[35] It may have made him nervous of the police, although by now he was a responsible adult with a wife and young child and, when interviewed on television in 2001, he came across as an extremely sincere and mild-mannered man.

At 8.30 a.m., after a night of snow, officers from Essex Police examined the call box. They found a cigarette butt in the coin-return shute, with saliva traces that later indicated an 'A-secretor' blood group.[36] The handset was removed to the lab and dusted for fingerprints. The Bell Motor Hotel's register was checked, and all guests and staff were questioned, although further snow had already covered any tracks that may have been left by the caller. The cigarette was a Piccadilly, the brand favoured by Nizamodeen Hosein.[37]

6

RUINS

Had a busy afternoon walking around the ruins – the Acropolis. Very pleasant mild day, delightful sunshine. Card doesn't take ink well so bye bye for present. Another from Vienna. Love to Carl. Hope you are well.

                                                    Muriel McKay, Athens.

The kidnapping was a desperate act, and so was its detection. The police were dealing with not only a new type of crime but a new type of newspaper.

In the stunned aftermath of the telephone call, both Alick and Walter Whyte agreed that for some of the time, the caller 'appeared to be speaking with a slight American accent'[1] along with a West Indian accent, although Whyte felt that the American part 'was not genuine, as the strength of the accent was not consistent throughout the conversation'.

Muriel's name had not been mentioned in the BBC news bulletin, but by now word of her disappearance was circulating within the media, so there was still a faint chance of the call being an unpleasant hoax, although Whyte says, 'I had little doubt that it was genuine.'[2] It was striking that there was no mention whatsoever of the police in the call, nor had there been any instruction left at the house for them not to be informed.

Also, as well as the ludicrous demand for £1 million (£1 million in 1969 is nearly £18 million in today's money), the caller said that Alick would need to obtain it 'by Wednesday', which was only twenty-four hours away. The imbecilic timescale was clearly because this was as much time as the Hoseins had to keep Muriel at Rooks Farm before Elsa and the children returned.

The other significant revelation on the call was the admission that 'we tried to get Rupert Murdoch's wife'. It quickly became clear that it was the Rolls-Royce that had erroneously led the kidnappers to Arthur Road, but the fact that they had mistaken 55-year-old, brown-haired Muriel for blonde, 25-year-old Anna shows just how little interest they had in the Murdochs beyond their money. Anna Murdoch had been well represented in profiles of the tycoon, and even pictured in the newly launched *Sun*, starting the printing presses, but clearly the Hoseins knew nothing about her and had no idea what she looked like. (Although there is the possibility that they knew that the woman at Arthur Road was not Anna Murdoch but reasoned that whoever it was had a close enough connection to Murdoch to be a potential route to his money.)

If we pause briefly to contemplate the timescale of the previous evening's events, certain conclusions can be drawn. The vivid sightings of men fitting the Hoseins' descriptions in a car matching their muddy Volvo and on Arthur Road place them in the village from about 4.30 p.m. until 6 p.m. George List's sighting of a car parked about 50 yards down the road and facing St Mary House is not especially conclusive, but if it was the Hoseins' car, it seems to have been parked at one of the two back gates of Ricard's Lodge High School. From here, one has a clear view of the entrance to St Mary House without being seen by the occupants.

Since this sighting was at 5.50 p.m., it is conceivable that the Hoseins lay in wait here for Muriel to return from dropping off Mrs Nightingale, being able to see easily from there her Capri turning into the drive and allowing ten minutes for her to garage her car and settle back into the house. Time would have been of the essence since they would have had no idea when Alick would be returning. Even if they had followed the Rolls-Royce on the three consecutive days the previous week when Alick was being chauffeured, one of which was Christmas Eve, when he finished at lunchtime, such surveillance would have given them no guarantee of when he would return on the first day back at work after the Christmas break.

It was Muriel's habit to leave the sound down on the television until the evening news came on, which on both BBC1 and ITV was at 5.50 p.m. that evening. Subsequently, neither Alick nor Inspector Anderson could recall whether the volume was up on the television, which could have indicated a tighter timeframe.

The reports of the passenger in the Volvo having 'some sort of headwear' are curious. One wonders whether this could have been a rolled-up balaclava. We know that Nizam owned a balaclava, as a villager later reported occasionally seeing him in it.[3] The passenger would appear to have been Arthur, since he was described as being 'a head shorter'. Eileen Butler, landlady of the Raven, also said that Nizam 'nearly always wore a hat, which was round with a small peak and looked soft'.[4]

The second sighting noted 'something around his eyes, possibly dark spectacles'. Arthur certainly owned spectacles with dark lenses; Griff Davies would remember him wearing them the previous summer.[5] Also, when Arthur was machining, he wore 'dark-tinted spectacles pressed on the nose which had no side pieces'.[6] The witness also said that both men had on 'a light tweed overcoat or something similar'. Arthur was consistently seen wearing a fawn overcoat over this period, while later that evening, Shauffie Ali remembered Nizam was wearing a 'rather long, old-fashioned blue or black overcoat'.

It was later established that it would have taken about two hours to drive back to Rooks Farm from Arthur Road, which means that about an hour later, Nizamodeen must have left to drive back to London again and appear at his relatives'. At some point in that hour, he must also have been instructed about what to say in the first call to the McKays, in the light of discovering that they had kidnapped the wrong woman.

It is also clear that other things had gone wrong with the operation too. They had left behind the billhook, the detritus in the hallway pointed to a struggle and Muriel having been trying to ring the police when the phone was ripped away from her, and there was nothing left behind to tell the family not to contact the police, which the events that followed suggest had been their intention.

There has never been a satisfactory explanation for why the chain was off the door when Muriel was so meticulous about security, and about that chain in particular. Most accounts of the case have reported the abduction as beginning with a ring at the doorbell. Alick would later tell the Old Bailey that 'she would always leave that chain on and when she opened the door, she would always open the door with the chain on',[7] even when he gave his special ring, because the glass in the porch doors was frosted and she could not be certain who was outside without opening them, also ruling out the possibility of her being forced at gunpoint by whoever was outside to unchain the door. So, either she took off the door chain or, on that occasion, she simply forgot to put it on.

Mrs Nightingale told the police, 'I don't think she would let anyone in.' She also said that the dog 'used to bark his head off'[8] when the doorbell rang and that Muriel tended to tuck him under her arm when she answered the door, rather than shut him in the den, where he was found. If she simply forgot to put the chain on, her refusal to open the main door would explain only the inner door being forced.

There is, of course, the possibility that on this occasion she forgot to put the chain on, perhaps because as she was entering the house the telephone was ringing, and she then forgot about it, but there was never any evidence of a phone call at that time. The possibility was also raised at the trial that the kidnappers were already in the house when Muriel returned home, having taken advantage of the chain being off when she left to drive Mrs Nightingale home, forcing the inner door, then closing it so that the returning Muriel did not notice any danger until she was back inside, the intruders having already been upstairs perhaps and taken the jewellery. Inspector Anderson accepted that from the outside, there were no obvious signs visible of the forced opening, and Alick himself didn't notice it at first.

There are several factors against this possibility. There was no sign of disturbance elsewhere in the bedroom, suggesting that the intruders had been told where to look for the jewellery. There was also no way that they could know that forcing the inner door would be guaranteed to make the door look undisturbed. If they had made a mess of it, it would have forewarned her. It would also mean that one of the two would have had to fetch the car after she had returned. The key factors against this are the unguarded fire, cup and saucer, and evening paper. Muriel was not ambushed immediately upon re-entering the house, and it is hard to believe that the Hoseins, having already gained entry to the house, would have lurked long enough for her to drink a cup of tea.

How she was taken away also remains a mystery. Was she bundled into the boot of the Volvo? Peter Rimmer, a temporary detective constable at the time, says:

> That was the big mystery, how did they get her away? Of course, she could have been unconscious. There wasn't anything that wasn't discussed. As I recall, it was decided that you could survive for quite a while in the boot, you would be semi-conscious. She may have been unconscious when she was taken out to the car, whether she had fainted or been knocked out.[9]

A police photograph of the boot of the Hoseins' Volvo reveals that it contained an LPG converter, which would have severely limited the available space, though if she was instead put in the back of the car, quite how she was controlled and prevented from attracting the attention of other motorists over a two-hour journey, much of it in London traffic, is puzzling.

By now, as well as the constant police presence at St Mary House and the arrival of Dianne and her husband – who, along with Jennifer and her husband, would remain there for over a month, during which time Alick did not leave the house once – friends of the family were appearing, incredulous at what was unfolding. One theory floating in the air was that Muriel may have been suffering from shock and amnesia after being attacked by the intruders. Lady Cudlipp, who arrived at the house with her husband at this point, later recalled that 'nobody was quite sure what had happened. Some people thought she had just walked out, perhaps had a brainstorm or something.' She remembered 'driving round that part of London, vaguely looking for her, thinking that I might see her if she had wandered off and lost her memory or something'.[10]

At 4 a.m., Detective Chief Superintendent Bill Smith arrived at the house to take charge of the inquiry, accompanied by his deputy, Detective Inspector John Minors. Smith, a 47-year-old Lancastrian, was a former RAF bomber pilot with a predilection for bow ties and cigars. He was a steadfast man, a bull who guarded his china very carefully, and was hugely respected by his colleagues. Roger Street, a detective sergeant on the case, has nothing but admiration for him, 'He guided everyone. He was an avuncular man who came across like a typical northern uncle, friendly and affable, but behind it all, he was a real shrewd cookie, as sharp as a knife.'[11] Peter Rimmer similarly describes him as 'a very good leader, a down-to-earth but very smart man'.[12]

Smith was only nine weeks into the role of head of V-division CID, but his experience as a detective was impressive, having solved over thirty murders so far in his career. Aubrey Rose considers him to have been 'a determined man, who wanted his way, but a nice fellow'.[13] However, his impression of John Minors, a 45-year-old Norfolkian who was also a former RAF bomber pilot, is that 'he felt himself to be a bit more advanced, thought rather more of himself. Smith was sort of hail-fellow-well-met, Minors a different type. They were upright men though, different in character but upright.'

The McKay family speak fondly of the young officers who were a permanent presence in their home, and of Bill Smith. 'I liked him,' says Dianne.

'I thought he was very dedicated and sincere, and my father had a great deal of time for him. But we did not feel the same confidence in Minors.' A heavy drinker, superior and unscrupulous, Minors was many people's prime suspect for the subsequent leaking of stories to the press.

Smith, however, was widely celebrated, among his colleagues, in the press and ultimately by the trial judge, for his indefatigable devotion to a case which saw him barely eat or sleep during its first four days, and left him commended but also blighted by stomach ulcers. It becomes clear to anyone studying the paperwork that there was also an impressive amount of diligence, sensitivity and diplomacy in his handling of the investigation, unfashionable currencies with which to credit police officers in this age of mistrust and misconduct.

Although not as crime infested as some metropolitan districts, Wimbledon was still a challenging beat, as Roger Street explains:

Wimbledon was division 2, not division 1. These were bad places to work in that all the resources went to the division 1s, West End Central* or what-ever. Division 2s, such as Wimbledon, Streatham and Peckham, could be enormously busy but didn't have the same impact, so you were always short of staff and never had enough time to investigate a crime.[14]

Any last vestiges of doubt about this being a genuine kidnapping were quickly dispelled by Smith. Although, as a good detective, he arrived on the scene armed with the possibility that 'there might have been something nefarious going on at the house', having met Alick McKay, 'I chatted with him for a while, and he was obviously a very genuine man. You can assess people very easily when you've talked to them for a little while. Seeing his distress ... you can't put on distress like that.'[15]

Walter Whyte remembers that there were repercussions for certain officers having 'pooh-poohed the whole thing at the start. That was addressed by Bill Smith. The uniformed officer was nearing retirement anyway. I wasn't very impressed with him, to be honest.'[16] Graham Birch was involved no further in the case either and left the police force nine months later. Roger Street says, 'I was on the inquiry within the first few days, and I don't remember it ever being considered a hoax or that she had left of her own accord.'[17]

---

* The HQ of C Division, covering the City of Westminster. The station, located on Savile Row, closed in 2017.

To Bill Smith's horror, the story was sprayed across the morning's front pages. The *Sun* scoop, which had gone to press before M3's first contact, came out as 'Mystery of Press Chief's Vanished Wife – London Hunt After Gems Raid' and, despite a couple of errors, was a reasonably accurate report of what was known at the time. The *Daily Mail* used the word 'kidnap' in its headline, and the *Daily Mirror* was even more bold with 'Hunt for Kidnappers as Wife Vanishes', though the *Daily Express*, while featuring the story on its front page, led with a report on hospitals appealing for volunteers to cope with a flu epidemic. By the time Smith had arrived on the scene, the genie was out of the bottle, and his attempts to limit the press coverage from this point on were constantly frustrated, by unscrupulous police officers as well as unscrupulous journalists.

At 8 a.m., Detective Sergeant Jim Parker collected all the physical evidence from Arthur Road, having been appointed exhibits officer. Parker had worked with twelve different murder squads by this point and on this case, as well as setting up and running the incident room at Wimbledon Police Station, which was operational within forty-eight hours of Muriel's abduction, he would be responsible for the movement, care and eventual production of what would ultimately run to over 150 separate exhibits. 'That case was held together by Jimmy,' says Peter Rimmer. 'He was a brilliant policeman who did a remarkable job. I learned so much from him.'[18]

★★★

An extraordinary incident occurred later that morning, after Jennifer arrived at the house with her husband:

> I wanted to walk round the house, try to understand what could have happened. As I got to the little room beside the kitchen, just past the back stairs, my eyes just happened to glance down and catch sight of something under the table. It was a photograph, a small black-and-white snap of three or four Indian men, wearing duffle coats and leaning against a campervan. It looked like the sort of snap taken at a motorway café or on the way to the airport.[19]

Jennifer asked to speak to John Minors in the dining room and gave him the picture, but he was disinterested, suggesting that it was probably dropped by

Mrs Nightingale, who would sit at the table there to have her break. 'It was absolutely nothing to do with Mrs Nightingale, and I told him so. But he just wasn't interested.' The photo was never seen again. 'I am absolutely certain that one of the men in that picture was Nizamodeen Hosein,' says Jennifer.

Many years later, Jim Parker, who as exhibits officer should have been given this photograph, was asked about the incident. He confirmed that he never received it, and pointed out that if he had been, it could have sooner identified the perpetrators as Indian rather than Afro-Caribbean men.[20] Jennifer later challenged John Minors about the matter and was given short shrift.

Since 2 a.m., radio news bulletins had been including Muriel's name in their reports of the disappearance. As the McKays were listed in the London telephone directory, this resulted in a flood of nuisance calls to Arthur Road which would continue for weeks. There were over thirty calls on that first day, three of which purported to come from Muriel herself. Among them was a call at 2.10 p.m., taken by David Dyer, in which a tired and distant-sounding voice, which he thought was that of his mother-in-law, uttered two words, 'grey Hillman', before hanging up. Four hoax ransom demands were also traced to a telephone kiosk at Belsyre Court, on Woodstock Road in Oxford, but prints taken from the receiver yielded no matches.

Alick was not fit to attend a press conference held that afternoon at Wimbledon Police Station, so David Dyer spoke for the family, appealing for the return of 'the greatest mother that ever was',[21] saying, 'Her greatest interest was her family. If you had talked to Muriel, she would have talked to you about the children. She was interested in people, sympathetic to people and a very modest, human person.'[22] He closed by saying, 'Please let Alex have Muriel home. I would dearly love to see this man whom we love so much get his wife back. You couldn't find a closer couple,' asserting that 'whoever may be holding my mother-in-law … is not going to crack this family. In time, we may well sway a bit, but we have plenty of reserves.'[23]

Bill Smith confirmed that the police were treating this as an abduction, but although everything had to be treated seriously at first, the 'grey Hillman' call was deemed within a few days to have been a hoax.[24]

Between 2.30 and 3 p.m., the Hoseins apparently visited the Patemans' dairy farm at High Cross, where they bought a calf. They stayed for about a quarter of an hour, Arthur telling Charles Pateman that he was missing his wife. Pateman noticed that Arthur 'was looking a bit rough that day. He hadn't shaved.'[25]

The evening papers were electrified by the £1 million ransom demand, and both the *Evening News* and the *Evening Standard* led with it, the latter quoting Larry Lamb, who had spoken to Alick by telephone that morning, that the call was one of several ransom demands that had been made by male callers. The *Evening News* was similarly non-committal about the ransom calls, which may all have been 'cruel hoaxes'[26] but had gleaned that one of them had led the police to Epping.

The *Evening News* also noted the curious similarities between Muriel's disappearance and that of Dawn Valerie Jones, seven months earlier. The 33-year-old housewife had vanished in extraordinary circumstances from her flat at Montfont Place, Southmead, where she lived with her husband and stepson, just 2 miles from Arthur Road. Her husband had returned from work to find the door open, two electric fires and the radio on, and her shopping bags containing the evening meal dumped on the kitchen floor. Her handbag and purse were found in the family cycle shed nearby.

Dawn's body was found five weeks later, over 500 miles away, in a disused hen coop in Anagach Wood, Grantown-on-Spey, in the north of Scotland. She had apparently never been to Scotland before and knew no one in the area. She had arrived in the town (which no longer had a train station) the day after her disappearance and checked into a hotel under a false name and address. She had stayed there for four days, during which time she had her hairstyle changed in a local salon and was wearing a newly purchased outfit. She had died of an overdose and there was no evidence of foul play. The case remains a truly remarkable mystery.

It may have been a memory of this case which fuelled ideas that middle-aged housewives who vanish sometimes choose to do so 'in a theatrical manner'.[27] Like Alick McKay, Dawn's husband, Frederick Jones, remained convinced that she had been 'taken hostage'.[28] Several newspapers linked the cases over the next few days.

While the country was devouring the latest news of Muriel's disappearance in the evening papers, at just after 4.45 p.m., the telephone rang again at Arthur Road. Since 3 p.m., all calls to the house were being recorded through a crude listening device which had been attached to the telephone via a suction pad. Now David Dyer activated the battery-operated tape recorder, then lifted the receiver.

The second call from 'M3', and the first one to have been captured on tape, remains the most puzzling of all. This time, the caller did not even think to check whether he was speaking to Alick McKay and gave David no chance to identify himself. After the pips of a call box, he said, 'This is M3 speaking again … Your wife just posted a letter to you.' After a pause, he added, 'Do cooperate … For heaven's sake, for her sake, don't call the police. You have been everywhere, you have been gone, you have been followed.'

David asked him to repeat this, to which he said, 'You have been followed, did you get the message?'

He replied, 'Yes.'

M3 asked, 'And the money?'

David replied, 'I'm sorry?'

M3 repeated, 'Did you get the money?'

David said, 'Just a minute,' presumably trying to alert Alick to come to the phone, and M3 abruptly hung up. A stunned David remembered that immediately after the call had terminated, he said to Alick, 'It's incredible that somebody can say "don't phone the police".'[29]

Playing the recording back, Alick and David were of the view that this was the same voice they had heard on the first call. Although the voice is not particularly 'deep', as the first call was described, it is a younger-sounding voice than that on the calls which would follow, and betrayed an unmistakeable West Indian accent, most markedly on 'speaking again', which has a hint of the characteristic 'h' intonation between the 'g' and the 'a' of 'again', as well as a West Indian lilt and perhaps a vaguely American lilt on 'Your wife just posted a letter to you'.

But apart from alerting the family that a letter was on its way, written by Muriel, there seemed little purpose to the call. There was no mention of how to deliver the money (which was supposedly expected to be paid the following day) and M3 got his words confused at one point with, 'You have been everywhere, you have been gone, you have been followed', presumably meant to be 'everywhere you have gone you have been followed', an example of the linguistic clumsiness and scrambled sentences which both Hosein brothers were prone to, this one typically echoing Nizam's characteristic clumsiness with language rather than Arthur's malapropisms and solecisms.

However, there were two particularly revealing moments in the call. The first is the warning to not 'call the police'. Nearly twenty-four hours after Muriel's abduction, this was the first time that the family had been told not to alert the police. Why on earth did M3 think that, up until this point, they hadn't done what anyone in their situation would do unless warned otherwise?

The other curious point was 'Did you get the message?' What message M3 was referring to, we will never know. There are three likely interpretations. The first is that M3 is reinforcing what he has just said, as in 'have you got the message?', though the delivery of the phrase doesn't quite suit that reading of it. The second possibility is that he is referring to the previous evening's call, which was made by someone other than himself, although it feels rather late in the game and unnecessary to be checking on that, and also, he begins by saying, 'this is M3 speaking again,' which infers that he made the previous call too.

The third possibility is that he is referring to some other message that was intended for the McKay family, but which they never received. It rather suggests that the Hoseins had intended to leave an instruction for Alick at the house. It is clear that something went wrong during the actual kidnapping of Muriel, besides the fact that they were abducting the wrong person.

The billhook carelessly left in the hall and the twisted Elastoplast show that this was not a slick operation, and that it did not go according to plan, so it is quite conceivable that, in the heat of the moment, they forgot to leave behind instructions. How else could they seriously assume that twenty-four hours later, the police had still not been informed? Also, if this was the case, it must also follow that they did not realise that they had failed to leave this instruction, since M3 on this call is still under the illusion that the police are not involved.

As for the strange and abrupt ending to the call, this may have been simply because someone approached the call box, panicking M3. The rather authoritative 'just a minute' may also have thrown him and made him uneasy. But most likely, he realised that after delivering the message about the letter, as he got drawn into conversation, he was making mistakes and so fled before incriminating himself. It does sound as if, for the first portion of the call, he was reading a script, which he then abandoned disastrously.

But there is one indisputable fact to be drawn from this call, and one which is essential to bear in mind when considering the events of the following forty-eight hours, which is that M3 at this point clearly *does not know* that the police are involved. This means that M3 had not seen any media coverage of the story so far, and presumably wasn't expecting there to be any either. As far as M3 was aware, on 30 December at 4.45 p.m. the police were not investigating Muriel's disappearance. Also, at this point, they were fully expecting their preposterous ransom demand to be met the following day.

That would all have changed four hours later. The *BBC Evening News* at 8.50 p.m. featured a major report on the case, a broadcast which Arthur Hosein must have watched. After newsreader Robert Dougall introduced the story from the studio, there was a film report by Richard Whitmore, containing shots of the Bell Common call box, a brief interview with Bill Smith on the drive of St Mary House, and an interview with a distressed but resilient Dianne, conducted by David Tindall. In the first part of the interview, she referred to the anonymous calls that her mother had been receiving recently, and how she had heard interference on the line when she had spoken to her the previous day, wondering whether someone had been listening in. She also spoke of the 'grey Hillman' call.

Despite these false leads, it was not only the revelation that their crime was now national news and the subject of a massive police investigation which would have shocked the Hoseins, but the next exchange:

DT: What about the ransom, the million pounds, I mean, your father's reasonably well off but demanding a million pounds …

DD: Well, it's just pathetic. Somebody doesn't know anything about money, that's all. It's just … it's just a sum I would think someone had their eye on and …

DT: What about the thought that they might want to extort it from the company, from the *News of the World*?

DD: Well, I don't know that the *News of the World* have even got a million pounds, it's a lot of money, isn't it?

DT: If the motive isn't money, what do you think it can possibly be?

DD: Well, it seems completely senseless and so pointless, I mean my mother is the most gentle person, she hasn't an enemy in the world.[30]

Arthur being told, through the television set, along with the rest of the country, that whoever was behind this crime 'doesn't know anything about money' would have enraged him. The report must have left the Hoseins aware for the first time of the full ramifications of their misbegotten crime. The McKays did not have £1 million and could not even conceive of how to acquire it, and a relentless search for Muriel and her captors was now underway by the police.

The following day, the day on which the McKays were meant to deliver the money, M3 did not call. The plan, like the McKay family, was now in ruins.

The significance of this news broadcast has never been fully identified before. As will be seen later, it has always been important in establishing the last point at which we can be certain that Muriel was still alive, since a letter sent some time later in her handwriting refers to Dianne's television appearance. What has not been explored before is this broadcast's role in establishing not only the last point at which we can be sure that Muriel was alive, but why, shortly after it, she was probably murdered.

The matter rests largely on establishing that the broadcast was the first media coverage of the crime that the Hoseins saw. This may be hard to comprehend in an age of rolling news, but it is demonstrable.

First, we have seen that at the time of M3's telephone call at 4.45 p.m. that day, he was unaware of the police involvement in the case. Although the case was on the front pages of almost every national newspaper, the Hoseins did not take a daily newspaper, only the *People* on a Sunday, and there were no shops in Stocking Pelham, the nearest being at Brent Pelham or Berden. There were no television news broadcasts on ITV that day until the early evening news. (Some Stocking Pelham residents were able to pick up the Anglia region as well as Thames, but that only offered an additional five-minute regional bulletin, *Anglia Newsroom*, at 4.15 p.m.) The BBC had a lunchtime broadcast, at 1.45 p.m., and both channels showed their early evening news at 5.50 p.m. M3 would have been busy at this time driving back from Tottenham, where he had posted the letter and presumably had made the 4.45 p.m. telephone call.

However, I initially found it hard to believe that, considering the amount of time spent in the Volvo, on the drive back from Thornton Heath via Epping the previous night, and to London and back that afternoon, M3 would not once have switched on the car radio and caught one of the hourly bulletins featuring the story.

Then, on a visit to Scotland Yard to look at their exhibits relating to the case, I enquired as to whether there were any photographs of the interior of the Volvo. There were.

The Volvo did not have a radio.

***

A couple of days after returning the hacksaw to Ernest Woollard, which he claimed he had needed to saw through some piping,* Nizam asked to borrow a garden fork. The excuse this time was that 'he wanted it to use in draining the water off the garden'.[31] He kept the fork for some time before returning it, and when he did, 'he thanked me, shook my hand, and said something about going away. I think he said he was going to Malta.'

At some point during the day of the 30th, a tailor, Gerald Gordon, had telephoned Rooks Farm about some trousers which he urgently required. Nizam told him that Arthur was ill in bed and offered to drive them down to London the following day but, exasperated by Arthur's dilatory attitude, Gordon said that he would rather collect them himself. He telephoned again that evening, just after the news broadcast. This time, Arthur spoke to him and said, 'If you wish, you can come and get them.'[32] He arranged to drive over the following morning.

Gordon arrived at Rooks Farm at 7.30 a.m. on New Year's Eve. It was dark and cold, and the dogs were barking. 'I would not walk around the back, no thank you, they were too near the back door for my liking,'[33] he later said, instead flashing his headlamps and sounding the horn. Nizam appeared and invited him in. They went through the front door, into the workroom, which was immediately to the left, sorted the trousers, then he left. He saw nothing suspicious.

---

* Elsa Hosein later confirmed to the police that no metal or piping had been sawn through at Rooks Farm.

7

VOICES

Had a barbeque last night, not even a cardigan on.
          Muriel McKay, Cala d'Or, Mallorca, September 1968.

The freezing final day of the 1960s began for the McKay family with the delivery of a letter postmarked 'Tottenham N17, 6.45 p.m., 30 Dec 1969'. With gloved hands, Bill Smith opened the envelope. It contained one sheet of cheap, blue writing paper, lined on one side. The handwriting and its alignment were faltering and messy. It read:

Alick Darling,
I am blindfolded and
cold. Only blankets. Please do something
to get me home. Please co-operate
or I can't keep going.
<u>Muriel</u>.

I think of you constantly
and the family and friends.
Have been calm so far darling.
What have I done to deserve
this treatment?
Can you <u>do</u> something
please
<u>soon</u>.

Although there was no reference to 'M3' or a ransom demand, the letter firmly established the link between the M3 caller and Muriel's disappearance. As to the content, this first letter is the one with the least suggestion of having been dictated or prompted by the Hoseins. The details are personal, physical and emotional, and the appeal 'can you do something soon' does not precede any instructions on exactly what Alick McKay must do. There is no mention of money and no threat (although there is the disturbing suggestion that Muriel was being ill-treated); in fact, there is nothing at all to suggest that the kidnappers were speaking through it to Alick.

Unfortunately, the letter gave no clue as to Muriel's surroundings or her captors, reporting instead merely feelings and physical discomfort, the sensory nature of them backing up the claim in the first sentence that she was blindfolded. However, although the first part of the letter is messy enough to suggest that it was written blindfolded, the postscript, after 'Muriel', is dramatically more legible, the alignment neat and indentation of each of six lines beginning about a third of the way across the page, something a blindfolded person would not be able to judge so accurately.

There are also two instances in the postscript where words or phrases are accurately underlined ('do' and 'soon'), which a blindfolded person could not have done. The underlining could have been done by M3, but the legibility of the postscript backs up the suggestion that the second half of the letter was written without a blindfold. Additionally, examining the collection of holiday postcards which Muriel had written over the years to Mrs Nightingale, I found that she did habitually underline words for emphasis, as she does in the letter. (Although the 'Muriel' which signs off the first and untidy part of the letter is also underlined, it is not so precisely done.)

The kidnappers may have removed the blindfold because she was finding it difficult to write legibly while wearing it, but it is also possible that she was told to say that she was blindfolded and to make her handwriting untidy at first because if she was believed not to have seen her captors, her family would think that there was a much greater chance of her eventually being released alive if the ransom demand was met.

Examining the envelope, however, is a very different matter. One is immediately struck by the fact that it has been addressed immaculately. The indentations at the start of each line, the neat handwriting, the parallelity of the four lines of the address, the unnecessary inclusion of 'Esq' after 'A.B. McKay', the underlining of the postcode, and the word 'Urgent' in the top left-hand corner, also underlined, scream out that despite its untidy contents, the envelope itself was certainly not written by someone wearing a blindfold.

The letter and envelope were given to DCI Brine of the Fingerprint Bureau, along with a control sample of Muriel's handwriting from a recipe that she had recently jotted down for a Polish chocolate gateau. Mrs Nightingale also provided the police with the postcards that Muriel had written to her over the past eleven years.

After examining the first letter and its envelope, Charles Fryd, Principal Scientific Officer at the Met's Forensic Science Laboratory in Holborn, said that 'without any doubt', the handwriting was Muriel's. However, he also stated:

> In spite of the wording of the letter it is clear that the writer was not blind-folded during the writing of the envelope or the bulk of the letter; and there are reasons for doubting whether, in fact, she was blindfolded during the writing of any of it.[1]

It proved impossible to detect Muriel's fingerprints on the letter. When collecting elimination prints from St Mary House after the burglary in September 1969, it had been established that she was a 'non-secreter'. Roger Street explains that, at that time, fingerprints were detected 'because of mois-ture, amino acid secretions from your fingers, and some people don't produce it'.[2] Techniques are much more sophisticated today, but at that time, some-one who had dry fingers and who did not perspire would leave no discernible prints on a dry surface that they touched.[3]

Nizam was supposed to come to London on 31 December to spend the day with Liley and had promised to telephone to let her know when he was arriv-ing. He never did telephone. Having given up on him, Liley was dressing to go out at about 7 p.m. when he and Arthur arrived at her home unannounced in the Volvo. Arthur waited in the car while Nizam went in to persuade her to come back to Rooks Farm with them.

Despite Liley's fear of Arthur, Nizam did manage to persuade her, saying that Arthur had promised that he would leave her alone. The three drove back to the farm and arrived at 9 p.m. She later told the police that Arthur was still unshaven, and when she arrived 'the two Alsatian dogs were chained up in the shed outside the kitchen door'.[4]

Harold Prime, a regular visitor to the farm to inspect the livestock, would also notice this change:

> Normally the two Alsatians were locked away when I called, but on the last two occasions in early January, the dogs were on chains so that I couldn't get to the door of the house and walk in as I used to do, so I sat outside in the car and waited for someone to come out.[5]

Had they been moved from where they were usually locked away because that was where Muriel had been kept, or at least to dissuade any visitors from approaching the house while she was being held there?

Liley's presence at Rooks Farm was clearly the Hoseins' attempt at an alibi for the period of the kidnapping, albeit a posthumous one, reminiscent of Nizam's late appearance at his relatives several hours after the abduction. Unwittingly, she performed the role adequately, since she told the police that from her arrival there at 9 p.m. on New Year's Eve until lunchtime on Friday, 2 January, when the brothers drove her back to London, she never left the farm, and the only people that she saw there were Arthur and Nizam, whom she prepared meals for, with Arthur not going out once. He did no work whatsoever. In fact, she had no idea that there was even a workroom at the farm. 'He sat watching television all the time and watched the news broadcasts.'[6]

The first of those that he may have seen was that night's *News at Ten* on ITV, which featured another interview with Dianne, this time accompanied by her husband, David, recorded earlier that day, in which she spoke to Michael Brunson. This is a transcript of that report:

> BRUNSON COMMENTARY: Mrs McKay's single-page letter came to her Wimbledon home with the normal morning post. The envelope had a north London postmark but apart from that, there were no details of her whereabouts. As the family read the letter, signed simply 'Muriel', police dogs searched a churchyard by the house. Later I asked Mrs McKay's daughter and son-in-law if they were convinced the writing was Mrs McKay's.
> DAVID: Absolutely positive.
> DIANNE: It's my mother's writing.
> BRUNSON: So, it's quite obvious that it was your mother's own letter. Do you think it was written though, under dictation?

DIANNE: Well, it's possible, but it was my mother's writing.

BRUNSON: Can you give me some idea of what the letter said?

DAVID: I think in answer to that, we'd rather keep that detail with the family and she used the phrase which I think you say, darling.

DIANNE: Well, she said very simply the sort of things you would say. She said, what have I done, why should this happen to me.

DAVID: I think this sums up the letter.

BRUNSON: Did she ask for help?

DAVID: Yes.

BRUNSON: And did the letter give you any indication at all of the people who were responsible for taking her from the house?

DAVID: None whatsoever.

BRUNSON: Was it quite clear to you from the letter that she was being held against her will?

DIANNE: That was quite clear even before we got the letter, but it's very clear now.

BRUNSON: But was there anything in the letter which suggested to you that she was being held against her will?

DIANNE: Oh, yes, absolutely.

BRUNSON: And was there in the letter any mention made of any ransom?

DAVID: None whatsoever.

BRUNSON COMMENTARY: The relatives then told me of the long day they'd spent waiting for further news. There'd been none. Mr Dyer then read a statement from his father-in-law, Mr Alick McKay.

DAVID: The statement from Mr McKay says 'Would you please inform me what I have to do to get my wife back. What do you want from me? I'm willing to do anything within reason to get my wife back. Please give me your instructions and what guarantee I have that she will be safely returned to me. I have had so many persons communicate with me that I must be certain that I am dealing with the right person.'

BRUNSON COMMENTARY: At the house in Arthur Road tonight the relatives appealed for well-wishers and others not to ring them on the Wimbledon number. 'The line must be kept clear,' they said, 'in case, just in case the kidnappers decide to talk to us.'[7]

Despite the family's desperate hopes, 1969 passed into 1970 without any word from M3. Liley spent the night with Nizam, during which he told her that he was feeling homesick on his first Christmas away from Trinidad. In the early hours of the morning, Arthur telephoned Germany to speak to his wife, but was unable to reach her.

The morning post at St Mary House contained nothing other than messages of sympathy.[8] The morning papers, however, were more about sensation than sympathy. Although the contents of Muriel's letter were not officially released to the press, the *Daily Sketch* gleaned the gist and paraphrased it, while the entire contents were published on the front pages of the *Sun* and the *Daily Express*. The *Daily Sketch*, a paper struggling to survive and only just over a year away from being swallowed up by the *Daily Mail*, was generally the most sensational and reckless, having already revealed the mentions of the Mafia, though thankfully it had not revealed the 'M3' code name.

Nizam rose at 9 a.m. to feed the animals, then went back to bed with Liley until 11 a.m. He then killed a chicken for her to make a curry with, and she and the brothers spent the afternoon and early evening watching television. At some point in the afternoon, Nizam complained of stomach ache and announced that he was going out in search of something to ease it, despite having assured Liley that he would not leave her alone with Arthur. He was gone for about an hour and a half, during which time Arthur once again tried to sexually assault her. 'He tried to get fresh with me, but I got annoyed with him and started to cry, so he stopped.'[9] When Nizam finally returned, she scolded him, later recollecting that he did not appear to have bought any medication and that he made no further mention of the pains.

Watching the news broadcasts throughout New Year's Day, Arthur would have seen reports of the arrival in England of Ian McKay and his wife, Lesley. A dignified and dutiful presence, although visibly bewildered and incredulous at the horror that had befallen his family, Ian told the crescent of reporters in the drive of St Mary House that 'we are going through hell'[10] in a situation that he could have perhaps understood 'if my father had been a millionaire'.

By this stage, the family, who he had not seen for two and a half years, were, in Bill Smith's words, 'very emotionally upset, particularly when telephone calls were received from the man calling himself M3',[11] so it was decided that since Alick was now under sedation, on future calls, Ian, as 'the more stable and level-headed member of the family', should negotiate with the kidnappers.

By that evening, Arthur had expected to be counting out £1 million but instead had endured twenty-four hours of news reports presuming that he was 'a crank', someone who knew 'nothing about money' and revealing him to be the target of a massive police search. Finally, festering and probably drunk, he must have reached breaking point. At 7.45 p.m., the telephone rang at St Mary House.

By now, with Alick under sedation and making no public appearances for several days, calls were being answered by Ian McKay. The first word M3 said was 'Dianne', which he pronounced 'Deanne'. A momentarily flustered Ian initially confused M3 by saying that it was 'Mrs McKay' when asked who was speaking. The voice then asked to speak to Dianne, who came to the phone. Initially, a monosyllabic M3 simply asked how she was, and when she asked who she was speaking to and was told 'M3', undermined him by playing the *faux naïf* card with, 'I'm sorry, I've never met anyone called M3'.

Getting nowhere, M3 said, 'I wanted to speak to your daddy.' When told that Alick was not in very good health, he said, 'Well, where's your mummy, can I speak to her?'

Dianne said that she wished she knew where her mother was, adding, 'Do you have any idea?'

M3, trying to regain ground, said, 'I'll contact you later.'

Dianne tried to keep him on the line, warning that she might not be there later, and M3 then said dismissively, almost wearily, 'You've gone too far, it has gone too far now.' Dianne questioned this, and M3 hung up.

The call lasted less than two minutes and was clear evidence that M3 was flailing, angry and bewildered. The call had gone badly, M3 clearly having no script and, it seems, no real objective. Then, after the time it would have taken M3 to smoke a cigarette, the phone rang again.

Once again, there was a tedious reticence from M3 to get to the point, with an unnecessary round of hellos and 'who's speaking' until eventually, in an embittered tone and a voice of last resort, he said:

Look, it's concerning your mum … Now you tell them they've gone too far … Tell them they've gone to the police … They've got to get a million, a million pounds, I'll contact them tomorrow, and they've got to get it in fivers and tenners.

Dianne came back with, 'Where do you get a million pounds from? I wouldn't know.'

M3 responded, 'Well I don't know. That's not my business.'

Immediately, Dianne upbraided him by saying, 'Well if you want it, it's your business, isn't it?'

Less than a minute into the call, M3 hung up.

These two calls, the third and fourth made by M3, are baffling, more because of the mystery surrounding how they were made than why they were made. The first thing to note is that the voice is certainly not the same voice as that of the previous call. This voice is older, deeper, less nasal. The initial hesitancy also suggests that this is the first time this person has spoken to the McKays.

The fact that the first thing M3 said was 'Dianne' is what establishes such a powerful link between these calls and the television interviews with her in the previous two days. These calls are petulant and restive, more about anger than instruction, and were clearly intended to bully and admonish her.

M3 did not count on Dianne's strength of character, however. In challenging everything he said, she effectively ridiculed him. Whatever M3 intended to say on the call, he was obstructed, and he hung up the first time in defeat. It must also be acknowledged that the fact that it was a woman who was challenging him would have been even more of an infuriation to such a misogynistic man. When he called back, he was more direct, but still cornered and weakened, making a half-hearted demand for the money but without much conviction or even much optimism that he would be obeyed.

It is certain beyond reasonable doubt that this call, and almost all future calls, were made by Arthur. Whereas Nizamodeen's calls seemed to have been more scripted and direct, relaying pre-prepared messages, Arthur's tended to be taunting and emotional, his volatile nature and hostility when challenged or frustrated being clearly in evidence here.

These two calls were made for scant reason, but this makes the mystery surrounding exactly how they were made even more perplexing. When making her statements to the police and giving evidence at the Old Bailey, Liley was adamant that Arthur did not go out at all on the evening of 1 January. In fact, she said that he did not go out at all during her entire stay at the farm. The only one who did go out was Nizamodeen, and although she said, 'I don't know if he took the car or not',[12] she seemed fairly sure that his absence was in the afternoon of New Year's Day, not during the evening.

This continues to be an utterly exasperating anomaly. There are several possible explanations, however. The first is that these calls were made by Nizam, whose ninety-minute disappearance on New Year's Day is curious. Nizam himself later claimed that rather than drive to Bishop's Stortford to find a chemist that was open, he had walked to the Cock and had a pint of beer for his stomach pains. No witness was ever produced to support this, and quite why, wherever he was going, he did not ask Liley to come with him rather than be left with Arthur, was never explained.

There was, and still is, a telephone box opposite the Cock, and all these points together might be thought of as a satisfactory explanation. Unfortunately, they are not. As well as the voice almost certainly being that of Arthur Hosein, and Liley being fairly certain that Nizam went out in the afternoon and not the evening, to complicate matters further, it seems that at this time, the village call box was not capable of making STD (subscriber trunk dialling) calls, non-local calls still needing to be put through the operator, yet STD pips can clearly be heard on the recordings of both these calls.

Another explanation is that Liley was lying about Arthur not going out at all on the evening of New Year's Day. This also seems highly unlikely. She had absolutely no reason to show any loyalty to him, and if she was covering up for the Hoseins, she would hardly have revealed that Nizam was missing for ninety minutes on New Year's Day and was not at Rooks Farm on the evening of the kidnapping, two pieces of hugely damaging evidence which she swore to on oath.

The most likely explanation, banal as it is, is quite simply that Liley was mistaken. She may not have understood, when she was asked whether Arthur could have gone out at all during that evening, that it might have been just for ten minutes. Moreover, her certainty that Arthur did not go out at all should be considered with caution. It must be remembered that her presence on the farm was clearly to provide the Hoseins with some sort of vague alibi, and therefore it would have defeated the object if Arthur had slipped out without slyly hiding the fact from her.

I find it implausible that, since she could not say whether Nizam took the car when he went out in the afternoon, she could be absolutely certain that at no point that evening did Arthur leave the farm at all. Could anyone in her position really be certain about the movements of both brothers over an entire three days? It is surely conceivable that Arthur slipped out while she was cooking a meal (her primary reason for being there), napping or bathing. There is also the possibility that he went out while she and Nizam were having sex and that she was shy of sharing this possibility.

There is another explanation, namely that a third person made these calls. However, the voice on these calls so strongly resembles those on the calls that we can safely say were made by Arthur, as does some of the prosody – 'who's speaking please', 'concerning your mum' – and the rambling, the impatience, the petulance and the sickly intimacy of using first names and asking how they are, that this being a third voice feels highly unlikely.

The only thing that the McKays and the police could take from the calls was the ominous statement that both they and the situation had 'gone too far'. The following day's *Daily Mail* reported that David Dyer had come to the door in tears at 1 a.m., saying that there might be developments, but he did not reappear. Supposedly a detective also told reporters, 'Something has happened. But we cannot say what it is at the moment.'[13]

Despite a gaggle of the world's media crowded around the entrance to St Mary House, an eerie silence now descended, a silence which yielded nothing and would remain unbroken, with no telephone call to the family from M3, for a further thirteen desperate days.

8

WHISPERS

Hope you, Brian and Carl are all well, as we are. My pills did me a lot of good.
Muriel McKay, Cala Gran, Cala d'Or, Mallorca, 30 May 1969.

Six days after lunching with the McKays, Dr Tadeus Markowicz was back at St Mary House attending to a shattered and sedated Alick, whose enduring heart problems were being exacerbated by the colossal stress that he was under. As he left the house, Dr Markowicz was surrounded by fact-starved reporters wanting to know whether he had any reason to fear for Muriel's health.

A vague attempt was being made to panic the kidnappers, by intimating that Muriel had medical conditions which could make her seriously ill without treatment. David Dyer told the press that her arthritis drug was only available on prescription and she also suffered from a number of other complaints, the details of which he could not divulge. Dr Markowicz played along with this, rather unconvincingly, it must be said, clearly uncomfortable at having to tell professional untruths. He did concede that, having seen how Muriel had reacted to stress once before (presumably after the burglary), then yes, her heart could be affected, and that it was 'very important' that she received her injections.[1] When the press pushed him on whether there was a possibility that her life itself could be at risk, the questioning was terminated.

In truth, Muriel suffered from an arthritic shoulder, for which she had been receiving regular injections and taking Arlef and Indocid capsules for the last two years. She had been due for her next injection and repeat prescription the day after her abduction. St Mary House was a warm and comfortable place, but damp and cold conditions would obviously intensify her pain. Despite this, Dr Markowicz told the police that in his opinion, she had a normal expectancy of life, and judged her to be in better health in 1969 than in the previous two years, adding that although she was probably more likely to be affected by shock than the average woman of her age, it was 'not nearly enough to cause any danger to life'.[2]

The squad on the case was now increased to twenty-eight officers, DS Brian Poole taking charge of the office staff as they dealt with more than 100 letters a day and a continuous flow of incoming calls. Poole was also responsible for the action books and the deputing of the actions of officers on outside enquiries, with over 1,500 individual actions carried out under his immediate control. All statements were personally checked by him and separated into 'inform', 'active' and 'evidential' bundles, before being passed on to Bill Smith. This was basic policing, based on paperwork and shoe leather, powered by diligence, detail and detection, but it was hampered, not only by a lack of useful information and a lack of technology, but by disinformation, distraction and doubt.

In the early stages of the case, Bill Smith was having to contend with scepticism among senior officers and the inference that too much was being made of Muriel's disappearance, and that she had 'probably run off with the milkman'.[3] In the face of this, as well as a constant police presence at St Mary House and a constant watch on the house, he launched Britain's biggest ever hunt for a missing person.

On one day, 18,000 police officers searched Wimbledon Common and Epping Forest, where they found the abandoned bodies of six newborn babies,* but no clue to Muriel's whereabouts. All open spaces and derelict buildings in the Metropolitan Police area were searched by police, assisted by all 240 police dogs. Every pond and lake in the capital, many of which were now frozen over, was searched by police underwater search teams, and exhaustive house-to-house inquiries were made in Wimbledon.

Preposterous as the ransom demand was, and asinine as the 'Mafia' references in M3's first call were, in 1969 there were rumours of the Mafia establishing operations in the UK, and so, however unlikely, the possibility that the Mafia claim was genuine had to be investigated. Bill Smith contacted the FBI via the American Embassy, for their opinion on the Mafia possibility

---

* The Abortion Act had come into effect less than two years previously, on 27 April 1968.

and their advice on dealing with kidnapping, a crime which was unknown in the UK but familiar in the States. The FBI came back to him on 2 January with their opinions.

On the possibility that the West Indian accent on the telephone indicated 'black men who were involved with the Mafia', he was told that while there were black Mafia operatives, in the FBI's experience, 'they don't speak like that, they're more American'.[4] The FBI's opinion was that the kidnappers were not Mafia men, and probably not even professional criminals, since only amateurs would demand such an impossible sum.

'On the evidence you have given us, we feel that Mrs McKay is already dead', was their conclusion, based on a comparison of dozens of similar cases in America over the past five years. Statistics from America released nine years earlier in the Australian case of R. vs Bradley* showed that in cases of kidnap and ransom, 70 per cent of the victims were murdered within seventy-two hours, and most of those within forty-eight hours.[5]

However, the unbusinesslike behaviour of M3 gave Smith a glimmer of hope that this case might be different. The fact that the kidnappers were unlikely to be professional criminals was in many ways a disadvantage, since it meant that there was no information to be tapped from the underworld about their identity, but it also meant that their behaviour would perhaps not be traditional. Memories were stirred of the kidnapping of Frank Sinatra Jnr, six years earlier in Nevada, by a gang of amateur crooks. Remarkably, the 19-year-old son of the singer had been released after two days, following payment of the $240,000 ransom.**

Curiously, although the McKay case was modern Britain's first ever kidnapping for ransom, only six days before it occurred, the *Sun* had reported that police were investigating allegations of a plan by Arab terrorists to kidnap

---

* Stephen Leslie Bradley was jailed in 1960 for Australia's first ever kidnapping for ransom, after abducting 8-year-old Graeme Thorne, whose father had recently won a much-publicised £100,000 on the Sydney Opera House lottery. Graeme's body was found five weeks later, but it was established that he had been murdered within twenty-four hours of being taken.

** The Sinatra kidnappers were captured almost immediately after the release of their hostage. All communications had been conducted by payphone, and Sinatra Snr had become so obsessed with ensuring that he always had enough change on him to make a call that the foible persisted for the rest of his life. He was even buried with 10 dimes in his pocket.

Charles Clore, the Chairman of Selfridges, Lord Sieff, President of Marks and Spencer, 'and other leading Jewish businessmen'.[6]

There has been criticism over the years that the kidnapping of Muriel McKay was regarded at the time as an 'un-British crime', and it is telling that immediately before it, a rumoured kidnapping was attributed to 'Arab terrorists'. Perhaps there is an inference of racial superiority in the phrase, and perhaps 'not a crime that was known in Britain' is less loaded, but it is an unavoidable fact that kidnapping for ransom was unprecedented in the United Kingdom.

Perhaps it was partly because the police were in uncharted territory that the public felt compelled both to assist and exploit the situation. In total, the police received some 1,300 letters offering information – most of it useless. Two calls from people claiming to have psychic powers were received at Arthur Road, both of which claimed that Muriel was being held in north London, the same area in which the letter had been posted.

The McKays were desperate. In the words of David Dyer, 'Maybe we are living on crumbs, clutching at straws, but we are glad of any help.'[7] Therefore, on the advice of a family friend, they consulted Dutch psychic Gerard Croiset, whom the *Evening Standard* described, erroneously, as 'a man who has had astounding success in finding missing people'.[8]

The newspapers, now running on empty, were revitalised by this intrigue, but to Bill Smith it was an open invitation for timewasters to jam the phone lines and clog up the in-trays. 'As soon as that was in the newspapers, every soothsayer ... dowsers, stargazers, you name it'[9] felt empowered to pester the police. Mediums as far away as Rhodesia and New Zealand were making predictions on the case. News of the consultation with a medium led to the police taking 157 calls in five hours. One caller held a pendulum over a map and decided that Muriel was in a house in Wrotham, Kent, while a music teacher from Llandudno claimed to have had a vision that Muriel was being held 'for spite, not money'[10] on the outskirts of Glasgow.

Over the years, reports of Gerard Croiset's intuitions have been somewhat garbled, with claims that he made remarkably accurate descriptions of a house which later proved to be Rooks Farm, although according to the *Sun* at the time, he pinpointed 'a bungalow in Hainault, Essex',[11] which happened to be just 8 miles from where the highly publicised Bell Common call had been made. He claimed that Muriel was in a green outbuilding beside a stream at a farm near a disused airfield and this led to a search of Canes Farm, at North

Weald in Essex, which again yielded nothing, although despite being woken at 6.45 a.m. on a Saturday morning, the owners were extremely cooperative.[12] Croiset was reported in the *Daily Mail* on 10 January as saying that Muriel would be found within two weeks, 'probably by someone confessing'.*

As well as psychic visions, physical sightings of Muriel were now being reported all over Britain, and wading through the weighty files of witness statements detailing them shows just how many eccentric events occur at any given time in our society. Aubrey Rose remembers going through 'what seemed like thousands of pages of sightings. People claimed to have seen her everywhere.'[13] Some of the sightings seemed plausible, some ludicrous, but reading them, they all share sincerity, if not verisimilitude.

Seemingly, a vast number of distressed or disorientated middle-aged women were roaming around Britain's towns and cities, and now, for the first time, were being noticed by those around them. A woman was seen waiting outside Southfields tube station, a mile and a half from St Mary House, in the early hours of the morning of 30 December. She strongly resembled Muriel and when asked, claimed falsely to be an employee at the station, before boarding a train without a ticket.

Another woman broke down to a stranger at the station buffet bar at East Croydon. A woman was seen being led across a sports pitch at Roehampton by two men in the early hours of the morning, while another, in a distressed state, was seen carrying a dachshund and looking for accommodation in Herne Bay. A woman in a Bournemouth café imparted to a stranger that she felt 'cold inside', while another who resembled Muriel was spotted browsing holiday brochures in an Aberdeen travel agency.

A park ranger in Liverpool reported an extraordinary story of an acquaintance who asked him for help, claiming that he was involved in the disappearance. An Oxford woman was convinced that she had chatted to Muriel in a Wimpy bar, while another reported having seen her entering a nunnery in Edmonton. A man exercising his dog on Wimbledon Common stumbled across items of women's clothing in thick undergrowth near Warren Farm, but even these proved not to be connected to the case. In the first week

---

★   Croiset was brought to England on 10 January 1970 and driven around London. The following day he made further claims about the case, all of them nonsense, including that Muriel had willingly left home to join a religious cult and that the owners of a mask shop in Wimbledon were involved, also naming various erroneous locations in north London. A recording of the session exists in the Gerard Croiset Archive.

of the inquiry, the police fielded more responses from the public than during the first month after the Great Train Robbery. Every single one was recorded and considered.

As well as the good-intentioned and the attention-seeking, inevitably the malicious and the criminal were also motivated by the McKays' desperation. A few days after Muriel's abduction, in the early hours of the morning, a telephone caller to St Mary House promised to return her in exchange for £5,000 in cash.* The arrangement was that Jennifer should take the first bus to Stamford Hill from Catford depot at 5.20 a.m. the following morning, where, somewhere along the route, a car would draw up behind it. The interior light would then be switched on and Muriel would be seen sitting in the passenger seat. At this stage, Jennifer was to leave the bus and hand over the cash in exchange for Muriel.

Even though the police were certain that the call was a hoax, there was never any chance of Jennifer herself taking part in the operation. Every CID officer on the case was male, and of those, Walter Whyte was the only one of a suitable build and shoe size. Made up by Jennifer and Dianne, and wearing a wig, false eyelashes, long, white boots, skirt and short coat and carrying a handbag containing the £5,000 cash – which Alick McKay had insisted was genuine and which he had arranged to have delivered from his bank – Whyte boarded the bus along with two other officers, one dressed as a train driver and the other as an Esso paraffin salesman.

The hoaxer did not keep the appointment and apparently telephoned St Mary House later to apologise for his actions.[14] Roger Street, who was one of the two disguised officers on the bus, smiles as he remembers that 'we never let Wally forget it'.[15] However, the incident was not without benefit. The sober Scot had 'carried out his duty with equanimity',[16] his disguise having aroused no suspicion, even from the bus conductor, and Bill Smith later recorded:

> Up to this point in the inquiry, relations between the McKay family and the police were strained, with not a great deal of trust one with the other. However, although this operation took us no closer to the actual kidnappers, the mere fact that police were prepared to go to such lengths to solve the case gained the admiration of the whole McKay household and cemented the bond of mutual trust necessary to enable family and police to work together.[17]

---

* £59,000 today.

Unfortunately, the hoaxes continued, including one for a rather more plausible £25,000,* which was accompanied by a note saying that 'a woman's life is worth more than money'. John Minors later reflected that each deceiver was 'a thorn in our side, because although we didn't believe any of it, the McKay family were clinging to every straw'.[18]

On 2 January, Jennifer took a call from a man who claimed that he had been in Soho the previous evening and had discovered where three armed men were holding Muriel hostage, one of them 'a trigger-happy madman',[19] who would shoot to kill if there was a rescue attempt. She handed the telephone to her father, who was told by the caller to bring £500** to Wimbledon Station that evening. When Alick said that he did not have that much cash in the house, he was told instead to bring £100 and some personal effects which the man would return when the balance was paid.

That afternoon, Smith and Minors dodged reporters by leaving Wimbledon Police Station by a back door and separately headed for the train station. Minors, disguised as Alick McKay and wearing his ushanka hat, waited as arranged by the public telephones at the station entrance. There he was approached by a 'slim, swarthy and darked-haired man',[20] who said that he would lead him to Muriel.

As he was joined by Bill Smith, Minors identified himself as a police officer. The man, 18-year-old William Alexander Peat, said that he would still lead them to her, and so Smith and Minors and, unknown to Peat, twenty-two other officers, trailed him to within 50 yards of the Strand Palace Hotel, at which point he tried unsuccessfully to flee.

A £25-per-week waiter at the hotel, Peat was the son of a doctor from Kingston, Jamaica. Claiming to be a disciple of Che Guevara, he said that since he lived in a capitalist society, he had decided that he might as well make some quick money from Alick McKay's situation. He was charged with attempting to obtain £500 by deception. Surbiton Quarter Sessions heard that he had been mixing with young people with 'half-baked' political notions, and that he was 'concerned about being the child of a mixed marriage'.[21] In court, he requested that reporting restrictions be lifted so that his apology to Alick McKay could be made public.

The other notable hoax, and the one which was dealt the most severe punishment, was perpetrated by Roy Edward Roper, a 25-year-old army

---

* £293,500 today.
** £5,900 today.

deserter from Leytonstone in east London, who had been a trooper with the Royal Tank Regiment but had gone AWOL at the beginning of November. Roper had written to Alick saying:

> You have suffered enough. I want £2,000 in used notes. You will send someone with the money to the toilets outside Maryland Point station, E15. Place it in the end toilet behind the seat. The person picking up the money doesn't know who I am or anything about this. If police are anywhere near or if they are told it will do you no good. So in your wife's interest don't do anything foolish or you will suffer the results for the rest of your life. If the money is delivered with no trouble your wife will be set free within a few hours. The money will be sent on Friday at exactly 3 pm. Don't do anything foolish.

Two police constables made the drop, and watched Roper arrive, arresting him after he had collected the package. Initially, he claimed that he was collecting it for someone else. Later he said, 'I don't know why I did it. I don't know how I thought I was going to get away with it. I suppose I will get a fair stretch.'[22] He was charged with attempting to obtain money by deception and demanding money with menaces and jailed for three years by South West London Sessions.

One telephone call not purporting to come from M3 was taken seriously by the McKay family. It was taken by Jennifer's husband, Ian Burgess, on 11 January, who noted it in his diary and remained for the rest of his life 'convinced that it was genuine'.[23] The call featured a woman who was shrieking hysterically, 'She's dead! Mrs McKay's dead!', amid what sounded like pub noise, before cutting out. Jennifer remembered that 'there was a communal glass of brandy kept by the telephone. You needed something after one of these calls, sometimes they were just silence, sometimes people offering to help, and then you became anxious that they were blocking the line.'[24]

The idea that the kidnapping was an act of terrorism against the tabloid press was fed by a letter which was pushed through the letterbox of the offices of the *Hornsey Journal* at 5.30 p.m. on New Year's Day. Addressed to the editor and marked 'urgent', the writer asserted that until the *Sun* and the *News of the World* stopped printing certain types of stories, Muriel McKay would remain a prisoner. The editor, Mr A.J. Chaple, described the letter as 'somewhat illiterate':[25]

They do not worry much about all the kiddies' souls. They pay out hundreds of thousands of pounds for no-good girls to write their stories. So why should they not pay me for not murdering Mrs McKay? I lost my 12-year-old daughter because she was influenced by the money these dirty girls get paid for telling everyone about it.

Claiming to have last heard from the daughter three months ago, the writer continued, 'A million pounds will not really compensate for the loss of my darling little girl but it was not me who asked for it.' The letter continued with tirades about the permissive society, using a four-letter word, according to the *Evening News*. A postscript added, 'I will let Mrs McKay go if the *News of the World* and the *Sun* publicly announce that they will not corrupt our kiddies anymore.'

Muriel McKay was not only the victim of the Hoseins' monstrous greed and cruelty. She was also a pawn in a desperate press circulation war. Fleet Street was electrified by the case, the rival tabloids already on a war footing since the Murdoch takeover of the *Sun* and the *News of the World*. Their hunger to outsmart the two newspapers which had an inside track on the case led to some deplorable behaviours.

'We were under a lot of pressure from the press,' recalls Roger Street:

Information would come in, go into the database, which was handwritten in those days, there would be an old sergeant in charge of the office who would turn it into actions, hand them out to the investigating teams, usually two of you working together, then off you'd go and do your inquiries. If any new actions came out of them, they'd be put into the database and handed out, and so on. The old nick at Wimbledon was very small and the press would be camped outside and would try to follow us to find out what we were doing. They were on top of us all the time.[26]

As well as journalistic persistence, the case was bedevilled by leaks, many of which came from police officers themselves – officers whom Bill Smith later described as 'idiots, just greedy … they can completely ruin a case just for getting a few quid from a reporter'.[27]

Michael O'Flaherty, a crime reporter on the *Daily Mail* at the time, who would later write a pulpy account of the case, *Have You Seen This Woman*, amiably confessed in 2001 that he regularly paid officers for information, on one occasion meeting an officer in a cubicle of an underground public lavatory and handing him £100 in a brown envelope in exchange for some documents.[28]

As well as corruption, there was invention. One senior police officer, Commander Bert Guiver, considered that the reporters weren't wholly to blame, since they were being pushed to extremes by their editors, and unlike the established crime reporters, the freelancers, many of them on lineage for the day,* were 'living on what they could feed to a paper to justify their expenses. The most outrageous stories were getting into print.'[29] Peter Rimmer says:

> The TDCs were all under threat of sacking for any involvement with the press, but other newspapers and newspaper groups resented that Alick McKay was able to control so much of the story, that he was the news, as it were. We did not have any contact with the press for a long time, but we were all aware who was having contact with them. What can I say … I won't name who we all thought it was. A certain officer enjoyed that side of things, the limelight. That was what we all thought. We were not allowed near any of the press or into the pubs which they drank in, not that we wanted to be. While there were some who were pleasant enough, who you got to know months later, in general we viewed the press as being beyond the pale for most of that enquiry.[30]

The *Sun* and the *News of the World* had little need to resort to such tactics, since they had constant access to Alick, who as a newspaper man was convinced that publicity could only help to save his wife's life. The presumptuousness and intrusiveness of the *Sun* and the *News of the World* frequently exasperated the police, with Larry Lamb visiting Alick daily to receive updates on the case.

However, the situation could occasionally be useful, as on 3 January, when the *Sun* devoted its front page to trying to panic the kidnappers with the headline 'Vanished Wife "In Serious Danger" – Doctor's Injection Warning', fleshing out the story with a full-page timeline of the events so far, and asking why, if Muriel had been kidnapped, had there been no further ransom demand.

The same day, *News of the World* reporter Noyes Thomas called at St Mary House to talk to Alick at his bedside for the next day's edition. Alick's remarkable statement deserves to be laid out in full:

---

*   Being paid per line of copy that the newspaper prints.

For five days now, I have been tortured by agonies of grief, dread and utter helplessness. So have all of us here in this bitter mockery of a once-happy home. I don't know how much longer we can go on living like this. I beg the person or persons holding my wife to show some mercy and humanity, to at least make some move towards ending this fearful ordeal for an ailing middle-aged woman. I appeal to them at least to tell me what they want, why they are keeping her, what I can do to get her set free.

She was so good and gentle. My wife and companion for 35 years and a childhood sweetheart. I find it hard to believe that it is all happening to me. I never thought I was that important. And I am certainly not wealthy – if that is what people think. Even as a newspaperman all my life, I have never heard of anything like this affair.

One bitter irony of it all is that we were just settling into a new and even happier way of life. Though we are both Australians, we made our decision long ago to end our days here in the Britain we both love, where over the past 14 years we have built our life and home. But my new appointment on the board of the *News of the World* organisation, which only began just before Christmas, opened up for us the prospect of more frequent visits to Australia, with which this company now has such close links. Muriel, always a happy person, was so happy about that. And so was I. We had all sorts of plans. And now … All I can say is, for God's sake, someone, somewhere, tell me what I must do to get Muriel back.[31]

Later that day, in his pyjamas and dressing gown, and against his doctor's advice, Alick gave a press conference at the house, pushing hard his message to the kidnappers, 'Do you realise, whoever you are, how dangerous will be the state of my wife's health if she does not quickly get the drugs she needs?'[32] Pictures were taken of him in his night attire to illustrate that his health was failing, in the hope that they might appeal to the kidnappers or panic them.

The same day, Lord Robens, Chairman of the National Coal Board and a family friend, issued a statement quashing any notions of the kidnapping being an act of retribution against 'a distinguished member of the press' whose *News of the World* position had only begun a few weeks ago. He knew the McKays as a:

… devoted couple … among the kindest and most charitable people, who have devoted their lives to public causes. Muriel is actively concerned with welfare for unmarried mothers and Alick's interests, too numerous to mention, include chairman of the appeals committee of the British Heart Foundation, a patron of the Wimbledon Hospital and, until recently, a member of the British National Export Council.

He dubbed the idea of a vendetta against him and his family 'monstrous … all his friends know him to be one of the most gentle, generous and respected men in the publishing industry and to submit Alick and his family to this cruel ordeal is both inhuman and unjust'.[33]

As the world's press hungered for anything to sustain this unique story, the police continued with door-to-door enquiries, forensic examination and public appeals. What was making the crime so challenging to detect was not down to any skill on the Hoseins' part, but because as well as being amateur criminals, whom police informants had no mutterings about and the police themselves had no data on, they also had no connection whatsoever to the McKays, to Wimbledon or to Fleet Street.

Vast numbers of statements were being collected from local residents, owners of grey Hillman cars and sacked staff of the *News of the World*, but at this point nothing was pointing the police in the direction of Rooks Farm.

Although, as Bill Smith later noted, relations between the police and the McKay family were 'strained' for a time, presentations of this have clearly been exaggerated over the years.[34] Family friend Chloe Baveystock says:

> I do not think it true to say that the McKays were at loggerheads with the police; they were just desperate and under enormous strain, which inevitably led to some degree of conflict as day by day suggested procedures were scrutinised and often found wanting. Despite police contact having been made with the FBI almost immediately, the idiosyncratic way that the Hoseins proceeded made any understood appropriate action frequently questionable. Alick McKay was unfortunately in a very difficult double bind, and he certainly was not a particularly easy man to deal with.[35]

Bill Smith himself reflected after the trial that he had 'never been closer to anyone'[36] in his professional life than Alick McKay, and Peter Rimmer adds:

> There certainly weren't quarrels when I was at the house. Bill Smith had the responsibility for the whole division, so whatever else was going on was his

responsibility too, leaving John Minors in charge for a lot of the time. They took on an awful lot of responsibility.[37]

On the morning of Sunday, 4 January, as millions of *News of the World* readers absorbed Alick's impassioned statement, the McKay children and their spouses attended morning worship at St Mary's Church at the top of Arthur Road. The Reverend Clifford Smith offered a prayer: 'For those who may be involved in Mrs McKay's disappearance, pray for them, that something of love may touch their hearts.'[38] He also led a prayer for the police and the press.

The congregation included many of Muriel's friends from the local Senior Wives Fellowship. The *Sun* were also in attendance and presented a picture of the family at prayer on the following morning's front page to sustain the story's high profile, even if no one was under any illusions that the image would prick the conscience of the kidnappers.

Peter Rimmer accompanied the family to church:

I spent that Sunday with them, we all took it in turns to be present. At the house, you were waiting for contact all the time. It was very uncomfortable. I lost my mother in sad circumstances just after my thirteenth birthday. My sister, who was fifteen, held the family together, my father was a broken man. I perhaps had an understanding of how the McKay family must have felt.[39]

Today, the initial response to a kidnap situation would be covert and structured, with an absolute stranglehold on press coverage; and, compared with the lack of professional victim support back then, today, trained officers 'would be seconded to the family to primarily support them during the traumatic hours spent waiting for news and to ensure they were constantly updated with the progress of the investigation'.[40]

One of the many dreadful consequences of a crime is the misplaced suspicion and guilt that it can plant in the minds of those who are devastated and desperate. Later that day, Jennifer's husband, Ian Burgess, mentioned to the police that when Alick and Muriel had stayed with them over Christmas, he had noticed that they were fractious with each other, mostly because of Muriel's dog.[41] These are the unreported, unresolved consequences of crime, the secondary, insidious torments that families of victims endure. Alick must have been haunted for the rest of his life by the memory of his testy mood with his wife on Christmas Day.

He was also by now being tortured by another realisation. 'He had genuinely thought that the publicity would make her too hot to handle,' remembered Bill Smith. But Smith was convinced it had in fact made her 'too hot ever to be let go'.[42]

9

SILENCE

Hope you are enjoying weather like us, it's perfect every day.
                              Muriel McKay, Ansedonia, Italy, 15 August 1959.

Friday, 2 January was the last day before Elsa and the children returned from Germany, and yet, tellingly, no letters were posted by M3, no telephone calls were made, and no ransom demands were issued. Rather than taking advantage of their final day of privacy, the brothers began the year under a guise of normality.

Before driving Liley back to London on 2 January, Arthur could be heard singing in the background when Nizam telephoned Rahim and Zaneefa to wish them a happy new year and to suggest that they come to the farm later in the month. It seems that, for the moment, the Hoseins had decided to pause or even abandon the operation.

Arthur continued to show little interest in his work, missing appointments with two tailors that day and briefing Nizam to say that he was bedbound if they telephoned. On the journey to London, he terrorised Liley into giving him the address of her sister, Farida, who by now was married. He arrived at her flat that evening demanding custody of their child, Michael, who was being looked after in Trinidad. Farida's husband supported her refusal. 'He just wanted the child and I kept telling him no,' she said later.[1]

The following evening, Arthur and Nizam collected Elsa and the children from Liverpool Street Station and headed up the A10 back to Stocking Pelham. Two astute police officers, Sergeant Roy Herridge and PC Sinclair of the Special Patrol Group, were on duty at Stamford Hill and noticed the muddy blue Volvo with no tax and which appeared to be missing its front number plate.* They stopped the car and approached Arthur to ask for proof that this was his vehicle. He immediately became alarmed and aggressive. Elsa tried to calm him down, but he continued to argue, boasting that he knew all the police at Bishop's Stortford and saying, 'I will report the sergeant if you don't let me go, I'll say he swore at me, my brother is a witness.' Nizamodeen then got out from the back of the car and said, 'I'll go witness.'

The officers asked to look in the boot but found that it contained only luggage. Arthur was told to produce his driving documents at his local police station and informed that he would be charged with having no road fund licence and no front index mark. Arthur boasted to them that he hadn't had one since October and that he would claim that he hadn't used the car since then. In his report on the incident, Herridge noted, 'Hosein appeared very anxious to get away.'[2]

Remembering the incident today, Herridge explains:**

We weren't satisfied with him that night, the abusiveness and then he and the brother trying a bit of a pressure job on us, so when we got back to the station, I told my governor what had happened, and he said that if we ever saw that car in the area again, to follow it.[3]

On returning to the farm, Elsa was shocked at how untidy the house was, but according to Freida, 'When we got home and went into the kitchen, there were bloodstains. I remember Mum asking, "What's happened in my kitchen?", and Arthur said that he had just chopped a chicken up.'[4] Elsa also noticed in the weeks after her return that Arthur and Nizam tended to whisper together on occasion, but her suspicion was that Arthur was involved with another woman.[5]

Two days later, two Hertfordshire officers, DS Summerville and DC Gray, called at Rooks Farm to question Arthur and Nizam again about the attack on Wilfred Lane. When they arrived, Arthur was being interviewed by PC Richard Felton about the road traffic offences. Surrounded by police

---

* The number plate was, in fact, bent up underneath the car, possibly from going over a large bump.

** Herridge retired from the Metropolitan Police in 1991, having been awarded the Queen's Police Medal for Distinguished Service and the most commendations for any officer to date.

officers, he protested his innocence about the attack again. 'I have already told you that we are not troublemakers and, as for using violence, no. My brother is a very timid man and would not hurt anyone,' he preached, with quite remarkable hubris, adding, 'As for me, my wife will tell you I am not a violent man.'[6]

At 7.30 p.m. that evening, Arthur was having his hair cut at his barber's in Stoke Newington. Roy Herridge was passing and noticed the Volvo parked outside. Still curious about the extraordinary behaviour of its obstreperous driver, he waited, while inside the shop, incredibly, Arthur was getting acquainted with another local policeman, Detective Constable David McEnhill, whom he immediately invited to visit Rooks Farm that weekend for some shooting. (McEnhill did not accept the invitation.)

Despite Arthur's usual overconfidence, and a gregariousness that verged on the pathological, it was noted that he was looking uncharacteristically shambolic, wearing carpet slippers, 'badly in need of a shave'[7] and complaining of money problems that might soon force him to sell the farm. He also made the officer aware that he had been ill with 'flu over Christmas. In fact, he was telling everyone that he had been ill with 'flu over Christmas, once again demonstrating his predilection for the posthumous alibi. Farmer Pateman, the visit to Thornton Heath and Liley's visit are all examples.

While Arthur was having his hair cut, the radio was playing in the shop. The news carried an item about Muriel's disappearance, and the barber speculated that 'she might have run away with somebody'.[8]

Arthur replied, 'Who knows, it might be for other reasons.'*

Herridge, waiting outside, watched Arthur and Nizam leave, and followed the Volvo as far as Stamford Hill, noting that the rear nearside light was not working.

The radio item came at the end of an exhausting and fruitless day of searching for Muriel. Britain was icebound on the coldest day of the winter so far, with temperatures well below freezing.

For the first time since Muriel's abduction, the *Daily Mirror* didn't carry a front-page item on the story, just a small piece on the back page reporting on the family's visit to church the previous day. The *Daily Sketch*, however, looked at the cases 'for and against abduction', taking the intruders' errors,

---

*   Although the hairdresser was unable to pinpoint when this exchange took place (at the trial he claimed it was the one o'clock news on a Thursday), the police officer who was present confirmed at the trial that it was 5 January.

such as leaving behind the billhook and not cutting the telephone lines, as evidence against it.

This twelfth day of Christmas marked a week since Muriel's abduction and the police were now considering mounting a reconstruction, while pedestrians were stopped and officers at Wimbledon Station appealed over the tannoy as commuters ascended the steps from the platform.

The following day, 6 January, should have been the day on which Muriel began her new painting class. Britain was blighted by fog, black ice and frost. Portions of the Thames froze over at Windsor and Hampton, and at Herne Bay even the sea froze for 100 yards near the sea wall at high tide. The chilly silence from M3 now forced the police to direct the publicity in a specific way, issuing the press with photographs of the jewellery and the billhook, which were on the front page of the morning's *Daily Mirror*.

It had now been established that Muriel had spent £60 on clothes on the day of her disappearance and had taken them to be adjusted, for collection in a few days, clearly not the behaviour of a woman planning to vanish. However, without any new developments, even the *Sun* was struggling to sustain the story, and, for the first time, relegated it to page 2, with a picture appeal showing details from family snapshots displaying Muriel's missing jewellery, which were also shown to pawnbrokers and second-hand dealers,* and a shot of the mystery 'meat cleaver' which, after a television appeal, was finally identified as a hedging bill.**

By now, newspapers were finding less cooperative ways of keeping the case on the front pages. The front page of the following morning's *Daily Express* claimed that doubt was now being thrown on Muriel having been abducted, due to the lack of evidence of intruders in the house and a man having claimed to have seen her boarding a tube train. It was old news and even older speculation. The following day, the police publicly rebuffed these claims, and Alick described the suggestion that the signs of a break-in had been planted as 'appalling'.[9]

That day, 7 January, saw Britain's biggest ever manhunt for a missing person, as 20,000 police officers searched, addressing the possibility that after

---

* Since Arthur's workshop in Kingsland High Road was above one of the many jewellers' shops in the East End, he was probably confident that he could sell the stolen jewellery easily at some point in the future.

** It was, in fact, a Hertfordshire hedging bill. Most counties had their own local design, matching the local style of hedge laying.

the kidnap Muriel may have been abandoned in a lonely place and was perhaps alive but unable to move or call for help. Every rank from London's 184 stations commenced at dawn, combing bomb sites, derelict buildings and waste ground, questioning landladies of boarding houses and hotels and checking hospital admissions. The ice and snow hindered the searches of ponds and rivers, while police with staves and beaters prowled the countryside.

In Essex, Bell Common and Epping Forest were searched, as were woodlands and countryside at Navestock, following anonymous telephone calls. In Surrey, open spaces at Hayes, Sutton and Chislehurst were searched, as well as churchyards and building sites, and every concealed well, tunnel and secret passage was identified from maps and inspected. Eight miles of banks along the River Mole were combed, while mounted police covered Oxshott Heath and Cobham.

The exhaustive operation, conducted in appalling conditions, produced nothing. The *Sun* presented the news poignantly, with a photograph of Carl, Muriel's adored dachshund, while the *Daily Mirror* attempted to sustain the story in a more reflective fashion, running an article about the vast numbers of people who disappear of their own accord every year. (The statistics were extraordinary: in Manchester, 400 women went missing every year, most of whom were under 30 and back home within a week, but on average, one middle-aged woman vanished per fortnight, and 3,000 people vanished in London every year, most of them turning up again within twelve months. Nearly 800 wives were reported missing to the Salvation Army every year. The most common group to vanish were women aged between 23 and 34, and only 3 per cent of women reported missing were over 50. Almost half of the women who disappeared had been married for between six and fifteen years.)[10]

It was now eleven days since Muriel's abduction, and over a week since any contact from M3. The press were by now resorting to stories of 'fears growing' for Muriel's safety and overreactions to a Suffolk man who claimed 'with great surety'[11] to have spotted Muriel on a No. 201 bus from Ipswich to Felixstowe. It was a timely moment to stage a press conference which, due to Alick's ill health, was held at St Mary House. Unfortunately, it proved counterproductive.

Space inside the house was limited and priority was given to television and radio reporters, and members of the Press Association. The nationals had to wait outside in the rain. They grumpily asked the news agency men to put questions on their behalf, but some of those questions were vetoed by Andrew

Henderson of Scotland Yard's Press Bureau on behalf of Bill Smith and the family. Smith, now keeping as tight a rein as possible on publicity, forbade any questions which could hamper the investigation, and the family had made it clear that their objective was to use the media to appeal to the now concerningly silent kidnappers. They were not there to be interrogated by a kangaroo court of insensitive journalists desperate for a new angle.

Flanked by his daughters and son-in-law, Alick McKay thanked the journalists present for their work. He mentioned that he had cancelled his joint bank account, which contained some £2,000, and referred to the 'far too many phone calls' to his home, including 'an extreme number of spiritualists who have offered help'.[12] Aided by sedatives, he said that he was now 'standing up to it much better than I was. I've got over the initial shock and I'm now trying to join the work of getting her back again.'[13] He appealed for proof that Muriel was still alive and exhaustedly read:

> I just cannot understand why those holding Muriel have not contacted me recently. I appeal to you to contact me by telephone, letter or telegram. My son or sons-in-law are ready to meet you or any intermediary anywhere on my behalf. I would come myself, but my doctor will not yet let me leave the house.

More concerned with his wife's comfort than anything else, he added that without her arthritis injections she would be all right 'as long as she was being kept warm'. As he returned to his bed, 100 police officers conducted another search of an icy Epping Forest.

The BBC introduced the report on the nightly news by noting the unusual vigour with which Scotland Yard were controlling the conditions, with a police representative sometimes cutting short an answer to avoid a future court case being hampered by certain information having been made public. They noted, 'The combined stresses of heart trouble and anxiety for his wife have left Alick McKay tired and strained, but he remained calm as, surrounded by his children, he appealed to the kidnappers to send him some proof that his wife Muriel was still alive.'[14]

While the appeal returned the story to the front pages, unfortunately, greedy for more information than they were being given, rather than prioritise the appeal, some newspapers chose to present the press conference as a story of censorship and conspiracy. The *Evening Standard*, in an article suspiciously bearing the by-line 'Standard Reporter', reported that an hour before the press conference, when proposed questions had been looked over by a police press officer, one reporter had four of his deleted. Outrageously, the article then proceeded to print them.

The questions were: 'Did you find a letter from your wife when you got home on the night of her disappearance?', 'What do you, in retrospect, think happened on the night?', a third asked how long it was before Alick had called the police and whether he had contacted any relatives first, and the last was 'Are you satisfied the police have been told everything?'[15]

The insinuations were clear. The *Evening News* went further, heading their report, 'The Case That Does Not Add Up', and claimed that Muriel had been 'disappointed' by Alick's decision to ignore his ill health and postpone his retirement and return to Australia, in favour of the *News of the World* job. The piece was also openly critical of police procedure – not always accurately – and disgruntled at them only having released portions of the letter from Muriel.

The following morning's *Daily Express* was even more contemptuous. 'Yard Man Censors Questions' was the front-page headline.[16] Embittered, they printed the questions in full, too. Having already put out a statement trying to quash such rumours, the police and the McKay family now refused to make any comment to the press in the days that followed. The response of the *Daily Express* was to run another aggravating story about the family consulting clairvoyants again and how the police placed them 'well down in importance',[17] a reference to Gerard Croiset's futile visit to London a few days earlier. However, the *Sun* remained loyal to the family, presenting the appeal simply and directly.

While the press conference was taking place, Dennis Saunders, a county court bailiff, called at Rooks Farm to serve Arthur with a summons for debt. No one answered the door, although the Volvo was there. A few hours later, as the evening papers were hitting the news-stands, Arthur, Elsa and Nizam were enjoying drinks at the Black Horse with Arthur's young solicitor, David Coote, and his girlfriend. At 7 p.m., they repaired to the farm. Arthur wanted a chicken cooked, but Coote said that there was no need and Elsa agreed.

Coote and his girlfriend went into the lounge, and Nizam was changing from shoes to slippers in the hallway when, from the kitchen, Elsa screamed out for him. He ran to the kitchen and found Elsa on the floor, clutching her stomach, with Arthur kicking and punching her. The following day, Elsa left Arthur, taking the children to stay with a friend in Hackney, Rose

Young. Her bruising and pain was severe enough for her to attend the Bethnal Green Hospital for treatment,[18] and a local chemist whom she called on also noticed that the very well-dressed lady that he used to know now looked 'untidy'.[19]

★★★

The ice had thawed over the weekend, allowing the searches of ponds and rivers to resume. The ice also thawed with M3. On the morning of Saturday, 10 January, the day that Nizamodeen's visitor permit expired,* an envelope addressed to 'The Editor, News of the World offices', postmarked London E1 at 4.45 p.m. the previous day and marked as 'urgent and personal', was received by Stafford Somerfield. It contained a letter on a piece of lined, white paper, torn along one edge, as if clumsily pulled out from an exercise book. It was composed in heavily disguised handwriting that jumbled upper- and lower-case letters:

> I am writing these lines to you because I can't get through to Aleck McKay by phone for it is bugged by police. If you are his friend you will contact him discretely telling him his wife is safe and well she is being treated by a doctor from abroad. How long this will continue depends on how much co-operation Aleck McKay will give us. When he authorise the police out of his home and he is free to talk I shall telephone him giving instructions and proof of his wife existance for a ransom of one million pounds to be collected on two occassion of half million each time if he cooperate he shall see his wife if he don't cooperate I shall not be contacting him any more and his wife will be disposed off. If he had obeyed me on the Monday when I telephone do not calling the police the matter would have been solved already
> 1 A clue for him to know she is alive
> Mauriel said that Rupert Murdoch left for Australia on Xmas Eve for six weeks
> Secondly, he has not paid ∧ off for ∧ St Mary House
> She said he hasn't the money but (PTO)
> He can borrow from firms he know

---

*   The return date for his charter flight had long since passed.

Immediate attention is important
And he is in no position to bargain

I shall telephone in few days to confirm
"   "   give a code number when telephoning.

I am WRITING These LINES TO you BECAUSE I CANT get THROUGH TO
ALECK Mc KAY BY phoNE FOR IT is BOGGED BY POLICE
IF you ARE His FRIEND YOU WIll CONTACT HIM
DISCRETELY TEllINg HIM His WIFE IS SAFE AND WEll
SHE IS BEINg TREATED BY A DOCTOR FROM ABROAD
HOW LONG WIll THIS CONTINUE DEPENDS ON HOW MUCH
CO-OPERATION ALECK Mc KAY WIll gIVE US. WHEN HE
AUTHORISE THE POLICE OUT OF HIS HOME AND HE
IS FREE TO tALK I SHAll TELEPHONE HIM
gIVINg INSTRUCTIONS AND PROOF OF HIS WIFE EXISTANCE
FOR A RANSOM OF ONE MIllION POUNDS TO BE
COllECTED ON TWO OCCASSION OF hALF MIllION EACH
TIME IF HE COOPERATE HE SHAll SEE HIS WIFE
IF HE dONT COOPERATE I SHAll NOT BE CONTACTING
HIM ANY MORE AND HIS WIFE WIll be disposED
off. IF HE HAD obeyED ME ON THE MONDAY
WHEN I TELEPHONE BY NOT CAllING THE POLICE
THE MATTER WOULD HAVE BEEN SOLVED ALREADY
① A CLUE FOR HIM TO KNOW SHE IS ALIVE
MAURIEL SAID THAT RUPERT MURDOCH LEFT
FOR AUSTRALIA ON XMAS EVE FOR SIX WEEKS
SECONDLY HE HAS NOT PAID FOR HOUSE OFF STMARY-
SHE SAID HE HASNT THE MONEY BUT
P.T.O.

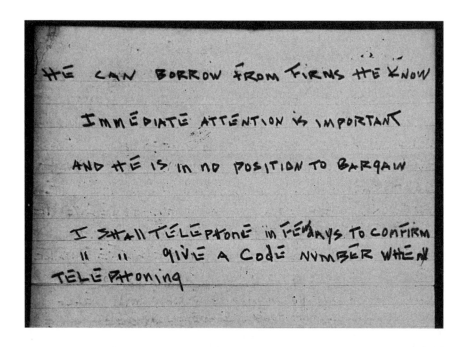

HE CAN BORROW FROM FIRMS HE KNOW

IMMEDIATE ATTENTION IS IMPORTANT

AND HE IS IN NO POSITION TO BARGAIN

I SHALL TELEPHONE IN FEW DAYS TO CONFIRM
" " GIVE A CODE NUMBER WHEN
TELEPHONING

Somerfield immediately drove to St Mary House and presented the letter to Alick and Bill Smith. There was little to connect it to M3 with any certainty, since the £1 million ransom demand was public knowledge and no code name had been included. Only the promised follow-up telephone call could determine how seriously to take the letter, which, if genuine, would be possibly the first ransom note received in Britain since the capture of Richard the Lionheart.

There was little to be gleaned from the letter, even if it was genuine, although some of it carried a faintly West Indian syntax, such as 'when he authorise the police out of his home' and 'he can borrow from firms he know'. Confusingly, the letter claimed that Alick should have 'obeyed me on the Monday when I telephone' about not calling the police. One assumes that the call being referred to is the first call, received at 1.15 a.m. on the Tuesday morning, yet that call contained no such instruction. Even if it had, coming some seven hours after Muriel's abduction, it would have been far too late for such an order.

Since that call was almost certainly made by Nizam, and this letter was almost certainly written by Arthur, we can deduce that Nizam simply failed to include the instruction in that call, and that Arthur was ignorant of that fact, or else that Nizam should have telephoned St Mary House much earlier in the evening but failed to do so. Even then, that would have been a bizarre method of delivering such a crucial instruction, the brothers surely knowing that the first thing Alick was likely to do upon arriving home that evening was to call the police. It must also be noted that if Muriel had still been alive at this point, M3 would surely have made her write the letter, rather than attempt to disguise his own handwriting.

The weekend yielded nothing further, although the absence of Elsa and the children from Rooks Farm was allowing the brothers their first opportunity since New Year to resume the operation. Although Arthur was probably arrogant enough to assume that he could persuade his wife to return in time, for now he certainly believed that she had left him, sharing the news with several of his tailoring contacts.

On Monday, 12 January, posters asking 'Have You Seen This Woman?' went up outside every police station in Britain, while police fruitlessly swooped on a train arriving at Glasgow from Euston following another bogus tip-off. The following day, after visiting Nizam at the farm, Liley returned to London and visited Elsa, whom she had met for the first time a week earlier. It seemed that as well as the assault that she had endured the previous Friday evening, Elsa had also been beaten by Arthur a few days earlier after discovering that Liley had stayed at the farm over the holiday and accusing Arthur of having an affair with her. Liley's visit was probably a well-meaning attempt to reassure her but, whatever the case, for now, Elsa remained determined not to return to Rooks Farm.

Elsa not having returned, on Wednesday, 14 January, M3 finally broke his silence and made telephone contact, though not initially with Alick McKay. His first call that day was to Stafford Somerfield. Usually, an anonymous call to the editor of a controversial newspaper would be fielded, but Somerfield's secretary took the 'M3' code name as referring to 'M', which was Somerfield's wry code for a contact in the security services. The call was terse, M3 asking gruffly whether Somerfield had received the letter, and saying, 'Tell McKay he's got to get a million, I'll send him proof of his wife's existence.'[20] When Somerfield demanded his name and telephone number, M3 became excited and abusive, then hung up.

Somerfield detected a West Indian accent in the voice of M3, and was played some of the previous calls, after which he identified one of them as strongly resembling the voice that he had heard. A few hours later, just after 4 p.m.,

M3 telephoned St Mary House. It was his first contact with the McKay family in thirteen days.

'This is concerning your madam, your mistress', was how M3 began the conversation. After referring to the letter that he had written to Stafford Somerfield, and without any prompting, he said, 'You want proof.' He said that he would be getting Muriel to write a letter, and that enclosed would be instructions on how to deliver the money. 'You got to cooperate and you'll get your madam back.' Alick asked whether Muriel had been receiving any treatment or medication, and M3 assured him that she was and that 'she's costing me a lot now'.

The zealous proffering of proof in the form of a letter from Muriel is what is most significant about this call. M3 does not actually specify whether this would be proof that he is holding her or proof that she is still alive, and since he has dictated the terms, he clearly already has a letter written by her and is contriving to make it sound like it will be written on his instruction shortly after the call. He also said that 'she is wearing a double coat, brown and black'. Presumably 'double coat' means 'reversible'. Whether this unfamiliar term could have hinted at some knowledge of tailoring, one cannot say, but it is certainly not the usual way to describe such a garment.

The promised letter did not arrive, M3 perhaps judging the call to have achieved its purpose in ascertaining that Alick McKay was prepared to cooperate and did not appear to have suspicions that his wife was now dead. Although M3 requested that Alick 'get the police out of there', there was no reference to the hysterical claims in the letter sent to the *News of the World* that the police were bugging the telephone at St Mary House.

A few hours after the call, Arthur and Nizam collected Liley from the Whittington Hospital and drove her back to the farm. They arrived there at 10.30 p.m. Elsa and the children were still away, and Liley was appalled to find that the brothers had left their young sister, Hafeeza, alone in the house. The following morning, she returned to London on the first train from Bishop's Stortford. At the same time, the morning's papers were offering a new angle on the story, summarised several hours later by the front-page headline of the *Evening News*, 'Kidnap Wife – It Looks Like Murder', under which was added, 'Today's police theory – her captors decided that she must die'.

10

EPIPHANY

Leaving train lunch time for Amsterdam. Pleasant with sunshine again. Hope you and Carl are well. See you Saturday.

Muriel McKay, Rhein, Germany, 13 November 1969.

'We all thought that she must be dead by now,' remembers Peter Rimmer. 'The letters had stopped, there was that long gap without any contact, but then greed got the better of them.'[1] According to the *Times* on the morning of 16 January, reports that Muriel was dead had left the police 'angered and embarrassed'.[2] As the press chewed over the rumours, Arthur called on a tailoring colleague, Harold Gordon, who was discussing the case with his father. Arthur stayed silent on the matter.

On an early shift at the Whittington, Liley had watched, fascinated, as an elderly lady patient on her ward had amused herself making paper flowers from tissue paper. Having been shown how to do it, on her way home Liley bought a box of Kleenex rainbow-coloured tissues from Boots in Crouch End and some paper clips from W.H. Smith. While waiting at home for Arthur and Nizam to collect her, she sat making flowers in different colours, showing them to the brothers when she got into the Volvo.

The following day, Arthur drove to Hackney, where Elsa was staying. Freida remembers:

He was begging her to come back, saying, 'Oh please, I'll never do it again.' He was crying and crying. I'd never seen a man in a state like that before. But all the time, I was thinking, 'Oh, please don't, Mum,' because I didn't want to go, I knew that it would just happen again. But he managed to persuade her. She packed up our things, and back we went.[3]

On the other side of London, Alick was at his lowest ebb. Bill Smith arrived at the house and asked to speak to him, preparing to deliver surely the most difficult and dreaded message with which a police officer can be entrusted. Sat on the edge of the bed in his pyjamas, Alick was 'so low'[4] but Smith had to make him aware of the outlook, as gently as possible, before he was exposed to any more press blabber. 'I said, "Now, one must expect that you'll never see Muriel again. Can you accept this?" And he cried. To see a man cry is a terrible thing, a man of his stature.'

Alick nodded, but while he agreed, he could not accept it, and had to keep hoping. Smith agreed that they must hope for the best but be prepared for the worst. 'That was the first time I saw him break down. I put my arm round him, he was sobbing away, he really was upset.'[5]

Commander Guiver later said that 'Alick never really accepted what we said. He went on hoping. But at the same time, he was willing to help us in any way that was within his power.'[6] Smith was aware that another call from M3 must be imminent and he explained to Alick that it was now imperative that M3 be made to believe that he was prepared to negotiate with him and that a meeting must be arranged. As Ian McKay later said, 'At the very worst, we had to catch these people'.[7]

Later that Saturday afternoon, 17 January, the Hoseins, now with Elsa, arrived at George Cuda's farm to buy a new calf, the one they had bought from the Patemans having died. Cuda refused to sell them one but did lend Arthur a billhook similar to the one left behind at Arthur Road, for Liley and Nizam to chop the dead calf up with, so that it could be boiled up then fed to the dogs.

While she was at the farm that weekend, Liley also taught Hafeeza and Freida to make paper flowers, and when she got into the front passenger seat of the Volvo on the Monday morning to be driven back to London by the brothers, she hung some of the creations on the hand grip above the glove compartment. About half an hour after she was dropped off, the telephone rang at St Mary House.

The agonising conversation that followed between M3 and Alick McKay was the longest of the calls made to the family and the most vivid proof that Alick McKay was now at breaking point, and that he was trying to reason with someone without any firm grip on reality. After confirming that he was speaking to Mr McKay, M3 greeted him with a perversely upbeat 'Oh, Alick!' and gave the code name, before immediately overreaching himself by saying that Muriel was 'very worried' and he had not sent a letter or been in contact 'because we got a tip from the CID that she contacted them'.

Alick pleaded with him to make a reasonable demand but M3 continued with his absurd sum of £1 million, to be delivered in two lots of half a million. Alick then demanded proof, which M3 again chose to interpret as proof that he was holding Muriel, not proof that she was still alive. His answer was revealing:

> She is with us. Ah, well now. She is wearing a low-heeled cream shoe with chains on the front with a piece of chain to the front of it. She's wearing a green skirt and bodice with buttoned-down bodice and a double-way coat, black and brown, light brown. She hasn't got her glasses, her eyes are going a bit bad now. She can't read. We gave her books to read.

In contrast to most of what M3 said on the call, which is rambling, clumsy, ill-considered and callous, this description stands out as strikingly detailed, informative and erudite. No attention seems to have been paid to it at the time, and certainly it was not a detail from the calls that was raised during the trial, but with the obvious benefit of hindsight, it surely betrays some sartorial knowledge. Would the average man in 1969 naturally have reached for phrases such as 'buttoned-down bodice' and 'low-heeled cream shoe', ornate terms that were more specific even than those carried on the missing person posters?

Alick tried to pin M3 down for proof that Muriel was alive and well by asking for her to write out the names of her children in full and to list what Christmas presents she had received. M3 made a vague promise of a letter and instructions for the first delivery, but when he again proclaimed that it would be for 'half a million', Alick snapped, erupting at him, 'Look, bring a gun here and shoot me rather than ask unreasonable situations, I mean I can't get that. It's ridiculous … nobody's got a million pounds and I mean, quite frankly, it's ridiculous to talk about it.'

M3 said that after receiving the letter, Alick would be given 'a few days', to which he replied, 'You could give me ten years. You might as well kill me now.'

M3 then responded that if Alick did not cooperate, he would be to blame for not seeing his wife again.

'I'll never be blamed for that, my boy, because I can't meet impossible situations,' Alick fought back, repeating his demand for a letter from Muriel listing her Christmas gifts.

M3 prevaricated again, saying that Alick would be able to speak with her after the first delivery.

There was now a deadlock, Alick firmly stating that he had nothing like that sort of money and asking M3 to make a 'reasonable' demand.

Implacable, M3 responded, 'This is not a one-person group, this is a world-wide international,' to which Alick replied that such a group must therefore know that he had not got that sort of money and if M3 had been to St Mary House he would have seen that it was not a millionaire's home, adding that it was still on a mortgage.

M3 was now trapped in his own false narrative. He cautiously asked Alick how much he would give.

In a desperate, faltering voice, Alick replied that he would give 'everything I've got'.

M3 was in a difficult position. On the one hand, he was readily being offered a considerable sum of money. However, he must have been aware that to lower his demand would have discredited the narrative about a worldwide criminal organisation, a narrative which, clearly, he believed was convincing. He prevaricated again, and Alick despaired.

'What are you trying to do to me … what have I done to deserve this?' he asked.

When M3 told him that he was sorry that they had to do this 'because your wife is such a nice person', Alick replied that Muriel was 'the quietest and most charitable person you've ever met'.

M3 changed the subject again, explaining how his 'boys' traced the Rolls-Royce and 'got her instead'. The most money that Alick could raise was £20,000*which he had arranged to borrow from his bank, and he offered this, only for M3 to reply that it was 'no use, twenty thousand only cost of cars'.

When he returned to the sum of half a million, Alick told him that he could solve the problem by killing himself. M3 again retreated behind fantasy, saying that he had another job lined up in Malta and that he was about to leave for the airport. Alick, by his own admission nearly out his mind, was reduced

---

* £235,000 today.

to a heart-breaking plea of 'Have me instead. Take me instead.' After nearly three-quarters of an hour, M3 hung up.

The references to a 'first delivery' in the call suggested that there was now a chance of M3 being tempted out of the shadows, but the delicate negotiations that would be required to realise this would need a cooler head than that of Alick, or his daughters, who, it was felt, were 'overanxious and consequently tended to dominate the conversation'.[8] Smith suggested that Ian McKay take over the role of talking to M3, having been impressed with his practical, calm demeanour. He was being given the appalling task of having to bargain for his own mother.

Since it was likely that M3 was using a script, even though he was prone to veering off it, a script was prepared for Ian too, while they awaited another call. He was to open by explaining that his father had suffered another heart attack after the last call and was now seriously ill, and that the family had been told by his doctors to expect the worst. It then listed a set of guidelines and questions:

1 LISTEN WHEN HE TALKS.
2 PROLONG THE CALL BUT LISTEN AS WELL.
3 Impossible to raise money through friends as they all believe Muriel walked out. Even the police suspect father and have searched the house and even dug the garden.
4 Why didn't you leave a note when you took Muriel, then the police would never have known?
5 How do we get the police off our tracks so that we can meet?
6 DELAY MEET AS LONG AS POSSIBLE. ABSOLUTE MINIMUM 36 HOURS TO GET ANY MONEY FROM BANK WITHOUT POLICE KNOWING.
7 We need proof. We cannot agree to hand over any money until we see Muriel. We've had so many demands for money, we must have proof.

He was also instructed to repeat himself as much as possible to keep in control of the call. The task was a hugely demanding one, having to win the trust of the kidnappers while also not arousing suspicion by being too willing to pay, and being sceptical without alienating them.

When the call came, two days later, just after noon on 21 January, Ian excelled himself, despite having to endure some appalling gambits from

M3. Once Ian had convinced him that Alick was too ill to come to the telephone, too drugged to drive a car to any rendezvous, and that his father's life was endangered and he had been asked to act on his behalf, M3, who was impervious to the idea that he might cause Alick McKay's death, resorted to telling Ian that his mother was 'very worried' and 'has been even trying to give herself to the doctor, our doctor, you see we've got a doctor from abroad to take care of her … and she has been offering herself to the doctor to get away'.

M3 then switched to enquiring about the police presence. Ian said, 'If we'd had a note right from the start, we would have known not to call them, but we can't get rid of them now.' Smartly, he added that the police were now even suspecting Alick and then returned to the point, 'If only you could have left a note, he would never have panicked, you see, in the start.' Although he hadn't quite managed to present this as a question, as had been intended in the script, M3 did make a vague revelation, 'Yes, yes, that's it, you see, we had the note delayed but it so happened that your mum, you know, she was a bit upset.'

This is the only time that any acknowledgement of the matter was made by M3, and it suggests that he had indeed intended to leave instructions at the house for Alick not to call the police. Presumably, the statement about it being 'delayed' because 'your mum … was a bit upset' suggests that the abduction took longer than intended and was more difficult than they had expected, and so they could not risk the time it would have taken to return to the house to leave the note and collect the billhook and twine, or, more likely, that in the heat of the moment, they simply forgot, something M3 would be too arrogant to admit. This theory reinforces the idea that the BBC news broadcast the following evening was their first realisation that the police were involved.

Ian then broached the subject of a rendezvous. M3 said that the instruction was now for one person to come, and that Muriel had written a letter last night which he had just posted: 'One is to your dad … the other is to Dianne.' He added that a few bits had been clipped off because 'she was trying to tell you all where she was'.

Once again, he prevaricated on whether it would provide proof that she was still alive, switching to a wild story about having sent a detective to intercept Ian when he arrived at the airport, but that he was 'guarded'. He then returned to fantasies about the M3, saying that it was not a question of what he wanted personally; he belonged to the M3. He then claimed that he controlled the M3, which was 'Mafia Gang 3' rather than 'Mafia Group 3', as it had been called in the first call. After reiterating that they had originally intended a different target, the call cut out.

M3 telephoned again a few minutes later, this time for a very brief and more pointed call, confirming that letters to Alick and Dianne were on their way, as well as instructions, and that the date would be 1 February. Before hanging up, he said that they would have to get half a million pounds. 'We want a million but the first delivery gotta be half a million.'

M3 had effectively halved the ransom demand, since clearly the idea was now to collect half a million and then vanish, even though to the rest of the world, half a million was still a ridiculous sum to expect. Things were gaining traction, with Ian having won M3's trust and a date for the rendezvous now having been set. The following day, an envelope arrived at St Mary House, in Muriel's handwriting, though rather more roughly written this time. It was postmarked '2.15 p.m., Wood Green N22'.

It contained three letters: one to Alick McKay, one to Dianne, and one giving instructions for the pay-off. What it did not contain was the promised proof that Muriel was still alive. The first letter read:

Darling Alick – I am deteriorating in health &
spirit – please cooperate
excuse writing I'm blindfolded and cold –

Please keep the Police out of this and cooperate
with the gang giving code No M3 when telephoning
to you. The earlier you get money
the quicker I may come home or
you will not see me again. Darling. Can you
act quickly please.
please. Keep Police out of this if you want to see me. <u>Muriel.</u>

The second letter read:

Dearest Dianne I heard you on T.V.
Thank you for looking after Daddy
Would you please persuade Daddy to cooperate

Darling Dick — I am deteriorating in health & spirit please cooperate excuse writing Im blind cold & cold —

Please keep the Police out of this and cooperate with the Gang giving Code No, M3 when telephoning. The earlier you get money the quicker I may come home or you will not see me again. Darling. Can you Act quickly please. Please keep Police out of this, if you want to see me. Muriel

with M3 gang – they will telephone you
giving that code No. M3.
You will then be sure you are speaking to the
right party. Act quickly for my sake dear.
Please keep Police out of it if you want
to see me alive.
Negotiate with Gang

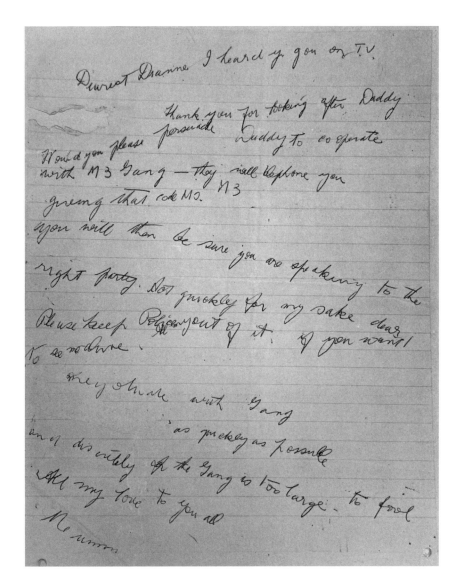

as quickly as possible
and discretely as the Gang is too large to fool
All my love to you all
Mumm

Both letters were again chaotically written, but this time they carried with them a suggestion of having been partially dictated by M3, particularly in the dubious claim that 'the gang is too large to fool'. The two most important details in the letters were Muriel saying that she had heard Dianne on television and the unnecessary restatement that the gang would telephone using the code number 'M3'. Unfortunately, both details only strengthened the case that Muriel was no longer alive.

Bill Smith was convinced that all the letters from Muriel had been written some time ago, and had been sent in the wrong order, especially since the code 'M3' had been established weeks ago, as long ago as Dianne's television appearance. The reference to that television appearance was the most vital detail.

Although Dianne was visible in the background of the television coverage of the press conference on 9 January – seen but not 'heard', which the letter states – her two television interviews were on 30 December and 31 December. Neither appearance made any specific mention of Dianne 'looking after' her father. The *News at Ten* on New Year's Eve did feature David Dyer reading out a statement from Alick, but it is much more likely that Muriel was referring to the BBC broadcast of 30 December, since this was an interview solely with a distraught Dianne.

As was set out earlier, by 31 December, visitors were calling at the farm again and by the evening Liley was staying there. By that time, Muriel must have been dead. Rather than providing proof that Muriel was alive, all the letter did was prove that she did not die before 9 p.m. on 30 December 1969. If she had still been alive, M3 would have readily provided as much proof as possible now that there was a hint that the money would soon be within his reach.

The envelope also contained the promised ransom note, which was unnecessarily lengthy and as rambling as the telephone calls had become. It was in a neat, careful hand which showed less evidence of disguise than that in the bizarre letter received by the *News of the World*:

> this is your instructions Please obey no error must happen you have no alternative you will be advice not to inform the police or any other party if you disobey you will be blame for the consequences we are demanding one million pounds in two occasion the first occasion you must place half million pounds in a black suitcase comprising of £5 and £10 notes, you must drive your wife ford capri car you must not accompanied by any one but your self from your home get into the north circular road keep driving until you approach into the A10 cambridge road as soon as you drive on the A10 cambridge road the first set of traffic lights on the left hand side

you will see a public telephone box on the junction of CHURCH Street N.9. you will find the telephone box No 01-360-3578X you will enter telephone box and wait for us to telephone you to give you further instructions at 10.^{00} P.M. on the 1st February∧ ^{1970} we shall we telephoning you. if in case you wish an earlier day for our business transaction providing you got the money of course. we shall use code number for identity (M3) your wife muriel is pleading with us that you cannot obtain one million pounds. but I am making no promises, but if you co-operate discreately and we collect the first half million, our gang will hold a conferance whether to satisfy with half million pounds, if we do agree, you will receive your wife two days after business is settled.

Make sure that suit case with money is locked. We can assure you that we will not be caught because we are sending P.t.o.

a totally strange person, who will be paid to do a job and that his job is to collect a black suit case, if he is caught by the police or any party of yours he will not be able to assist you or the police, my men will be surrounding the time you leave your house until money is collected, any error on your behalf it will only take two minutes and you shall never hear from us or see your wife alive you will see her dead and deliver at your door

your wife have been blindfolded for our security just in case we have to release her back to you

on the 1st FEBRUARY 1970
at 10 ^{00} .PM
   on A10 CAMBRIDGE ROAD
   Junction CHURCH STREET N9
   further instruction will be given
   on telephone

we shall keep in touch with you

M3 could quite easily have sent just the postscript, since it contained all the necessary information, but he was clearly rather enjoying both the power that he believed he was holding in the situation and his imagined eminence in the criminal world. One point to note, however, is the use – twice – of 'party', which echoes its rather jarring use in one of the accompanying letters from Muriel, which refers to ensuring that 'you are speaking to the right party', and is evidence of dictation by M3. Also, the superfluous claim at the end that Muriel has been blindfolded 'for our security just in case we have to release her back to you' is significant. Considering this statement in conjunction with the evidence of some of the letters and envelopes having been written without a blindfold gives some weight to the suggestion that M3 wanted the family to believe that there was always a chance of her release even though he never had any such intention.

The locations identified in the ransom note, a call box in Edmonton, close to the districts where the letters had been posted, and the A10 heading north-north-east out of London, coupled with the awareness that the first M3 call had been made from Epping, on the A11, which ran out of London and into Hertfordshire parallel to the A10, pointed tentatively towards a base of operations somewhere in that direction. Either M3 was cunningly misdirecting the police, or his apples were not falling very far from the tree.

While the McKays and the police were receiving these three letters, at Rooks Farm, in the morning post, Arthur received a bailiff's summons for debt. He replied, outraged and incredulous that 'an English Court would exercise such injustices'.[9] He was playing for time, while the McKays now had just ten days to find an impossible half a million pounds, M3 again showing his idiocy by demanding not only an impossible sum but the impossible feat of fitting half a million pounds in £5 and £10 notes into a single suitcase.

The next day, 23 January, Arthur was in London, visiting various tailors in the East End. At just before noon, the first of three calls that day were made by M3 to St Mary House. M3 fared badly on the call, floundering as Ian's controlled aggression pushed him as far as possible without permanently alienating him. Pointing out that there was no actual proof in the letters that his mother was still alive, Ian repeatedly listed practical ways that M3 could offer such proof, and said that without it the family would not pay him any money. M3 again fell back on the offer of describing what Muriel was wearing. In fact, he offered to describe again what she 'is' wearing, when in fact, three weeks on, surely they would have had to give her a change of clothes by now. He added, 'Do you want me to take her clothes off and send them to you?' and 'If our phone was not bugged ... she could have used a telephone now, we don't want to take her out, you see.' (Nonsensical as this was, with hindsight, it carries a faint suggestion that Muriel's captivity had been at Rooks Farm.)

Ian reminded M3 that a description of Muriel's clothing had already been widely publicised. M3's response is important. He said, 'The police have issued according to the shoes, driving shoes, but they didn't say the colour of the shoes, I saw, you see.' Nothing was made of this at the time, but it strengthens the case for M3 having seen the 30 December BBC news report. During that report, Bill Smith mentioned that Muriel's driving shoes were missing, a detail that was not included in the other news report to feature an interview with Dianne, which was broadcast on New Year's Eve.

Ian boldly put it to M3 that his mother was dead and that he would not cooperate without proof that she was still alive. M3 said that unless his attitude changed, 'You shall get her dead at your door' and Ian would be to blame. Ian retorted, 'Your gang will blame you if you don't get the money.'

M3 hung up.

Two hours later, he called back. This time Ian was even fiercer, deploying the technique of repeating himself to avoid being led astray by M3, who was becoming more and more ill-considered, emotional and eccentric with each call, now claiming that his organisation even had men in the Post Office. Aware that to suddenly agree to pay half a million pounds now would be highly suspicious, Ian told M3 that through friends and relatives, the family had raised a quarter of a million, which they would deliver if they were given proof that Muriel was alive. When M3 tried to take control of the call and stated that no further proof would be given, Ian said:

Because you haven't got it, you've got a corpse, you've got a corpse, you've got a corpse, you've got a corpse … You've got a dead person, you haven't got her at all, you know she's not alive so you are just trying to trick us, you're trying to trick us, you're trying to trick us.

In confusion, the scorned M3 tried to claim that this would be 'on our conscience'. Ian kicked back with, 'You couldn't have much conscience, or you wouldn't have kidnapped her.'

Although the call was terminated in a hostile manner, it seemed that M3 was considering taking the bait. A quarter of an hour later, he made his final call of the day. He wanted to talk to Alick rather than Ian, and when this was refused, he tried emotional blackmail, claiming that Muriel had told him that she had been 'a good wife to your dad and … a very good mum to her children' and was asking 'why have they forsaken her'.

Ian remained resolute, demanding that his mother write out the headlines from the evening newspaper, and then took his boldest stance, repeating this demand three times and then finishing with '… and I'm going to hang up on you. Goodbye, goodbye, be reasonable, goodbye.'

Three days later, on 26 January, another envelope arrived at St Mary House, again postmarked Wood Green N22, and again addressed in Muriel's hand, but an even more rough and untidy effort than the previous letter. There were several items inside, perhaps everything that M3 had left to bid with. Two pieces of shabby, blue, lined paper contained messages from Muriel. The first read:

Darling Alick – you don't seem to be helping me. Again, I beg of you to cooperate with the M3 Gang. You do understand that when the

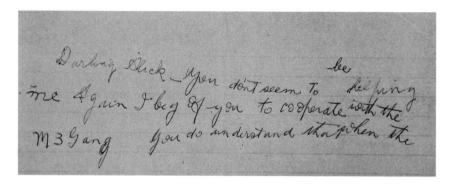

The note was written on the top portion of a piece of lined writing paper and had been untidily cut from the rest of the page after the third line of script. This suggests that it was the letter that M3 had referred to on the telephone call five days previously, which he warned he had clipped bits from because Muriel had been trying to reveal her location.

The second letter was the most chaotic, with lines intersecting and a tear in the centre, probably caused by unsteady use of the pen.

Alick Darling – if I could only be home
I cant believe this thing happened to me
Tonight I thought I see you
But it seems hopeless that is all I can say
at the moment
You betrayed me by going

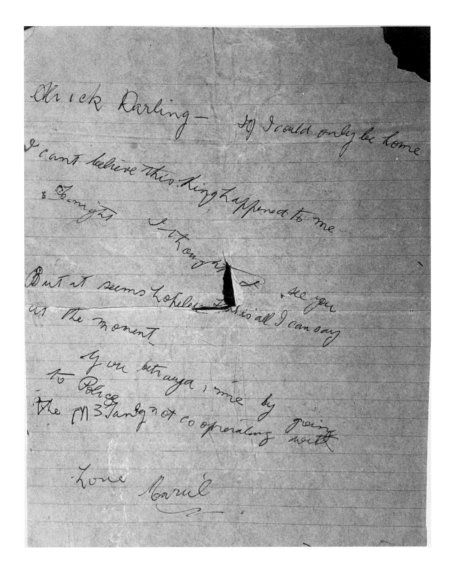

to the Police and not cooperating
with the M3 Gang
Love <u>Muriel</u>

This letter is further evidence of M3's outrage at the police involvement, and Muriel's claim that she had thought that she might see her husband that night perhaps suggests that after the news broadcast, when the remaining letters were probably written, she had briefly hoped that the Hoseins would release her. Most deplorable is the final sentence, clearly the words of Arthur Hosein, in which she has been forced to tell her husband that he has betrayed her, something that she has tried to countermand by adding 'Love Muriel'. The phrase 'Tonight I thought I see you' is oddly ungrammatical, causing one to ponder whether it was dictated by Arthur, or whether perhaps Muriel was trying to give a clue to the West Indian speech of her captors.

Accompanying the letters were three pieces of material cut from Muriel's clothing. The first was a square from her overcoat, fawn on one side, black on the other. The second was a square of green, woollen material, and the third a triangular fragment of cream-coloured patent leather. Muriel's dressmaker identified the materials as having been cut from the collars of the costume and the coat and from one of her shoes.

A third piece of paper, in the same careful handwriting as M3's previous ransom demand, tried to regain some of his ground after the bruising exchanges with Ian McKay:

I am sending you final letter for your wife's reprieve, she will be executed on the 2nd february 1970. unless you keep our business date on the 1st of February without any error. we demand the full million pound in two occassion, when you deliver the first half million your wife life will be saved and I personally shall allow her to speak to you on telephone

We will not allow you to tell us how to run our organisation
we are telling you what to do you cannot ~~have~~ eat the cake and have it too. this is our 4th Blackmail we have absorb 3½ million pound we did not murdered any one, because they were wise to pay up and their family were return to them, you do the same and she will return safely my next blackmail will be in Australia some times this year.

Looking forward in settling our business on the 1st february at 10pm as stated on last letter in a very discreet + honest way, and you and your children will be very happy to join muriel mackay and our organisation also will be happy to continue our job elsewhere in Australia we shall look forward to see your son IAN when we visit Australia.

you see we dont make our customer happy we like to keep them in suspence in that way it is a gamble that is why
we dont accept you IAN telling us what to do
we give the order and you <u>must</u> obey
<u>M.3</u>

Amid the clumsy spelling and grammar, and the rambling, facile boasts, some of which were delayed responses to points which Ian had tripped M3 up with during the telephone conversations, the note showed that M3 was likely to take the bait.

While the police spent the next few days preparing for the operation, Arthur was restive. On 28 January, he telephoned Audrey Strube, accusing her of making allegations and insinuations against him and saying that Yasmin and her friend had been doing the same on the school bus, and that if it happened again, 'he would hound me out of the village and send me a solicitor's letter'.[10] The Strubes were bewildered as to why they had been targeted in this way, particularly since they had been so neighbourly to the Hoseins, but the teasing that Hafeeza was enduring from some local children on the bus was obviously being used against the Strubes out of spite because of the incidents at Rooks Farm just before Christmas.

Two days later, on the morning of Friday, 30 January, M3 telephoned St Mary House again. Ian handled this call particularly skilfully, pulling back from his tone of imperiousness and mistrust to lull M3 into a false sense of security, saying that since receiving the most recent delivery, 'we know you're the right people, and we want to cooperate'.

For the police's plan to work, they needed Ian to persuade M3 that he must take the Rolls-Royce to the drop, rather than his mother's Capri, and that he should be accompanied by the chauffeur. Ian achieved this by claiming that he had damaged his arm, that he was unfamiliar with north London and that the press camped outside the house would be inquisitive if they saw him driving the Rolls, or the Capri, which had been garaged for weeks. M3 accepted, saying that if the exchange went according to plan, he would see his mother that night, but warned that 'any error would be fatal'.

Later that afternoon, Arthur visited a tailor, Sid Flecker, pressing what he surely believed were two of the last pairs of trousers that he would ever need to press. Back at Rooks Farm, having just been visited by Liley, Nizam wrote a letter to the nurse he had been seeing the previous summer, Dolly Premchand, who was still living in Wakefield:

Dear Darling Dolly,

I am very sorry for not writing earlier to you. I must apologise and do hope you accept my apology. I hope that these few lines will meet you and greet you with health, happiness and prosperity. I shall now state my reason for not writing earlier. As you know that I had applied for a PERMIT to stay in England but unfortunately the home office gave me notice to leave the country. I should have left on the 10-1-70 for that was the dead line date for me remaining in England. I therefore had to keep moving around so that they would not find me. I am now back at my brother at the above address who's phone number is BRENT PELHAM 317 which you got. I wanted to come down to Yorkshire to see you but I was not certain if you will be there. I could not contact you for you don't have a phone. Secondly I forgot the name of the hospital. I have decided to remain in England which is illegal but they cannot find me here. I do hope that you would reply to my letter. I received your Post Card of which I am very thankful.

I did not send any Post Card to anyone even at home for I was terribly worried. I cannot write more at the moment. I hope sincerely that you have not changed due to I not corresponding with you but I will see you soon in the near future.
I must say Goodbye now.
Awaiting your reply.
I wish you good health, and a Bright and Prosperous 1970.
Until I hear from you,

I Remain,

Your Forever, Nizam Hosein.

You could phone me any day you wish to. Preferably at night after 7pm.[11]

While his excuse for not writing – that he 'had to keep moving around so that they would not find me' – is pure invention, what is detectible in the letter is a tone of both jumpiness and optimism. He claims, 'I did not send any Post Card to anyone even at home for I was terribly worried. I cannot write more at the moment.' This is probably a reference to Christmas cards, although quite what was worrying him so terribly at that time, in the run-up to the kidnapping, he does not divulge, nor does he divulge why he 'cannot write more at the moment'.

He openly admits that he will be staying on in England illegally and that 'they cannot find me here'. Considering the supposedly torturous existence that he was suffering at the hands of Arthur, it is presumably not just his reluctance to return to his reproachful father in Trinidad but the fact that two days from the date of this letter, he was expecting his share of £1 million, that has made staying on in Britain illegally an attractive option.

However, the operation would not go according to plan – for the Hoseins or for the police.

PAPER FLOWERS

The garden here is so colourful, pink geraniums hang along both balconies, large rose bushes heavy with red blooms, the longest godetias I've ever seen, yellow marigolds and others to vary colours. A very pleasing effect.

Muriel McKay, Mallorca, 7 May 1967.

The desolate countryside around the sorrowful hamlet of Cold Christmas should have been an apt place for this midwinter tragedy to conclude. Driving north out of London along the Great Cambridge Road, the city and the suburbs swiftly strip away into plain, airy countryside riddled with signposts bearing arcane place names. Cold Christmas Lane crosses the road just before the village of High Cross and leads to the deconsecrated and now desecrated ruins of a church which, according to local mythology, is haunted by a band of children who froze to death one ancient Christmas.

Standing today at the roadside where, on the snowy and sleety night of Sunday, 1 February 1970, Nizamodeen Hosein planted two of Liley's paper flowers to mark the spot where the ransom money was to be laid, one is struck by the irony of two men as unpoetic as the Hosein brothers inadvertently choosing such a fitting place for what was intended to be the story's end. But despite that, although the dainty flowers survive in a display cabinet at Scotland Yard's Crime Museum, there are no ghosts of that Christmas past here today, the bleak spot merely a reminder of the unhappy reality that the story did not end here, nor did the night of Sunday, 1 February end with Muriel McKay being reunited with her family.

Arthur and Elsa worked all day on Saturday, 31 January, getting ahead because they would be losing a day on Tuesday, Arthur having been summoned to appear at Old Street Magistrates' Court for motoring offences. Meanwhile, the police were preparing for the drop, with conferences held at Scotland Yard, at which it was decided that, since there was no question of Ian McKay or the chauffeur, William Nunn, being allowed to take part in the operation, Detective Sergeant Roger Street, a dynamic presence on the inquiry and its youngest CID officer, should impersonate Ian, to whom he bore a vague resemblance. M3 had accepted Ian's claim to have injured his hand, so Street's arm would be put in a sling concealing a two-way radio. John Minors would masquerade as the chauffeur and carry a loaded .38 revolver. Although M3 had failed to provide evidence that Muriel was still alive, there was also no firm evidence that she was dead, so botching the operation could have fatal consequences.

Alick McKay loaned the police £300 in £5 notes, which were placed on the top and bottom of each bundle of 100 specially printed fake banknotes. While they were produced on authentic paper, at the centre of each note was a large white bar, so when the edge of a bound bundle was flicked through, it appeared genuine. 'The hilarious thing,' says Street, 'was that we just had this suitcase, when in fact if we'd really had the amount that they were demanding in fivers and tenners, we'd have needed a van to move it.'[1]

Aware that he would have to answer the telephone as Ian McKay, Street spent time learning to mimic his voice and had his hair dyed a lighter colour. No one could predict how the events of the evening would unfold. 'Everyone asks whether it was nerve-racking, but at that age, as a young officer, rather than being fearful, you're just excited. It's like going on a 999 call to a serious crime, you aren't thinking about the consequences, you're thinking, "Let's get there and do this".'

The Hoseins had guests for Sunday lunch, tailor Gerald Gordon and his family. While entertaining them, Arthur faced the indignity of a visit from the paper boy, who presented him with a large unpaid bill from the newsagent. The Gordons left at 6 p.m., and Arthur and Nizam then left for the East End to make some collections and deliveries. As they were leaving, Arthur Rosenthal, a trimming merchant, arrived at the farm, and chatted to Arthur briefly, gifting him a packet of Piccadilly tipped cigarettes before being invited in to watch television with Elsa and the children.

Between 7 p.m. and 7.30 p.m., Nizam collected some trousers from Lillian Skinner in Whitechapel, asking her for sixpence to make a telephone call. At 7.50 p.m., the phone rang at Arthur Road. M3 announced that this would be his last call to the house, the rest that night being to the telephone box identified in the letter. He then made a ludicrous attempt to suggest that Muriel was still alive by asking Ian for his 'solemn word' that when she was returned, she would not be 'interrogated by the police or by any member of the press. You see, this is orders from the head office which I got to confirm tonight.'

Street sat in the back of the Rolls-Royce and the cases were placed in the boot. The car would be followed by an unmarked police car containing Bill Smith, both vehicles also equipped with a tracking device, a new piece of technology which it was hoped would become an essential tool in the transportation of high-risk prisoners and large sums of money. Although it had proved only to work within a 5-mile radius at its first demonstration a year previously, its range was now promised to be up to 50 miles. At 9 p.m., Minors moved off from Arthur Road, heading for the call box 20 miles away on Church Street, Edmonton.

As soon as the operation was underway, problems became apparent. The first was that the tracking device was, in Street's words, 'useless. It just never worked. It turned out that the tracking vehicle had always to be within 200 yards of us or it couldn't function':[2]

You must remember that this was a completely different era and a very different atmosphere and environment, technologically as much as anything else. When I retired, twenty-seven years ago, the tech had moved on enormously since 1969, but even then, it was nothing compared with what they can do now. The Home Office boffins had given us a tracking device in the suitcase, but it never worked. It was absolutely prehistoric. Similarly, they'd given us these horrible radios that you held in your hand rather than plugged into the car, and they never worked either. The radios in the cars too, once you'd gone out of London, you couldn't talk to each other, the signal wasn't even being relayed between the two cars.

Undaunted, at 9.55 p.m. they arrived at the call box, on the noisy junction of Church Street and the A10, where a telephone box still stands today. The light in the box was not working, so Street waited in the dark for twenty minutes, until finally he discovered that the bell on the telephone was also not working. He lifted the receiver, answered as Ian McKay, and listened as a West Indian voice said, 'This is M3, these are your instructions.'

The voice then directed him a couple of miles down the A10, away from London, to another call box, this one at the junction with Southbury Road, Enfield. M3 displayed no doubt that he was speaking to Ian but warned again that 'any error will be fatal'. This second box was also unlit, and this time, when the telephone rang, Street was told to look down at the floor where, in the dark, he saw an empty Piccadilly cigarette packet. He gingerly picked it up and opened it delicately to avoid obliterating any fingerprints that it may have held. It contained a rough map of the junction, indicating the direction he should proceed in and a further set of instructions, which M3 talked him through:

From South Bury Road ∧ ^{AFTER telephoning} continue on CAMBRIDGE ROAD A10 to HODDESDON continuing into Ware and then you will approaching into <u>HIGH</u> <u>CROSS</u> you will continue not far from HIGHCROSS there is a narrow road on your LEFT HAND SIDE known as <u>DANE</u> <u>END</u> to recognise DANE END you will see on your right hand side there is a board mark DANE END 2 ½ miles with the Board pointing to direction Before you approach DANE END you will recognise a PETROL STATION NAME = HIGH CROSS ESSO SERVICE STATION. Before approaching the pointing board

To be more exact from the corner junction at Southbury CAMBRIDGE Road to (DANE END) HIGHCROSS is exactly 15 ½ miles, you will no doubt clock the mileage in your car. so that when you travel 15 ½ miles you will be in the area as mentioned above.

THE DESTINY
  DANE END
    HIGH CROSS
      HERTFORDSHIRE
        I hope you
        will endeavour
        to co-operate.   <u>M.3</u>
        Most sincerely.

The gist of the rambling instructions was to drive 15½ miles north along the A10 to High Cross, where, just after passing what M3, significantly, referred to on the call as the Esso 'gas station', at the turning for Dane End, two paper flowers would mark the spot where the money was to be placed. After leaving it there, Ian was to return to the first telephone kiosk at Church Street, where he would receive a call saying where Muriel was to be found. Street returned to the Rolls and he and Minors headed into the dark Hertfordshire country-side with 'absolutely nothing to give any impression of what might be waiting for us'.

From the back of the Rolls, Street radioed Bill Smith, who instructed two officers waiting in the vicinity, Tony Stevens and William O'Hara, to leave the area and drive to High Cross. Smith continued to tail the Rolls, which also had an escort of four officers on motorcycles disguised as Hell's Angels. Disastrously, the Rolls was no longer being discreetly followed by a few unmarked police cars, but was now leading a convoy, being trailed by so many unmarked police cars that, once it was stripped of its camouflage of city traffic, it began to resemble a cortège. Senior officers at Scotland Yard had been so anxious about so much supposedly genuine money being transported and the risk of the operation being hijacked by someone other than M3 that they had asked for the assistance of the Flying Squad and the Regional Crime Squad to provide extra protection for the cargo. As a result, there were forty-eight carloads of detectives, 180 officers and three commanders on the ground, as well as Bert Guiver at Scotland Yard. The operation was over-planned and over-subscribed but uncoordinated. Detective Sergeant Kenneth Rextrew would later recall that 'senior officers were arguing over the airwaves about who should take command, different squads all wanting a bit of the action'.[3]

Street and Minors arrived at High Cross at 11.45 p.m., spotting the two sodden and windswept paper flowers, one apricot and one green, stuck into a muddy bank about 1ft apart, at the junction of the A10 and the turning for Dane End.* It was 'very, very dark and quite eerie', and Street was quite startled when a voice from the hedge said, 'It's all right, we're already here.'[4] Minors lifted the hundredweight suitcase from the car, placed it by the flowers as instructed, then drove the Rolls back to Church Street, where he and Street waited for the promised call concerning Muriel's location.

---

*   Now called Pest House Lane.

Stevens and O'Hara passed the Dane End turning just as Minors was setting the suitcase down and drove on until they arrived at a roadside café, 600 yards further up the A10, the same café that Arthur Hosein had regularly visited since befriending its proprietors, the Westlakes, some months earlier. O'Hara, armed with a pistol and equipped with a radio, was deputed to watch the suitcase and headed back across the ploughed fields on foot to the Dane End junction to lie in wait. He remained there for two and a half hours, enduring snow and sleet in saturated clothing.

Bill Smith's car turned into the unlit forecourt of the transport café. His driver switched off the headlights and parked behind a hedge, hidden from the road. About five minutes later, a dark, mud-splashed Volvo turned into the forecourt from the direction of London, passing a few feet away from them. It drove around the café and then out again, heading back towards the Dane End junction. Its headlights were dipped but Smith noticed that the front nearside light was out, and that the car contained a passenger. O'Hara and Stevens had also noticed the Volvo when they had turned into the forecourt but had made out little in the dark other than that the man in the passenger seat had very bushy hair.

By now, the police presence was overwhelming. As Kenneth Rextrew turned into the roadside café, he looked back down the A10 and 'all you could see were headlights coming up from the direction of London, and they all finished up trying to get into this one car park. It was complete and utter chaos.'[5]

At one point, detectives approached a suspect vehicle, only to find that it was another police car. At this time of night, usually the traffic was mostly comprised of heavy-goods vehicles. The police logged less than a dozen cars during the operation, one of which was the Volvo, although its registration number could not be discerned in the dark.

Quite what happened inside the Volvo that night remains uncertain, but some sort of argument broke out between Arthur and Nizam, whose subsequent account of it is unlikely to be the whole truth. It certainly culminated in violence, with Nizam ejected from the car and left to walk home in the rain, hitching a lift part of the way. It was probably the result of the brothers' tension and frustration over the obvious police presence, Nizam perhaps defying Arthur by refusing to risk retrieving the cases.

Arthur arrived home alone. Elsa was concerned as to what he had been up to if Nizam had not been with him all evening and suspected again that he had been with another woman. Nizam eventually returned, soaked. She made the brothers a meal, Nizam eating his by himself in the kitchen.

Eventually, at 2.30 a.m., with the money unclaimed and Street and Minors still waiting in vain at the telephone box in Church Street for the call that would reveal Muriel's whereabouts, Smith gave orders for the operation to be abandoned and instructed Minors and Street to return to High Cross to collect the suitcase and the paper flowers. He was now faced with the unenviable task of returning empty-handed to Arthur Road and to the waiting McKay family.

There was little doubt that the saturation of the area with officers and cars had sabotaged the operation and panicked M3. 'They'd made too much of this, there were too many people,' Smith would later mourn.[6] Roger Street reflects:

> They had recruited the Flying Squad to do the tailing, but there were no surveillance units, just cars of detectives. The fear of losing them meant that they just put in far too many people. In 1981, we set up our own sur-veillance team, as C11 surveillance were always so busy and we couldn't always get them, and trying to do it yourself is a nightmare, so we set up our own team, a couple of people off each of my four squads and some drivers. We had our own limited surveillance team, but they had nothing like that at all back then.

The operation had been leaked to the press and the *Evening News* prepared a humiliating front-page splash, but after Commissioner Sir John Waldron pointed out that this could destroy the chances of ever negotiating again with the kidnappers, the story was dropped. Publicity was also narrowly dodged when a member of the public who regularly tuned into police messages mis-took the name McKay for McVicar and thought the officers were on the scent of the armed robber who had recently escaped from HMP Durham.[*]

★★★

The spot that Arthur had chosen for his fortune to be laid at is just 10 miles south of Stocking Pelham. The operation had again pointed police in the same

---

[*] John Roger McVicar (1940–2022) escaped from HMP Durham in October 1968 and was not recaptured until November 1970. A notoriously violent armed robber, after education and parole, he became a journalist.

north-north-easterly direction out of London, so inquiries were made in the vicinity of High Cross for any West Indians known to be living in the area. The local police told them that they knew of no West Indians in the area, but on further checking, a postman mentioned that there were two brothers living on a farm at Stocking Pelham, who were possibly Pakistani.

It was enough for Tony Stevens and another officer to visit the village, posing as insurance salesmen. They learned that the brothers were strange and unpopular, but not that they were criminals. They viewed the farm from a distance, noting a Volvo car, and returned the information to the incident room for processing. It was surely only a matter of time now, one way or another, before the police would close the nets on the Hoseins. Since it seemed outrageous to imagine that M3 would continue with the ransom demands after this, all other leads to find him would be pursued zealously.

The day after the Dane End fiasco, Arthur missed all his tailoring appointments, Elsa having to field telephone calls for him with the excuse that he was ill. On Tuesday, 3 February, he failed to attend the Magistrates' Court, Elsa again having to lie that he was sick. He did use the telephone twice that day, however.

M3's first call to Arthur Road came in the late morning, opening with him telling Ian, 'What a nice boy you are, aren't you? You know who is speaking, don't you?' It was a torturous, sadistic exercise, but as the call progressed it seemed that, amazingly, M3 was prepared to set up another meeting, even if, to maintain his authority, he was going to make Ian McKay wait for his decision and also punish him for having betrayed his trust.

Before referring to the events of the previous Sunday, M3 delivered possibly the only part of the call he had thought out beforehand, regarding a supposed meeting he was on his way to:

> This is a meeting now, well, first our business is being handled by the intellectuals, the heads. Now there's to be a meeting of the semi-intellectuals, to be passed on to the third party, the ruffians, ruffians we call them. Er, this meeting is, er, in consideration with your mum, what time she be executed, er, whether she should be executed and what time you see.

'What a hardship for the family, having to listen to that stuff about this supposedly huge organisation, which was bizarre in the extreme,' says Aubrey Rose.[7] While the claims were moronic, they were also menacing, and coupled with the most sustained threats to Muriel's life, although this time, M3 was reporting them from the point of view of a blameless observer:

> I … spoke to your mum this morning, and er, I just don't know what to say … I took your word for granted, I believed you, I trusted you … I'm going to plead for your mum … She pleaded to me. 'Please. Please don't hurt me,' she said. I'm very fond of your mum, you know, Ian, I'm very fond of her because she reminds me of my mum, you see.

M3 said that his own life would be in danger if it became known that he was making this call, and that he was thinking of 'resigning … let this thing go through, when I resign then I assist you. I don't know what to say now. I well, look, I had said she, my mind's so jumbled up. I've got to go to this meeting. I don't know what they're going to decide.' Perhaps this was a moment of genuine insight into Arthur's state of mind at this point, tantalised by the memory of that bulging suitcase at the side of the road, a temptation that was battling loudly in his mind with the risk of a police sting.

He went into detail about the obvious police presence at High Cross, but Ian tried to convince him that he must have been followed, by either the press or the police. His contrition seemed to work, M3 saying that he would call back after the meeting, regaining ground with a vile slur which he presented with a tone of wounded concern:

> I'll let you know whether, er, we'll be able to pursue this or whether they're going for execution. But Ian, I really don't know what to say, boy. Just imagine, the person who bring you into this world, you have condemned that person. Just think of it.

M3 rang again two hours later, announcing that a decision had now been made. He was prepared to allow one final chance but would now only deal with Alick. Ian put up a gallant fight to remain as the intermediary, saying that his father was now so ill that any further upset could finish him off, also suggesting that if he died, the money would then immediately be frozen, and that even while his father was still alive, only he had been granted the authority to move it from the bank.

Amid his usual unconvincing fantasies, which this time, in his new tone of embattled benevolence, included a claim that he had 'broke down into tears during the meeting there', came the revelation that he was now reading news-paper coverage of the case, since he made a reference to reports of detectives recently acting on anonymous telephone calls.[8] He claimed he was unable to do a deal with Ian separately, since his own life was now in danger, as were the lives of his wife and children. When Ian tried once more to elicit proof that his mother was still alive, M3 switched back to spite, 'She says this, after thirty-three years of marriage, this is what she get from you all'.

However, Ian's behaviour on the call was highly effective. As well as tempt-ing him again with the money, he told M3, 'We have got to shake the press off so let's do it in the middle of, you know, a crowded place where we can lose these people, you know.' Since M3 was also claiming to be acting outwith the organisation now, there was a contrived sense of collusion which, in his addled, confused state of mind, appeared to be ensnaring him.

The following day was Muriel's birthday. She would have been 56 years old. The only news was an alert that a woman's body had been dragged from the River Lea near Nazeing in Essex. The proximity to Epping immedi-ately alerted the McKay squad, but whoever the poor lady was, she was not Muriel McKay.[9]

Arthur drove to London the following morning to collect some trousers from various finishers to press at the farm. He took Nizam with him, purport-edly to show him where to go in case he lost his licence after the postponed court appearance.

At about 10.15 a.m., Jennifer answered the telephone at St Mary House, and a quite extraordinary call began. M3 asked to speak to Alick, and Jennifer, immediately recognising the voice from the tape recordings, identified herself as her sister Dianne, since Dianne had spoken to M3 previously, and when asked, used this as an explanation for how she could tell who was speaking.

When Alick came to the phone, it was the first time that he had spoken to M3 in more than two weeks and it was striking how different the positions of both men now were. Rather than indignation and despair, Alick was now stern, aloof, even sardonic at times. M3 was muted, less certain of himself and his authority. Early in the call, when he referred to 'the boss', Alick said, 'I thought you were the boss. The last time I talked to you, you were the boss, have you been demoted?' He added, 'For a smart organisation you haven't worked very smart.'

Alick still had to try to flush out M3, and he did this with a tone of weary resolve. He said that he had been mourning but now was determined to return to work, since he needed to repay all the money that people had loaned him to pay the ransom, which they were now starting to doubt was genuine. It was enough to put pressure on M3. Alick also said that since such a crime had not occurred in England 'for 400 years', there was no specific charge to cover it, and so there was nothing to stop M3 returning Muriel after collecting the money that Alick wanted to pay him.

M3 wanted time to consider, and then, clearly in command of the call, Alick moved to a different matter. He asked if M3 had written the letter that he had received that morning, signed 'R', which bore a Balham postmark. The writing was similar and claimed to be from someone who was not a kidnapper but had information on where Muriel was and it would cost Alick far less than the ransom demand.

The matter confused and irritated M3, but every time he dismissed it and tried to move on, Alick simply elaborated, reading him extracts. Whether this was because there was a faint belief that the letter was genuine, or simply to force M3 into action, it demonstrated that in the period of these interminable phone calls, the power shift from M3 to the McKays had been seismic, and not simply because of the growing sense that Muriel was no longer alive, but also because of the McKays' stamina and M3's diminishing bargaining powers, his diminishing grip on reality and his lack of focus. Alick finished by informing him that if M3 did not arrange something swiftly, he would appeal in every newspaper offering a reward for information, fiercely telling M3, 'You've done enough harm to this family, and I don't believe my wife is alive any longer. If she is, she's a wreck.'

M3 called back within the hour with his decision. His condition was that the delivery be made by Alick and Dianne. They were to be at the same telephone box on Church Road, Edmonton, the next day at 4 p.m., with the money in 'two small briefcases', although he amended this to 'suitcases' when Alick pointed out that the money would not fit in them. He tried to intimidate with his fallback threat that 'any error will be fatal', but Alick also warned him against sending him on 'a Cook's tour' like the one that had led to High Cross. Also, to avoid arousing suspicion by being too accepting, Alick insisted that he would not hand the money over until he saw his wife.

At 2.15 p.m., a crash-helmeted Nizam appeared in the public bar of the Cock to buy cigarettes, where the friendly baker, Bernard Law, was drinking. In the weeks since Nizam's visitor permit had expired, Elsa had been telling anyone who had asked that he had returned to Trinidad, and so, surprised, Law said, 'Hello, are you back again?'[10]

With his brother's gift for the ridiculous, Nizam replied that he had returned because the British Government thought that he was an asset, even though he didn't think he was, he just helped his brother on the farm.

Nizam then asked the landlady, Joyce Bunkall, whether the pub was for sale since she had now given in her notice to the brewery. Nizam said that he would like to buy the place. 'He also said he would like plenty of businesses everywhere and especially one in France.' Law warned him that France was 'all women and wine', and Nizam said, 'I don't want women, I would sooner have animals, I talk to them, and they listen to me'.

Law offered him a lift home as he was going to Rooks Farm, but Nizam said that he would walk.

While Nizamodeen Hosein was somehow planning to spend his future in hiding but also constructing a business empire, in Wimbledon more practical plans had commenced, all the while with the knowledge that although it was staggering that M3 had set up a second meeting, it would surely be the last.

12

PAPER CHASE

We eat out under the stars in the evening and the hotel cat always finds me as he knows I'll give him a piece of fish or meat.

Muriel McKay, Mallorca, 4 October 1959.

Friday, 6 February 1970 was the fortieth day since Muriel's disappearance. It was a day which the police had less than twenty-four hours to prepare for but, having learned bitter lessons from the events of the previous Sunday, they devised a plan which was bolder, more intricate and less hysterical. Although commentators have gleefully described the Dane End operation as farcical and incompetent, the adept operation that brought the case to a close has inevitably been less remarked upon.

Alick McKay loaned the team two cream-coloured suitcases, which again were packed with the fake banknotes sandwiched between genuine money. There was never any possibility of Dianne and Alick complying with M3's orders and taking part in the operation themselves. Instead, John Minors, shorn of his trademark moustache, was kitted out in Alick's vicuna coat and ushanka, as he had been on 2 January when meeting hoaxer William Peat at Wimbledon Station. He already had experience of driving the Rolls-Royce, and he was a gifted mimic, so he was confident that he would be able to pass himself off as Alick to M3 on the telephone.

Convinced that Muriel was no longer alive, Smith was aware of the possibility that the order for Dianne to accompany her father was because M3 required another hostage to ensure payment of the ransom money. Detective

Constable Joyce Armitage of the Flying Squad, an officer with sixteen years' service, and of similar height and build to Dianne, was asked to take her place.

At Scotland Yard, the rules of the operation were established. Radio silence would be maintained throughout, contact to be made only by public telephone to the operations room. It was most significant that the kidnappers had chosen the same starting point for this exercise as last time: the telephone box at Church Street, Edmonton. It was fair to assume, therefore, that the Rolls would once again be drawn into the Hertfordshire–Essex area. Anticipating this, Detective Chief Superintendent Ron Harvey of Hertfordshire CID was asked to assist in the operation, and teams of Flying Squad and Regional Crime Squad detectives were posted to all main roads in the area. The idea was that, rather than following the Rolls, they would be waiting at wherever its destination was to be.

John Minors would be armed and he was also given a replica gun 'to fool the kidnappers if they caught me and ordered me to throw my gun in. That pause might have given me a few vital seconds.'[1] However, because of the sparse police presence around the Rolls itself, it was decided that an armed officer would be concealed in the car boot. Volunteering for the nauseating task was another Flying Squad man and skilled marksman, Detective Inspector John Bland.

The two most feared outcomes were that the car would be ambushed at some point on its journey or that the press would blow the whole operation. Although the leak about the High Cross handover had been contained, this time the Commissioner decided that prevention was better than cure, issuing a directive to the Press Association requesting that editors refrain from publishing any further reports about inquiries in the Ware, Hertfordshire, area in relation to the McKay case and insisting that careless talk could cost Muriel her life.

Friday, 6 February was a perishingly cold day, heralding a wave of appalling weather. Arthur and Nizam drove Liley back to London in the morning, Nizam also posting the letter that he had written to Dolly a week ago at lunchtime in Stoke Newington. They then did the rounds of Arthur's tailoring associates.

When calling on Abraham Eckhardt, Arthur was encouraged to dance to an Elvis Presley song that was playing on the radio. Eckhardt later said, 'If he had murder on his mind while dancing in my workshop, he's the best actor I've ever known.'[2]

Meanwhile, in Wimbledon, the suitcases, purportedly containing £250,000, all but £600 of which was in fake £5 notes, were placed on the back seat of the Rolls-Royce. Joyce Armitage met Dianne at St Mary House and, with cosmetics and a dark, long wig, was made up to resemble her, also wearing her distinctive pink coat and outer clothing, so that if Muriel was waiting at the end of the trail, she would recognise that this stranger was legitimately representing her daughter.

Shortly before the Rolls moved off from John Minors' home in south London, John Bland climbed into the boot. He carried a supply of water and a portable oxygen bottle and mask, in case of exhaust fumes. 'It's pitch black, no air getting in there and no light. You daydream, you go back, you think about other jobs you've done,' he later recalled.[3] At 2.45 p.m., the car began its journey to Edmonton, passing St Mary House at 3 p.m.

M3 had made his final telephone call to Arthur Road at 2.30 p.m. Sounding uneasy, he asked to speak to Dianne, but Ian informed him that they had already left. M3 replied, 'I hope no tricks this time because, eh, as a matter of fact, why I phoned up is because I, eh, you see, I just get some information, so I wanted a bit of time more, you know.' Clearly, he was nervous at the risk he was taking and perhaps wanted to backpedal.

Unmarked police cars were never far away from the Rolls as it crossed London, though they were ordered never to get too close. Minors hit heavy Friday afternoon traffic when he reached the East End, Bland having to resort to his oxygen supply in the boot, but the car arrived at the Edmonton kiosk punctually, at just before 4 p.m. Minors told Joyce Armitage to lock the doors behind him, before entering the call box. He waited three-quarters of an hour for the telephone to ring. Waiting anxiously in the car, Armitage later said that they both believed that they were 'going to be hijacked somewhere along the line. All the time, one's looking around, seeing who's about … it was an awfully long time.'[4]

At 4.45 p.m., the telephone rang. Minors answered it as Alick and M3 told him to go to Bethnal Green, to a telephone box outside the police station. Minors asked if he would be there and M3 said, 'I'll be phoning you. I want to speak to Dianne', then rang off. Minors didn't actually know the way, so at one point John Bland had to shout directions to him from the boot of the car.

The car being directed back into London was a worrying development when the police were banking on being led out into Hertfordshire again, where the strongest support was lying in wait. Arthur and Nizam must actually have been close by at this point, having been in the area and within sight of the Bethnal Green call box at 4.30 p.m. when they visited tailor Percy Chaplin.

Minors arrived at Bethnal Green just before 6 p.m., and five minutes later, M3 called again, requesting that Dianne come to the phone. Warning her that 'any error will be fatal to your mum', M3 ordered them to go with the suitcases to the nearest underground station, take a tube to Epping and expect a call at the station kiosk. To allow Minors to hear the instructions too and jot them down, Armitage pretended to be upset and passed the phone back to him. Minors was told, 'If the police are about this time, we will execute Muriel, and no one will ever see her again.'

The two detectives now faced a ferocious dilemma and limited time to make a decision. It was approaching the rush hour, and the tube trains heading east out of central London and into the Essex suburbs would be jammed with commuters, providing convenient camouflage for M3 if he planned an ambush, and potentially risking the lives of members of the public. Equally, disobeying his instructions could be catastrophic if he was already watching the Rolls-Royce.

An impressive compromise was reached at the operations room. Minors was told to drive to Theydon Bois, the stop before Epping on the Central line, and take the tube from there. He was also told to drive slowly, to allow time to populate the train with disguised detectives and ensure a discreet police presence at Epping Station.

Arthur and Nizam were now heading back to Hertfordshire. At Bishop's Stortford, Arthur left Nizam with the Volvo and took a minicab to the Raven at Berden, inviting the driver in for a drink, which he declined. Arthur was the first customer of the evening, arriving just after 7 p.m., ordering his usual double Scotch and ginger and standing the landlord, Frederick Butler, an Arctic ale.

Arthur sat watching Butler and his wife playing shove ha'penny in the public bar, establishing an alibi for himself that was strengthened with the chance arrival of his actor chum, Griff Davies, and two young friends, Beverley Grice and Marilyn Dodds. The group were in good spirits, Davies currently a chiming face from starring in a KitKat advert and having completed a busy decade of television work, including six separate appearances for *The Wednesday Play* and roles in popular series such as *Doctor Who*, *The Newcomers* and, most recently, *Softly, Softly*. Arthur joined them in the saloon, buying them several rounds as the evening progressed and ordering 'at least eight double whiskies with ginger ale' himself, according to Butler.[5]

As Arthur was drinking his first whisky of the night in the Raven, on what would be his last night of freedom, Minors was parking the Rolls-Royce in the station car park at Theydon Bois, 25 miles away. By now, Bland had been travelling in the boot for over four hours. Lifting himself out, as Minors and Armitage waited with the cases on the eastbound platform, he dashed to the gents, only to be caught short when he heard the train coming in. All three boarded the 7.15 p.m. train, which thankfully was fairly quiet, having shed most of its passengers as it neared the end of the line. Bland sat away from Minors and Armitage, all three pondering how this odyssey would end. Minors felt that 'we couldn't keep going forever, from phone box to phone box, it had to end sometime, and I felt that it couldn't be much further than Epping. It was getting us closer, which is what for weeks we had been striving for.'[6]

Bland 'couldn't visualise' what could possibly be about to happen, but although M3 had said to expect a call at Epping Station, he was aware that it could also be a good place for an ambush.[7] So, when they arrived, he alighted and took up a position at the bus stop outside, Minors and Armitage in his line of sight as they waited by the telephone kiosk. At 7.30 p.m., M3 made his final telephone call.

Heavy weather was made at the trial of how Arthur could have made this call, for although there was a call box near the pub, it would have been difficult (though not impossible) for him to reach it without being seen leaving. The call was almost certainly made by Nizamodeen Hosein, and possibly from a payphone in a house converted into flats in Bishop's Stortford.[*]

In a muffled voice, M3 warned him that he was being watched. The instructions now were for he and Dianne to take a taxi up the A11 to Gates Used Cars at Bishop's Stortford, where one of the six cars parked was a minivan, registration number UMH 587F. The cases were to be left opposite that car, on the pavement next to the hedge.

Minors told M3 that he could not leave the money without seeing Muriel, and M3 told him that after depositing the suitcases, he should return to Epping Station, where he would speak to her on the telephone:

---

[*] Although the call was probably made from Bishop's Stortford, since Nizam dropped Arthur there between 6.30 and 7 p.m., and was seen there again from 8 p.m., this oddly specific detail regarding its location seems to be unique to the account of the case in Gordon Honeycombe's *Murders of the Black Museum* (Comet, 1983) and I have been unable to substantiate it.

She is around your home area now … Leave the money and trust us. Any error will be fatal to Muriel and Dianne. You see we deal with high-powered telescopic rifles, anyone illegal that attempts to interfere with the cases we shall just let them have it, you see … Any sign of the police or a trick we will use high powered rifles and shotguns. We're watching, you see.

After M3 hung up, Minors called the operations room at Scotland Yard to pass on the latest instructions, while outside, Bland moved up the lane to hide in a hedge.

At 8 p.m., the driver of a dark-blue Volvo asked the attendants at Gates garage to check his tyres, but after this had been done, he remained on the garage forecourt for about half an hour before being asked to move on by the attendants, who noticed that he was studying a piece of paper.

It took longer than anticipated to get a taxi, but finally, at 8.25 p.m., Minors and Armitage were collected from Epping Station by Robert Kelly. They told him to drive them up the station approach and, before reaching the junction, to flash his headlights and stop for a moment 'to pick up a friend'. There, John Bland crawled into the back of the car and lay on the floor beside Armitage. Kelly was then told to drive on to Bishop's Stortford. He later said that during that strange, silent 16-mile journey, he decided that he must be driving three villains with stolen property, but that he was 'more intrigued even than frightened'.[8]

The minicab arrived at Gates garage at 9 p.m., Armitage noting that at this point, 'it was brilliantly lit and the street lighting was very bright'.[9] As M3 had stated, there were six cars lined up on the forecourt in front of a high, white, slatted wooden fence, and second from the right was a white minivan.

What M3 did not know was that behind that fence, two armed Flying Squad sergeants, Jack Quarrie* and Nicky Birch, were already lying in wait.

Minors and Kelly got out and Minors opened the back door to let Armitage out. As she stepped on to the pavement, John Bland crawled out on his stomach and disappeared into the hedge so deftly that even the watching Flying Squad officers did not notice him. The cases were set down beside the hedge just a few feet from him, on the opposite side of the road to the

---

* After retiring from the police, Jack Quarrie BEM was the technical adviser on the ITV drama series *The Sweeney* (Euston Films, 1974–78).

garage. Kelly then drove Armitage and Minors back to Epping Station, where they would remain until 1 a.m., waiting for a call from Muriel McKay which never came.

Less than five minutes into his vigil, Bland and the other officers noticed a blue Volvo slowly approaching. It slowed to a halt beside the suitcases and the driver leaned over, looking intently at them. 'It appeared he was about to get out of the car,' remembered Birch, but at that moment, the silence was shattered by the impatient driver behind him sounding his horn and the alarmed Volvo driver sped away.[10] According to Bland, 'That driver was frightened, and he wasn't the only one that jumped.'[11] He had noticed, however, that the driver was a 'young man of colour' with long hair, and that the nearside rear light of the car was out.

By now, the garage attendant, Michael Byers, was becoming increasingly concerned about the driver of the Volvo whom he had seen driving past the garage six or seven times since being told to move off at 8.30 p.m., and so at 9.15 p.m. he telephoned the police, fearing that the man 'may make an attempt to attack me and steal the money from the petrol kiosk'.[12] Thankfully, the coordination of the operation with Hertfordshire Police meant that rather than them innocently sending a constable into the middle of the situation and sabotaging it, they were able to inform the caller that there was some police activity near the garage and that he need not fear for his safety.

Ten minutes later, the operation was nearly jeopardised again when two passers-by on the way to the local football club to collect their wives from bingo stopped briefly to look at the cases. They returned a few minutes later with their wives and stopped again, only to hear a voice from the hedge say, 'Would you go away, we're police.'

At 9.35 p.m., the dark Volvo reappeared, being driven slowly down the road from Bishop's Stortford. This time, when it reached the cases, it turned into the alleyway beside Gates garage – the one that Birch and Quarrie were watching from. The driver was clearly looking to see if there was a trap laid. The officers held their breath, trying to keep out of the beam of the Volvo's headlights as it turned around, very slowly drove back to the top of the alleyway, and stopped, facing the main road. The driver looked all around him, then turned right on to the main road and drove away.

Six miles away, in the Raven at Berden, Arthur was still drinking with Griff Davies and his two friends. According to Davies, 'During the evening he behaved perfectly normally. He had plenty to say and seemed very happy. He was always friendly and talked repeatedly about money. At one stage he said he was going to become a millionaire like his father in Trinidad.'[13]

Arthur told the group that he was waiting for Nizam to pick him up on his way back from London. He was typically flash with his money on his last night of freedom, carrying about £15 on him, offering to change a fiver for Davies and plying the party with drinks. Beverley Grice, who had met Arthur before and found that he always had 'a boastful manner', said that during the evening he bragged of wanting to be a millionaire and that he 'already had three-quarters of a million pounds'.[14]

All evening Arthur had been talking in a loud voice as usual, always 'conspicuous', but at 10 p.m., just as Davies and the two girls were leaving, Nizam arrived, and after (bizarrely) pressing the party to stay for another drink, which they declined, Arthur became quiet, which, according to Fred Butler, the landlord, was 'most unusual'.[15] Arthur bought Nizam a beer and the pair moved to a table at the far corner of the empty saloon, away from the servery, where they had a whispered conversation for ten minutes. Butler observed that 'They were quiet, no raised voices and their conversation appeared in earnest.'

Butler left the bar, after which Arthur asked Eileen, his wife, to change a two-shilling piece for six pennies and three sixpences. She did, and then also briefly left the bar. When the Butlers returned at just before 10.30 p.m., the brothers had gone, which was equally unusual as Arthur habitually stayed until closing time.

At 10 p.m., the floodlights on the forecourt of Gates garage had switched off. At 10.40 p.m., as Arthur and Nizam were approaching, another car drew alongside the cases and stopped. It was a Ford Prefect driven by Peter Abbott, who had first noticed them on his way to collect his wife, Joan,[*] from her evening shift at the local telephone exchange. The couple thought that perhaps someone's luggage had fallen from a roof rack on the way to nearby Stansted Airport. They drove on to a call box and informed the police at Bishop's Stortford, who told them that the matter would be dealt with. However,

---

[*] Joan Abbott devoted her life to charity work. She was a standard bearer for the Royal British Legion, sold from a market stall to raise money for Help for Heroes, and volunteered for a local hospice for thirty years, as well as for Meals on Wheels, a local rehabilitation centre, the RNLI and the British Heart Foundation. The morning after her ninety-seventh birthday, she was conned out of £482 by a telephone scammer. She died, aged 98, in 2020. Local people lined the streets for her funeral cortège, in honour of her outstanding community service.

rather than leaving matters there, the public-spirited Abbotts decided to drive back to the cases and guard them until the police arrived.

At 10.47 p.m., from his frosty look-out point, John Bland saw the Volvo once again approach the scene. It slowed almost to a halt opposite the cases and Bland noticed that there were now two men in the car, the long-haired driver and a passenger with bushy hair and a moustache. The officers had orders not to apprehend anyone unless there was a dire emergency, so the wait went on. The Volvo moved on and, a few minutes later, the Ford Prefect carrying the Abbotts appeared again. They got out and inspected the luggage more closely, noticing that the tag read, 'McKay, Arthur Road, Wimbledon'. Overhearing their conversation, Bland gleaned that they had informed the local police and were now going to remain with the cases until the police took charge of them.

At Bishop's Stortford Police Station, senior officers were despairing of the good Samaritans who were unknowingly wrecking the operation. PC Alan Smith remembered, 'Eventually the comment was, I believe, "Will you tell that couple to fuck off out of it and leave them suitcases alone".'[16] After waiting fifteen minutes, the Abbotts decided to take the cases to the police station themselves but found them too heavy to lift into their car, so Mrs Abbott waited with them while her husband drove down to the police station to hurry them along.

By now, the Volvo had vanished into the night and, despite a pocketful of change, M3 made no further phone calls. Arthur and Nizam arrived home to find Elsa watching the television. She made a meal for a very drunk Arthur, and they retired to bed. At 11.40 p.m., the cases were collected in a panda car by PC Smith.

However, even though such kindly souls as the Abbotts had managed to frighten M3 away, the operation had actually been a success. John Bland had endured four hours in the boot of the Rolls-Royce and then lain hidden in the frosty hedge for a further three hours, keeping the control vehicle, hidden some distance away, informed of the situation. Later recommending him for a commendation, Bill Smith wrote, 'a more harrowing and exhausting tour of duty could not be visualised' and that at the end, 'he showed signs of great physical strain'. But Bland was the hero of the hour for another reason too. To Smith's delight, he had also, on its very first appearance that evening, noted down the registration number of the Volvo: XGO 994G.

Smith immediately sent an officer to County Hall, who was admitted by the night security staff, and who, within an hour, telephoned Bishop's

Stortford Police Station to inform Smith that the car was registered to a Mrs Elisabeth Hosein, of Rooks Farm, Stocking Pelham, just 8 miles away. The name Hosein was also noted as having just been uncovered by the two officers making enquiries about West Indians in Hertfordshire. Smith and Harvey prepared for a coordinated swoop on Rooks Farm.

Meanwhile, back in Wimbledon, the family were frantic. 'That was the worst night of all,' remembers Jennifer. 'Waiting and waiting by the window, until finally the Rolls-Royce drove back up the drive, and desperately looking to see how many people were inside it, and whether one of them was my mother.'[17]

13

DISCONNECT

We did a day trip to Amalfi, which was breathtakingly beautiful, even though it was showering. Since then, sun all the way.

Muriel McKay, Naples, 14 November 1966.

Through the night, as sleet and snow drifted into Hertfordshire, a conference was held at Bishop's Stortford Police Station and it was decided that a warrant would be obtained to search Rooks Farm for the stolen jewellery, to be executed in daylight. At first light, police observation was set up on the lane connecting the farm with the rest of the world, with police cars waiting in the car park of the Cock while the RAF air photography unit performed aeriel observation of the site.

At 1.45 p.m., DCS Ron Harvey of Hertfordshire CID led a troop of CID men on to Arthur Hosein's land which, by now, was surrounded by police officers. As they approached, they saw the unloved Volvo parked beside the house, still mud-splattered, windows left down, the same model as had been seen at High Cross six days earlier.

Harvey rang the bell, which was answered by Arthur's son, Rudi. Arthur then appeared behind him. Harvey introduced himself, presenting the warrant to search the premises for stolen jewellery. As Harvey, Smith and Minors entered Rooks Farm, Arthur casually told them that they could search wherever they liked.

They had, in fact, arrived at a chaotic moment. The mains water pipe connected to the washing machine had just burst and flooded the dining room carpet, which was being dried by an electric fire because the farmhouse had no heating system in operation, the Aga cooking and heating unit having been out of order for some days.

The trio followed Arthur into the kitchen while John Bland went upstairs, discovering Nizamodeen in his bedroom and immediately recognising him. He brought him down to Smith and announced, 'This is the young man who was driving the Volvo car last night.' Jack Quarrie agreed and added that Arthur 'was the passenger when I saw the car for the fourth time at 10.47 p.m.'.[1]

Smith told them that he had reasonable grounds for suspecting that they both knew something about Muriel's disappearance and that, at the same time that she disappeared, a quantity of jewellery also went missing from her address. The brothers were cautioned, Arthur insisting, 'I know nothing. I earn over £150 a week. I don't deal in stolen property. I am a wealthy man; you can look where you like.' Nizam said nothing.

Relations with Elsa Hosein got off to a poor start as she stressed about this invasion of strangers trudging over the wet carpet and complained about the searching until, regrettably, she was told to shut up and that the men were simply doing their job. While the brothers were detained in the kitchen, police combed the farmhouse.

When Minors entered the children's bedroom, Freida picked up two paper flowers from a chair beside the bed and innocently handed them to the visitor. She told him that she had made them and that there were some more in the car.

Searching Nizam's bedroom, Minors found another flower, as well as three pieces of coloured tissue paper in the wastepaper basket, two whole pieces of thin, blue writing paper, lined on one side, three-quarters of a sheet of the same paper, the top quarter of which had been torn off, and a page torn from an exercise book. In the bathroom, they found an empty twenty Piccadilly cigarette packet. In Arthur's bedroom, under the bed, they found a double-barrelled sawn-off shotgun.

In the lounge, on top of the radio, was a tin of Elastoplast. Behind the cocktail cabinet, in a leather case, Minors found a barrel from the shotgun, which had been sawn short a few inches from the breach, and an air rifle and pellets. In one of the cupboards of the cocktail cabinet, he found a box of shotgun cartridges and a plastic phial of small and large white tablets, which Elsa knew nothing about.

Smith told Arthur that he now intended to search the car and outbuildings and asked Arthur to accompany him. 'I'm not leaving the house,' said Arthur.

Smith then suggested that Nizam accompany him, but Nizam said, 'No. I want to stay with Arthur.'

Quarrie waited with the brothers while Smith and Minors searched the Volvo, which revealed a pink paper flower on the floor. They tested the lights and found that the nearside ones were not working. In the outbuildings, they found some bailing twine.

They returned to the house and showed the brothers the items that they had found. Arthur claimed to know nothing about the paper flowers and could not explain how one came to be in his car. As for the writing paper, he never did any correspondence and, 'as it was in Nizamodeen's bedroom, you had better ask him'.

'I don't know anything,' was all that Nizam could contribute, although he did admit to recognising the flowers.

When asked what brand of cigarettes they smoked, Arthur said, 'Peter Stuyvesant now, but I did smoke, until recently, Senior Service untipped.' Nizam told them that he smoked anything that he was given but admitted to having smoked the contents of the empty Piccadilly packet in his room, which had been given to him by Mr Gordon the previous Sunday.

The police confiscated two pairs of tailors' shears from the workroom and, from the kitchen, a familiar-looking billhook that was lying on a shelf. Arthur was summoned back to the kitchen and asked how many of these he owned. He replied that this was the only one and that it was borrowed from a local farmer, George Cuda, in January to chop up a calf that had died. Smith asked where the calf was chopped up and Arthur replied, 'Well, it was Nizam that did the chopping, and it was done in the space between the two sheds.' Smith asked him what he did with the calf after it had been chopped up, to which he said, 'We fed it to the dogs.' What happened to the bones and head? 'The last time I saw the head and the big bones they were out with the rubbish to be collected by the refuse men.'

Smith then informed the brothers that he was looking for Muriel McKay and that he intended to have a thorough search made of all the buildings and grounds. Arthur replied, 'That's all right by me, carry on.'

The brothers were told that they would be taken to Wimbledon Police Station for further questioning. Brazenly, Arthur replied, 'Certainly, I want to help you if I can. Can I tell my wife to inform my friend, David Coote, who comes here with his girlfriend weekends? He is a solicitor and can vouch for my honesty.'

Nizam then turned to Arthur and asked, 'Do I have to go?'

Arthur replied, 'Yes, don't worry, you will be with me.'

Nizam said, 'What about the animals?'

Arthur responded, 'Elsa can look after them.'

The brothers were placed in separate police cars, Smith, Minors and Quarrie travelling with Arthur, and John Bland with Nizamodeen. They were driven away from Rooks Farm, never to return.

A few minutes into the journey, after waving to a mounted Captain Barclay, Arthur pointed towards Sleepy Hollow, saying that this was the home of George, the farmer who had loaned him the chopper. Since this chopper was borrowed in mid-January, and the one found at St Mary House Arthur had stolen from Leonard Smith in mid-October, this was another instance of him concocting a posthumous alibi.

On the journey to London, Arthur jabbered incessantly about himself, his wealth, and how popular he was with the local people and the police. The officers were told all about his plans to stand for the local council, and that his father was an important and wealthy man in Trinidad, who had influence in high places. He also boasted about making money greyhound racing.

By the time the cars carrying the brothers were approaching Wimbledon, the press had heard of the arrests and encircled the station, so the vehicles were diverted to Kingston, the headquarters of V Division. The media were waiting for them there too, television cameras capturing the arrival of Arthur, sitting in the back seat in his fawn overcoat, face covered, though Nizam was crouching out of sight on the floor of the second vehicle.

They arrived at 5.30 p.m., were fingerprinted, and placed in separate cells. Arthur asked for a meal and both were served up a plate of sausage and mash before the long-awaited evening of questioning began.

At 6.30 p.m., Smith and Minors visited Arthur in his cell. He was cautioned again and told that he would be questioned and that Minors would note down his answers. He said, 'All right.' They then told Nizamodeen the same, to which he said, 'Why don't you see us both together? I know nothing.'

At 6.45 p.m., Arthur was fetched from the cells, keeping up 'a non-stop conversation about his personal life' all the way to Smith's office.[2] After delivering him, Jim Parker then brought up Nizamodeen and sat with him. Nizamodeen said, 'When I was at the farm, a man said something about me driving the Volvo on Friday night.' Parker reminded him that he was under caution and, despairingly, he said, 'Oh my, what has Arthur done to me? I was driving the car last night because I had a date.'

Nizam now invented a story about having had a date in Bishop's Stortford the previous evening, then began to moan and kept repeating, 'Kill me, kill me, oh my God, what have I done? Arthur always gets me into trouble. Kill me now.' According to Parker, 'he then broke down completely, threw his arms around my shoulders and cried. He suddenly stopped crying, sat down and stared straight in front of him.' Parker gave him a glass of water; he then started rocking from side to side, but after five minutes, 'he was completely composed and refused to speak'.

In his office, Smith was asking the questions that the entire country was desperate to have answered, but although Arthur talked constantly, he was saying absolutely nothing.

On Monday, 29 December, he was on the farm all day with Nizam, and sometime in the early evening, he went to see his finishers. When asked which finishers he visited, he replied that he would have to think as he had so many. He claimed that he got home at 8.30 p.m., and Nizam was there. When asked whether he was ever in Wimbledon, he replied, 'Where is Wimbledon?' On whether he had heard of Muriel McKay or Arthur Road, he claimed that he didn't read the newspapers or watch television news.

Smith then showed Arthur the phial of white tablets. He explained, 'I suffer from headaches and can't sleep. Nizam's girlfriend got them for me, she is a nurse.' He said that she got them for him at Christmas, not on a prescription because 'I don't believe in doctors, but I wanted something to make me sleep'.[3]

On the shotgun – he had owned it for some months but didn't want to say from where he got it. He dodged a question about whether he had a licence for it and claimed that he only used it 'on the farm to shoot pigeons from my bedroom window'. Smith drew his attention to the barrels, which appeared to have recently been sawn short. After examining the gun, Arthur pointed out a small dent a few inches from the muzzle and said, 'It would be dangerous to use with that dent'. When asked who sawed it down, he said, 'Nizam did that.' He then added, 'I am very tired, I can't think. I want to help you as I know you have a very difficult case. I must sleep. Will you let my wife know where I am?'

Smith suspended the interview at 7.45 p.m., but when asked to look over the notes that Minors had made of his answers, Arthur refused to sign them.

At 8 p.m., Nizamodeen was brought to Smith's office and cautioned. He was asked to sign the caution but refused. Smith explained that he would be asking him some questions about the disappearance of Muriel McKay, to which he nodded his head.

With his first question however, 'Where were you on 29 December 1969?', the same question he had put to Arthur, Nizam 'made no reply and started trembling violently. He closed his eyes and shook his head a number of times.'

Smith asked again where he was that day, to which he replied, 'Where did Arthur say I was?'

Smith said, 'I want you to tell me where you were.'

He replied, 'I was with my brother, Arthur.'

When asked if he went to Wimbledon between 5.30 p.m. and 7.45 p.m., he made no answer, still shaking violently. When Smith asked him what the matter was, he said, 'I want to die, let me die.'

Smith asked, 'Why do you want to die? What is troubling you, nobody is going to hurt you.'

He said, 'My brother, Arthur, will kill me, he beats me.'

Smith asked why his brother should want to kill him, and he said, 'I mustn't speak, I can't speak. Let me see Arthur.'

Smith asked him again whether he had travelled to Wimbledon that day.

'Why don't you kill me,' he replied.

Smith said, 'Don't be ridiculous, what is the matter with you, why are you behaving like this?'

Nizam said, 'Ask Arthur, ask Arthur, ask Arthur.'

Smith said, 'I'm asking you, what do you want me to ask Arthur?'

Nizam made no reply but closed his eyes and shook his head from side to side. There seemed little point in continuing, so Smith asked him to sign the notes that Minors had taken. Nizam made no reply but sat with his eyes closed, shaking his head from side to side.

The interview was concluded at 8.20 p.m. It was decided to resume the questioning in the morning. Officers remained in and around Rooks Farm overnight, including a WPC who had been placed there to assist the family.

The following morning, at 11.45 a.m., Nizam was again brought to Smith's office and reminded that he was still under caution and need not answer any questions unless he wished to. Smith asked him whether he felt better today, but he pretended not to hear. Smith then asked whether he'd had a good night's sleep and had breakfast, to which he nodded. He was told to answer aloud, and he asked to speak to Arthur, saying, 'What has Arthur said to you, is he blaming me for something?'

Asked again about his movements on 29 December, Nizam said that he couldn't remember where he was and didn't know the names of places in

London, 'I just go with Arthur'. However, when asked whether he was with Arthur that day, particularly between 5.30 p.m. and 7.45 p.m., and in the Volvo, he said, 'Yes, I think so.'

As to where in London they were, 'Whatever Arthur told you will be right, I guess.'

Smith said, 'If Arthur told us he had been in Wimbledon, would that be right?'

Nizam replied, 'No, we wasn't in Wimbledon.' When asked how he could know that if he didn't know the names of places in London, he fell silent.

He did make one useful admission, that Arthur did used to get a newspaper delivered at the farm, the *People*, but it was stopped about three weeks ago 'because he hadn't paid the bill for a long time'.

The brothers were offering no firm alibis, simply denial.

Smith moved on to Sunday, 1 February, the day of the High Cross drop, on which day, Nizam admitted, he and Arthur went out as it was getting dark to deliver trousers to the finishers in London, with Arthur driving. He said that after the last delivery, Arthur sent him to a pub to get three packets of cigarettes. While inside, he bought himself a Black Label lager and stayed drinking it for ten minutes, and when he got back into the car, Arthur hit him because he was in a hurry. He said that they went home up the Cambridge Road, through Ware and High Cross, but did not stop on the way. He made no telephone calls, but as for Arthur, 'I don't know'.

When shown the paper flowers that were found stuck in the mudbank at High Cross, he made no reply but again started shaking and closed his eyes, having been much more open when talking about the innocuous events of earlier in the evening. Again, he started to cry and sob, 'Let me die, let me die.'

Smith and Minors decided to conclude the interview at 12.45 p.m., and Smith asked him to listen to the answers as they were read back to him and initial them, but Nizam gave no sign of having heard. Instead, he lay back in his chair with his eyes closed, muttering incomprehensibly.

Arthur's solicitor, David Coote, had now arrived, having had to curtail a weekend in Yorkshire with his girlfriend after getting Elsa's telephone message. He told Nizam that if there was any possibility that Muriel was alive and if he knew anything about it, he must tell the officers. Nizam hung his head and made no reply.

At 2 p.m., Arthur was brought to Smith and Minors again. He declared, 'I want to help you all I can. I realise you have a very difficult case.' On

Sunday, 1 February, he had been at the farm all day. Gerald Gordon and his family had arrived at 1 p.m. and stayed for lunch and tea, leaving just before 6 p.m. Arthur Rosenthal had called half an hour later, and Arthur and Nizam had then visited four finishers, for whom he listed precise details. When Smith asked whether he could now remember the ones that he had visited on 29 December too, he said, 'Oh yes, the same ones.' (The four finishers, along with all the others who had dealings with Arthur, were interviewed and all denied that he visited them on 29 December.)

Arthur claimed that after visiting the finishers on 1 February, he and Nizam went straight home, arriving there at about 11 p.m., though interestingly, his account of the route mentioned both High Cross and the petrol station. He admitted that he used to take the *People* but stopped it because it was too expensive and he never read it. When asked again about the paper flowers, he started to shout. He then apologised, explaining that he was upset and wanted a cup of tea, which he was given at 3.20 p.m.

Smith then asked him for some specimens of his handwriting, which he gave, copying a few paragraphs from a newspaper, but rather slowly. Smith decided that he was attempting to disguise it.

When shown the bailing twine, Arthur said that it looked like 'the rope they tie up bales of hay with', and when asked what the billhook was, he said, 'A meat chopper.' He said that the air rifle belonged to David Coote, 'a great friend of mine, he visits my farm a lot and brings his lady friend. He leaves the rifle at my farm because he likes to shoot.' He said that he had never seen the Elastoplast before.

Smith now asked about Muriel, to which Arthur said, 'I am sorry for the poor lady and her family. I only wish I could help you in some way.' He knew nothing of the ransom demands or the pieces of clothing that had been sent to the family. Did he write any letters to Mr McKay?

'No, no, I don't write any letters to anybody.'

Smith got as far as the cigarette packet found on the floor of the telephone box in Southbury Road when Arthur complained about 'all these questions. I have a headache and can't think.' Before taking a break, his answers were read back to him, but again he refused to sign them, saying, 'I want to cooperate, but I am not signing anything. I have done enough writing for you today.' The interview concluded at 4.45 p.m.

At 9.30 a.m. on Monday morning, Nizam was brought to Smith's office again, this time to be asked about the events of the previous Friday at Bishop's

Stortford. Again, he refused to make a statement, but said, 'You ask questions and I will see if I answer or not.'

He said that he and Arthur left the farm at 10 a.m., then listed all the tailors and finishers that they visited, finishing up at Percy Chaplin's at about 6.15 p.m. for five minutes – which happened to be opposite Bethnal Green Police Station and the call box where Minors and Armitage were at 6 p.m. – then headed home half an hour later. They went 'Bishop's Stortford way' and got home 'after the pubs close', so after 11 p.m.

Smith asked why it took them over four hours to get home, and he replied that they stopped at Bishop's Stortford just before 7 p.m., Arthur leaving the car with him and taking a taxi home because Nizam 'had a date with Susie' at 7.30 p.m., although she did not show up where they had arranged to meet, which was near where she lives. When asked where that was, he said, 'In between Gates garage and the traffic lights going into Bishop's Stortford', on the main road, but he didn't know her address because 'her parents don't like coloured men, so I've never been in the house'. He said that she worked on the sausage bar at the local Tesco and he had been out with her six or seven times since Christmas.

He waited until 9 p.m. and got some petrol at Gates. He eventually gave up waiting and went to the Raven for a drink on his way home, where he was surprised to find Arthur, who asked him to head back to Bishop's Stortford as he 'wanted to go for a drive'.

Nizam then provided some handwriting samples and was given a cup of tea.

When the interview resumed, he was asked whether he had written or posted any letters to Mr McKay. He denied that he had, but when shown the billhook, he started to shake and closed his eyes. He was then shown the sticking plaster. He shook his head, started trembling and muttered, 'Let me die, let me die.' The notes from the interview were read back to him but again he refused to sign, and after an hour and a half the interview was suspended.

Peter Rimmer says, 'In the days before PACE* it was quite common for people to refuse to sign,' but beyond that, the behaviour of the brothers when they were in custody was quite bizarre:

---

* The Police and Criminal Evidence Act 1984 regulated police powers and included the obligation for all interviews with suspects to be recorded.

When they were arrested, whatever we might have expected, none of us expected them. Very quickly it became obvious that they were not professional criminals. It would probably have been easier if they were, we'd have got an idea from somewhere. Someone in that world would have said something. But their behaviour was very unusual. A lot of stuff was said about Arthur having control over Nizamodeen, but that never struck me at all. Nizam was a sulky, moody person. I never believed that Arthur would have been able to subdue him physically. If you look at the photographs, look at Nizam's eyes, they never changed. He didn't look quite right, and he had a terrible chip on his shoulder.[4]

Smith and Minors saw Arthur again at 11.15 a.m. When reminded of the caution and that he need not answer any questions, he again said, 'That is all right, Mr Smith, you have a very difficult case, and I am genuinely sorry for you.'[5]

When asked about last Friday, he said that he would tell them where he was but regarding signing a written statement, 'Oh no. I sign nothing. You ask questions and I will try and answer them.' He said that he and Nizam left the farm at 9.30 a.m. with Liley and after dropping her home, they visited various tailors and finishers, then he loaned the car to Nizam at Bishop's Stortford at 7 p.m. Even though Nizam had no licence in Britain, Arthur admitted to letting him drive the Volvo sometimes.

Arthur spoke cheerfully about his evening at the Raven with 'my actor friend' and his girlfriend, the truthful part of his account, and claimed that Nizam arrived and took him home at closing time. When Smith informed him that Nizam said that they drove back to Bishop's Stortford, he said, 'Nizam is a fool to have told you that.' He said that they did not return to Bishop's Stortford, and their accounts also differed in that Arthur claimed to have arranged for Nizam to collect him from the Raven, whereas Nizam claimed to be surprised to have found him there.

Smith then arranged for a test call to be recorded on the Arthur Road tape recorder, and asked Arthur whether he would speak some sentences into the telephone, to which he said, 'Yes, anything to assist you, Mr Smith.' The call was recorded and when played back, Alick McKay 'noticed many similarities in that man's voice to the voice of M3'.[6]

Smith told Arthur that his prints had been identified on the *People* newspaper, the letters and envelopes, cigarette packet and note found in the call box.

Arthur said, 'That is impossible. I have never touched any of those things. You are just trying to trick me, Mr Smith.'

He sat with his head bent down, shaking it from side to side, and felt his pulse. 'All these questions, Mr Smith. I'm feeling unwell you see.' He was offered a doctor, but said, 'No, you see, I get headaches, I will be all right.'

Asked again whether he could explain how his fingerprints came to be on those items, he said, 'I'm sorry I can't help you there, you have a very difficult case, Mr Smith.' His answers were read back to him and again he said, 'I am sorry Mr Smith, I don't wish to sign.' Then he smiled. The interview concluded at 12.40 p.m.

Nizam was brought back in at 2.45 p.m. This time he was shown the phial of pills found at the farm and whispered, 'I don't know,' but made no further reply. When asked why the shotgun barrels had been altered, he whispered, 'Don't know,', but admitted that it was done by him and Arthur.

When shown the cuts of Muriel's clothing, he closed his eyes and slumped in his chair, again muttering, 'Let me die, let me die, why don't I die?'

Smith tried to appeal to him that if something was worrying him, to tell him. Nizam 'did not appear to hear, but leaned his head back, staring at the ceiling. He was trembling and shaking.' Smith said, 'Nizam, is Mrs McKay dead? If you know you must tell me.'

He showed no signs of having heard the question 'and appeared to be in a trance'. Smith announced that the interview was terminated, at which point Nizam, having clearly heard that, got up from his chair and walked to the door.

Ten minutes later, at 3.30 p.m., Arthur was brought back yet again and asked whether he understood the caution. He said, 'I should do by now.' He continued to deny everything put to him, but agreed to provide a further handwriting sample, after which he was asked again where Muriel was. He stressed that he couldn't help and asked when he could go back to his farm. When Smith asked why he kept refusing to sign his answers, he said that his answers were true and 'that's all, all right'. The interview concluded at 4 p.m.

At 4.35 p.m., David Coote returned to the police station and visited Arthur and Nizam in the presence of Smith and Minors. He appealed to each of them to say where Muriel was if she was alive, but to no avail.

At 6.10 p.m., Nizam, having complained of abdominal pain, nausea and vomiting, was seen by Dr Maxwell Muller, who found that 'there was evidence of vomiting in his toilet'.[7] 'On examination, his pulse, temperature, respiration and reflexes were found to be normal. He had a soft abdomen with no abnormal physical signs. He declined to speak and mimed deafness.' The doctor concluded that his symptoms were hysterical and that he was fit to be detained with supervision.

Nizam was seen again the next morning, Tuesday, 10 February. Once again, he refused to sign his answers. 'I must not sign.'

Were his answers wrong?

'No, they're okay.'

He also refused to speak some phrases into the telephone and suddenly became defensive, saying, 'It's a trick. Has Arthur done it?' When told that Arthur had spoken into the telephone, he said, 'I don't believe it. My brother won't be tricked … I don't want to do it. All right.' Smith asked him, 'for the last time', what happened to Muriel, but again he made no reply, gazing at the floor and giving no sign of having heard.

They saw Arthur again, Smith giving him every opportunity to tell them what had happened, but he continued to deny everything, 'I have nothing to tell. If you think you've got anything on me then book me.'

It was now three days since their arrest, but in all that time the brothers had said absolutely nothing that could help to establish what had happened to Muriel. Whether other officers could have got through to the brothers is doubtful; to have experimented with this would have risked collapsing the fragile rapport which Smith had created with them. 'Bill Smith would have tried to put them at their ease,' says Roger Street. 'He was masterful at that. I read the transcripts of the interviews at the time, and you could see that.'[8]

Bill Smith and John Minors visited the family that evening, after which Ian Burgess recorded in his diary:

Bill Smith & John Minors [sic] call. Minors 'worse for drink'. Very objectionable. Smith marvellous. Said that after 72 hrs the Brothers would not break & just laughed, said that he hoped they would 'break' when charged with murder.[9]

Nizam allegedly attempted suicide during his time in custody, once by trying to throw himself from the window of the interrogation room and once by repeatedly banging his head against the cell wall. He would later claim that he also tried to strangle himself.[10] Arthur, on the other hand, was apparently suggesting that a film should be made of the case with Sammy Davis Junior playing his role, Richard Burton playing Bill Smith, Roger Moore as John

Minors and Frank Sinatra as the judge whom Arthur was yet to face, supposedly a reference to the 1963 kidnapping of Sinatra's son.*

At 6.20 p.m. on Tuesday, 10 February, Arthur was told that he and Nizam would now be taken to Wimbledon Police Station and charged with murder and demanding money with menaces. He was cautioned and said, 'Nothing to say, Mr Smith. You have your job to do.'

At 7.45 p.m., they were formally charged and cautioned. When asked whether they now had anything to say, Arthur said, 'Nothing,' and Nizam made no reply.

The following morning, both men were taken across the road to the courthouse, Nizam with a grey blanket over his head, which remained draped around his shoulders throughout the hearing. Smith requested a week's remand and objected to bail.

The Hoseins were then taken back to the police station before being transferred to HMP Brixton. Before leaving the courtroom, Arthur slipped on a pair of dark glasses.

'Smith said to me later that it was as if they'd both brought shutters down in their minds,' says Aubrey Rose.[11] Having been disconnected from each other for three days, the brothers also seemed strangely disconnected from reality – and from their crime.

---

* The events described in this paragraph are 'alleged' since they are not recorded in the available case papers.

14

MIDWINTER

Arrived to see fresh snow everywhere. I had a very enjoyable walk through it, very dry and pretty.

Muriel McKay, Zermatt, Switzerland, 18 April 1961.

The final blast of the winter that saw off the 1960s was savage. Immediately after the brothers were removed from Rooks Farm, a gigantic search operation began there in conditions that quickly worsened from rain and hail to ice and snow.

Dogs were brought on to the site first, so that the scents weren't confused. The ground was quartered, the search initially focusing on a 14-acre area of the farm and surrounding fields and hedgerows. When they found nothing, a specialist commando search unit moved in, and then came blanket coverage for two weeks over 112 acres of land, with 200 policemen covering the countryside on foot daily, from dawn to sunset, their only tools wooden staves, forks and the naked eye.

On the Sunday morning, the first day of the operation, the inside of the farmhouse was searched, but while no trace of Muriel could be found there, plenty of clues were being catalogued to connect the Hoseins with her abduction, including, in the pocket of a pair of Nizam's trousers, a torn strip of paper on which was written, in red biro, 'Gates Used Cars one car Mini # UMH 587F'.

The Aga cooker was dismantled and ash samples and chippings from the flue were collected. The builder who had done some alterations to the house was consulted over whether there were any secret compartments.

While the search progressed, Alick and his daughters attended church, still hopeful of explanations, if not of being reunited with Muriel.

Ironically, for a case which had been so valuable to the press, the final arrest of the kidnappers played badly for them. Coming on a Saturday afternoon meant that the more reflective Sundays scooped the story. Nevertheless, Stocking Pelham was now in the eye of a journalistic storm, as the world's media descended on the usually hushed hamlet.

Barred access to the farm, and impatient for a promised police statement, enterprising reporters even managed to charter a light aircraft and helicopter to capture photographs of the location. Audrey Strube wrote a cherishable piece for the *Herts and Essex Observer*, capturing – with that plentiful detail in which local newspapers were once rich – how with no shop, no post office and a broken telephone box, the Cock had become the nerve centre for communicating the police activity to the outside world.

The landlords of the pub, the Bunkalls, were about to vacate the premises to return to their native Cheshunt and had been letting their stocks run down. Suddenly, they had to send out for emergency supplies from the brewery and employ help behind the bar and in the kitchen. Joyce Bunkall said, 'I must have used thirty or forty loaves during the three days, gallons of soup, tea and coffee, and pounds of cheese and ham. We just kept going continuously. Twice we ran out of whisky and had to send out for more.'[1]

She opened up at first light each morning to make tea for the BBC newsmen sending their pieces for the 8 a.m. bulletins and was herself interviewed by Anglia Television and the BBC News, though she was too busy to see either. Her 12-year-old son, Trevor, said, 'Nothing like this will ever happen to us again, we must keep a scrapbook of everything these newspaper chaps write on the strength of mum's soup and sandwiches.' She called the pressmen 'a lovely bunch of boys. Most courteous and appreciative of what we were able to do for them.'

A quintessentially English brouhaha bubbled up that evening when a local couple, the Lakes of Tinkers Hill, arrived back in the village from a day out and, chatting to a reporter in the Cock, described themselves and the community as 'country bumpkins'. After this was broadcast on BBC Radio, another local couple, the Bradfords, took offence and started a petition, saying, 'The so-called country bumpkin is an educated and skilled man who can pay his way. We are not prepared to be sat on as our grandfathers were.'[2]

However, despite the colour that the media circus splashed into village life, and the parish-pump politics that it sparked, Elsa Hosein and her children were living in dread, trapped at Rooks Farm as photographers lined the perimeter, and besieged by abusive telephone callers and unwanted visitors. Elsa appealed to Ron Harvey for police protection, which she was granted, but Freida told me that they would ultimately have no choice but to leave England, 'We were getting murder threats. Loads of people wanted to kill Mum and to kill us. We were even escorted by the police just to go to school.'[3]

'We could see Rooks Farm from our cottage,' says Yasmin Strube:

… and after this we didn't want to go anywhere near it. The place was crawling with police, in a line across the field behind us looking for clues. It was a mixture of fear and excitement. Nothing like that had ever happened to us before. Did I find it plausible from the start that the brothers could have been involved in it? Yes, I think I did.[4]

Monday morning began with 150 police officers arriving in coaches and vans and a mobile HQ being set up at the farm. Hedges, brambles and undergrowth were cut down and a vegetable garden and a rose garden were dug over. The fire brigade pumped out three nearby ponds and a moat, and all outbuildings, pig huts and cowsheds were rigorously searched.

The concrete passage between the 'dark, gloomy sheds'[5] led to a dumping area where farm rubbish and manure had been left beside a small stream, but again, it yielded nothing. Those stark, dank outbuildings would have been a hostile environment for anyone to be kept for any length of time, but over Christmas and New Year, when the frost was at its cruellest, if Muriel had been kept there, she would have endured excruciating, ravaging cold.

'As a young, uniformed officer, I was one of the many who tramped across those muddy fields,' recalls Des Hillier:

I was stationed at Berkhamsted, so quite some distance away; officers were called in from all over. You were looking for any disturbed soil. We did this for a few days, with Met officers who were not so enthusiastic, to say the least. The then Inspector, Ron Smith, was in charge of the search and had some problems encouraging them. It was freezing and very muddy. We went backwards and forwards with spades, God knows how many times.

Every time we saw a mound that might be a grave it had to be dug up, but we found absolutely nothing.[6]

The promised press conference was postponed several times, and when it eventually took place at 5.15 p.m., there was still little to report. DCI Cyril Thomas of Hertfordshire CID told shivering reporters that an intensive search across 25 acres had taken place, which would continue tomorrow. He appealed for anyone who had seen anything suspicious in the last two months to come forward. He quelled rumours of Muriel's fingerprints being found in the farm and of a shallow grave having been found and stated that, as yet, they had no evidence that Muriel was not still alive.[7]

On Tuesday morning, the search spread out into a wider area, including the garden and outbuildings of the nearby Old Rectory Cottage and the woods around Stocking Pelham Hall. Huge areas of undergrowth were cleared as a bitter blizzard cut across the ploughed fields. Officers were warmed a little by tea and coffee from a mobile canteen.

The police's appeal for reports of recent suspicious activity showed some promise when three residents came forward regarding Sleepy Hollow, an isolated smallholding on a dead-end track, a mile across country and just over the Essex border. The witnesses claimed to have seen a large car pass by and head down a track leading to a water tower and fields on 27 January in the morning, and then again in the afternoon, that time carrying a female passenger who had vanished when the car left again, fifteen minutes later. After lowering an officer down a deep well at the farm, the search was paused at dusk, with an announcement that the following day it would be extended out into Essex.

On Wednesday, while the search of the farm surroundings continued, a large operation moved to Sleepy Hollow. At the end of the lonely mile-long cul-de-sac, beside a humble timber house, was a tree-shaded duck pond and a swollen stream, beyond which stood a water tower, and beyond that, across the fields, a major National Grid substation. Battling dense mist and freezing conditions, two skin divers smashed the morning ice and sunk themselves into the pond.

After initially cordoning off the area, later in the morning the police allowed pressmen on to the site, making this slight settlement, not even named on Ordnance Survey maps, front-page news. The bleak conditions and the poetically eerie name, painted on to a sorrowful, slouching signpost, were immortalised in moody newsreel of the time and are now readily reached for in any documentary about the case.

Unfortunately, Sleepy Hollow proved to have played no significant role in the story, and by 2.30 p.m. that afternoon, the last of the search teams had left the patch. A few days later, the mystery car and its occupants were identified as a local businessman dropping off his secretary, who lived on the other side of the fields. Both were eliminated from the inquiry.

As police returned to Rooks Farm, a brief burst of sunshine brought carloads of binocular-wielding sightseers to Stocking Pelham, but they were driven away by returning snow. The following day, the search was brought to an early close when sharp rain, brutal gales and a colossal snowfall which totalled 6 inches finally defeated the squads.

A considerable number of reports came in of suspicious activity in the district over Christmas and New Year, but none of them produced results. Stella Hill of neighbouring village Furneaux Pelham reported to the police that one morning, soon after 6 January, since the children had returned to school, at 6.40 a.m. she let her dog into the garden, a Saxon Leopard Hound, which hunted by windborne scent. The dog became interested in a smell coming from due north across the fields, which Mrs Hill was certain was identical to the smells that she had been used to when she lived near Golders Green crematorium.

Rooks Farm was ¾ mile due north across the fields, but by 6 January, Elsa and the children had returned to Rooks Farm. Although they left again a few days later, no evidence or remains of a burned body was ever found at the farm.

Horace Dover, a heating engineer, saw two men, one of whom resembled one of the Hoseins, give him 'such a stare' when he noticed them parked in a Ford Anglia in Cut-Throat Lane, a rough road leading to some disused gravel pits which was being used as a dumping ground by local people, somewhere around 11 January. Another villager had seen lights in the woods at Much Hadham in the middle of the night, several weeks previously, while Samuel Moule remembered seeing two Indian men parked up in a grey Morris 1000 van in Lime Kiln Lane in late December or early January.

'I reported to the police that I'd seen people digging at the bottom of Whitebarns' back drive, where it joins Violets Lane, and along the road towards Washall Green,' remembers Sharly Hughes. 'It turned out to be people digging up badger setts. As far as I could see, the police were very thorough, they followed up everything that we reported to them.'[8]

'There was a whole host of statements from people who had seen in cars in Epping Forest, things like that, a great bundle of them,' says Roger Street:

> We had no computer to feed everything into back then. I was slightly involved with the Fred West case, twenty-five years later, as I was at the Home Office then and had to look after the security for it. I went to the HQ that the murder squad was operating from, and even then, it wasn't computerised. HOLMES* was first used on the Kensington bombing in 1986, and it was going to be the answer to all this, that you could put a mass of information into it, but on that first occasion, it collapsed within twenty minutes of being set up. In the era of the McKay case, you had all these statements and you said, 'those are the relevant ones', the others were put to one side, and you simply went through however many hundreds there were to see how many mentioned a brown car or whatever.[9]

Since the physical searching at the Pelhams was producing as little as the questioning of the brothers was, 40 miles away at Kingston, reporters were becoming restless and inventive. Fuelled by the knowledge that Arthur had sold his remaining Wessex saddlebacks at Hertford market in January, the monstrous and nonsensical rumour that Muriel had been 'fed to the pigs' was born. Journalist Peter Hardy claimed in 2021, without any discernible remorse, that it was his invention, inspired by a trashy American thriller that he was reading at the time.[10]

Arthur had in fact been trying to arrange a sale of the pigs, via Leonard Smith, for some time before the kidnapping.[11] However, it is extraordinary how audible the whisper was, long before it appeared in print. On 2 March, Stephen Burgess, a prisoner at Brixton alongside the brothers made a statement that, in his three weeks on remand, there was 'a strong whisper' around the prison that Mrs McKay had been 'fed to the pigs'. Burgess said that he was told this by 'a junkie who was speaking to Arthur'.[12]

'People make these kinds of stories up,' says Peter Miller, a Hertfordshire officer who briefly worked on the case:

---

* Home Office Large Major Enquiry System, a computer system enabling the collating and fast cross-referencing of information in major crime investigations.

A few years later, not far from Stocking Pelham, we had the case of Helen Hooper, who disappeared and whose body was also never found.* On that occasion, the rumour was that her husband had relatives at a zoo, and that she had been fed to the lions.[13]

'Before I joined the Met, as a boy I had worked on a farm in west Wales, so I knew farming from the age of 10,' says Peter Rimmer. 'I was one of the few officers who had an experience of it, and I made the point that the rumour about pigs was absolute rubbish. It was a very cruel story, absolutely beyond the pale.'[14] Aubrey Rose called it 'as unfeeling and unfounded a comment as there could be'.[15]

When considering why no trace of Muriel could ever be found at Rooks Farm, one must remember not only that this was an age of severely limited forensic techniques but that by the time the Hoseins were arrested, nearly six weeks had passed since Muriel's disappearance and probable death. Elsa had returned soon after New Year and, as well as day-to-day life at the farm trampling over and blowing away evidence, the house would also have been cleaned several times since then.

Before Elsa's return, it is hard to imagine Arthur and Nizam, however thorough, managing to remove every last trace of evidence, since they were both domestically incompetent as well as chauvinistic when it came to cooking and cleaning. We know that no fingerprints would have been left by Muriel, but the lack of any other forensic evidence must be primarily down to the rudimentary level of forensic science at the time.

Des Hillier says:

Without a doubt, forensic science has improved so much since then, so she could have been kept somewhere there. There was some talk at the time about how effective the searching could be considered. However, although we didn't have the technology back then, we were far better in terms of dedication. I know every generation says this sort of thing, but when I joined

---

* Helen Hooper met her husband, Walter, when she was 16 and he was 50. She tried to leave him several times and was planning to elope with her lover on Valentine's Day 1976, but the previous day, on which it is believed that she intended to tell her husband, was the last time that she was ever seen. Walter Hooper was charged with her murder but after an eight-day hearing, magistrates ruled that there was no case for him to answer. He died in 1996.

the CID, we worked some horrendous hours, and if you said, 'Sorry guv, I'm getting tired', you were told, 'Well, we didn't ask you to come on CID, did we?'[16]

Another Hertfordshire officer, Peter Miller, remembers:

I had two days at Rooks Farm. Our task was to look after Mrs Hosein, to act as a barrier from the media. It was such open land that the press could potentially get in from any direction. She had no animosity towards us, she accepted that we had to be there and at times seemed almost disinterested in what was going on. I remember her asking me to kill a chicken for the dinner, but I refused, I couldn't kill a chicken, so she went out and did it, and had it plucked in double quick time and in the pot. There was a level of hardness there, a sort of country hardness, you could say.[17]

The first interview with Elsa was conducted on Monday, 9 February by Ron Harvey and Jim Parker. 'You do ask a lot of questions, questions, questions, questions,' she remarked at one point, saying that her solicitor had told her not to answer them, but that she was happy to since she had nothing to hide.[18]

Nevertheless, she wasn't above the odd fib. She told the officers that she never looked at the times of Arthur's comings and goings, only that, 'it is my job to get his meals'. She confirmed that no metal or piping around the farm had been sawn by Nizam since he had borrowed the hacksaw and blades but denied staying in London from 12 January, saying that she had gone to town on a pretence of seeing Nizam off at the airport, since his visa had expired and he had decided to stay on in England illegally.

In her next interview, she admitted that, in truth, she had been staying in London because she and Arthur had rowed over Liley. Elsa had accused him of having an affair and then left him after he assaulted her. She said that she had lied because she didn't want any trouble for the old lady with whom she had stayed with. She downplayed Arthur's brutality, obviously out of fear, and seemed completely unaware during questioning that Farida, the mother of Arthur's son, Michael, was still in London.

The press still awaited details of the two suspects being held by the police, so began the week's coverage of the story with photographs of the area around Rooks Farm, accompanied by occasionally inflated accounts of the police operation. The *Evening Standard* stuffed its inside pages with rubbish about a fifth columnist in the gang who had supposedly been tipping the police off ahead of each instruction on the ransom runs – a garbled version of Arthur's pretence at collusion with Ian on the M3 calls – and there was also a fictionalised account of John Bland's role in the final sortie, which had been impressive enough without exaggeration.

After questioning Elsa, police attention inevitably moved to Adam Hosein, the third Hosein brother living in London. A self-employed insurance broker, he lived with his wife, Marion, and their three children, at 2 Leander Road, Thornton Heath. Born in 1942, he was six years younger than Arthur and six years older than Nizam, but a more formidable character than either of them. I asked Arthur's daughter, Freida, for her memories of Adam, reassuring her first that he had died in 2021. She says:

> Thank God. He was horrible, a real horror. I didn't like him at all as a child. He felt dangerous. They came to visit us a few times with their kids. His wife was lovely, I liked her and felt sorry for her, I used to listen at the door as she told mum of how Adam would beat her up, they both obviously had the same experiences. I loved to play with their children, but as for him, being a child, you know who is good and who is not good, and I had an instinct about him.[19]

In his first statement to the police, on 12 February, Adam said that he had seen little of Arthur between 1964, when he married, and August 1968, only making occasional visits to Ongar, and he had not seen Arthur at all since April 1969, nor had he spoken to him at all since he had taken Nizam to live at Rooks Farm. (There is no evidence to contradict this.) He claimed to earn about £4,000 per year, but said, 'I budget month by month and have about £600* in my bank.'[20] He was asked for his movements on 29 December. He said that he had stayed at home in the morning, as it was his wife's birthday, and had gone to his office in Wembley at 1 p.m. He returned home later in the afternoon and at 5 p.m. had taken a train to Turnpike Lane Station, where he had an appointment with business associate Victor Pinheiro and his brother-in-law.

After discussing life insurance, Adam and Pinheiro had then left at 7.30 p.m. for Balham, where they collected Pinheiro's children and dropped

---

*   £4,000 was £49,033 in 2021, and £600 was £7,335.

them off at his home. The pair then drove to the Effra Residential Club* in Brixton, then Pinheiro drove Adam to 205 North End Road, where he had a 10 p.m. appointment with a limbo dancer, Keith Warrell,** to whom he delivered an accident claim cheque for £125. Pinheiro had then dropped Adam back to his home in Thornton Heath at about 11 p.m. and he had gone to bed.

Despite the enviable clarity of Adam's account of events six weeks previously, his statement makes no mention of Pinheiro coming into the house for a drink after dropping him home, nor does it mention Nizam's visit at 11.45 p.m. Adam was interviewed again on 25 March and was asked specifically whether he received a visit from Nizam over Christmas; that time, he said that he saw him twice over Christmas but was uncertain of the dates.

When one considers Freida's words about Adam and, as will be revealed, his later criminal associations, it is tempting to read significance into the thoroughness of his statement and its one glaring omission. However, despite his dislike of him, he may well have been covering up for Nizam at this point out of familial if not fraternal loyalty. If this was so, it was particularly unfortunate for Nizam that Adam failed to recall that visit, considering that the visits to Adam and to his cousin on the night of 29 December were clearly Nizam's limp attempts at an alibi, or at least attempts at recording an air of normality in his behaviour during the hours immediately after the kidnapping (even though his relatives thought that his unannounced visit at such a late hour was quite abnormal).

As for Adam's well-documented movements throughout that day and evening, their thoroughness could well be because they were recalled with the aid of a diary or work documentation. Whether it was typical of his schedule to have business appointments so late in the evening, we will never know, but his 10 p.m. appointment was with a fellow Trinidadian, so it is plausible that it was partly a social call.

---

* The Effra Club, at that time one of London's many drinking clubs for the West Indian and African community, is still trading today, as the Effra Social, its décor perfectly recreating the style of the 1960s.

** Under his stage name, Rocky Allen, Trinidadian-born Warrell appeared in the eccentric British sci-fi musical *Pop Down* (1968). No complete print of the film is known to survive, although Warrell's sequence and some other portions were recently recovered.

The statement makes it very clear that Adam was nowhere near Wimbledon at the time of Muriel's kidnapping. Similarly, on Sunday, 1 February, the day of the High Cross operation, after lunch with a Mr Sheikh and his family in Balham, he called again on Mr Pinheiro, who then drove him to various appointments. At 8.30 p.m. he arrived home, where he saw his wife and some visiting friends who left at 10.30 p.m.

On 6 February, while Arthur and Nizamodeen were directing the Rolls-Royce from London to Bishop's Stortford, Adam had appointments until 11.30 p.m. Whether such overwhelming evidence is so conclusive as to be suspicious depends on one's readiness to overcomplicate the story and to embrace conspiracism.

The day after Adam made his first statement to the police, the *Evening News* reported that Shaffi, the Hoseins' father, was flying to England, his wife having collapsed when she heard the news. 'I don't believe my sons are in this business,' he said, 'it must be a mistake.'[21]

Also that day, at 2.30 p.m., an agricultural worker at Stocking Pelham, William Bell, was asked by a man, who was between 30 and 40 and 'appeared to be of Indian origin', whether he could get to Rooks Farm across the fields.[22] The man was given directions but gave up walking in the snow after a few minutes, returned to his car and drove away. This may have been Adam, but if so, his unfamiliarity with Rooks Farm corroborates his statement about having barely seen Arthur since 1968.

The snow was indeed thick by now, as evidential photographs taken at this point illustrate, while at Wimbledon, the garrulous Arthur had now descended into icy silence. On 18 February, Smith saw him in the presence of David Coote and questioned him about the shotgun. He made 'no comment' answers and refused to give a blood sample. Nizam also refused to provide one, saying nothing whatsoever.

While officers made laborious house-to-house inquiries in Bishop's Stortford regarding the non-existent Susie from Tesco who Nizam claimed to have been stood up by, at the forensic laboratory, John McCafferty, the Senior Experimental Officer, completed his report on the firearms that had been discovered at the farm. The right barrel of the shotgun was found to be fouled from firing, but the left barrel had been partially cleaned since it had last been fired. The sawn barrel in the gun case comprised the original 28in barrels for the gun, sawn across in two parts, the barrels having been in good condition before the mutilation, while the saw cuts appeared to be recent. Both the muzzle ends were fouled from firing and contained some steel filings, showing that they had been fired through and not cleaned prior to the sawing. The breach ends had been partially cleaned and were lightly oiled. The condition and appearance of the ends suggested that they had been fired through after the sawing and then cleaned and oiled.[23]

The tablets found at the farm were tranquilisers, six of them Mogadon and the others Largactil. Both were only available on prescription, although possession of them was not restricted by the Dangerous Drugs Act.[24] The fact that they were found hidden with the shotgun cartridges suggests that they too were considered by the Hoseins as weapons.

On 18 February, the *News of the World* applied to have the registration number of the Rolls-Royce changed. While actioning this, a clerk at County Hall found the record of an application for the owner's details, dated 19 December 1969. The form was collected by the police and the handwriting was judged to be that of Nizamodeen Hosein, despite it bearing the name 'Sharif Mustapha' and the address 175 Norbury Crescent. When he arrived at that address, Bill Smith was greeted by Nizam's relative, Rahim Mohammed, who told him that he had never heard of anyone called Sharif Mustapha. (The name was actually that of a school friend of Nizam's.) Although the clerk who had dealt with the original inquiry, Maureen Callanan, could only give a rough description of the man who had so insistently tried to obtain the address of the Rolls-Royce owner, in conjunction with the handwriting, the document still proved to be powerful evidence.

The same day that the form was discovered, Leonard Smith identified without doubt the billhook found in Arthur Road as the one that he used for hedging and which he had lost at Rooks Farm after the auction in October. The wooden handle was loose, the wood having shrunk after getting dry and warm from being kept on the floor of his car. Additionally, he was left-handed and had sharpened accordingly for the bevel to strike the wood in the most effective way. The only discrepancy was that, as a farmer, he always kept his tools sharp for everyday use, whereas the edge of this bill had dulled and there was a new orange stain on the handle. He was even able to produce a receipt for the replacement that he had bought.[25]

While the evidence against the Hoseins mounted up, the brothers were reacting to their confinement at HMP Brixton in different ways. Sometime around 17 February, Liley received a letter from Nizam:

My dear darling,

I do hope sincerely that this letter would reach you bringing a lot of relief and joy to your heart.

I must say that what has happened was a great surprise and an impossibility. I must now tell you the truth. I knows nothing of what they are trying to accuse me of. You know for a fact that I would not indulge myself in anything stupid or to get in the hands of the police. There it is I was taken into a cell for the first time on Saturday at Kingston Police Station. I was transferred to Wimbledon Police Station where I stayed for a night and day. I went to court and was remanded until Wednesday 18th February to appear in Wimbledon Magistrates Court at 10am. I am not at the above address Prison. Could you find out and let me know if my mother knows and what are her reactions. Is she still alive. Please tell me the truth. The charges of which I am not guilty off and knows nothing off are as follows

(1)   MURDER

(2)   BLACKMAIL

You never thought that your boy would be called by these names but there it is the Police did it. Do you still love me after hearing this. I love you Liley. I will waiting to see and hear you as soon as possible.

I Remain,

Yours Forever,

Love Nizam[26]

A heart was drawn around the signature.

For most people who are unfamiliar with jail, to be facing a potential life sentence while being locked up for the first time with some of society's most brutal miscreants would surely be a petrifying experience. Arthur, however, was typically boastful.

Also at HMP Brixton at the time was Michael Patrick Kelleher, a habitual petty criminal, on remand this time for cheque fraud. Three weeks into his remand he was working as a cleaner in the hospital wing, where he met the Hoseins and befriended Nizam. Arthur was 'always poking fun at the screws and was quite unconcerned about the murder he was charged with', boasting that the law could not hold him as they could not find the body.[27] He was still boasting that he had plenty of money, and asking why, as a wealthy man, he would commit such a crime.

Unlike Nizamodeen, who was 'very moody and nervous', Kelleher thought that Arthur was controlling himself very well. Only on one occasion did he show any nerves, when a prison officer claimed that Nizamodeen had scrawled a confession on his cell wall. Arthur was not goaded until the officer added that the press had photographed it, and 'he then showed his nerves by going very quiet and closing his eyes', but only momentarily, before laughing.

As the snow cleared, police resumed the search, following up the sighting of two malevolent-looking men near a gravel pit on Cut-Throat Lane and trawling areas around Violets Lane in Furneux Pelham, Washall Green, 140 acres of land adjacent to Grays Cottages at Brent Pelham, a Dutch barn near the farm, and the hedgerows of surrounding corn fields. A rubbish tip near the farm was searched by dogs and then with a mechanical digger for anything unusual, including jewellery. It all came to nothing.[28]

On the morning of 27 February, Kelleher was cleaning in the bathroom of the prison hospital while Arthur was shaving. A prison officer commented that if Arthur was found not guilty, he would immediately resign.

Arthur replied, 'What makes you think I killed her, I wouldn't kill anybody. I've got no reason to kill anybody.'[29]

The officer walked away, and Arthur apparently then said to Kelleher, 'All this cunt don't know, there could be someone higher in this.' He then 'said something to the effect that he had to have information to do the job, and went on to say, "there's somebody working outside for us, in the papers".'

A day or two later, Kelleher passed Arthur near his cell. Arthur appeared to be very happy about his imminent court appearance, and said, 'Well, I've got nothing to worry about, for a start they haven't gone to a higher court and they're looking in the wrong place for the lump.' Kelleher laughed at the word 'lump', and Arthur then laughed proudly and said, bluntly, 'body'.

On 2 March, while Nizamodeen was having a bath, Kelleher asked him if he had killed Muriel and 'straight away he said, "Yes, but they won't fucking prove it".' He then fell silent and Kelleher 'got the impression that he wished he had never said it'. Kelleher asked why, and Nizamodeen said, 'They haven't found the body.'

Kelleher asked, 'Well, if you did kill her, where would you put the body?'

According to Kelleher, Nizam then said something in a whisper, of which he could only make out the words 'Windsor' and 'Thames' and 'I have been there'. They were then called by the officers, and Kelleher never saw the brothers again.

Kelleher made his statement to the police just over a fortnight after this event, saying that he came forward because after his release he was drinking and related the conversation in the presence of a policeman, who urged him to report it. However, he was not considered a reliable witness and his evidence was not used at the trial.

'Mickey Kelleher went to my school, Corner Hall in Hemel Hempstead. I think he was in my year,' says Des Hillier:

> I came across him while I was on the CID at Hemel. I can't remember what that was for, so it must have been something minor. As for his statement about the brothers, I would have paid some credence to it. He would real-ise that saying something like that wouldn't hold him in good stead with the other prisoners. I don't think that he was somebody who exaggerated, claiming that he was the biggest thief in Hemel Hempstead or whatever.[30]

However seriously the police may have taken Kelleher's statement, they were aware that as a witness he would have no credibility. Yet his impression of both brothers is astute, and his straightforward reporting of Arthur's gran-diose nonsense about 'somebody working outside for us, in the papers' has a ring of truth – or rather, ridiculousness – to it. Nizam's 'Thames/Windsor' comment can probably be rejected, since Kelleher claims to have asked him 'Where *would* you have put the body?'.

There is one piece of information however, which must be given serious consideration – Arthur's comment that 'they're looking in the wrong place'. The Hoseins were certainly not scrupulous when disposing of evidence such as the paper flowers and the writing paper, but Arthur's reaction to being told about the fingerprint evidence is in marked contrast to the strange con-fidence that both brothers showed throughout the later stages of the crime, and throughout their arrest, custody, remand and imprisonment, that Muriel's body would not be found. Given their lack of care in removing other incrimi-nating evidence, it is likely that the failure to find Muriel's body was not down to ingenuity on the Hoseins' part, but because, in Arthur's words, the police really were looking in the wrong place.

EVIDENCE

Lovely sunny days, little breeze. Have a flat roof for sunbathing. The Spanish couple keeping house have an Alsatian pup, Amego. He's getting friendly gradually. Hope you are well. Pats for Carl.

Muriel McKay, Pollensa, Mallorca, 19 September 1968.

Alick McKay returned to work on Monday, 23 February. By now, Rupert Murdoch had returned to England, having been advised by Alick and the police to remain in Australia until the kidnappers were captured. Both men were returning to a booming enterprise in Bouverie Street. The sales figures for the *News of the World* had increased by 389,000 over the past six months, creating a gap of 1 million copies between the paper and its nearest rival, the *People*.

One of Murdoch's first duties upon his return was to summon Stafford Somerfield to his office, where he terminated a twenty-five-year newspaper career in a three-minute interview. Asked whether he would be making a statement to the press later, Murdoch said, 'I doubt it.'[1]

Somerfield retired to the long bar of the Falstaff at lunchtime and reminisced with journalists about his long career on the scandal sheet. He was forbidden by the terms of his expulsion to work for any rival newspaper for a number of years, and instead wrote a book about boxer dogs and became a judge at Crufts.

A report of Somerfield's sacking featured on that evening's television news, alongside an item on the continuing police search in south Hertfordshire. Shortly after this, Alick was required to make another statement to the police in relation to the M3 telephone calls and the exhibits. At the close of it, he reflected that from the amount of publicity that surrounded the arrival of Ian from Australia, 'I am certain that my wife, who had not seen him for two years would ... have made some reference to him in her letters', and 'the tremendous affection which she held for her children, grandchildren and myself would cause her to get in touch if she was able. As time goes by, I am more and more convinced that she must be dead.'[2]

On 13 March, Adam visited Nizam at HMP Brixton. Immediately they faced each other in the cubicle, Nizam stood up and held a piece of paper against the glass partition for him to read. A prison officer, John Lodge, spotted this and told Nizam to sit down, noticing him stuff the paper into his jacket pocket as he did. When the visit ended, Lodge searched him and confiscated the paper. It read:

> Don't say anything to no one not even the Solicitor. That I was by you on Monday night. 2 farmers are saying that Arthur was down by them on that day at 6.30pm. I was home.

Presumably Arthur had been putting pressure on Nizam by lying to him that he had alibi witnesses for the time of the kidnapping. Nizam must have then decided that his visit to Adam was placing him in London and dangerously close to Wimbledon, albeit several hours later. Adam made a second statement to the police on 25 March but claimed that he could not remember the contents of the note.

Principle Scientific Officer Charles Fryd brought in powerful evidence from the papers found at Rooks Farm. The exercise book, which belonged to Hafeeza, was clearly the source of the paper on which the letter to the *News of the World* had been written. The torn edge bore the impressions from two partially opened staples and complemented the remainder of the edge that was still in the book. There were also indentations on the paper from the words 'St Mary' and an omission mark having been written on top of it, indentations which tallied with the dimensions and spacing in a line of the *News of the World* letter, 'Secondly, he has not paid ∧ off for ∧ St Mary House'.

Detective Chief Inspector Arthur Brine submitted more damning evidence from the fingerprint bureau: Arthur's prints were identified on a page of the *People* newspaper; on the envelope that contained the first letter; on the ransom demand sent on 21 January; on the inside flap of the Piccadilly cigarette packet

from the Southbury Road call box; and on the 'Alick Darling' letter and envelope sent on 26 January which had contained the pieces of Muriel's clothing.
Brine had 'no doubt that they were made by the same fingers, thumbs and
palmar impressions'.[3] Bill Smith later commented that by sending the samples
of her clothing, the Hoseins were proving that they had Muriel, not only to
her family but, ultimately, to the courts.[4]

The handwriting on the letters was confirmed as Muriel's, the writing on
the GLC form as Nizamodeen's, and the writing on two of the ransom letters as Arthur's, though the writing on the *News of the World* letter was too
persistently disguised to be matched. A visit to the Smith & Nephew factory
in Welwyn Garden City confirmed that the Elastoplast found at Arthur Road
and the red tin found at Rooks Farm were of the same manufacture.

Vegetable dyes extracted from the paper flowers corresponded with those
on the flowers found at the farm and with the remaining unused tissues in the
box which Liley had bought. The blue paper used for some of the letters was
airmail paper and again tallied with that found at the farm.

Less yielding was a breakdown of all telephone calls made from Brent
Pelham 317 (the telephone number of Rooks Farm) through Bishop's Stortford
exchange between 1 December 1969 and 6 February 1970. There were no calls
made from Rooks Farm at all between Boxing Day and New Year's Day, a
five-day silence which is as curious as the 'curious incident of the dog in the
night-time'.*

Since there were extensions in the barn at Rooks Farm and the master bedroom, as well as the main telephone in the lounge, if the New Year's Day M3
calls to Dianne had been made from one of those, it could explain how Arthur
managed to make those calls despite Liley saying that he never went out.
However, STD pips at start of the calls rule out this possibility, while the list
dispels the possibility that the 'grey Hillman' call could have been by Muriel in
captivity after glimpsing the grey Morris parked at the farm.

However, on that last point, I asked Andrew Wood, Treasurer of the
Communication Museum Trust Limited, whether it was possible that calls
could have been made from Rooks Farm at this time without the need to
go through the operator at the local exchange. Britain was in the process of

---

* 'The dog did nothing in the night-time – "That was the curious incident," remarked
Sherlock Holmes' in *The Adventure of Silver Blaze* (*Strand Magazine*, December 1892).

switching all exchanges over to STD, which enables a caller to make a call to any area without the need to be connected by the operator. He explains:

> Brent Pelham was automatic at that time but that doesn't necessarily mean that customers could self-dial trunk calls [STD]. Initially, automatic exchanges could only self-dial local calls. For long-distance, you would dial '0' and ask the operator to connect you. The ability of Brent Pelham to self-dial trunk calls would depend on the main exchange at Bishop's Stortford going automatic as well. The records I have show that in March 1973, Brent Pelham could self-dial trunk calls, and that it was automatic from 1960, but in 1960 it could not do STD, as the Bishop's Stortford exchange was not yet automatic. The crucial factor then is which year between 1960 and 1973 did Bishop's Stortford go automatic, thus giving Brent Pelham STD ability. If the exchange supported STD, then it is 99% certain that all call boxes on it would be STD too.[5]

Unfortunately, Andrew wasn't able to confirm that detail. The breakdown of telephone calls made from the farm via the operator over the winter of 1969–70 suggests that STD was not possible, and this would also mean that the village call box opposite the Cock was unlikely to be able to perform STD calls, as was stated at the trial. It might be that STD calls were possible but that the Hoseins lazily used the operator most of the time for convenience. Although we know that the Hoseins made a call to the *News of the World* when attempting to ascertain the details of the Rolls-Royce, that number does not appear on the call sheet, so presumably they always made potentially incriminating calls from call boxes, although seemingly, not from local call boxes. The conclusion is that we can be reasonably sure that no M3 calls were made from the farm, or from the village call box, leaving us no nearer to ascertaining how Arthur made the calls on New Year's Day, but also making it fairly safe to rule out the 'grey Hillman' call.

On 25 March, Alick left St Mary House for the last time, and moved into a flat in Rutland Gate, Knightsbridge. Dianne explains, 'We had to get him out of that house. He was never going to leave by himself. Eventually, we moved him out while he was at work, I remember even taking the pyjamas from under his pillow.' A few months later, the house was sold to Chloe Baveystock and her husband: 'On the basis of a chance remark I made to Muriel and Alick at Dianne and David's wedding, we were approached regarding possible purchase when Alick was selling the house, thus bypassing an open sale which would have created a flood of gawking sightseers.'[6]

On 12 April, a couple from Rochester complained to their MP, Anne Kerr, about the length of time that the Hoseins had been detained before being committed for trial, requesting that a question be asked in Parliament about prisoners being held indefinitely. However, their concern was misplaced and the law was found to be perfectly intact.[7]

On 22 April, the brothers were further charged with kidnapping, secreting Muriel McKay against her will, demanding £1 million with menaces, and with threats to kill or murder. Arthur said, 'I am innocent of all those charges and all those charges are false.'

Nizam said, 'I know nothing about those charges.'

David Coote had been representing both brothers and had instructed barristers to conduct their joint defence, but Nizam then dispensed with their services and replaced Coote with Aubrey Rose, therefore now requiring separate counsel for a defence that would perhaps be hostile to Arthur. Rose had a long and impressive relationship with the Caribbean:

> I acted as a lawyer for most of the Caribbean governments. I was very concerned about people being treated fairly, and about discrimination, particularly towards West Indians. The Trinidad high commission asked me whether I would take up the case, so I went to see the brothers.[8]

Immediately he met the brothers, Rose was stunned by their differences, not only in appearance but in temperament:

> I thought Arthur was peculiar. While anybody on such a charge would behave strangely, he was strangely confident. Nizam spoke in this subdued manner and looked so drawn and unhealthy. Nizam was very much the bottom dog and Arthur the top dog. Nizam had only been in the country a short time and felt obligated to Arthur, he looked up to him and seemed to have little confidence himself.
>
> They both wanted me to act for them, but it was clear that their defences were going in different directions, so I chose to act for Nizam. Both protested their innocence but said very little. The police had a terrible job getting any information out of them, as did I. Their behaviour was most unusual.

The case gripped Rose so much that despite employing two sets of inquiry agents, he drove up to the Pelhams himself and spent a day scouring 'the fields and barns and byways of south Hertfordshire',[9] and met Elsa, whom he found to be 'very much a hausfrau, and very decent'.[10]

Arthur continued to be represented by his friend David Coote. 'I wasn't 100% impressed with him,' says Rose. 'He was very young and seemed not to have much experience of criminal cases, not a bad man but a bit overawed by what Arthur's strongminded barrister told him.'

Elsa was struggling financially by now, so Coote billed the police for £6 for their use of the telephone and electricity at Rooks Farm. An obstinate John Minors quibbled with this amount, pointing out that no calls were made from the farm once the mobile HQ was set up two days after the arrest, and that the farm had no heating system in operation at the time. He also considered that Elsa herself owed 'a great personal debt' to the officers at the farm, who had provided her with police protection and without whom 'she would have been unable to cater for the needs of the livestock, or the personal needs of herself and her two children'.[11]

Tom Pateman, whose parents had the dairy farm at High Cross which Arthur had bought the calf from, which had died in January and Liley and Nizam had chopped up, remembers sweetly, 'After the arrest, my mum and dad visited Elsa at the farm, and since she had no money, Dad bought a Jersey cow from her to help her a little.'[12]

It seemed as if the seriousness of his situation was only now beginning to dawn on Arthur, but his response to it was typically desperate and reckless. On 8 June, during committal proceedings at the Magistrates' Court, as soon as the tape recordings of his voice were played, he jumped to his feet and made towards Bill Smith, shouting, 'You bastard, you bastard, I'll get you, don't worry you bastard!' He was restrained by four officers and taken back to his seat as he yelled, 'Even if I have to do thirty years, I'll get you!'

A few minutes later, he calmed himself and apologised to the Bench. When the court rose, on his way out he stopped by Smith and Minors, smiled, and said, 'I'm sorry, Mr Smith. I lost control. It's being cooped up so long, you see.' He then shook hands with Smith and said, 'No hard feelings, eh?'

The following day, during further proceedings, Arthur sent David Coote over to Smith to ask the name of the man sitting behind him, Commander Bert Guiver. Coote noted it down, and when the court rose for lunch, as Arthur passed, he said to Guiver, 'I've seen you before.' Guiver replied that he had seen him before too, and Arthur said, 'You were in the interrogation room and helped to beat me up.'[13] His next tactic was even more injudicious.

Arthur spotted a story in a newspaper about Rupert Murdoch's nemesis, Robert Maxwell. He then dreamed up a tale, which he told Nizam to play along with, that one night at the farm he had discovered Nizam in the presence of four men, one of whom was Maxwell, who were pressing him to take part in the kidnapping, in return for which Nizam would be granted permanent residency in England. The story is rather typical of Arthur's latter-day 'M3' fantasies, which painted him as the moral conscience and reluctant puppet of higher forces.

In the same way that Arthur sent Nizam into the GLC offices, told him to make the first M3 telephone calls, and left him to prowl around Gates garage while he was securing an alibi at the Raven, it shows how much he was prepared to incriminate his brother. Arthur shared his Maxwell story with his gullible father, who was shocked to discover that Nizam was refusing to countenance it. Nizam's continued defiance enraged Arthur, who resorted to attacking him, after which the brothers were separated.

On 12 June, Nizam was at Wimbledon Police Station again, awaiting further committal proceedings. He asked to see Smith and Minors in his cell at Wimbledon without his solicitor present. Smith reminded him that he did not have to say anything, and Nizam said, 'Could you tell me if anyone is stopping Liley seeing me? She hasn't been to see me, you see.' Smith knew nothing about this, and Nizam then said, 'Would you know if my brother, Adam, has told her not to visit me?' Again, Smith wasn't aware of any such matter. Nizam said that he wanted to speak to Liley today, and that this was all for the moment, but that he would like to see Smith again before going back to Brixton.

After the day's proceedings ended, Aubrey Rose and Leonard Woodley, who had now been appointed as his junior barrister, saw Nizam in his cell, and then told Smith and Minors that Nizam wanted to see them again, alone. Rose and Woodley left the cell, and Smith again reminded Nizam of the caution and asked what it was that he wished to say.

'Well, you see,' he said, 'I can get out of 90 per cent of this trouble if I put my cards on the table.'

He did not want to make a written statement and so Smith asked what he wanted to tell him. Nizam thought for a few minutes, then said, 'I want to think some more about it, Mr Smith. I'll leave it 'til another day.'[14]

Three days later, the Hosein brothers were committed for trial at the Old Bailey on seven counts: murder, abduction, secreting, two counts of blackmail and two of sending letters threatening murder. In a memo, the Crown estimated the trial would last three weeks and with thirty-four of the seventy-five witnesses being called, the chances of success being 'strong really'.[15]

Peter Rimmer travelled back from that final visit to the magistrates' court with the brothers:

> We were inside the black maria, which was very small, with benches down each side. I had Arthur strapped to my left wrist and the other officer had Nizam strapped to his left wrist, because you always kept your strongest arm free. Nizam was sitting opposite me. As we got to the gates at Brixton Prison, I think one of the officers said something like, 'We won't be doing this again', meaning that the next thing was the trial, and it was obvious by then that they had an awful lot to answer for. In between the gates, as they were opening the second gate, Nizam, who always looked resentful anyway, just suddenly launched himself across at us, more towards Arthur but at that close range there was just a big kerfuffle. That was the only time he went for him.[16]

The brothers would not see one another again until they stood side by side in the dock of Court Number 1.

There were some legal concerns over a charge of murder where no body had been found, but the matter was not unprecedented. After the murder of 10-year-old Mona Tinsley in 1937, for which, despite strong circumstantial and physical evidence, her killer, Frederick Nodder, could only be tried for abduction and secretion charges similar to some of those drawn up for the Hoseins alongside the murder charge,* there had followed a number of successful convictions for murder without a body having been found. Confidence was drawn particularly from the most recent incident, the conviction of the Kray twins and their associates for the murder of Jack McVitie on 4 March 1969,** which provided strong reassurance that such a conviction would be possible for the Hosein brothers.

---

*   Mona's body was discovered three months after the trial and Nodder was then tried for murder and hanged. The case is considered pivotal in the abolition of the 'no body, no murder' principle, which was finally abolished in 1954.

**   There were subsequent claims that the body was thrown into the sea from a boat off the Sussex coast or buried in a newly dug grave at Gravesend Cemetery.

Nevertheless, further searching was done over the summer. 'We considered we were handicapped by the weather in the early searching,' said Ron Harvey.[17] Once again, however, it produced nothing.

David Ryan was one of the dog-handlers involved in this search. He explains that:

> Back in 1970, we did not have dogs specifically trained to search for and locate human remains. That was to come along later. The method used was to search designated areas, quite often employing a staggered line of handlers and dogs, or, a specific area would be covered by one handler and dog.
>
> When I was a dog sergeant many years later, I attended a week-long course that included observing the methods of search by body dogs. It was totally different to the tactics of years ago and one of the most impressive aspects was the field craft employed by the handlers. As the sergeant running the course explained, it's virtually impossible to bury a human body without leaving visual evidence on the surface and that particular disturbance can remain visual for quite some time.[18]

With a date for the trial set, the Hoseins applied for legal aid. Considering Arthur's obsession with wealth and status, it must have been humiliating for him to declare, 'I have no other source of income. My liquid capital (if any) is minimal. My wife and two children are maintaining themselves with the assistance of social security payments.'[19]

He estimated the value of Rooks Farm at £15,000 and his outstanding mortgage at £8,000, with assets of £700 in cash at the house and livestock valued at £800–1,000, making his capital and savings £8,700.[20] This was then updated to include the Morris car, which was valued at £30, and the Volvo, valued at £1,000, and to include his liabilities. He had an overdraft with Barclays Bank at Ongar for £346, and further debts of £103 for his carpets and £81 for animal feed, plus costs, as he had been sued for both, £49 national insurance contributions, a county court judgement of £44, an additional £160 debt for animal feed, an uncalculated income tax liability, £81 outstanding fines from Bishop's Stortford Magistrates' Court, and £200 outstanding on a finance agreement for the Aga. With the additional costs of the legal actions, his liabilities totalled £1,245.[21] Since July 1969, a total of £2,000 had been paid into his bank account, but his outgoings had always exceeded his income. At the time of arrest, he was apparently earning £5,000 a year. Nizam declared that he had 'no means at all'.[22]

On 22 June, their alibis were submitted, with Nizam's defence team lamely claiming that the testimony of seven witnesses 'will tend to show that' Nizamodeen being in Norbury and Thornton Heath several hours after the kidnapping suggested that he was unlikely to have been 'where the offences are alleged to have been committed at the time of their alleged commission'.[23]

Although this caused the Crown little concern, David Coote produced a supposed alibi witness for Arthur – John Bailey, the man whom Nizam had invited to the farm after meeting him in the Plough the night before the abduction. Coote claimed that on Monday, 29 December, after finishing his shift as the wines and spirits manager at Tesco in Ware, Bailey had gone for a drive and saw a car at the farm at 5 p.m. However, when Smith and Minors interviewed Bailey, it became clear that he in no way alibied Arthur, nor was there any certainty that his statement referred to the correct farm or the relevant day. It transpired that it was only because of 'Mr Coote's persistent questioning' that he had said this, merely to get rid of him, and having had quite a lot of drink bought for him by Mr Coote, he had not appreciated the seriousness of the matter.[24]

On 8 July, Adam made a further statement, finally detailing Nizam's visit to him on the night of 29 December. It only alibied Nizam between 11 p.m. and midnight and fatally placed him en route from Thornton Heath to Stocking Pelham immediately afterwards and therefore in the vicinity of Epping at precisely the time that the first M3 call was made from there.

Adam now recalled that he got home just after 11 p.m., accompanied by Victor Pinheiro, whom he invited in for a Scotch. They were drinking in the breakfast room when the bell rang, and Pinheiro answered it, returning with Nizam, who had a drink but did not sit down. Pinheiro and Adam continued their conversation, and 'at this time I had no discussion with Nizam'. When Pinheiro left to go, Adam asked Nizam what he wanted, and he said that he had come for the shirts from his father that Adam had brought back from Trinidad in October. Adam told him that they were in the bedroom but his wife was sleeping, to call back for them whenever he was down again, and that he was tired and wanted to go to bed.

Adam watched him drive away in the Volvo at midnight, but Nizam never returned for the shirts. 'He phoned after that about his visa problems. I told him it served him right. He had created his own problems. That was the last time he phoned.'[25]

Nizam was now alienated from Adam and Arthur, and from his father. Relations between Arthur and David Coote were also becoming strained. On

15 July, Coote visited Arthur at HMP Brixton and, not for the first time, had to wait nearly an hour to see him due to no officer being available. Arthur assumed that Coote had arrived late and so refused to see him.[26]

Arthur's defence team briefed an independent forensic expert, Dr Julius Grant, to be called on the fingerprint, handwriting and paper evidence, and commissioned an inquiry agent to time the journey from Rooks Farm to Arthur Road which, travelling via the city rather than the A10, was two hours and five minutes. They pondered calling a Mrs Hall of Ilford as a witness, who supposedly overheard a call on a crossed line on New Year's Eve in which a £1 million ransom for a dead woman was discussed and on which it was mentioned that the woman was dead. This would potentially take issue with elements of the prosecution's case regarding the date of Muriel's death, but this line was quickly abandoned.

Notice was served on all witnesses except Marilyn Dodd, who was found to have left the country two months earlier to safari in Afghanistan and was now incommunicado, her father having no knowledge of who she was travelling with and her only contact address being the Central Post Office in Kabul. The trial also brought to a standstill the final rehearsals for Joan Littlewood's production of *Forward, or Up Your End* at the Theatre Royal, Stratford East, due to Griff Davies being required to give evidence.

The preparation for the trial had involved over 300 pages of depositions and evidence, 150 exhibits and hundreds of statements. Aubrey Rose worked a total of 234 hours preparing Nizamodeen's defence. Arthur was to be represented by Barry Hudson QC and his junior, Hubert Dunn, and Nizamodeen now by Douglas Draycott QC and his junior, Leonard Woodley, who would go on to become the first person in Britain of Afro-Caribbean heritage to become a QC. The prosecution of the Hosein brothers would be led by the Attorney General, Sir Peter Rawlinson QC and MP.*

Yet, the most powerful piece of evidence that had been uncovered would never feature in the trial.

'My mum found something at the farm,' says Freida:

---

* The Attorney General is the principal legal adviser to the Crown and traditionally always prosecuted in cases of murder by poisoning. Sir Peter Rawlinson's predecessor, Sir Elwyn Jones, had personally chosen to prosecute this case. After the change of government with the June 1970 General Election, his successor fulfilled the obligation.

On the landing, there was a long corridor with stairs at each end. In the middle of this corridor there was a small gap behind a cabinet, just below where the roof started, which you could hide something in. And that was where she found the jewellery.[27]

Rather than inform the police, Elsa apparently telephoned Adam, and they threw the jewellery into the Thames. Elsa never shared the discovery with the police, but Freida says that she did tell an alarmed Arthur about it when visiting him.

It is impossible to ascertain when this discovery was made but being told of it may have been the reason for Arthur's marked change in temperament during his remand – the switch from casual arrogance to 'no comment' answers, frantic accusations of police brutality and attempts to force Nizam to collude in fantastical stories about Robert Maxwell. It may have been made before the full search of the farm had been completed, or it may have been as late as the start of the trial, since Elsa stayed with Adam and his family for three nights while attending the Old Bailey.[28] We will never know. She continued to cover up for her husband for some considerable time, partly because he was still able to manipulate her and also, presumably, through fear for her safety if he was acquitted and a desire to protect her children from the truth.

Arthur and Nizamodeen were both pronounced fit to plead. The trial was set to start on 14 September 1970 and estimated to last a colossal eight weeks. As lawyers stacked the papers up neatly and the McKays prepared to relive their ordeal, Arthur's obsession was with whether his new mohair suit would be ready for the occasion. When it finally arrived, he quarrelled with the tailor, refused to pay, and so never got to wear it.

'The brothers were absolutely dead as far as the kidnapping charge went,' says Peter Rimmer:

> … but quite a few of us couldn't make out why they didn't plead guilty to kidnapping and then say that she had died of natural causes and say where she was. Obviously, they had threatened to kill her, but they could have then argued for a charge of manslaughter.[29]

The brothers may have been stupid, arrogant or deluded enough to believe that a blanket denial was their best hope. However, there was perhaps another reason why they were refusing to confess that Muriel had died of natural causes and to reveal the location of her body – because its discovery would make it abundantly clear that she did not die of natural causes.

16

JUDGEMENT

Walked around the Louvre yesterday, looked at the wonderful paintings.
Muriel McKay, Paris, 7 November 1969.

The trial began on Monday, 14 September 1970. Although the public gallery in Court Number 1 at the Old Bailey can only seat twenty-six people, queuing ghouls waited in hope every morning for a glimpse of the unremarkable brothers accused of such an extraordinary crime.

Each day began with the Hoseins standing in the dock, in the glare of the public gaze if not now in the shadow of the noose. Each day ended with a fleet of crime reporters rushing to the telephone kiosks to call in their copy. For those who were not personally affected by the horrors which were heard there, the stern solemnity of that palace of legality was romanticised by the swirl of silk gowns, the immaculately woven wigs, the might and command that shrinks the stature of whoever stands accused, even a man as deluded and self-important as Arthur Hosein.

The wives of the aldermen and city dignitaries were regular attendees at Regina versus Hosein, having ready access to tickets because of the Old Bailey being run mainly by the City of London.[1] Alick McKay attended every day of the trial, seated with Ian at the end of the press benches, enduring the dispassionate presentation of his family's tragedy because 'I just want to know what happened to my wife'.[2] However, after the early witnesses had been called and described the events of Monday, 29 December, Muriel's name was barely mentioned in Court Number 1, as the court built up an increasingly bewildering picture of the behaviour of the Hoseins in the ensuing six weeks.

'The judge was my old friend, Sebag Shaw,' remembers Aubrey Rose. 'Years before that, as a prosecutor, he did a case for me against Rachman. We very nearly got him into prison. We were trying to protect immigrants from monsters like that.'[3] One is struck, reading the trial transcript, by not only the brilliance of Shaw's judgement throughout an unprecedented case but his impish sense of humour. When John Bailey gave evidence and said that as well as being a barman at the Plough, he worked at Tesco in Ware, Shaw couldn't resist asking, 'Tesco's where?'

'Ware,' Bailey replied.

'Where?' repeated the judge.

'Ware, Hertfordshire,' he repeated.

'I suppose you have heard people make that joke before now?' said the judge.

Bailey replied wearily, 'Yes, many times.'[4]

While it may read as irreverence or insensitivity, judges' occasional light quips, like their fondness for playing the *faux naïf* card, are skilled, gentle tactics for enlivening a jury and keeping it attentive. This was the first trial in modern Britain for kidnapping-for-ransom, which was a common-law offence but not a statutory one, with no prescribed punishment. There was a colossal amount of evidence to be heard, and concentration was essential.

Commentators were struck instantly by how little physical resemblance there was between the Hosein brothers in the cold light of the courtroom, how little they resembled each other in temperament, and how, side by side, they seemed devoid of any emotional bond. A pattern was immediately set when they were asked how they pleaded to the charges. Arthur said, 'Not guilty,' while Nizamodeen, only just audible, said, 'Not guilty, sir.' As the jury of nine men and three women was sworn in, Arthur undid his collar and loosened his tie.

William Cooper, who wrote a detailed account of the trial, noted Nizam's 'strange stillness' and that he hardly ever turned his head, and never once towards Arthur. Cooper noted that while he continually looked straight ahead, there was nothing trance-like about it; it suggested neither stupor nor stupidity.[5] 'Something is going on in his mind and it is probably quite a quick mind.'[6] Nizam fascinated him, but also made him doubt whether Arthur really was the cleverer of the pair.

Arthur's performance at the Old Bailey was increasingly bizarre. 'He appeared in a different suit almost every day, and on the final day in what looked like a dinner suit,' says Aubrey Rose:

But it was monstrous that his mental health was never mentioned once throughout the trial. Arthur himself probably prohibited it, but had they gone into that, it would have been a shorter case; he would probably have been sent to a mental hospital. A question arises here about the process of British criminal law. How can you conceal the most important element in the whole case? Throughout the committal hearings and the trial, Arthur's mental condition showed in his behaviour, yelling at the top of his voice, his clothes, rebuking the judge, yet it was never addressed. He'd been kicked out of the army because of his mental health. How can you have a criminal case of this magnitude tried without the most important factor ever being discussed? It has worried me ever since, when dealing with criminal cases.[7]

The first day of the trial was devoted to the opening speech for the prosecution, delivered by the Attorney General, Sir Peter Rawlinson. Sitting behind him was the Director of Public Prosecutions. Such senior forces were appropriate for a trial which, whatever the outcome, would forge legal history. A tone of solemn theatricality was established the moment he delivered his opening line, 'Mrs McKay disappeared from her home at 20 Arthur Road, Wimbledon. She has never been seen again.' He then presented the Crown's account of the crime and its stern assertion that Muriel was murdered very soon after being kidnapped.

The skeleton of the story would have been familiar to everyone in the courtroom from the vast media coverage of the case, but the second day of the trial began with something no one expected. Observers noticed the intense conversation taking place between Douglas Draycott and his junior, Leonard Woodley – Nizam's defence team. Then, after the Attorney General had completed his five-and-a-half-hour opening speech, but before the first witness was called, Draycott rose and announced to a stunned courtroom that his client wished to make certain admissions. He made clear that they did not involve any knowledge of or intention to commit the offences in the indictment, and after a protestation from Arthur's defence, Barry Hudson QC, the judge made it clear that none of these admissions were to be attributed to Arthur, who was continuing in his denial of everything. Nizam's admissions were:

• He made the application on 19 December 1969 to the GLC for details of ownership, etc. and the handwriting on it is his.

Muriel McKay in the garden of St Mary House, on her way to Ascot for the day.

Alick and Muriel McKay holidaying on the Continent, in the mid 1960s.

The McKay family (standing, from left to right: Ian, Jennifer and Dianne) at home in Australia, February 1957, shortly before they emigrated to England.

St Mary House, Arthur Road, Wimbledon.

The hallway of St Mary House on the evening of 29 December 1969. Note the neat arrangement of the keys and other items on the stairs.

The billhook found at St Mary House.

The porchway of St Mary House.

The entrance to Rooks Farm.

The Volvo boot. Note the large LPG converter, which would have made this an even more appalling place in which to have been enclosed.

Arthur Hosein.

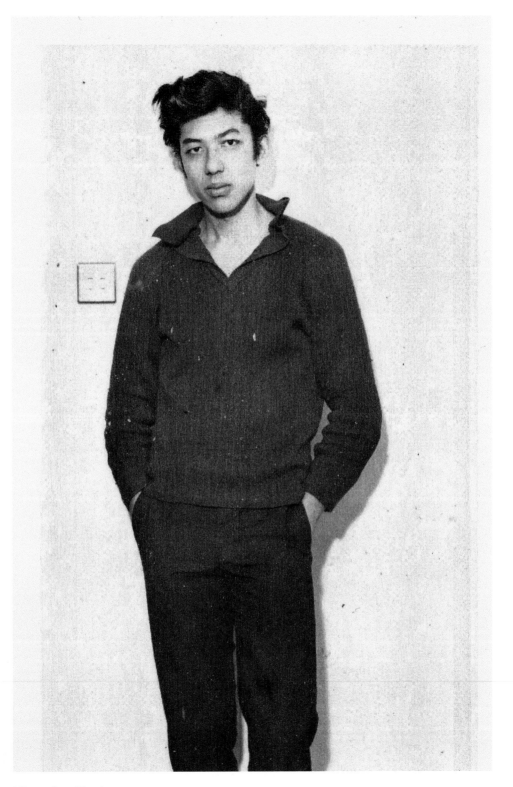

Nizamodeen Hosein.

Rooks Farm.

The ramshackle shed adjoined to the house, where the guard dogs were kept.

Inside Rooks Farm.

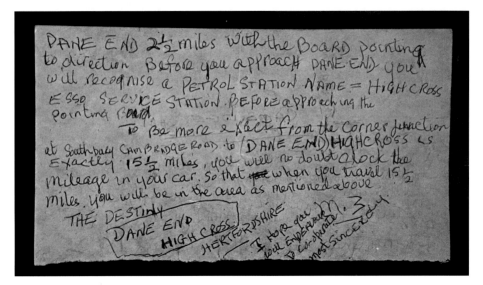

Instructions written on a cigarette packet and left in the Enfield call box on 1 February 1970.

Pieces of Muriel's clothing and shoe sent to the family alongside the final letters.

The grass bank at High Cross, where paper flowers marked the place where the ransom money was to be left.

Detective Inspector John Bland re-enacting his role in the operation which broke the case, with John Minors disguised as Alick McKay. This reconstruction was performed for the BBC's *Worse Than Murder* documentary.

Elsa Hosein and daughter Freida.

Liley Mohammed.

The McKay squad. From left to right: DC Weatherson; DCS Cyril Thomas; DCS Ron Harvey; DS Ken Rexstrew; DCS Bill Smith; DC Keith Robinson; DI John Minors; DC Ray Carter; DS Jim Parker; and Mr F Jackson, a laboratory technician.

The McKay family during the trial. From left to right: Ian, Jennifer, Alick, David Dyer and Dianne.

- On 1 February 1970, he placed two paper flowers where they were subsequently found by the police near the junction of Dane End and Cambridge Road.
- On 6 February 1970, at about 8 p.m., he drove the Volvo motor car, registered XGO 994G, to Gates Used Cars, and he did so in order to look for two suitcases. He drove around and waited at the garage for about an hour and at about 9.50 p.m., he saw two white suitcases on the pavement opposite the minivan.
- On 6 February 1970, he drove the said Volvo motor car to the Raven public house at Berden, arriving there at about 10 p.m.
- At 10.47 p.m. on 6 February he returned in the said Volvo motor car to Gates Used Cars.
- The note containing the registration number of the minivan is in his handwriting.
- The note found by the prison officer that he showed to Adam is in his handwriting.

Draycott made clear that 'neither expressly nor by implication do these admissions involve any knowledge or intention of the offences set out in the indictment'.

The admissions shortened the trial by several weeks and destroyed any last vestige of loyalty between the brothers, but Nizam's defence team now had the challenge of presenting a credible plea for innocence on the charges of murder, blackmail and kidnapping after having admitted his involvement in these connecting matters. The insinuation was that Nizam was acting merely as a lackey, but the success of that claim would depend as much on his performance in the dock as on his barristers' advocacy.

The jury then withdrew while a legal matter was considered. The Attorney General wanted the tape recordings of the M3 telephone calls played in court when the evidence turned to those instances. The judge pondered whether there was any advantage in this beyond dramatic emphasis, to which Sir Peter replied that it would bring out the emphasis and tone of the calls, conveying the full horror of the blackmail to the jury.

Draycott and Hudson acknowledged this point, but Hudson objected to the tapes being played because that could prompt some 'amateur detection by the jury' on whether they could identify the voices as those of the defendants, empowering them to determine the brothers' guilt or innocence without any qualifications in this field.[8] After hearing all the arguments, the judge ruled against the recordings being played, explaining that they did not add much to the weight of evidence and would take up unnecessary time.

The jury returned and the story was then told, piece by piece, by the prosecution witnesses, beginning with Alick McKay. 'Everybody must recognise that this for you is a very difficult ordeal,' he was assured by the judge.[9] William Cooper would later note a poignant moment when, identifying the exhibits, Alick was presented with his wife's handbag. 'It has a special catch,' he explained, and as he demonstrated it, the bag sprung open and Alick smiled, transported for a moment back to happier times.[10]

Dianne remembers:

> At no point did anyone ever prepare us for what was going to happen when we went to court. No one said, 'You go in, you'll see the Hoseins standing there,' there was nothing. It was horrific. To me, as I looked at them, the older brother was mad, and the younger one was evil. I felt that he was the one who killed my mother.

The evidence of the first prosecution witnesses was unchallenged by the defence. The first moment of conflict in the court was curious because it was hard to decipher what motivated it. Tailor Arthur Rosenthal was giving evidence regarding his arrival at the farm on Sunday, 1 February, just as Arthur and Nizam were leaving for London. Arthur was short of cigarettes and Rosenthal had given him a packet of Piccadilly tips, like the one found in the Southbury Road call box with instructions written on it.

After the prosecution had established this, Hudson rose and immediately there was a collision. Hudson asked if it was correct that up until 29 December, he had called at Rooks Farm every month. Rosenthal's reply was, 'Why?'

After the judge intervened, he answered that he had not called every month, more like once in three or four months. Hudson then suggested Rosenthal had not told the truth accurately. Rosenthal was extraordinarily defensive, saying that he only called on 1 February as he had not seen Arthur for some time and felt it was time that he saw him for some business.

'That is the truth, I can't help it, that is the truth. I can't help the truth,' he protested.

The judge assured him, 'Nobody is asking you to.'[11]

Hudson pressed on, suggesting that he went there to deliver some trimmings, referencing a bill which Elsa later received, and also suggesting that, in fact, Rosenthal only gave Arthur one cigarette. This triggered more defensiveness, with the judge saying, 'There is no need to get into a tizzy about it. Just keep cool.'[12]

Things then deteriorated further, despite the judge trying to make light of the disharmony. Rosenthal seemed terrified of being associated with the farm and protested that at the time that he planned to visit, the place was not 'taboo'.

Incredibly, Hudson said, 'You see, I suggest, quite bluntly, you are lying about this.'

When Rosenthal withdrew, the judge thanked him, to which he replied, 'It has not been a pleasant experience, sir.'[13]

Hudson had gone rather a long way over the top seemingly just to try and disassociate Arthur from the cigarette packet, which suggested an air of desperation about the defence, even this early in the proceedings. He fared badly with the next prosecution witness too, DCI Arthur Brine, who remained impervious as Hudson challenged his findings, albeit with a lighter touch this time. Brine had served as a fingerprint officer for twenty-two years and, impressively, revealed that it was seven years before one was permitted to give evidence.

At the end of Bill Smith's cross-examination by the Attorney General, his sincere denial of ever having struck Arthur was put on record, although Arthur's retraction of the claim after his outburst at Wimbledon was not mentioned. Hudson then asked Smith to confirm that his investigations had revealed no previous convictions for violence or dishonesty from Arthur, only an army court martial for desertion, a further conviction for escaping from custody and motoring offences. Draycott had no questions for Smith and no need for any similar denials, since Nizamodeen had made no complaints of ill-treatment from the police.

An important prosecution witness was farmer Leonard Smith, who confirmed that the billhook found at Arthur Road was the one that he had lost at Rooks Farm. When the Attorney General repeated back part of his evidence, the judge wryly remarked, 'I am not sure that Mr Smith has not put it more picturesquely than you.'[14]

Smith was an elderly man with a strong rural accent, who hobbled rheumatically, but he was unshakeable as Hudson continually challenged his damning evidence, although his demonstration of how to sharpen the billhook evoked laughter even from the dock. Hudson challenged him on a piffling matter of the Hoseins visiting him on 27 December, trying to bolster Arthur's limp claims of being ill at the time and over the days of the kidnapping. Clearly moved by the pastoral flavour of the rustic-voiced farmer's evidence of runaway pigs and cattle waiting at the gate, when Smith withdrew, the judge said, 'Thank you, very much. You go back to your cows and pigs and look after them.'[15]

Liley Mohammed looked frightened as she stepped into the witness box to give evidence against Arthur, who was watching just feet away. Although she was a prosecution witness, on one matter her evidence worked for him, not against him. She repeated that he did not go out on New Year's Day. She was unshakeable on this point, so the prosecution's line was rather to suggest that Nizam could have made the calls to Dianne that evening, since Liley stated that, unlike Arthur, Nizam did go out, for about ninety minutes, albeit in the afternoon rather than the evening (the calls were at 7.45 p.m.). The fact that Nizam had left Liley alone with Arthur, despite promising not to, and that the details of his absence could never be explained adequately, were enough to suggest that one of the brothers could have made those calls – and that was enough for the Crown, though Liley's evidence on this point would remain something of a puzzle.

Regarding Boxing Day, Draycott asked, 'Now, I am not going to ask you any details about it, but there was some trouble that night, between Arthur and Nizam, was there not?' It was detrimental to Nizam's defence and the prosecution's case not to bring up these aspects, although perhaps the evidence of the attempted rape of Liley by Arthur risked, for the prosecution, giving credence to Nizam's defence of being terrified of Arthur. Draycott made it clear that Nizam complained to the police and stayed with Liley through the night because she was frightened, and also that he had been 'very upset' when the calf died. He ended by asking Liley to confirm that Nizam had 'always been quite gentle and kind to you', which she did.

The second week of the trial began, and the case for the Crown concluded, with forensic evidence regarding the handwriting, paper and paper flowers. The jury then retired while Hudson made a potentially devastating submission. He argued that as the evidence stood, count one – that of murder – should not proceed. He cited the case of Michael Onufrejczyc* and quoted,

---

* Onufrejczyc was tried in 1954 for the murder of Stanislaw Sykut, who it was alleged he had murdered for possession of his half of the farm they owned. His death sentence was demoted to life imprisonment, of which he served eleven years. Like the McKay case, the absence of a body and the backdrop of a farm inspired stories that Sykut had been 'fed to the pigs'.

'On a charge of murder the corpus delicti may be proved by such circumstantial evidence as leaves open no other rational hypothesis than murder.'[16] In that case, there was evidence that inferred that if the victim was dead, the circumstances pointed to the death not being a natural death, but Hudson stressed that here, there was 'not one scintilla of evidence' that Muriel was ever at the farm, although he accepted that there was prima facie evidence of abduction and kidnapping.[17]

However, the judge was firm that the letters challenged a charge of manslaughter. Draycott suggested that Liley's evidence pointed to a possibility of Muriel still being alive in January and held elsewhere, but the judge stated that the initial calls from M3 made it clear that if they did not have the money by 31 December, 'we will kill her'. The judge acknowledged that the defence were right to make the submission, but he ruled that the count of murder would remain for the jury to decide upon. The trial resumed, and Hudson began his defence by calling his client, Arthur Hosein.

Arthur's puffed-up performance was, at times, as preposterous as the scheme that had led him to the Old Bailey. He crossed to the witness box wearing a black, single-breasted suit with a U-shaped waistcoat, black bow tie and white shirt, the collar and cuffs of which were black with white polka dots. Hudson asked him to confirm that he was a tailor and designer, and he replied, 'By profession I am a fashion designer, cutter, clothing manufacturer, including trousers.' He had lived at Rooks Farm for 'approximately two years before my apprehension'.[18]

When asked about his work routine, he immediately put his closure of the shop in London in the context of 'the last Labour Government', and his move to the farm down to selective employment tax and 'pressure on the small business man'.[19] On whether he pressed the trousers after finishing at home or at a steam press, he said that if the material needed 'experience and craftmanship, I do it myself'.

He spoke of his life before his arrest in the present tense, as if this trial was merely a brief interruption in it. Trade did not get slack for him at Christmas because 'I am well known'.[20] He described being ill over Christmas as having ''flu internally, although my out-showings do not show my suffering inside'.[21] His lofty, clumsy sentences bore out the words of the owner of the drinking club, who spoke of him using big words but in the wrong places.[22]

Arthur claimed that on Monday, 29 December, he woke as usual, between 11.30 a.m. and noon. Contradicting his original answers on the night of his arrest, he said that between 2.30 p.m. and 3 p.m., he and Nizam visited the Patemans for half an hour to buy a calf, which they put in the boot, and returned to the farm. Arthur strived to be ornate and came across as odd. When asked whether he saw anyone else when visiting Pateman, he replied, 'At the time I trespassed on his land, there was nobody visible.'[23]

He was asked several times to take his hand away from his mouth so that he could be heard and confessed that he was 'a bit nervy'.[24] He said that David Coote telephoned Rooks Farm between 5.15 p.m. and 5.30 p.m., and that he spoke to him. Unwisely, Arthur referred to 'David Coote, there', causing the judge to ask whether he was in court. Hudson confirmed that he was but that he would not be called as a witness.

Arthur testified that, after Nizam had made him some coffee and biscuits, which was all that he could manage due to being ill, he retired to bed at 7.30 p.m. with a bottle of whisky and a couple of bottles of ginger ale. When asked whether he went to the toilet subsequently, he said that he did, at about 9.45 p.m., a degree of accuracy that seemed highly suspicious. He said that when he looked from the toilet window, he saw that his Volvo was gone. He had ignored a call at 8 p.m. (presumably he based this detail on having heard Liley's evidence about calling the farm that evening) but had telephoned his wife to say that he was ill and to come back.* He said that he answered the 10.30 p.m. call from Liley thinking that it was Elsa.

Tuesday, 30 December was the other day for which the brothers badly lacked alibis. Arthur's recall for this day was rather less impressive, something which, with dreadful irony, he blamed on being 'kept in captivity'.[25]

Moving to the M3 calls, Arthur said he not only did not make them, but generally did not telephone people at all, despite just having told the court about trying to telephone his wife. He was asked whether he had ever heard anyone else talk in such a way, and after waffling a little – and saying that if Bill Smith had not treated him badly he would have revealed this earlier – he gave the court his moronic yarn about how one evening he woke at 2 a.m. and heard voices, and when he came downstairs he saw four men with Nizam, drinking his whisky. 'I believe one is British, one is American, and I believe two is French, sort of Maurice Chevalier** sort of type,' he said, adding that they had influence in the House of Commons and were going to get Nizam

---

* The only call he made to Elsa was on New Year's Day, as the call logs prove.

** Maurice Chevalier (1888–1972), debonair French actor and singer.

permanent residence in the United Kingdom. He did not dwell as he was embarrassed at being 'in his shorts' and could not say when this was as he was 'not equipped with any computer'.[26]

When describing Nizam, he called him 'a stranger in a strange land', a useful phrase which Nizam himself would then regularly deploy when striving to evoke sympathy, and Arthur said, 'He respects me. It is sort of fear … the correct word is respect.'[27]

When pressed about his movements after leaving the Raven, Arthur started to ramble and tested the patience of the judge and his own counsel. The upshot was that Nizam drove him straight home from the Raven and he went to bed. He denied asking for change from the landlady, but in a typically boastful way: 'I spend a considerable amount of money, and if I wanted change, I had enough change in my possession'.[28]

Arthur denied all knowledge of the billhook that Leonard Smith identified. When asked why he had borrowed another from George Cuda, he said that a heifer calf had died, 'not from any disease, being not fed very well'[29] and they had intended to bury it but Pateman suggested that it could be skinned, boiled and fed to the dogs, which Nizam then did.

He denied owning the tin of Elastoplast, insisting that the police must have planted it, despite Elsa having said that she had seen it about the house. He claimed not to know where Wimbledon was, but he knew it from the days when he raced greyhounds.

He said that Bill Smith 'beat the hell out of me while he was under the influence of liquor', and that Smith had a bottle of scotch in front of him and had been 'drinking while he spat on my face and kicked my belly and I fell to the ground'. He claimed that Minors held his head to avoid him fainting when he hit the ground, that he was beaten for two days and starved for three, and that he was woken every ten minutes for two nights.[30]

After Hudson had finished collecting Arthur's round of denials and untruths, none of which he seemed inclined to make capital from, Draycott rose. He adopted Arthur's description of Nizam as 'a stranger in a strange land' and from there, got him to agree that he was a comparative stranger as far as the detailed geography of London and its surroundings went, implying that he could not have travelled to certain places without Arthur's guidance.

When asked about the men supposedly talking to Nizam, after some nonsense about how, if he were bailed, he would 'most probably take up detection' himself to find them, Arthur stunned the court by claiming that he recognised one of the men though, not being a vindictive man, he did not wish to say who it was.[31] He was then asked, and said, 'I believe it is Robert Maxwell, the Member of Parliament.'[32]

Because of this, the police had to visit Maxwell at his home, Headington Hill Hall in Oxfordshire, to collect a statement from him confirming that he had no knowledge of Rooks Farm or the Hoseins.[33] 'Maxwell's lawyer arrived at the Old Bailey the next day,' says Aubrey Rose, 'instructed to say that on no occasion was he ever in that house. Arthur had made the whole story up. There was an element of racism in him, as Maxwell was Jewish, and Arthur's anti-Semitism came out vividly at the end of the trial.'[34]

Finally, it was the Attorney General's turn. Arthur probably felt worthy of the attention of such an eminent figure, but he was far from deferential, becoming openly combative at times. Arthur did admit to having seen the interview with Rupert Murdoch on television, which he had been interested in because of the Christine Keeler confessions. 'I have a difference of opinion against him for republishing a person who have already been damaged in his political career,' he explained.[35]

Sir Peter returned to Arthur's alibi for the day of the kidnapping again and asked him to point out David Coote in the courtroom. He asked, 'Mr Coote here is a solicitor, a solicitor of the Supreme Court. Is he going to come and give evidence?'[36]

When pressed on the Volvo sightings in Wimbledon, Arthur said that it wasn't as if 'Mr Hosein was the only person to have a Volvo' and if the witness was so certain that it was him, why did he not take down the registration, to which the judge crisply replied, 'He did not know somebody in the vicinity was going to be kidnapped.'[37]

Arthur suggested that Leonard Smith's identification of the billhook was because he probably had a grudge against him over a deal on some livestock, his claim that 'farmers collaborate amongst themselves'[38] echoing the psychiatric report that noted how many of Arthur's utterances 'had a flavour of persecutory ideas'.[39]

Struggling to avoid being linked to the pages of the *People* found at Arthur Road, one of which bore his fingerprint, Arthur suggested that perhaps one of the mysterious four men took it with them after leaving the farm and added that while he was not 'an intellectual genius as you, Sir Peter', he had enough common sense not to take his own paper or drive his own car on a crime. The judge asked him to remember his good manners and warned him not to try to score off counsel 'because it will not help anybody'.[40]

Arthur claimed that the fight between him and Nizam over Liley was due to him diligently trying to prevent Nizam from driving her back to London when he had been drinking. His explanation of his fingerprint being over the stamp on the envelope containing the first ransom letter was that he had stamped many envelopes in his house and this one was obviously then used by someone else, hence why his print was only on the stamp.

When asked to point out in a photograph of the farm where one entered the dog shed, he left the witness box, saying to the jury, 'It is all right, I am not dangerous,' only for the judge to order him back to the witness box.[41] He displayed complete confidence that he would be freed, saying of the shed, 'As a matter of fact, I am going to have it taken away.'

Sir Peter successfully trapped Arthur in his own narrative regarding his story of the mysterious four men. Since he had offered to cooperate with the police all he could, in their 'very difficult case', why did he not mention this to them at the time?

However, a potentially incriminating piece of evidence revealed by Arthur was not picked up on. It seems that no one at the trial registered it. Arthur told the court that the four men said they would never be caught because 'a strange person would be used',[42] namely Nizam. That unusual phrase 'strange person' also occurs in one of the notes, regarding the person who will be collecting the money: 'We can assure you that we will not be caught because we are sending a totally strange person, who will be paid to do a job.' (The phrase presumably should be 'a total stranger'.) When Sir Peter turned to the ransom letters, which displayed a similarly rambling and chaotic use of language, two misspellings were highlighted, both of which Arthur said he spelled that way. On the phrase 'his wife will be disposed off', he was asked whether he thought any word there was misspelled, and he said, 'No.'

Arthur conceded that the pieces of Muriel's clothing could have been cut with tailors' shears, and his vanity and eccentricity returned when he was asked whether his hair was bushy on 6 February, the night that he was spotted in the Volvo by Gates garage. He seized the opportunity to tell the court that 'once a week I attend the barber for a wash, set, face massage and scalp massage, and so on'.[43]

Arthur's final declamation in the dock was that he was in sympathy with the McKays, having a mother himself, a line which inadvertently echoed something that M3 said about Muriel reminding him of his own mother. He finished by holding his hands up and decrying, 'These hands are artistic, not destructive. I believe in the preservation of man, all man, and not the destruction, and that is what I am living for.'[44]

Those would not be the last words the court heard from him, but for now, he had exhausted them with his cockamamie stories and word salads. After watching his performance in the witness box, William Cooper sensed that Arthur felt that he could do anything, an outlook which would certainly have empowered him to enact such an outrageous crime. And while, like Nizam, with his fictitious checkout-girl romance, Arthur had no great gift for invention, Cooper was struck by the occasional flash of verisimilitude in Arthur's nonsense stories, such as his embarrassment at being in his shorts when coming downstairs and finding the four men in the house. He pondered whether the reason was that when Arthur lied, it was 'as real to him as reality'.[45]

Now the parade of witnesses trooped in to build some vague defence of Arthur, but for the most part, claims that Arthur behaved in his usual way over Christmas and New Year, or that he did things that no person would surely do while engaged in such a crime, rather than casting doubt on his guilt, merely confirmed his strangeness and irrationality. The first defence witnesses were the Patemans, the farmers whom Arthur and Nizam had bought a calf from on, according to the defence, the afternoon of either 29 or 30 December. The defence strove, without success, to suggest that it was the former.

Charles Pateman told the court that the brothers visited at between 2.30 p.m. and 3 p.m. on one of those two days, and stayed for about a quarter of an hour, Arthur looking unkempt and complaining that he was missing his wife. Pateman's mother maintained the ledger, and Charles Pateman had reported the sale to her that evening, 'but she was queer at the time. I don't know whether she booked it a day or two afterwards.'[46] He became fairly certain that the visit was on the 30th and examined the ledger for the day. The entry read, 'Friesian calf sold, Hosein, Rooks Farm' and the '3' of '30th' appeared to have been written over an erroneous '2'.

Draycott then tried to put more weight on the 29th being the date of the sale. Pateman said that they were expecting their cow to calf on Christmas Day, but it calved on Boxing Day, and 'we never keep a calf on a cow less than three or four days', which got no nearer to the date. The conclusion was that his mother had written '2' first, then altered it to '3'. Hudson, surprisingly, said that the visit was not an alibi, since the timing did not preclude the possibility of Arthur being in Wimbledon at 6 p.m. (although it would almost rule him out of being sighted there at 4.40 p.m.).

Hudson merely wanted to establish that Arthur had his mind on buying a calf that day, yet time and again we see the Hoseins behaving with a perplexing detachment at key points in the case, such as with the visits from the police, the visits to Thornton Heath and Norbury, relaxing in the Raven during the final ransom drop, giving Captain Barclay permission for the hunt to cross the land on Boxing Day,* and entertaining Liley in the wake of Muriel's disappearance. Since the calf the brothers purchased would soon die of neglect, the visit to the Patemans was surely, if not to establish an alibi, to assume a pose of normality.

However, if the visit was on the afternoon of the 30th, Muriel must have been alive, so why risk leaving her unattended? The previous evening it was considered enough for Nizam to go to London by himself and leave Arthur unaccounted for, so why did both brothers feel the need to be seen somewhere else on this day?

I think the most likely explanation is that this visit was actually made on 31 December, shortly before the brothers drove to London to collect Liley. Herbert Pateman followed his brother into the witness box and said that his mother made the entry on about 2 January 1970, which conveniently explained the erroneous '2' and also drew possibilities further away from the 29th. The confusion worked slightly in the Hoseins' favour, but also makes it just as likely that the visit had been on 31 December.

The next peculiarity was Gerald Gordon's evidence of visiting the farm at 7.30 a.m. on New Year's Eve to collect trousers. Interestingly, he added that he ticked Arthur off when he next saw him, and Arthur said, 'Man, I was well ill.'[47] The telephone operator said that the M3 caller from Epping had used 'man' several times, yet Arthur had said during his evidence that he did not tend to use it. However, this illustrated Arthur's dishonesty more than it linked him with the Epping call, which everything pointed to Nizam having made. Additionally, Nizam had been in England less than a year and had a more pronounced West Indian accent and more frequent use of patois than his highfalutin brother.

Elsa Hosein's evidence only further added to the confusion. Publicly loyal to her husband, she described the relationship between him and Nizam as 'brotherly. Quite good.'

Did she ever see Arthur ill-treat or threaten him?

'Never.'[48]

---

* It was not established at the trial whether Arthur granted permission for the hunt to cross his land generally or just for Boxing Day 1969.

Elsa said that Arthur complained of a chesty cold for a long time before she left for Germany and though he was still complaining of it when she returned, he worked normally. 'He is a very hard worker,' she said, 'You will never find another like him.'[49]

She got flustered and muddled when trying to remember which evening Nizam came home soaked, and Arthur interjected that she should be given a glass of water. When she recalled fifteen or twenty policemen arriving to arrest the brothers, she said, 'and they were not very nice either.'

The judge quipped, 'It was not a social call, was it?'[50]

Arthur was apoplectic. 'He is impartial?' he yelled. 'I refuse to sit down here. That judge. If he is partial. Take me down.'[51] He was hustled down the stairs and out of sight while his defence requested a short adjournment. When the court returned, a doctor relayed that Arthur wished to apologise.

'Oh, do not worry about it,' said the judge, perhaps aware that he had been rather insensitive.

Adam Hosein's role in the trial was a small one, but it showed that while there was some vestige of fraternal loyalty towards Arthur, the unpopular Nizam was now an outcast. He confirmed Nizam's visit on 29 December and that he had been told that Arthur was ill in bed. He also said that when he next spoke to Nizam, in January, Nizam mentioned 'some people helping him to obtain a visa, a permanent visa in the country'. This was Adam backing up Arthur's story. He also stated that Nizam had never complained to him about Arthur striking him, and that he was not particularly excitable, but he only knew him for a short while, having not seen him between 1960 and May 1969.

The other interesting piece of evidence was that Adam visited Malta on business in June 1969, while Nizam was staying with him.[*] It of course rang bells with the reference in one of the M3 calls to having to 'leave tonight for Malta' and to Nizam telling Ernest Woollard, when he returned the fork that he had borrowed, that he was going to Malta. The suggestion was that Nizam had remembered the name from his time staying with Adam and had used it when talking to Woollard and as M3 because it sounded impressive. In fact, those M3 calls were probably made by Arthur, so perhaps Arthur was eager to emulate Adam too. Watching him leave the witness box, William Cooper felt

---

[*] Nizam did not accompany Adam on the trip, instead having the use of his car while he was away.

that he would 'like to have heard a lot more from Adam' and perceived him to be 'the ablest and most powerful of the brothers'.[52]

The turning point of the trial came with the evidence of Dr Julius Grant, whom Arthur's defence team had called to give opinions on the handwriting, paper and fingerprint evidence. Grant was a small, slight man, and Secretary of the Forensic Science Society. He was regularly called for the defence, though he had no recognisable credentials as a fingerprint expert.

Possessing a doctorate in chemistry, Grant had begun his career working for a large firm of papermakers but had become fascinated with forgery after discovering that a supposedly erasure-proof paper for cheques could easily be treated with a chemical to erase the amount, which could then be overwritten with a different one. He assisted in making wartime ration books virtually forgery-proof by protecting the paper with chemicals and, in a later investigation for the *Sunday Times*, had judged the Mussolini diaries to be fakes. 'I had great respect for him,' says Peter Rimmer. 'I spent a lot of time with him, and he struck me as a gentle soul. But it was his evidence that wrecked it for the brothers more than anybody's.'[53]

Grant agreed with the prosecution that the torn page used for a ransom note and the pages left in the exercise book were similar, based on the weight per square metre of each sheet.* He also noted that the dimensions, the number of lines, the line intervals and the line colour, the staple indentations on the centre pages and the distance of the staples from the top and bottom of the page tallied. (On a similar exercise book that he bought as a control the line colour was a deeper blue.) The verdict was that both sheets were likely to have come from the same double page in the centre of the book. He also felt that the paper flowers were almost certainly made from the same paper as that found at the farm. Grant's meticulousness was impressive, not that these judgements aided the defence – but so far, so good.

---

*   One way in which paper is categorised is by weight per unit (grams per square metre, or gsm). Paper is bought and sold on this measurement. Exercise books are bought by retailers on weight and sold by area, since if the paper is too heavy, they get fewer books from it. The trade tolerance is 5 per cent, so for a 50 gsm requirement, you could get 47.5g or 52.5g on different pages. Grant deduced that these sheets were 58.4 gsm and 56 gsm, the difference between them being 2.4g, which is 4.3 per cent of 56g and therefore an acceptable variance, meaning that they could have come from the same exercise book.

He disputed much of the fingerprint evidence but agreed with the Crown that the handwriting on the letters was Muriel's. As for the ransom notes, he found similarities on them to Arthur's handwriting, but had reasonable doubt that Arthur wrote both. Also, he concluded that when compared to Nizam's writing, 'Arthur's resembles the questioned documents more closely than Nizam's, without hesitation'.[54] Not wanting to end his cross-examination on that point, Hudson asked Grant to reassert that there was nothing definite in the handwriting, which he did.

Draycott then referred him to Nizam's handwriting again, and Grant pointed to the name, written in block capitals at the top of the page, and some of the handwriting in the ransom notes. What Grant had not realised was that the name 'Nizamodeen Hosein' at the top of the page was not in Nizam's handwriting but was merely a heading. Aubrey Rose remembers, 'At this point, I was seated beside John Minors. He leaned over to me and said, "Aubrey, this man's a fool. That's my writing at the top of the page".'[55]

The judge helped Grant to regain some credibility by saying that, even so, there were some common features. 'Mr Minors, no doubt, breathes again,' said Draycott. The general conclusion was that neither brother could be said conclusively to have written the notes or not to have done, but if one of them did, it was more likely to have been Arthur.

Now the Attorney General stood up. He began by reminding the court that on the three areas on which Grant had given his opinion, paper, fingerprints and handwriting, the Crown had provided three separate experts, and added that Grant had also been giving evidence in Court Number 3 earlier that day, on footprints. Rather than suggesting that Grant was a polymath, the implication was that he was a jack of all trades and master of none.

Grant was asked whether he had worked in a fingerprint bureau. Grant could only admit to three weeks' work earlier that year in Cyprus, in relation to the attempted assassination of Archbishop Makarios. Had he even been to the fingerprint branch at Scotland Yard? Once, he said, many years ago, on an afternoon visit. He was forced to admit to no formal training but said that he read widely and attended lectures. Sir Peter compared this with DCI Brine telling the court that he had been with the Fingerprint Bureau for twenty-two years and had to serve seven years with them before being allowed to give evidence.

Sir Peter got Grant to agree that the eight different marks on five separate exhibits were all made by the same palm or finger, whoever it belonged to, and did some astounding work getting him to concede on certain points.

Grant was given some respite when the court rose for the day, but on the following morning came the disaster. Sir Peter summarised that Grant did not deny that the marks were all made by the same person, and the points on which Grant agreed with Brine totalled sixty-two, 'And those coincident sequences, on those two particular exhibits, combined with the fact that there are 62 marks of Arthur Hosein's on those objects, does that not point, to you, to whose palm and finger impressions were on those objects?'[56]

'Yes, it does point,' agreed Brine.

'It points to Arthur Hosein?' asked Sir Peter.

'Yes,' conceded Grant.

'British policing was one of the strictest in the world with fingerprints,' explains Peter Rimmer:

Some countries only required six points to prove that it was a match, but in the UK, you needed more points; I think at that time, eight was a partial and ten was a full print. He had argued that there weren't enough visible to say that it was a full print, but then he agreed with the prosecution, and at that point I thought, 'That's it, it's over, the defence took a big chance with him and those were the nails in the coffins of the brothers now.'[57]

After some paltry evidence from further witness, the flimsy case for Arthur's defence was complete.

Now Draycott rose and called his client, Nizamodeen Hosein. Remarkably, even before he had opened his mouth the court had cast him in a sympathetic light, the judge telling him to say if he felt under any stress or strain or if he needed a glass of water.

Draycott began by asking him some basic questions about himself to get him used to being in the box, but immediately the judge told him that he couldn't be heard. The answer to every question, including whether he had ever seen Muriel, was a denial, but his constant failure to make himself heard openly exasperated even his own counsel. The judge requested that a microphone be hung around his neck.

When asked about trouble between him and Arthur, he said, 'Whenever I don't do something he told me to, he have a go at me,' and when asked to elaborate he said, 'Punch me … on my chest and face.'[58] It was the beginning of a narrative that was at times plausible, and at times exasperating in its lunacy. Having admitted to making the GLC application, he said that he was merely obeying orders from Arthur, who told him to give a false name, but he did not ask what it was about because he did not want any trouble from him. This suggestion that he was robotically carrying out instructions is somewhat contradicted by the statement of the clerk, Maureen Callanan, who noted how persistent for the information Nizam was, and that he would not accept merely being told that the car belonged to the *News of the World*, claiming that he had already established that and had tried enquiring there.

It was noticeable that when Nizam was being truthful, such as in his account of Liley's night of fear at the farm, he was considerably more detailed. He claimed to have been at the farm at the time of Muriel's abduction and that Arthur had been ill. Interestingly, when talking about his late-night visit to Thornton Heath, he said that he needed to check that Arthur was asleep first because he would not be given permission to use the car, and looking into his bedroom, 'I saw the feather bed. I could not see him, he was under it', a detail clearly robbed from a detail in Arthur's testimony about being ill on the night of the kidnapping. This was not the first and would not be the last instance of Nizam purloining his brother's words.

As for his mysterious absence on New Year's Day, he said that he went out just before 3 p.m. to the pub, since there is no chemist nearby, had a pint of bitter, and returned twenty-five minutes later, going straight to the barn to start the feeding. His voice dropped whenever the evidence centred around an incriminating period, such as the night of 1 February, on which he obeyed Arthur's instruction to stick the paper flowers in the bank but did not ask why.

His evidence reached its most absurd level with the Gates garage sightings of him. He said that Arthur had told him to collect two black suitcases, but when he drove by and saw them, he was looking for an excuse not to pick them up and saw that they were white, not black. (One wonders how Arthur would have treated the news that Nizam was empty-handed when he arrived at the Raven because he had not seen any white suitcases, only a couple of black ones.) And if his excuse for not collecting them was because they were the wrong colour – but he had no reason to think there was anything sinister about them – why did he circle them so much?

The jury was sent out while Hudson made a submission for Nizam's previous convictions for violence to be brought out. Interestingly, Draycott argued that he had endeavoured throughout the trial:

... not to bring in any more than I have to the character of Arthur ... I have not brought in evidence relating to his relationship , which could be relevant to this case, with his wife; and I do not want to be pushed into the position where, in order to corroborate these matters, I have got to call his own solicitor, which I would find very distressing.[59]

Draycott seemed to be saying that bringing in evidence of Nizam's previous convictions would result in a dirty fight, a muck-slinging war of attrition. The judge considered that if Nizamodeen was giving evidence which undermined the defence of his co-accused, or supported the prosecution's case, it let him in for cross-examination on his character.

The court rose for the weekend. Hudson was hopeful that he could shatter any illusions that the court were under about Nizamodeen being a sympathetic victim in this case.

Hudson started the following week as he meant to go on, asking the mumbling Nizam whether he was trying to disguise his voice. Why had he refused to speak into the telephone at the police station?

'I never knew what it was about, sir.'[60]

Hudson proposed that Nizam's fear of Arthur was a complete invention and proceeded to try to prove it. He began with a brilliant point. Nizam was supposedly scared of Arthur all though his custody, yet he had been brave enough to report him to the police on 28 December.

He could glean no intelligent answer, and when it came to Nizam's 'I could get myself out of 90 per cent of this' remark and why it did not progress, Nizam said that he simply couldn't speak the words, despite in fact having said, 'Let me think about it a little longer'. Rather than it being hard for him to have told tales on his brother, his silence was surely because he hadn't got his invented story straight. He eventually fell silent.

Hudson was now relentless. On 29 December, if Nizam was at the farm at 8 p.m., why did he not answer Liley's telephone call?

'I never heard it.'

Why did he not return to Trinidad?

'I wanted to roam, sir, I wanted to further my education.'[61] Adam saying that Nizam had told him that after Christmas some people were trying to help him get a visa was, he said, untrue.

Hudson then played his ace. He suggested that, in truth, Nizam was not frightened of people but was quite capable of dealing with a situation involving violence. 'You were brave enough apparently to use a knife in Trinidad, were you not, when you came before the magistrates' court for using a knife on your brother aged 35?' he scolded.

'It was an accident,' insisted Nizam, claiming that his brother collared him from behind while he was peeling fruit in the kitchen. He turned around 'and the knife caught him in his tummy'.[62] On the charge of beating his father, he said that it was because he had come home drunk, but denied that he had beaten anyone. He ended with his usual plea that he was new to this country, which was hardly relevant to the matter in hand.

It was now the Attorney General's turn, but Hudson had already done some of the heavy lifting. Sir Peter felt that while visiting family over the octave of Christmas was traditional in Trinidad, driving out late at night from Hertfordshire to London in the cold and rain to see people for ten minutes strained credulity.

There was a telling moment when he was asked about going to the pub on New Year's Day at 3 p.m. When asked whether the pub was open when he got there, he suddenly changed his mind and said that it was either midday or in the evening that he visited it, realising that it probably closed at 3 p.m. When things got tricky, he fell back to bleating, 'It is very confusing because it was my first year in England.'[63]

After Sir Peter had finished with him, the court adjourned for ten minutes to allow a tearful Nizamodeen to compose himself. When it returned, Draycott decided to even the score with Hudson on the character of his client, by bringing up the matter of Elsa being scared of Arthur, which would mean that she would have been unable to help Nizam if he had complained to her about his beatings. Pre-empting the evidence, the judge said, 'It may be that he was a wife beater, but it does not necessarily follow that he should knock his brother about.'[64]

After mentioning the beating of Elsa in front of David Coote and his girlfriend, Nizam said that there were other heated incidents, but Arthur always appeared to be perfectly in control of himself, 'He is a ruler, sir, the master', or, as Captain Barclay called him, 'King Hosein'. To try and leave a palatable impression, Draycott asked Nizam to confirm that on neither occasion before the court in Trinidad was he convicted. There was some confusion about this, and on this occasion the judge let it go. The statement was probably not entirely accurate, since one of the judgements was effectively a suspended sentence, with Nizam saying that he was provoked, and on the second occasion, the same magistrate took into account his 'age and previous good record'.

In ending Nizam's seventeen hours in the witness box, Draycott asked him about his reference to Malta when borrowing the fork, and he explained that he always thought how lucky Adam was to go there. Adam enjoyed such places as he did not like the cold. Draycott ended on a decidedly weak note, asking Nizam to confirm that not once in the month since his arrest did he ever ask Arthur where Muriel was.

William Cooper, after hearing of Nizam's violence in Trinidad, while believing that his fear of Arthur was not total invention,[65] now decided that his was 'all a performance, a performance which can be so convincing as to be touching'.[66] He also noted that Nizam's English was better than Arthur's, which was cluttered with pidgin eccentricities, and when Nizam was audible, he could come up with 'the perfect, evasive, side-stepping, self-preserving answer'.

Sir Peter made a cannily slick closing speech, with Hudson stressing in his that Muriel may have died not from brutal murder but from criminal irresponsibility. He attacked Nizam, suggesting that his fear of Arthur was an invention 'to escape the possibility of conviction at this trial. He has a quick and ingenious mind and when a man is in a desperate position, he is prepared to look for every possible way out.'[67]

Draycott found Nizam's defence to be almost unique because 'there is no conflict with the prosecution evidence about him but only on the interpretation to be put on that evidence'. He referred to two previous murder trials without a body, that of Gay Gibson,* who disappeared from her cabin during a sea voyage, and the aforementioned Michael Onufrejczyc case. He accepted that Muriel 'has now been disappeared and not heard of for a very long time. The probability is, poor soul, she is dead.'[68] The next step from there was that she died in captivity, the difficulty being that 'she may well have died as opposed to being killed. She was a nervous woman, subjected to a course of treatment which would have put anyone under the greatest strain' and he argued that the jury had to be sure of intent to kill in order to convict of murder.

To the consternation of the court, Douglas Draycott then addressed the gruesome rumour about the pigs. He pointed out that forensic scientists were

---

*   Gay Gibson (1926–47) was a British actress whose killer, James Camb, confessed to having pushed her body out of the porthole of her cabin as the ship crossed the Atlantic.

not easy to fool and 'if anything had gone on like that at the farm, neither of these men has the skill or ability' to fool them. It was, in retrospect, a terrible mistake to put the rumour on the record, fatally legitimising it and empowering the press to splash it about without shouldering any blame. It made no odds that the rumour had been raised purely to be quashed. So much talk of choppers and of carving up a calf and feeding it to the dogs allowed it to gain currency, and it has endured ever since, with the most extraordinary and depressing persistence.

Draycott accepted that there was 'plenty of evidence against Nizam', and plenty of evidence that Nizam feared Arthur, including the attack that led to them being separated in prison. He also revealed that one of the first things Nizam said when asked to tell what he knew was 'Arthur will kill me'. He addressed and dismissed Arthur's claims of police brutality, acknowledging that Nizam's confidence in the police 'was such that he asks to see them alone, and was obviously about to spill the beans'. As for Arthur, he concluded, 'almost everybody else in this case is lying if Arthur Hosein is right'.

The closing speeches ended the week, and Mr Justice Shaw's summing up took the whole of the next Monday and a little of Tuesday. He made the excellent point that if Muriel had died by accident, 'another horrifying coincidence occurred there; she died when her captors had threatened her death'.[69] He explained that he had detained the jury for so long because this was a case of the 'greatest gravity'. He paid tribute to their concentration and attention in the course of their heavy responsibilities but stressed that 'your heaviest ones remain'.[70] At 12.35 p.m., the jury retired.

Seated by a window in the lobby of the Old Bailey was Elsa, with two women looking after her. The McKay family stood on the opposite side. Between them, the place was thick with gossip, the speculation being that the brothers would be found guilty on all counts except the murder charge.

At just after 4 p.m., the youngest member of the jury, acting as foreman, sent for tea. At 4.40 p.m., they returned to the court. The trial had lasted for over three weeks, but the future of the Hoseins had been agreed in a little over three hours.

The jury was asked how it found each defendant in turn on each of the seven charges. Despite having to answer fourteen times, the answer was unchanging. Arthur and Nizamodeen Hosein were found guilty on every count. The foreman remained standing after delivering the verdicts, to say, 'It is the unanimous decision of the jurors that I should ask your Lordship and the court if you would kindly consider leniency towards Nizamodeen Hosein. Thank you.' For all his dreary incompetence, Nizamodeen had successfully manipulated the jury.

Hudson reminded the judge of Arthur's antecedents, saying that he was of previous good character, and Draycott asked the judge to give effect to the jury's recommendation. The clerk then addressed the prisoners at the bar and asked whether either of them had anything to say about why the court should not give them judgement of imprisonment for life, according to law.

The penultimate occasion on which the two brothers would ever stand side by side also illustrated most explicitly their difference in temperament. Nizam had nothing to say and said nothing – not even a word of remorse. Arthur, however, was apoplectic and incapable of going quietly:

> I claim this privilege expressly this afternoon, that injustice has not only been done but also been seen and heard by the public gallery has not been done. The provocation by your Lordship, you have shown impartiality from the moment I have stood in that box and named Rupert Maxwell. I realise you are a Jew. I am not anti-Jew …

The judge interjected, but Arthur ranted on:

> My Lord, I was given permission to express myself. Whatever I have to say, if I am asked, would be abandoned, or in a certain degree. I have been given an alternative of expressing things and this is my privilege. You have shown throughout this case, you have directed the jury here and I have produced nearly thirty witnesses and you have not at one time mentioned anything on my behalf regarding the facts.[71]

An embarrassed Hudson asked that he speak to his client, but the judge told him, 'I don't think he needs your assistance but if he does, he will ask for it.'

Arthur ranted further, 'Again, partiality exists, my Lord. Counsel wishes to advise me on certain things, and you have denied me that advice. I think my word would be useless. Thank you. Thank you, members of the jury. This is a gross injustice done.'

Mr Justice Shaw's words were both fierce and compassionate:

The kidnapping and the confinement of Mrs McKay was cold blooded and abominable. She was snatched from the security and comfort of her home and for so long as she remained alive, she was reduced to terrified despair. This conduct must shock every right-minded person and the punishment must be salutary, for law-abiding citizens would not be safe in their homes otherwise.[72]

Both men were sentenced to life imprisonment on the charge of murder. On the kidnapping and unlawful imprisonment, he sentenced Arthur to twenty-five years' imprisonment. He continued:

You, Nizamodeen Hosein, are many years younger than your brother. I am not at all sure that you are in any degree less culpable or less evil. The jury have taken the view that your part in this matter was influenced by your brother, and I have regard to the possibility that was so.

Consequently, on those counts, Nizam was sentenced to fifteen years. On each of the two counts of blackmail, they were each given the maximum sentence of fourteen years' imprisonment. 'There could not be a worse case of blackmail. You put Mrs McKay's family on the rack for weeks and months in the attempt to extort from them your monstrous demands.' For each of the two counts of threatening murder, again, he passed the maximum sentence for each of them, ten years' imprisonment. All these sentences were to be concurrent.

Sebag Shaw thanked the jury on behalf of the City of London, and then asked Bill Smith to stand. He said:

I don't want to part with this case without saying that the community owes a debt of gratitude to you, Mr Smith, and to your colleagues who collaborated with you in this investigation. It was brilliantly done, there is no other expression to describe it, and it has enabled justice to be done in this court and I address the thanks of the community to you and your colleagues for that.[73]

The court dispersed after a cry of 'God save the Queen'. It sealed the Crown's dreadful judgement that another lady, of a more modest household, had not been saved. The trial offered no closure because it could offer up no answers. It ascertained the brothers' guilt, but they were so strange and their behaviour during the crime and during their trial so bizarre and erratic that all that remained was confusion and misery.

Elsa had been led sobbing from the courtroom when the guilty verdicts were delivered. In the foyer, a WPC broke the news to her of the sentencing. The *Daily Mirror* quoted her protesting her husband's innocence, though how sincere this was, we shall never know. Despite her having found the stolen jewellery at Rooks Farm, Arthur's last letter to her during the trial read, 'Dear Wife, It is a terrible thing that happening with our lives, but I can assure you that I am innocent', before blaming the whole affair on the British Government having a grudge against him that had first become apparent when his passport was confiscated in Trinidad in 1967.[74] She was at a loss as to how she was going to explain to her children their father's actions, and predicted that it would be 'a living death for all of us'.[75]

Shaffi Hosein was quoted as saying, 'There is nothing dearer in life to me than these two sons. I will not desert them.'[76] However, according to the *Daily Sketch*, he was preparing to fly home and wipe out the memory of Nizam, describing this as a 'Cain and Abel' story, in which the police had turned the brothers against one another. He could not accept that it was Arthur who Nizam was frightened of and said that he had pleaded with Nizam to reject his counsel's advice and revert back to Arthur's story, but that he had refused.

'I feel for this poor woman, Mrs McKay,' he said. 'But my son has violated family tradition.'[77] If these words are accurate, perhaps we have within them the most candid glimpse of the dynamics of the Hosein family: Nizam, despised and disposable; Shaffi, sternly judgemental and scripture-obsessed, yet gullible; Arthur, deceitful and manipulative. During the trial, Arthur said of his treatment of Nizam, 'You can beat a dog many times, but you can only beat them so much … I believe he can see my father's figure in me when he watches me. He saw my father's face in me, so he get a sort of respect.'[78]

The only support for Nizam came from Liley, who told the press, 'I will always be Nizam's girlfriend. He was a good boy. I know that it was Arthur who made him do what he did, but I will never believe that he had anything to do with Mrs McKay's death.'[79]

★★★

Arthur Hosein began his life sentence at HMP Wandsworth, and Nizamodeen at Winson Green.* The *Evening Standard* suggested that Arthur would be

---

*   Now HMP Birmingham.

eligible for parole in eight years and three months; Nizam even sooner, since under the Criminal Justice Act 1969, every prisoner can be considered for parole after serving a third of their sentence.[80]

Due to the overwhelming support of Alick's friends around the world who had offered money towards Muriel's safe return, raising the gigantic ransom could perhaps ultimately have been achieved, but it would have done no good. 'They have got a life sentence,' Alick told the press. 'I, too, have got a life sentence, wondering what has happened to my wife.'[81]

A few days earlier, Elsa had seen Alick entering the Magpie and Stump pub opposite the Old Bailey while she had been lunching with her solicitor, and had very much wanted to talk to him. Asked about this later, Alick said that he would have spoken to her, tenderly adding that he felt sorry for her and her children, and that Elsa was another innocent person in this dreadful crime.[82] He gave a full statement to the *Sun*:

> One can accept death in the ordinary way. It is something which has to be faced and one has to adjust one's life to take account of it. But in these circumstances, one is unable to accept the explanation of death without finding a body, although I am convinced Muriel is never coming home again. I must face this situation, of course, and live my life as best I can.
>
> I suppose I do not want to know the brutal facts really – and yet I must always ask, how did she die, what happened to her, where is her body? However much I try to escape the tragedy and hurt of it, I suppose I really would like to know the answers.
>
> My family try to help me not to think about it. They are extremely good to me, and I am never left alone for long.[83]

On Thursday, 8 October 1970, the McKay family returned to Wimbledon and to St Mary's Church, a few yards from their once-happy home, gathering with 200 mourners, including friends, relatives and senior police officers, for a memorial service. Printed on the front of the order of service were the words:

To remember, with Love, Muriel McKay.

17

ECHOES

Forgot to suggest that you order yourself a chicken sometime. Hope you are both well and happy, as we are. Pats to Ruby and Carl. Kindest regards.

Muriel McKay, Mallorca, 1959.

On the day that Bill Smith wrote his final report on the case, the *Times* claimed that most officers on the inquiry believed that Muriel had died 'from a combination of ill-treatment, shock, fear and probably exposure during the sub-zero temperatures of last January',[1] but as for her disposal, any traces that could have connected her with Rooks Farm 'would have certainly disappeared during the five weeks it took the police to track down the two brothers'. It went on to state that senior officers felt that even if £1 million had been made available within two days, the kidnappers would have been completely unprepared to negotiate.

Smith said they had learned a lot in the last nine months:

We may have made a few mistakes, but we faced a crime which had never been committed in this country before. There was no precedent, nothing we could fall back on to help us. The whole thing was a new experience and not one any of us would want to go through again. The kidnappers held the initiative from the start. They held the whip hand and knew it. It was a battle of wits which we finally won, thanks mainly to a team of skilled and brave officers.

A great deal of soul-searching was performed over the unprecedented levels of publicity and exposure that the case had involved. The *Sunday Times*, the weekend after the trial ended, asked, 'Did publicity help to kill Mrs McKay?' with Commander Guiver being careful to stress that arguing that the publicity hindered the police was not a criticism of any specific person. However, if the story had not immediately been made public, the police could have established a link with the kidnappers. 'We were embarrassed by the intensity of the publicity,' he said, adding that it may have 'forced the kidnappers beyond the point of no return'.[2]

Bill Smith was convinced that the farrago of publicity was the cause of the long silence from M3 which followed the initial contacts. In later years, he lectured at police colleges, advocating that there should be no publicity whatsoever in kidnapping cases, a wish that was granted when Scotland Yard created a specialist unit to deal with such crimes and agreed this condition with the media.

Endorsing Bill Smith's recommendation for high commendations for some of the key officers on the case, Commander Garrett wrote:

> The vital importance of this case in the sphere of public confidence in the police was vividly emphasised by the trial judge when passing sentence. Had the investigation failed then a disastrous acceleration of this horrible type of crime would have been inevitable. Events this year on the American continent show only too well how the disease of kidnapping can spread unless crushed quickly.[3]

While accepting this, the Deputy Assistant Commissioner pointed out that high commendations are usually awarded to officers performing spontaneous acts of outstanding bravery and so, since the principal officers had already been seen and thanked by the Commissioner, the Assistant Commissioner preferred that the case be seen as a team effort, with all the officers being treated alike. A note of their good work, including the Commissioner's commendation, and commendations by the court, the Attorney General and the Director of Public Prosecutions, would be placed on the files of each of the named officers, though in accordance with policy, the commendations would not be so named in police orders.

Aubrey Rose wrote to Commander Guiver, congratulating the police on 'a tremendous job of work'[4] and acknowledging the courtesy and assistance of his officers. While, on reflection, he says that there were flaws in the operation, 'I don't blame them, because they had no preparation for such a case.'[5]

Sir Peter Rawlinson singled out Jim Parker for special praise, due to his 'complete mastery of the detail'.[6] Peter Rimmer endorses this. 'I actually knew Jimmy again after he retired from the police, when he was chief security officer at Selfridges. He was the star of that inquiry, no question. And it was undoubtedly one of the cases on which we learned the most.'[7]

Bill Smith took his first break in two years, indulging his passion for the water with a holiday deep-sea fishing.* As he stepped away from the case, he told the BBC that he had never been so personally consumed by an inquiry, and had never been so close to anyone in a professional capacity as he had been to Alick:

> I feel very, very sorry indeed for Mr McKay. Nobody has profited and a lot of people have lost. I think it's the most hideous crime that can be perpetrated against anyone. Kidnapping is worse than just a straight murder. It's tied up with blackmail, threats, it's working on people's innermost feelings, their whole life is disrupted, they're in terror, it's a terror thing. It just mustn't happen here again.[8]

★★★

It was announced that an auction of Rooks Farm, its contents and the Volvo would be held on 18 November. By now, all the livestock had been sold. What remained, including Arthur's tailoring equipment, was expected to total fewer than 100 lots. The farm was described in the brochure as an 'attractive detached character farmhouse with approximately 10 acres of land, situated in this pleasant part of Hertfordshire amidst rural surroundings and in complete seclusion'.[9] Those wanting to view the farm were warned not to visit without prior appointment, due to the extremely dangerous guard dogs which, since Arthur's arrest, had already bitten a local child.**

---

* Smith was also a champion swimmer, awarded the Bronze Medallion of the Royal Life Saving Society when he was 12 and later holding the society's Award of Merit with Distinction.

** One of the dogs had also been responsible for savaging and killing two goats, which the landlord kept at the rear of the Cock, in May 1969 (*Herts and Essex Observer*, 21 March 1969, p. 22).

Rooks Farm was bought within ten minutes of the auction starting. Bids commenced at £5,000, the freehold going for £18,500 to Mrs Kathleen Liley, who outbid three rivals and then posed for photographs outside the house. The purchase was not a macabre one, since she had happy childhood memories of visiting the farm when her uncle had lived there. Despite this, a reporter asked her whether she would consider opening the grounds up for the public to visit.

John Minors and Jim Parker attended the auction, explaining, 'We want a last look before the files are closed.'

The Volvo was sold for £910. The net profit of the auction was expected to exceed £9,000, which Arthur had instructed must go to his father, but Elsa obtained an emergency injunction under the Married Women's Property Act 1882, pending a further hearing on Monday, 30 November. She asked for a judge's ruling on her entitlement to an equal share of the proceeds, for her children's future. A few days later, flanked by four prison officers and wearing 'a well-cut blue lounge suit with white shirt and matching tie', Arthur was led down to the well of the High Court, handcuffed to a prison officer, to conduct his own defence, since he apparently no longer had confidence in the British legal system. The absurd scene summed him up with the aperçu of a satirical cartoon.

When the judge told him that he had a duty to maintain his wife and children, and, 'in view of the present situation, it may be that you will not be able to earn money for a long time', Arthur laughed.[10] Remarkably, he was still claiming that his father was a wealthy man, and said that he was only intending for the money to be passed to him so that he could ensure his children's security, his wife being 'very extravagant'.[11] There followed a short hearing before a divorce registrar, with Elsa divorcing Arthur on grounds of cruelty.

The judge advised Elsa to take the children away from England which, in time, she did. For now, it was enough to leave Hertfordshire and relocate to Thornwood, Epping. However, she lacked the funds to emigrate for the moment, as the sale of the house fell through, leaving Rooks Farm to sit empty throughout that winter. Vandals visited too, stealing fixtures and fittings and smashing windows.

★★★

Before the first month of their sentences had been completed, both brothers were instructing solicitors in the hope of an appeal. Arthur planned to conduct his appeal himself, having by now dispensed with both his counsel and his former friend, David Coote. (Coote not being called as a witness at the trial to support Arthur's false alibi for the night of the kidnapping and his claims of police brutality was probably what ended their professional relationship.) The registrar wrote to Arthur, advising him to consider very carefully the risks of conducting his own appeal with no legal experience, and warning him that he had no appeal against the convictions unless the court granted him leave to appeal which, without solicitors or counsel, the court would consider only upon the papers. He could not be present to conduct this personally and any refusal would then be final.[12]

Arthur had the Christmas period to ponder the registrar's guidance. As the festive lights went on again in London, the McKays faced their first Christmas without Muriel, and a time of year which, from now on, would always evoke their tragedy.

On 5 January 1971, Arthur wrote back to the registrar:

Dear Sir

I have received your letter. And after reading the contents I considered it to be valuable advice. I must express my worthy thanks to you for your enthusiasm on my behalf.

I must express though that I am terrible hurt, after residing here for 16 years as a law-abiding citizen, never would I suggest crimes far more to be a participant and worst of all, to be accused and convicted on charges that the good Lord know that I haven't got the slightest idea about any missing person.[13]

The registrar advised his new solicitors, C.N. Astill & Sons of Leicester, that while no counsel had yet been appointed, there would be a considerable advantage in having at least the junior counsel from the trial in place. Nizam, meanwhile, requested that Draycott and Woodley act for him again, despite them informing him conscientiously that they could not advise any reasonable grounds of appeal.

Arthur's grounds for appeal were presented as the learned judge failing to direct the jury to consider whether Muriel was killed by someone other than the Hoseins – unless they could exclude this possibility, they could only convict him of murder if they were sure that he had murdered her himself or shared a common purpose to murder her with whoever did. There were quibbles with the fingerprint evidence, Leonard Smith's identification of the billhook and the identification of Arthur at Gates garage, and submissions that the judge failed to remind the jury that Arthur denied giving the police his alibi for the 29th about visiting some finishers. It was also asserted that the judge had not reminded the jury that Arthur had never previously been convicted of any offence involving violence or dishonesty.

His lawyers also appealed the sentence, saying that, despite the 'great gravity' of the crimes, twenty-five years' imprisonment on counts two and three – the kidnapping and secretion charges – was excessive when compared with other sentences for exceptionally grave crimes.[14] It was also added that the judge misdirected the jury about the time that Arthur claimed he arrived back at Rooks Farm after visiting the Patemans' farm on 29 December, since the journey time from Rooks Farm to Arthur Road made it impossible for him to have then been seen by Mr Anderson at 4.40 p.m. by Wimbledon Common.

Nizam appealed against all seven convictions, the grounds being that the judge did not adequately warn the jury of the danger of convicting him of murder in the absence of any direct proof of the death or killing of the alleged victim, and that there was no proof of death and hence the verdict could not be supported.[15]

On 29 March 1971, the brothers were brought to the Court of Appeal, each handcuffed to a prison warder. William Cooper, surveying the brothers from the press benches and comparing them with his memory of them less than six months previously at the trial, noted that Arthur now looked terrified, while Nizam looked unchanged.[16] After hearing the submissions, the judges retired to confer.

Lord Justice Edmund Davies began his judgement by saying, 'In the combined experience of the three members of this Court of Appeal, both at the Bar and then at the Bench, this is in some ways the most terrible case with which we have ever had to deal, whether as counsel or as judges.'[17] Arthur's new counsel, Edwin Jowitt QC, could not contest that Muriel was dead, nor did Draycott challenge this, but the appeal judges went further, 'There can be no doubt ... that the lady was, in fact, murdered.'[18] They called Arthur's denial of initiating the GLC application and Nizam's claims to have been merely obeying orders unquestioningly 'a packet of lies'.[19]

A case which, 'in its nature arose horror',[20] called for 'a most temperately expressed summing up, lest the jury, being human, might jump too hastily to conclusions and justice might be prevented' – and that was precisely what the judge had delivered, in their view. The 'temperature was kept low', as Sebag Shaw had reminded the jury, 'in unimpeachable terms', to act solely on the evidence, taking 'consummate care' to remind them that it 'did not follow as night the day' that guilt on one or more of the charges necessarily meant guilt on others. The summing up was 'extremely balanced, fair and clear'.

They pronounced that there were no grounds to grant either brother leave to appeal against the convictions. As for the sentences, they were 'justly merited' as 'no more terrible case ... could be conjured up' than the one proved against the two men 'in this dreadful case'.[21]

The Hosein brothers were led away from the outside world, for now, and from each other forever, having failed first in their appalling plan for becoming wealthy men and now in their attempts to persuade the courts that they had been treated unjustly.

★★★

Immediately after the appeal process was completed, the BBC was able to broadcast the film which journalist Tom Mangold had been preparing on the case. *Worse Than Murder* had originally been intended for broadcast on 29 December 1970, the first anniversary of the crime, in the *Tuesday Documentary* slot. Instead, it now formed part of the *24 Hours* series, and was transmitted on 21 April 1971.*

The BBC first proposed the project within a fortnight of the Hoseins' arrest. The Commissioner thought it an excellent idea, and the Assistant Commissioner added, 'If done properly, it will bring a good deal of prestige to the Met.'[22] However, they were cautious, having found the same team's earlier film, the impressive *The Name is Kray*,** to be 'sensational'. This time it was felt prudent to work more closely with the BBC, offering them unprecedented access, but forbidding the filming of any interviews until the trial was over.[23]

---

*   A ten-minute report by Jonathan Dimbleby featuring extracts from the programme was broadcast as part of Radio 4's *The World This Weekend* on 18 April 1971.
** Broadcast on BBC1 on 13 October 1969.

In view of the film's importance as 'an historical record and a dramatic lesson for the public', the police even waived the traditional embargo on filming in the operations room at Scotland Yard. The police saw the film as both a good public relations exercise and a useful deterrent 'against any repetition of a crime hitherto unknown in this country'.[24] It was also agreed that, as with the Kray film, if the accused were found not guilty and acquitted, the film would not be transmitted.*

Worse Than Murder (the title was a quote from Bill Smith) is a meticulous, level-headed film, typical of the impeccable journalistic standards of its age. Watched today, its fair-minded presentation of the police is so unfashionable that it could easily be mistaken for reverence and suggest that the price the BBC paid for such access to the investigation was its impartiality, but Tom Mangold stresses, 'We had completely free rein, they had no control of the film at all.'[25]

In 1972, he reflected:

The police had completely mucked up the first extensive operation to catch the kidnappers. The execution of a none too brilliant plan had degenerated into farce. How far could any investigation highlight the mistakes made? Would this be fair? Would it reduce confidence in the police? Scotland Yard had co-operated to the hilt … was this little exposure the right way to repay them? What effect would it have on future relationships between the police and the BBC?[26]

The film was the first time that police officers had re-enacted their roles in a televisual reconstruction of a case, and as such, it is an invaluable record of the inquiry, containing a particularly good recreation of the final ransom run on 6 February. Its weakness is in its simplistic explanation for the relationship between the brothers and their motivations for the crime, particularly Nizam's, as being born of 'his respect and fear for family tradition' and

---

* Similarly, Mangold's later *Panorama* film on the Jeremy Thorpe scandal was planned for broadcast after Thorpe's trial for conspiracy to murder in 1979, but on that occasion, the shock acquittal prevented that. Mangold guarded the film patiently, however, and finally, after Thorpe's death, he presented an aural version the following day on Radio 4, *Jeremy Thorpe: The Silent Conspiracy* (5 December 2014) and then for television, the original film, edited and updated, on BBC4, as *The Jeremy Thorpe Scandal* (3 June 2018).

its suggestion that the brothers are perhaps an example of *folie à deux*, which Mangold summarised as being, 'When two people have a very close relationship, and one of them has severe personality disturbances, he can infect the other and they will act in concert, but as soon as they are separated, that infection vanishes'.[27]

The problem with this explanation is that there is little evidence that the brothers ever had 'a very close relationship'. Arthur left Trinidad when Nizam was 6 and did not see him again for any prolonged period until Nizam moved into the farm, little more than a month before the plan for the kidnapping began to form. Other presentations of the case have elaborated on the *folie à deux* theory, but while to this day, Nizamodeen continues to both blame and imitate Arthur, to my mind, his complicity in the crime was driven by no more sophisticated condition than greed.

The film provoked some strong reactions. Sean Day-Lewis in the *Daily Telegraph* dubbed it an 'unjustified intrusion into private grief', despite it being 'most meticulous and indeed artistic', and expressed concern at Alick McKay's involvement.[28] Similarly, James Thomas in the *Daily Express* found it, 'not only compelling but also disturbing', and felt that the sound of Alick pleading for his wife on the telephone calls was 'a very personal exposure of the worried husband still facing up to his tragedy, which caused me some distress'.[29]

The most sympathetic review was from Henry Raynor in the *Times*, who appreciated the clear and unambiguous presentation and how that raised awareness of the gulf between reality and 'even the most scrupulous fictional attempts to simulate it' in crime drama. The use of the telephone calls 'frighteningly showed a sense of reality growing more and more tenuous as efforts to secure a wildly unrealistic ransom became more and more desperate' but 'Mr McKay faced what must have been a painful reconstruction with moving dignity and gentleness'.[30]

Despite hopes that the film would act as a deterrent to such crimes in the future, two days after the broadcast a letter was received by the Commissioner, Sir John Waldron, from David Keddie, managing director of the Keddie's department store chain in Essex. He accused the police of 'gross irresponsibility' and 'crass stupidity' because, the day after the broadcast, while he and his wife were away in Yorkshire, his childminder had taken the first of several calls from an unknown man who had slyly induced her to impart to him the movements of the family.[31]

Keddie was a wealthy and well-known member of the local community, and although there was no suggestion that the caller was planning kidnap, and may well have been planning burglary, a plain-clothes officer was posted to the family for three hours a day when the household was at its least-guarded.

Perhaps surprisingly, *Worse Than Murder* would remain the only presentation of the story on television for over two decades, as a case which had obsessed the world's media now vanished from sight. The case was evicted from Fleet Street and moved into Grub Street, to be sometimes crudely regurgitated over the next few decades in magazines and compendiums. However, just before that move, in 1971, no less than four books were published telling the story.

Have You Seen This Woman? by *Daily Mail* reporter Michael O'Flaherty was a throwaway account marred by hyperbole and invention, while the more respected *Murder in the Fourth Estate* by *Observer* journalists Peter Deeley and Christopher Walker was a careful and insightful study, if marred by occasional bizarre observations, such as the baffling remark that it was a measure of Arthur's conceitedness that he was contemplating carrying off the first-ever kidnapping in Britain 'without enlisting any help from known criminals. He did not even contemplate asking for advice from the underworld', which implies that the underworld is something that one might locate via directory enquiries.[32]

Shall We Ever Know? by *Observer* writer William Cooper is a perceptive account of the trial, though its racial references have not aged well. Probably the best of the four books is the well-researched and unsensational *The Murder of Muriel McKay: The Crime, The Detection, The Trial*, by Norman Lucas of the *Sunday Mirror*.

★★★

A ramshackle Rooks Farm, which had by now become a monument to the chaos that Arthur had left behind him, was reauctioned on 10 June. Elsa watched the £17,500 sale go through on her final visit to Stocking Pelham. She was now planning to remarry, 'and quickly, so that she could get rid of the name "Hosein",' says Freida. Her petition for divorce was heard undefended at the Royal Courts of Justice, four days later. It was the last time she ever saw Arthur.

After being granted a decree nisi, she took her children away from England to start their lives over again. Years later, she was remembered as having been 'a popular lady in Stocking Pelham', who had 'kept in touch with one village resident for many years afterwards'.[33]

Elsa and her daughters had no further contact with Arthur or Nizam. 'Mum protected us very well,' says Freida. 'When it was time to tell me what had happened, she did, but we have had to keep it secret all these years, because we were scared.'[34]

Elsa's remaining years were happy. She married a good man and ran a successful business. 'We were her world. She always looked after us. Everybody loved her. She was a very lovable woman. I looked after her at the end. She lived with Alzheimer's for thirteen years.' Elsa died in 2010.

★★★

On 28 July 1971, a *Daily Mail* headline proclaimed a 'seance clue to Mrs McKay' in the first of a steady stream of red herrings which would fill up several police files over the next two decades.[35] Two months later, Owen Alan Hughes, a driving instructor, told his local police that while Muriel was missing, he was driving along the B4406 and, about a quarter of a mile along on the Ysbytty Ifan side of Pont yr Afon Gam, he saw a dark saloon parked on the nearside facing Ysbytty Ifan, with a dark-haired woman in the offside rear passenger seat, smiling, and two men of colour, the younger one sitting in the driver's seat.

Hughes took an officer to the location and seven officers then conducted a basic search. Likely areas were dug but nothing was found. The land was wild and desolate with no dwellings in sight, described as 'very lonely, with the risk of people walking about at this time of the year very remote indeed'.[36] The road runs through open moorland and there are no hedges and no fencing. The ground was covered in reeds and heather, quick-growing plants, making any digging two years earlier hard to detect. Nothing was found, and despite the descriptions of the two men, it was considered that the area was 'so vast and so overgrown' that without a definite pointer it would be a waste of time. However, the information was filed in case any suggestion of the Hoseins having visited Wales came to light.

Arthur had now been moved to a special wing at HMP Chelmsford, from where he appealed to the European Commission of Human Rights, 'claiming colour prejudice at his trial'.[37] He was unsuccessful. He made a further attempt to appeal the following year. This matter is covered in the final chapter.

The new owner of Rooks Farm was a publican, Anthony Wyatt, who ran the Black Boy on Mile End Road. The local paper welcomed him, his wife and two children with a piece in which the family posed with their newly acquired horses and extolled the pleasures of pastoral life. Mrs Wyatt planned to make her own butter and cheese, to have a few chickens, ducks, pigs and cattle, and to start a pig-breeding business. Wyatt said that anyone approaching to snoop got 'short shrift' from him and – in an eerie echo of the recent past – his large Alsatians.[38]

Grotesquely, however, less than a year later, the wholesome hopes of the family were wrecked when the farm became the scene of a second murder investigation.

The farm had been the site of a wedding reception for Wyatt's sister-in-law, 'a dressy affair', but a scruffy, uninvited guest, John Scott, a regular at the Black Boy and, coincidentally, a tailor's cutter in the East End, had gate-crashed, drunk on brandy, and had 'made a nuisance of himself with women guests'.[39] In the ensuing scuffle in front of the fireplace, Scott had wielded a champagne bottle and Wyatt had struck him with a sickle, stabbing him in the heart. (The sickle had been to hand because Wyatt had used it that morning to clear weeds near the marquee.)

Wyatt drove the body to London in Scott's van, throwing the sickle out of the window while driving through Epping Forest, abandoned the vehicle in a side street in Leytonstone, then hitchiked back. After initially denying the crime, he told police, 'This is stupid. I have ruined my life.'[40]

Wyatt had two previous convictions for theft and, five months before his arrest, one for actual bodily harm. He impressed a prison psychiatrist as 'an industrious, ambitious and well-adjusted person' whose main interests were his wife, family and business.[41] The jury at the Old Bailey found him not guilty of murder but guilty of manslaughter. He was jailed for three years. Seven days later Rooks Farm was auctioned again, the Wyatts' extensive improvements raising its value to £46,500.

On 8 January 1973, the *Daily Mail* reported that Nizamodeen had been attacked in prison.[42] He had already ignored all appeals to reveal where Muriel was buried and apparently was later beaten up again, this time by a gang of inmates at HMP Gartree, who were trying to learn the location of the body in the hope of selling the information to the McKay family for a £10,000 reward.[43]

On 31 May 1973, Alick McKay married Beverley Hylton, the widow of impresario Jack Hylton, at Caxton Hall Registry Office. Rupert Murdoch was his best man.

The Murdochs, however, were soon to leave the UK. They were shocked by the actions of the Hoseins, which had resulted in such tragedy for the McKay family, when they had actually been the intended target. While living at Coopersale, a seventeenth-century mansion just outside Epping (and actually a five-minute drive from the call box at Bell Common), the Murdochs' daughter Elisabeth had attended Oaklands Kindergarten where, after renewed fears of a kidnap attempt, a policeman stood guard outside throughout the school day.[44]

★★★

In January 1975, 17-year-old heiress Lesley Whittle was kidnapped from her home in Highley, Shropshire, by Donald Neilson, later dubbed the 'Black Panther', who demanded a ransom of £50,000 for her safe return. He was subsequently sentenced to life imprisonment for her kidnap and murder. It was later claimed that he had been inspired by reading about the McKay case, although it is equally likely that he was inspired by the thriller *Dirty Harry* (1971), in which a teenage girl is held to ransom and, like Lesley Whittle, is imprisoned in an underground shaft.

Later that year, the Home Secretary received a letter from Charles Connelly, serving time alongside Nizam in HMP Parkhurst. Connelly claimed that he could help with the case, having spoken to Nizam in prison. Bill Smith visited Connelly, who then admitted that he had hinted that he might be able to help purely to assist in obtaining parole for himself; in truth, he had no information whatsoever. He had tried to engage Nizam in conversation about where the body was, saying that revealing it might assist his case when he came up for parole, but Nizam had refused to discuss it.

However, after concluding the interview with Connelly, Smith enquired whether Nizam would be willing to see him while he was at the prison. Nizam agreed, and after discussing family matters, Smith steered the conversation around to where Muriel's body was. Nizam 'stated that such knowledge would serve no useful purpose to anyone, least of all the McKay family, and went on to say that he took no part in the disposal of the body'.[45]

This is interesting because, unlike Nizam's usual denials, here he was not claiming innocence but ignorance. Whether his claim that such information would serve no useful purpose demonstrated a total lack of empathy or implied that in this matter, the truth was unpalatable, is something which cannot be determined, but the additional claim that he took no part in the disposal of the body is striking in that it implies that he was involved in the surrounding events.

In 1976, a series of anonymous letters were sent to the police claiming that Muriel was buried in a basement of business premises in Seven Sisters Road and that a third person was involved. They were shown to Bill Smith who, significantly, confirmed that on the original investigation 'no evidence ever came to light that any other person other than the two Hosein brothers was involved in this crime' and added that 'the ad-lib digging up of basements in Seven Sisters Road, a road of no short distance, is too ridiculous to even contemplate'.[46]

On 9 February 1979, from his cell at HMP Parkhurst, Nizam wrote to David McNee, the Metropolitan Police Commissioner:

Dear Sir,
It is now over nine (9) years since I have been imprisoned. From the beginning I was placed on the Category 'A' list by the Metropolitan Police Department. Since, I have been trying my utmost to be taken off that wretched 'A' list without success.

As you would understand, it is causing me many hardships in my present circumstances.

I am a stranger in a strange land, and I cannot understand why the Metropolitan Police is still wanting to keep me on the security list.
I now humbly beg you sir, please, please assist me in being taken off that list, thus making life a little more bearable as it has been far, far too long.

Thanking You In Anticipation
Sir,
I Remain,
Yours Faithfully,
N Hosein[47]

It is extraordinary that, ten years on, he was still employing Arthur's phrase 'a stranger in a strange land' when trying to win favour.

The Commissioner had no sway over this matter, so the letter was forwarded to the relevant department at the Home Office, who considered it but decided that Nizam should remain a category-A prisoner.[48] He would remain in prison until 14 February 1990 when, still not having revealed the whereabouts of Muriel's body, he was released from HMP The Verne in Dorset, and deported back to Trinidad.

He was befriended in his final years in jail by a prison visitor, Leela Ramdeen,* who took pity on him and accepted his protestations of innocence. After his release, they were married, but the union was brief and ended in an annulment.

In 1980, Arthur attempted to contact Freida. 'I was contacted saying that he wanted to see me,' she says. 'I said that I didn't want to see him at all, I didn't want to visit him, I didn't want anything to do with him.'[49]

That year also saw Arthur make his final attempt at challenging his conviction. He wrote to the registrar at the Court of Appeal Criminal Division, following a letter from the European Commission of Human Rights, asking for a copy of the trial transcript 'pertaining to the wrongful conviction imposed on me'.[50] The registrar replied with a copy of the Court of Appeal's original judgement. Arthur wrote back, in red ink, that he was requesting a transcript of the trial itself, all fourteen books of it, 'I again beseech you to assist me in this matter'. Three days later, he wrote a further letter, cancelling the request.

It was the last attempt he would ever make. By now he had served ten years of his sentence. He would eventually be removed to the high-security psychiatric hospital at Ashworth.

Alick McKay became group managing director of News International. He died in 1983. Dianne told me that after his death she saw a photograph of his second wife, Beverley Hylton, when she was young 'and then suddenly I realised that when she was young, she looked like my mother'.[51]

Throughout the 1980s, amateur sleuths and self-professed psychics sporadically posted nonsense to the police. Every contact was courteously acknowledged, even if privately the police considered them to be absurd. One 'self-taught criminologist', Douglas Batten, claimed that decoding one of the letters revealed that the body was in a crypt, in a graveyard close to Rooks Farm.[52]

---

* Leela Ramdeen (b. 1950), a dedicated campaigner for racial and social justice.

The police were 'at a loss as to how she could have written the letter after being murdered and buried in the crypt. The best explanation Batten can give is that he has extra-sensory perception. A more accurate description would be "a well-meaning eccentric".'[53] Batten's letter included a recent clipping from the *Sunday Express*, which had suggested, to his disgust, that since many lifers serve between ten and fifteen years, the Hoseins were perhaps 'looking forward to their first glimpse of freedom after 10 years'.[54]

Other anonymous letters over the years suggested that Muriel was buried in locations ranging from Cornwall to Teddington.[55] A shop assistant from Abingdon wrote to the police about a dream she supposedly had about Muriel's abduction on the night that it occurred, saying that she later located the place where it happened and was chased away by the occupants, enclosing photographs of Rooks Farm.[56] Thames Valley Police did try to contact her to acknowledge her letter, but to no avail. Roger Street, now Detective Superintendent Street, was acquainted with the facts and it was decided that if the woman was located in the future, a visit would be made to thank her.

In 1996, an anonymous letter was sent to Hoddesdon Police Station claiming that Muriel was buried at 14 Kenning Road, Hoddesdon, which in 1969 was the home of Arif Ali, a Guyana-born publisher whose remarkable career began with a greengrocer's shop in Tottenham Lane selling Caribbean provisions. He later launched an impressive publishing business to represent the stories and experiences of black Britons. The letter was shown to the now retired Bill Smith and Roger Street, both of whom felt that there was no substance to the claims and it was 'inappropriate to resurrect this matter and thereby cause unnecessary distress to the remaining members of the McKay family', and that, after twenty-seven years, it was 'ill-advised to act on anonymous information which appears to have no connection with the original investigation'.[57]

Rupert Murdoch had returned to England in the 1980s. Perhaps it was because of how vividly it had affected him personally that, if the case was ever spoken of at all in the British media, it was in hushed tones. Then, in 1992, a short dramatisation was made for ITV, entitled *Gone Too Far*, part of a Granada true-crime series, *Crime Story*.* Cast as Alick McKay was Ed Devereaux, who had in fact met Alick in 1971 after arriving in the UK from Australia. Clutching a letter from the Australian High Commissioner, he had

---

* Broadcast on 23 October 1992.

been told to see Rupert Murdoch, in the hope that he could provide the young actor with some publicity. Murdoch was away, so he met Alick instead. 'I was told beforehand not to mention his wife,' said Devereaux. He found Alick 'very polite ... but he was someone who had an invisible shield about him that you just couldn't get past'.[58]

Unfortunately, *Gone Too Far* is a truly awful piece of work – undercast, badly lacking in insight or compassion and littered with hackneyed dialogue, shallow characterisations and broad performances, although there are passable sketches of the Hosein brothers. More adequate was a straight compendium of newsreels on the case with linking narration, for the *Great Crimes and Trials* series the following year.

★★★

Arthur's mental state in the remaining years of his life was such that there was no hope of ever eliciting the truth from him about Muriel's death. He remained in Ashworth until shortly before he died. 'I saw Arthur later on,' recalls Roger Street:

> When I retired from the Met, the Home Office asked me to look after the three high-security hospitals, Broadmoor, Rampton and Ashworth. I was the adviser to the chairman of the board of the Special Hospitals Service, which was a joint operation by the Home Office and the Ministry of Health. It no longer exists; hospitals are all independent now. My job was to ensure that they employed proper security, because the most dangerous people in the world are in hospitals rather than prisons. I visited Ashworth one day and the head of security there said to have a look around. And he said, 'See that funny little man over there? His name is Arthur Hosein, he was involved in a kidnapping years ago, you probably won't remember it.'
>
> I said, 'I bloody do.' And there he was, this little wizened old man sitting there.[59]

In 1995, the *Sunday Mirror* gave Arthur his final moment in the public gaze. He was pictured posing in a line of offenders during a day trip to Alton Towers, which had been arranged to assess within a community setting the progress of their rehabilitation. A typically alarmist tabloid concoction headed 'Psycho Towers', with suspiciously unattributed quotes from supposedly outraged staff, it pictured him alongside other killers and child molesters, now nearly 60, grey and slight, and described as having 'fed his victim to pigs'.[60] He died of ischaemic heart disease on 22 January 2007, at the age of 70, not in Ashworth Mental Hospital but in a small care home in Watford for those with mental health issues.[61]

Liley died in Whipps Cross Hospital in 2001, aged 60.[62] She had never remarried. Her grave in Manor Park Cemetery is well tended. I visited it to see whether I could glean from the inscription the names of any surviving relatives, a trail which unfortunately led nowhere. I laid a bouquet of pink lilies on it for one of the many women terrorised by Arthur Hosein, although one who, unlike Muriel, has been allowed a decent, dignified resting place.

At the end of that year, ITV broadcast *Manhunt: The Press Baron's Wife*, a well-produced fifty-minute documentary which efficiently expressed both the tragedy and menace of the story. It was modest but fair, particularly when presenting the feats and flaws of the police investigation and, despite a couple of factual errors, was a respectable and effective account.*

Less praiseworthy was the presentation of the case for the series *The Real Prime Suspect* in 2020.** Bafflingly entitled *The Kidnap and Murder of an Heiress* (were the makers confusing the case with that of Lesley Whittle?), it started with the jaw-dropping statement that since the McKays 'were Scottish, they were probably looking forward to celebrating New Year' and descended into lurid shots of grunting pigs and a final dedication to Muriel which misspelled her name.

The tragedy of Muriel McKay electrified critics when it was shoehorned into James Graham's play *Ink*, which opened at the Almeida in 2017 before becoming an international success. A writer who tends to write political plays with the politics left out, Graham offered a typically compelling but gossipy take on a meaty subject – here, the creation of the Murdoch red tops in England. However, one struggles to justify the inclusion of the kidnapping of Muriel. Within the play, the character of Larry Lamb maintains, as the play seems to want to, as it strives to find the case's relevance to the narrative, that the crime was a crime against the *Sun* and the *News of the World*, which is complete nonsense. While that claim captures, perhaps inadvertently, the

---

*   Broadcast on 27 November 2001.
**   Broadcast on 17 March 2020.

pomposity and self-importance of tabloid editors, it also feels like a poor attempt at justifying the inclusion of a tragedy purely for dramatic punch.

★★★

During the preparation for this book, I decided to attempt an interview with Nizamodeen Hosein. In the thirty years since his release from prison, he had struggled to find employment due to his past, instead occupying his days with heavy drinking. I located him living in the old family home built by his father, in Railway Road, Dow village, but as I pondered how to make an approach, news was announced of a forthcoming documentary containing an interview with him, *The Wimbledon Kidnapping*.[*]

Unfortunately, the result was grossly disappointing, and resorted to some fairly dirty tricks in straining to reshape the kidnapping of Muriel McKay into a plea for sympathy for Nizamodeen, whom it implied may have been a blameless victim of racism, police brutality and mistaken identity. It was publicised with the line, 'Was there a miscarriage of justice?'

After a religiose introduction in which a shuffling Nizam meekly says that it is time to give his version of the truth 'before I go to my maker. He is my judge. I think I deserve that ... I know I have a clear conscience', he speaks of now having the courage to tell his story. Then, for the rest of the programme, he contrives to say almost nothing that could be considered revelatory or even credible. He claims never to have been to Wimbledon, to know nothing of the crime, and that during his trial he was 'like a zombie in the dock', listing off (in suspiciously uncharacteristic detail) the drugs that he was supposedly on at the time, while a forensic report is flashed up on the screen supposedly corroborating his words but which is, on closer inspection, a report on the tablets found at Rooks Farm, which has no relevance whatsoever to what he may have been taking seven months after his arrest.

'It's absolute rubbish,' says Aubrey Rose. 'I think he's a very cute fellow, very careful about saving his own skin. As for being drugged up, we had conferences with him each morning, at lunchtime and at the end of each day.'[63]

Nizam also parrots Arthur's claims in 1970 that the police 'beat the hell out of me', ignoring the fact that the doctor who examined Nizam during his custody found no signs whatsoever of any mistreatment, ignoring that Nizam

---

[*]   Broadcast on 21 August 2021.

requested to see the supposedly terrorising Smith and Minors alone, without his solicitor, when he was considering making a confession, and ignoring the fact that he made absolutely no complaints about his treatment in custody at the time, despite having a solicitor and junior barrister who would both become staunch campaigners against police racism. Instead, his legal team at the time stressed that the police had treated Nizam very well. 'In all the time I spent with him, there was never any suggestion of him having been ill-treated,' says Aubrey Rose.

One is in a precarious position when questioning the relevance of race issues to the case, but writer Gus John claiming on the programme that he could not believe that the brothers could have pulled off 'a heist as massive as this' (as if it was successful) and that there must have been 'white seasoned criminals' behind them is, frankly, ridiculous. While it would be madness to suggest that Britain did not have severe issues with race in the late 1960s, as it still does today, not one piece of evidence was brought forward to suggest that this had anything whatsoever to do with the kidnapping of Muriel McKay; in fact, the jury's plea for clemency in the case of Nizamodeen directly contradicts it.

Personally, I have been rather impressed by the picture that has built up while studying this case of the treatment that the brothers received within the community of Stocking Pelham, and of the hospitality shown to them. The film inevitably references the local hunt and implies that Arthur was deluded to imagine that he would ever be accepted by such a body, but in fact, Captain Barclay was on friendly terms with Arthur and agreed to write to the NFU to help Nizam get a work permit, only being rebuffed because Arthur was already in a dispute with another of their members. Arthur was unlikely to have ever joined the hunt primarily because he couldn't ride a horse.

While Hafeeza was bullied by older boys on the bus to school, Freida told me that she personally has no memory of any racism while living in Stocking Pelham. 'While I think that all the people who came to visit us came because of Mum and not for him, I don't remember any problems, even with the other children at school.'[64] In fact, the most regrettable remark on racial grounds that I have found in the whole case was actually made by Elsa, who told the *Daily Sketch* after the trial that Arthur had first impressed her with his smart dress sense, but that 'I did not mind his colour because he is tanned, not black'.[65]

While we may wince now at terms such as 'coloured' – which, it must be noted, was used in court and in statements as much by people of colour as it was by white people – we must accept that there is a difference between wilful racism and naive confusion, and in an age when we are striving to understand and accept those things that challenge us, we must also understand and accept the past and not misinterpret or misrepresent it from our more enlightened and elevated vantage points.

It is extraordinary, when watching Nizam in the documentary, how much he still blames Arthur and yet how much he still imitates him. His supposed beating by the police is described almost exactly with the words that Arthur used in court, and his description of everything after his arrest being 'like in a dream', so apparently inconceivable were the charges that were being put to him, echoes Arthur's words in court, 'I thought it was all fictional. I did not think it was real.'[66]

Villains have little regard for the truth, and decent people can easily be deceived by their protestations of innocence, perhaps because when presented with an ordinary-seeming human being, it is hard to relate them to an inhuman act. While he makes a dull impression, if one momentarily forgets the weight of his crime, one is reminded of William Cooper's assessment of him at the trial: 'It is all a performance, a performance which can be so convincing as to be touching.'[67]

Daring to present himself as the victim of the story, when asked how Muriel died and where she is buried, he deploys his favoured phrase, 'I have no knowledge'. When reminded that this means that Muriel's family will go to their graves never knowing the truth, he says, 'So will I.'

Having long ago killed off Nizamodeen Hosein in their memories and assumed that he was long dead in reality, the McKay family were stunned by the appearance. Seeing him on screen, 'we thought "why don't we talk to him?".'[68] While he still existed, albeit in a state of denial, perhaps there was still some hope of finally establishing the truth.

18

LEGACY

*Another beautiful morning – we are on this beach with the children, they are build-
ing a castle ... so grown up ...*

Muriel McKay, Cala d'Or, Mallorca, 9 September 1968.

A crime committed against one person has countless victims, even unto the
next generation. Dianne McKay has spoken of how her father endured years
of guilt, feeling that he was to blame by bringing the family to England. She
did not see him for a year after the trial because 'she reminded him of her
mother'. Her own marriage was destroyed by stress and trauma, and a fractured family remained.[1]

Meeting the McKay family today, I am repeatedly reminded of the words
of the police officers who have all spoken of them to me in both sympathy and
admiration. Despite their lives having been disfigured by their tragedy, and
despite them having suffered the familiar symptoms of crime – the sorrow,
injustice, broken marriages and strained relationships, as well as the continuing torment of being denied closure and of appalling possibilities swirling
around their many unanswered questions – they are decent, civilised, attractive people, blessed with a fierce, proud determination. They are a family not
of victims but of survivors. I am also reminded of the words of the late David
Dyer, Dianne's first husband, who told the press at the time that whoever was
behind this crime was 'not going to crack this family. In time, we may well
sway a bit, but we have plenty of reserves.'[2]

After the broadcast of *The Wimbledon Kidnapping*, which the family had
hoped might provide some answers, but in fact merely muddied up the issue,

the McKays instructed Matthew Gayle, a solicitor in Trinidad, to make contact with Nizamodeen. Dianne struggled to compose a letter to a man who had caused her family such enduring pain, eventually beseeching him simply to tell her where her mother was.

Gayle gradually built up a relationship with Nizam, who was living in squalor, the tin-roofed home his father had built in 1952 now merely a dirty shell with litter-strewn, unsteady floors. Despite having briefly been cleaned up for his interview on the documentary, his everyday existence was undignified. He was a lame, unkempt figure, ravaged and addled by drink. Ironically, he was probably at the same end point that he would have reached if he had successfully extorted money from the McKay family in 1969.

Remarkable persistence and skill from Gayle guided Nizam on a journey from his traditional denial of any knowledge of the crime to, astonishingly, a moment of apparent confession. He finally admitted to having been involved in the kidnapping but told a vague and ultimately ludicrous account of it. He said that no violence was used against Muriel. She sat beside him in the back of the car on the drive to the farm, befriended him and told him that she had a son of a similar age and that she could see that he was not an evil person. She was apparently kept in the farmhouse throughout her captivity, where she was fed and kept warm before suffering a fatal heart attack while watching a television news broadcast featuring her family.

While this account offered reassurance after years of appalling speculations, as soon as it is examined, it begins to crumble apart. If Muriel was placed in the back of the car and could see not only where she was going but the faces of her captors, there would never have been any hope of her being released alive, nor any need to blindfold her to write the letters. If she dropped dead of a heart attack while watching a news broadcast featuring the family (which can only have been the one on 30 December, featuring Dianne), how did she manage to write a note saying that she had seen it? If she died unexpectedly of natural causes, why had the Hoseins already got her to write four further letters to send over the coming weeks? Furthermore, healthy middle-aged women with no history of coronary problems do not drop dead instantaneously of a heart attack.

It did interest me that, despite how far-fetched his account was, he did mention the detail of the news broadcast, which I had long believed was what led to her death, albeit through wilful murder. However, his revelation of where Muriel was buried was potentially valuable.

He claimed that after she collapsed, he wrapped her in a coat and carried her on his shoulder out of the farm via the wooden gate which led to the fields and dug a deep grave by the manure heap. Again, the account was wildly improbable, not least because of the challenge of carrying a dead body, which only has a default centre of gravity, on one's shoulder. Digging a hole, which he claimed was 4 or 5ft deep, would be exhausting work even in cooperative conditions, but when one considers the winter cold, which would have made the heavy Essex clay virtually impenetrable, credulity is stretched to the limit. However primitive the tools for conducting the search in 1970 were, it was unlikely that the police could have missed a recently dug grave in a spot so near to the farmhouse. Any search is only as strong as its weakest link, but the sheer relentlessness of that search must be remembered, and that while it was initially conducted in brutal weather conditions, it was resumed in the spring.

When asked whether Arthur helped him, he said that he did it all by himself. He made no mention of Muriel having portions of her clothing cut away between her death and her burial, and his description of the precise location contradicted itself, somehow being '10ft from the wooden gate', yet also 'five minutes from the house'. He said, 'I never killed her', and claimed that she had a heart attack, significantly, after being asked, 'Then how did she die?', rather than 'Then who did?' Arthur is curiously absent from the entire account.[3]

However inconsistent and improbable the confession was, for the McKay family it was the most powerful development in more than half a century. Yet almost immediately after making the claim, Nizamodeen denied all knowledge of it, despite it having been recorded by Gayle. He gave an appalling interview to CNC3 Television in which he mourned, 'I still going through it, I still living it, I suffering because of it, look where I sitting here, I broke, I can't say "let me go and buy a biscuit to eat"'.[4] Not once did he seek forgiveness, so whatever else might be achieved, there was little chance of restorative justice.

By now, he had already been faced by Dianne on a Zoom call arranged by Gayle and claimed that talking to her, he had 'felt a deep emotion inside, if it were my Mom I would feel the same way', parroting not only Arthur's final declamation in the dock that he was in sympathy with the family, having a mother himself, but M3's words to Ian McKay, 'I'm very fond of your mum ... because she reminds me of my mum, you see'.

He showed no remorse whatsoever, instead, as always, casting himself as the victim, merely a messenger whom the jury recommended leniency on but the Crown 'penalised', for which 'I suffered dearly'.[5] Not for the first time, he tried to blame 'other people involved that never came to the fore, the names never came up, whose name, I choose to forget', immediately contradicting himself by saying that he was the only one left because Arthur had died. As well as claiming to 'have no disease, so I am not paying for no deeds, you know they say when you have diseases you paying for your deeds', when asked if he would help to locate the body, he said, 'Tell Scotland Yard if they have five million they can come and talk to me, other than that, don't worry.' Gayle responded that Nizam had a track record of 'telling untruths and half-truths to the media, who he clearly enjoys manipulating', and hoped that the Metropolitan Police would now 'conduct the necessary, first non-invasive search' to locate Muriel's body.

Dianne and Gale visited the farm accompanied by Norie Miles, director of Aerodata Forensics and a close friend of Dianne. The farm is encircled by a public footpath, so Dianne took flowers to lay at the site where she now believed that her mother lay, but unfortunately she was refused access to the land. The current owner's argument was that since Nizamodeen had served twenty years for murder, why was he claiming now, and not then, that his crime was in fact manslaughter, since he would have got a lesser sentence if he had confessed to it and revealed where Muriel's body was at the time. He also felt that if an excavation of part of his land produced nothing, Nizamodeen might then merely direct them to a different part of it. However, he did concede that if the police were conducting an official search, he would cooperate.

'We then got permission to get on to the neighbouring land, which was very close to the fence where Nizam was claiming she was, and from there we could lift the airborne radar up and run it along the area,' explains Norie Miles. 'We ran it from one end of the fence to the other three times, and it showed that the ground had been disturbed in three areas, each down to about 4 or 5ft.'[6]

Having been hindered in their attempts to conduct their own personally funded private investigation, the family then approached Hertfordshire Constabulary but were told that since the case had been a Metropolitan Police inquiry, any matters relating to it needed to be directed to them. They were initially frustrated by the slow response of the Met., so wrote directly to the Commissioner, Cressida Dick. The timing was unfortunate, since Dick was at that point severely embattled by continued and increasingly aggressive criticism of her handling of a number of recent police controversies. However, in one of her final acts as Commissioner,* she wrote a sensitive reply to the McKays:

> Please may I begin by offering my profound sympathies for the pain that your family still experience.
>
> I cannot imagine the anguish you must feel to have lost your mother in these circumstances. This is made worse, of course, that all these years you have not been able to properly say goodbye.
>
> I want to reassure you that my investigation team are exploring every opportunity available to us.
>
> I know that a member of my team has recently met with you and undertaken to keep you updated. I have also asked him to update me as he progresses to the next stage.
>
> Yours sincerely and with every good wish.[7]

Since this was a solved crime, the police would not conduct a reinvestigation, but with a duty of care to the family, shortly after Cressida Dick's letter, Scotland Yard's cold case team announced that it was reopening its files on the case.

The police could not obtain a warrant to excavate the land, since search warrants are only permissible in the search for evidence in pursuit of a prosecution, but the landowner granted them access for what was to be probably the only opportunity to search the area again using modern technology.**

The ground was waterlogged when the police first visited in February 2022, but finally, at the beginning of April, they cleared the area and using the GPR data, Nizamodeen's account and historical data and pictures, along with advice from forensic archaeologists who were on site throughout the process, they began to excavate. Unfortunately, after a week, the search had yielded nothing.

---

* Dame Cressida Dick resigned on 10 April 2022.

** No search records from 1970 could be located by the police, although David Ryan, a dog-handler on the search of Rooks Farm in 1970, told me that an operational report of the dog search would have been submitted to the HQ at Nine Elms at the time and, if it has survived, could be at the police's dog training establishment in Keston, Kent, although I have been unable to ascertain this.

It was a crushing disappointment, but it seems unlikely that there will be a further opportunity to excavate at Rooks Farm during the lifetime of Muriel's children.

Matthew Gayle persisted in his conversations with Nizamodeen, in the hope of eliciting more precise details of Muriel's burial place and the circumstances of her death. Living on scraps, although somehow also on substantial amounts of alcohol, Nizam was shown nothing but consideration and decency by Dianne, with Gayle taking him food, beer and cigarettes when he took part in Zoom calls, but he continued to exasperate the family with his vague, evasive and contradictory answers.

However, since I had spent so long immersed in the case and knew the intricate details of the known events of the crime, the family asked me whether I would consider talking to Nizam.

Obviously, it had been my intention at the outset of this project to come face to face with him and put my questions to him – questions that crime historians too have wanted answered for more than half a century. However, I was wary of dismantling the version of events that the family had been offered, and even more wary of building up a less palatable, if more plausible, account of the crime. At the same time, I was disturbed that Nizam was still controlling the narrative, and that his version of events had now been reported in the media unchallenged. However unlikely that version was, there was a danger of it becoming the final word on the subject and of history remembering Nizamodeen on his own terms.

The dilemma was resolved, however, when Dianne assured me before I spoke to him that, more than anything, what the family wanted was the truth, and in their minds they had gone through every version of events imaginable, every horrible possibility, so there was no need to hold back and protect them from anything.

As well as the considerable physical and emotional distance involved, attempts to build any kind of rapport would be challenged by the glitches of digital conferencing. Furthermore, open questions had proved to be an excuse for him to avoid giving direct answers, and closed questions tended to be met with denials. Instead, I decided to construct some 'Hobson's choice' questions, such as 'Did you both plan the kidnapping or was it just Arthur', to try limiting his opportunities for diversion.

I also prepared two icebreakers. First, I arranged for him to be shown a photograph that I had taken of Liley's grave. I wondered if it might somehow create a twinge of nostalgia and even make him understand that the family wanted only to give Muriel such a dignified resting place. The other idea was to relay to him the words that Freida had shared with me about how affectionate she still felt towards him, despite his recent confession (she told me that she still could only put his involvement down to fear of Arthur) and see whether her continued refusal to see him in a bad light might have some effect on him. He had talked fondly of her in the documentary, and although I was suspicious of the rather posturing mawkishness, it was worth a try. Both areas would, if nothing else, give a measure of just how much humanity and empathy, if any, still resided within him.

He had been taken to a hotel in Port of Spain, where he had washed and was being fed, and where, according to him, he had enjoyed the first decent night's sleep in years, at home being woken at 6 a.m. every day by the traffic noise on Railway Road. After keeping us waiting for over an hour, perhaps to establish who was in control of the situation, there he was – a figure who has, for decades, illustrated newspapers, magazines and books – being introduced to me and gesturing a vague hello with vivid indifference, while devouring a meal that he had ordered and showing no respect whatsoever for the matter with which he was being asked to assist.

He is a complete shambles of a human being. When beholding someone so lacking in dignity, it is difficult not to be lured into feelings of sympathy, just as a jury was in 1970, so it was to my advantage that he clearly disliked me on sight.

Neither Liley's grave nor Freida's words yielded any emotion in him except hostility. He was aggressive and used our different ethnicities as a divide between us. However, his reaction did establish two things. One was that he was far more perceptive than he was leading everyone to believe, as he clearly could tell that he was being manipulated. The other was that he had no discernible empathy or compassion. What little had ever existed probably fell away during his time in prison, where, he claims, with a faint pride, that he was befriended by the Great Train Robbers and the Krays.

Dianne had previously asked him why, when Muriel had supposedly collapsed, he had not called a doctor, his response being that he had tried to contact Liley. This was a provable lie. Liley had been expecting a call from him between the time of the kidnapping and the brothers collecting her on New Year's Eve, but it had never come. Now he was claiming instead that they had called a friend of Arthur's who was a doctor, who then came to the farm and pronounced Muriel dead. It was part of an increasingly improbable story in which his involvement in the crime was still merely as a bystander, everything that happened having been under Arthur's instruction, his actions only being kindly and humane. Whether he was incapable of telling the truth directly to the family or was simply enjoying the attention, it felt to me increasingly unlikely that any progress would be made. He did admit to giving Muriel the Largactil tablets but, typically, absolved himself of any blame by claiming that she asked for them.

However, he was fairly consistent on his claim that Muriel was buried on the farm, by the manure heap, even if his directions were rather different this time and no more specific. He refused to be pinned down any further and suddenly complained of feeling unwell. When he returned to the room, he slumped down in his chair in what seemed to be a state of trance, motionless and unresponsive. Small tears were running down his face. For a moment, I thought that he had broken, and that this was the long-awaited moment of catharsis. Then I realised that I was watching a precise re-enactment of an event from fifty-three years ago, when he was being questioned at Kingston Police Station: eyes closed, tears, feigning deafness and appearing 'to be in a trance'.[8]

After half an hour, during which he appeared to be catatonic, showing no physical response even to sudden loud noises, we decided to take a break. If the interview did resume, I had permission from the departing family to ask whatever I wished in their absence.

Finally, three hours later, it was announced that he had rested and was restored. With Matthew Gayle beside him in the hotel conference room, a magnificent mediator, only Norie Miles and myself now remained online to interview him. We fell into a pattern of good cop/bad cop, Norie focusing on the burial, and me on the details of the kidnapping. I deliberately prefaced questions with phrases such as, 'When you took that terrified woman from her home', which antagonised him but also interrupted his attempts to white-wash the crime. Surprisingly, it worked quite well, despite the fact that trying to hold a conversation with him is rather like doing a jigsaw puzzle by post, and while there were no moments of dramatic revelation, some progress was made, albeit more in calling out his lies than in eliciting the truth.

I tried to take him back to Wimbledon on that winter afternoon in 1969 and discover just how the brothers gained entry to the house. He disputed that the inner door had been forced open, claiming that they had simply opened the door, then altered this to a claim that he called out to Muriel that he needed help, both of which were pure invention.

Although those moments cost him twenty years of his life, as hard as it is to believe, the details are probably long forgotten because they held little significance for him. However, to try and avoid him disputing another matter, I asked him, 'Remember when she told you where her jewellery was – which one of you then went to get it?' and he answered directly, 'She did.'

We could progress little further with the events within St Mary House, but however hard he was pressed on Muriel surely having been transported in the boot, he insisted that she was put in the back of the car. As to when they had discovered that she was not Mrs Murdoch, he said it was 'when we saw the papers', again an untruth, since M3 knew who she was when he made the first telephone call a few hours after the abduction. He then said that they found out 'somewhere along the line in the car'. I suggested that Muriel would have been hysterical if she was in the back of the car, and he said, 'She was gagged.'

'With the Elastoplast?'

'Yes, maybe.'

'Then you cannot have had a conversation with her.'

'That is a difficult question.'[9]

It was at least giving the lie to his claims that they chatted all the way to Rooks Farm and that 'she treated me like a son, I called her "Mum" and she called me "Son"' – an insult to the family's intelligence and to her memory.

I arranged to have a recording of one of the M3 calls which he must have made played in the room. It was the second call, made on the afternoon of 30 December, in which he warned the family, 'For heaven's sake, for her sake, don't call the police', and after asking 'Did you get the money?', suddenly hung up.

Looking at Nizamodeen Hosein while that cold, monotone voice was heard again, a voice that was now so clearly recognisable as the foundation of his deeper, wearier voice today, was an eerie experience. He had perpetually denied making any of the telephone calls, but after the recording ended, I asked, 'Why did you hang the phone up?' and he replied, 'Because someone came to the door.' He was referring to the door of the farm and I pointed out that the call was made from a coin box, and he then amended this but, whatever the case, he had, at last, not disputed that – on that call – his was the voice of M3.

He also admitted that the kidnap plot was inspired by watching Rupert Murdoch being interviewed by David Frost on television, although he did not remember when Arthur first put it to him. He said that the kidnapping was planned not by both of them but just by Arthur, making no mention of a third party. I asked him how much his share of the million would have been, something which, ridiculously, he claimed was never discussed. Many people have a price, but if this was true, his price for participating in such an appalling crime was very low indeed.

When pressed again on the doctor who supposedly was called to the house, and whether he really existed, he said, 'Maybe, maybe not.' When asked why, if Muriel had seen both their faces and seen where she was being taken to, she had to be blindfolded to write the letters, he claimed not to have thought about it, later suggesting that she had been blindfolded in the car, something that made it even less likely that she travelled in the back seat, from where nearby drivers could easily have been alerted.

His account of the crime, with no violence being used and Muriel chatting to him, having free rein to wander around the farm, helping him feed the animals and ultimately dying of natural causes, was so genteel that it suggested that virtually no crime had taken place. It was clearly a constructed version that was easier for him to live with or, at least, was easier to tell the family.

If Muriel had seen their faces, seen where she was being taken to, talked to Nizam 'like a son' and been told his 'life story', as he claimed, how precisely would the brothers ever have been able to let her go?

'I didn't think about that.'

I asked him whether the reason that he was making this so difficult for the family was because he didn't care or because he was ashamed. Defensively, he said, 'I am not ashamed.'

It was interesting that throughout every account he had given of the kidnap and burial of Muriel, one person was repeatedly absent from the picture: Arthur. He was only ever referred to as 'the boss', 'the one in charge … I just did what he said'. I put it to him that if Arthur was in charge, he must have dictated how events played at the farm when Muriel was held hostage. I asked whether he found it difficult to talk about Arthur's behaviour at that time.

'Very much so.'

It was a rare moment of apparent sincerity. I asked whether, given what we now know of Arthur's behaviour towards women, the truth was that he had mistreated Muriel. He gave a vague, 'No', but an uninformed one. After arriving at Rooks Farm with Muriel on the night of the kidnapping, Nizam must have left again within the hour to drive back to London, leaving Arthur alone with her for nearly five hours.

Despite the increasingly vague and contradictory details, he continued to insist that Muriel was buried at the farm. When, at one point, I told him that Arthur had said that she was somewhere else, he angrily complained, 'He's a liar. He's a liar.'

I finally asked him if Arthur was the boss and dictated everything that took place, why then it was entirely down to Nizam to determine where Muriel was buried. There was a long pause, and a faint smile.

'That is a very good question.'

I told him that I thought there was not one word of truth in his account.

'That is your choice,' he replied. He began to complain of fatigue, and we left things there. It did feel that there had been sparse flashes of light in the darkness.

It was nearly midnight, London time. He was led away. I said no goodbye, and not because I wished ever to see him again.

19

CONCLUSIONS

Now at Gibraltar. Having smooth trip. Home on Friday about 2.30.
Muriel McKay, Gibraltar, 1959.

Crossing the Thames at Westminster Bridge has meant a walk along Belvedere Street. Six days before Christmas in 1969, when most of the capital was planning to spend money on others rather than extort it from them, a muddy blue Volvo was parked here, with Arthur Hosein waiting, while within County Hall, Nizamodeen Hosein tried in vain to obtain the address of Rupert Murdoch from the vehicle registration department of the GLC.

With a strange circularity, it was a vehicle registration that led the brothers here, and then erroneously to St Mary House, and it was their vehicle registration that led the police here and then to Rooks Farm. Already in the back of the Volvo that December day was the shotgun, and perhaps also the Elastoplast. Both are now housed just a few hundred yards away, within the building that stares directly across the river at County Hall: New Scotland Yard.

In 1969, in a Britain with more deference and less suspicion, the Metropolitan Police had just settled into their futuristic headquarters on Broadway, a building that lasted less than half a century, while its predecessors remain standing today. The Met's current home, on the Victoria Embankment, sporting tinted windows and fortified against terrorist attacks, is the product of a different age.

Few of the officers who worked on the McKay case are still alive, although both Roger Street and Peter Rimmer are enjoying well-deserved retirements,

Peter having served in the Organised Crime Squad and the Flying Squad before returning to Wimbledon to run the crime squad there. Roger rose to the rank of commander, having joined as a cadet and then attended the police training college at Hendon immediately after his A-levels. I asked him about his early years in the force, and how he learned to cope with all that an officer must face in his tour of duty.

'I learned not to get involved personally,' he explains:

That first eighteen months on the beat, you're being absolutely broken by things that happen, a child getting hit by a car and lying dead in the road, another crash where I took a guy out of a car and he died in my arms. You are not inured to it, you're sensitive to it, but you cannot get involved yourself, and it's the same when you're investigating. You mustn't get upset or make it personal, however much you want to catch the perpetrator.

The police have now become more of a fire brigade. Many years later, when I was a DCS at Brixton, I would sit with the radio on in the evenings if I was in my office, listening to what was happening out on the ground. By about 8 p.m. most nights there would be people lying in the street, there would be burglaries, fights, whatever, and people screaming as they tried to find someone who was available. I had 500 staff at Brixton and by 8 p.m., there was no one left. At Streatham, occasionally I'd find the youngest constable on the night duty shift and say, 'Come on, we'll go out and walk around your beat'. And night after night, by about 11:30 p.m. everyone else had prisoners, and we were the only two left on the ground, trying to police the whole district.[1]

I am at Scotland Yard today to meet Paul Bickley, the curator of what was previously known informally as the 'Black Museum' and today is known as the Crime Museum. In reception, people are gathering for a conference on the scourge of 'county lines', the recruitment of vulnerable children by traffickers to transport drugs into smaller towns and rural areas and away from the major cities. 'Most crimes that are handled here today did not even exist in the era of the McKay case,' he tells me.[2]

There is one unchanging truth, however. Crime remains the most pernicious of human activities, a disease that a person can create with their bare hands, its effects wrecking the lives of not only victims but their loved ones, its misery within families both contagious and hereditary.

Nothing can prepare you for how swiftly fascination turns to trepidation as you move around the Crime Museum, in the basement of Scotland Yard, a beautifully curated collection of relics of the ugliest extremes of human behaviour. You are at eye level with a vast and hostile parade of weapons to stab, weapons to shoot, weapons to maim. The appalling history of the stained bath and stove that were lifted out of Dennis Nilsen's Muswell Hill home instils the most mundane of domestic appliances with horror. Nearby, in a display cabinet, lies a crime scene photograph of the concealed body of one of his victims, a man who, at his young age, should have been closer to the cradle than to the grave.

Then I notice, on the far side of the room, an envelope bearing now-familiar handwriting. Gathered around it are a handbag, two dainty and sorrowful-looking paper flowers and the box of rainbow tissues that Liley bought – a splash of colour and kitsch amid the grim exhibits. Contrasting with their tweeness, and with Muriel's graceful handwriting and seemly reticule, is the brutal and unpleasant sight of a huge pair of tailors' shears, the massive, fearsome billhook and the shotgun, on close inspection still displaying the jagged results of Nizam's hacksawing.

I am shown the original letters, written in Muriel's terrified, unsteady hand, the page of the exercise book found in Nizam's bedroom with the incriminating indentations and the photographs of the crime scene at Arthur Road, in which, through a magnifying glass, we can identify some of the possessions dribbled down the stairs, including the keys, which appear not to have fallen at random but, bizarrely, to have been positioned ornamentally.

Since the museum's role is primarily as a teaching resource for police officers, the McKay case will always be enshrined here, not only because of how much was learned from it but because of its cruelty, senselessness and lack of closure. No matter how familiar these exhibits may be, nothing can prepare you for the menace and pathos they emit when seen up close. Our minds can only go some of the distance towards imagining the fear that those weapons must have unleashed when they were wielded, and the torment that those letters must have induced when they were delivered.

In the 1960s, most people held the law in high regard, trusting those who enforced it and believing their conclusions. Today, however, we live in an iconoclastic age, a time of suspicion, mistrust, cynicism and conspiracy theories, eager to embrace any suggestion that shadowy, uncaring authorities behave ineptly, corruptly, callously and at the expense of their subjects. Even with a crime as simple and senseless as this one, there have been attempts to search for more purpose to it – more motivation, more complexity.

Criminals, in truth, are mostly not particularly clever or imaginative. It is tempting to believe that a story is larger or more highly motivated than it appears because it is easier than believing that two such insignificant men could cause such enormous devastation.

The shadowy figure who has inevitably been moved into the McKay case is Adam Hosein, the brother who came between Arthur and Nizam and who was living in London at the time of the crime, at 2 Leander Road, Thornton Heath, 6 miles from 20 Arthur Road, Wimbledon. (No significance should be drawn from the proximity of the houses, since the Hoseins did not identify St Mary House until a week before the kidnapping.) I detailed Adam's strong alibis for the key dates of the crime in Chapter 14, acknowledging then that, to some, his alibi for the day of the kidnap might be so exhaustive as to be suspicious. Given what is now known about Adam Hosein, it is essential to consider the possibility that he was a party to the kidnapping of Muriel McKay.

Adam arrived in England in 1960, initially lodging at Mare Street with Elsa and, when Arthur was discharged from the army, helping with his tailoring. He 'got fed up with the hours'[3] and instead joined the RAF, which he served in for four years before being medically discharged, although, unlike Arthur's discharge, I have been unable to locate the reasons in Adam's case.

He told the police in 1970 that he did not go back to Arthur because they did not get on. Instead, he moved into a flat in Streatham and married Marion in August 1964. He lived at addresses in Norwood and Richmond before moving to Thornton Heath and setting up as a self-employed insurance broker. Freida found him to be 'horrible' and confirms that he was an occasional guest in Arthur's home. (Nizam also told me that he and Arthur did not get on, for what that is worth.)

He claimed in 1969 to be earning about £4,000 per year, but said, 'I budget month by month and have about £600* in my bank.'[4] He moved from Thornton Heath to a larger house in Kenley, south of Croydon, in 1973, an elevated modern property overlooking a valley. In 1977, he moved again, back to Streatham, but by 1979 he had left Britain, moving to South Florida and opening a series of companies, the main one being Maradam Oil.**

---

* £4,000 is £49,033 in 2021, and £600 is £7,335.
** Named after himself and his wife, Marion.

Clive Stafford Smith, the human rights lawyer and founder of Reprieve, has been investigating Adam for a long time. He explains:

Maradam Oil later became one of the fronts for Adam's money laundering. Marion however, who has now died, was a nice if much abused woman.* Adam appears to have got into cartel work in the early 1980s. He worked with Derrick Moo Young, who began small but then worked up to serious narco-laundering.[5]

Stafford Smith's interest in Adam is in connection with the 1986 murder of Derrick and Duane Moo Young in a Miami hotel room. Krishna Maharaj was convicted of the murder in 1987, after an appallingly conducted trial, and sentenced to death. Although the death sentence was later reduced to life imprisonment, he has remained in prison ever since, and is now in his early eighties.

Stafford Smith is convinced that he is innocent and that the murder was committed by Adam Hosein, who was in debt to the Moo Youngs. When a BBC *Newsnight* team travelled to Trinidad in 1995 to investigate the matter, at Adam's home they were confronted by Nizamodeen Hosein, who was 'abusive and unhelpful'.[6]

Stafford Smith said that he also visited the Hosein family home at this time and spoke to someone whom he took to be the mother of the brothers. She told him that Adam was behind the crime for which Arthur and Nizam were convicted, although I find that a most surprising admission to a stranger from a mother who was broken with shame about her sons. The claim was perhaps based on what Arthur and Nizam had told her, characteristically shifting the blame away from themselves and on to an equally wayward member of the family.

Like Arthur, Adam was clearly a man who would never be satisfied making an honest living. William Cooper observed him at the brothers' trial and described him as 'short, stronger and heavier than Arthur', with a deep, strong voice, who seemed 'the ablest and most powerful of the brothers'.[7] Aubrey Rose feels that 'he was the cleverest of the three of them. I was very suspicious of him.'[8]

---

* Marion divorced Adam in 2001.

However, tempting as it is to draw Adam into the case, there is not a shred of evidence that he was in any way involved in the kidnapping of Muriel – and quite a few common-sense reasons why he would not have been. While, as Stafford Smith points out, clever criminals often get 'small-time guys' to do their work for them, such criminals do expect a modicum of success. No clever criminal would have employed two such incompetent, erratic, unstable and unsubtle characters as Arthur and Nizamodeen to execute a crime.

Adam would have known his brothers well enough to know that both of them, particularly the loudmouthed Arthur, would have been major security risks, who would inevitably have given themselves away within days of taking possession of such a colossal sum of money. He certainly seems far too smart to have been under the ludicrous illusion that anyone could have produced £1 million in cash in thirty-six hours, an idea so outrageous that it could only have come from Arthur.

The fact that Adam later became a major criminal does not in any way connect him with the McKay case and, if anything, counts against him as a suspect. Kidnapping is a desperate crime, perpetrated by desperate men. Would such a shrewd operator really have been involved in such a deluded scheme? Would he not have looked further from home for his henchmen, particularly since he cared little for either brother nor they for him?

Why, if he was involved, would Nizam visit Adam five hours after the kidnapping, and for so little reason? If he had some vital message to relay to him, he would surely have done it by telephone, since Adam's house would be the last place to be seen if Adam was involved. And why, if Adam needed Nizam to keep silent, did he refuse to support Nizam at the trial, knowing that Nizam had already betrayed Arthur, who he was supposedly terrified of, and could just as easily betray him?

Moreover, if the M3 had been three men, exactly what would the role of the third man have been? It is not simply a case of him deploying Arthur and Nizam to do the legwork – what else was there to do, since there is not a single element of the flimsy planning and clumsy execution of the crime that cannot be linked to Arthur and Nizam? How exactly would a third man have warranted his share of the ransom?

The trial of Kris Maharaj for the Moo Young murders was extremely inadequate, and the guilt of Adam Hosein in the case is extremely plausible. However, I honestly do not believe that Adam Hosein had any involvement whatsoever in the kidnapping of Muriel McKay. While the suggestion of his involvement would certainly bolster his profile as a suspect in the Moo Young case, one must remember the words of Bill Smith, who knew more about the McKay case than anyone else could ever know, except the Hoseins, 'No evidence ever came to light that any other person other than the two Hosein brothers was involved in this crime.'[9]

Arthur's delusional fantasies about the Mafia and higher forces being involved in the crime should not be indulged. Such notions belong with his desperate claim that Nizam had fallen into the clutches of Robert Maxwell. That a third Hosein brother was living in London at the time who later became a career criminal creates no connection with Muriel's kidnapping, but merely shows the Hoseins of Dow village to be a family with more than its fair share of criminal elements. It certainly contained three criminals, one who was successful and two who were perhaps inspired by him.

Half a century on, the tragedy of Muriel McKay must not become the new Jack the Ripper, exploited as a vehicle for outlandish conspiracy theories. Every known event in the case can be linked to Arthur and Nizamodeen – and to no one else. The fact that both Arthur and Nizam boasted of or blamed imaginary co-conspirators should be reason enough not to indulge in baseless embellishment. There was no third man. Arthur and Nizam's personalities are expressed all too vividly in the arrogance, rapaciousness and preposterousness of the plan, and in the incompetence and callousness of its execution.

Despite *The Wimbledon Kidnapping* inevitably closing with the ominous suggestion that a third man was involved, offering Adam as a suspect and implying that there was a third voice on the tapes of the telephone calls, Dr Dominic Watt, an expert in forensic phonetics, who appeared on the programme and analysed the recordings, told me that he would not commit to there being any more than two voices.[10] Arthur and Nizam managed to create such carnage all by themselves. Let us move on.*

When I interviewed Freida Hosein, she told me that Elsa wrote a book telling her story. 'I've been trying to locate it,' she said. 'It was written with someone else. I have the receipts for the money that she received for it. She used that money to buy the hotel that she ran after we left England.'[11] Unfortunately, Freida has been unable to find it, and I can find no record of such a book having been published. I suspect that it was actually a newspaper that she sold her story to, which presumably then chose not to run it.**

---

* Adam's voice can be heard on the *Newsnight* report, and bears no obvious similarities with M3.

** Elsa did receive a 50 per cent share of the net income from overseas sales of *Worse Than Murder*, the receipts for which Freida showed me.

However, in 2012, John Lisners, a former journalist for the Murdoch press, published *The Rise and Fall of the Murdoch Empire*. He devoted several pages to the McKay case and claimed that he secured Elsa's exclusive story after the brothers were imprisoned, a story which he then presented fragments of for the first time.

Unfortunately, Lisners has not responded to my enquiries asking for confirmation that this is the account referred to by Freida and confirmation of its reliability. Nevertheless, while his account of Muriel's kidnapping itself is not strictly accurate, claiming, for example, that 'police believe she was fed to pigs',[12] if Elsa's story is reliable, then it is of enormous significance.

Elsa apparently believed that Muriel was held prisoner in a spare bedroom at the farm and at some point before the family returned from Germany, she was murdered, either strangled or shot by Nizamodeen. Lisners said that Elsa found the house in a shambles when she returned, 'Upstairs curtains in our bedroom had been ripped off railings. It looked as if there had been a fight. I tried to speak to Arthur about it, but he went berserk.' Hafeeza's bed had been slept in and, in that bed, Elsa found a flimsy blue-green woman's vest, which she angrily threw on the fire, and which, apparently, she later told the police about.

Most extraordinary is the claim that when she left Arthur in January, Nizam begged her to stay, holding out his hands and saying, 'You see these hands, Sis? They can kill.' She said that he was 'guilty of something terrible' and that 'without a shadow of a doubt', he killed Muriel. 'Arthur could be violent, but he could not kill. He could not stand the sight of blood.'

Lisners also claims that he and Elsa visited Nizam in Winson Green, so that she could appeal to him to reveal where Muriel was. Apparently, Nizam said, 'Yes, Sis, we had her.' He said that he and Arthur went to the Victoria Sporting Club in 'the early part of the evening' on 29 December, and 'Arthur got quite drunk'. Although he said that Muriel was not shot, he would not reveal what had happened because 'the prison governor had advised him not to do so for his own sake'.[13]

The detail about the Victoria Sporting Club is uncharacteristically specific for Nizamodeen, and I felt that if a connection could be made between it and the brothers, it would give some credence to his portion of the account. The Victoria Sporting Club was a casino on the Edgware Road and is today the Grosvenor Victoria Casino. Sadly, no membership records for the 1960s have survived the many changes of ownership down the years, but in one of Elsa's interviews with the police, she said with regard to whether Arthur gambled, 'Not now, he used to. He is a member of some sporting club, but so far as I know he doesn't go there.'[14]

The Victoria Sporting Club was also just half a mile from the club that Arthur frequented at 78 Bell Street which its proprietor, William Baker, confirmed that Arthur was visiting during the period leading up to the kidnapping. Nizam described Arthur to me as 'a gambler' but claimed that he never visited any gambling clubs with him, also denying that any such conversation with Elsa took place when he was in prison.

I have always suspected that Arthur was drunk when he carried out the kidnapping, since such a heavy drinker would surely have needed alcohol to fuel such a crime, and the idea that his final inspiration for it was mingling with those with money to burn in a gambling club is a persuasive one. It is also conceivable that the Volvo, if driven from the Edgware Road, would have entered Wimbledon via the Putney Heath road, where it was spotted at 4.40 p.m. (Although it was spotted driving in the wrong direction initially, since they were then seen ten minutes later driving back towards Wimbledon, it is conceivable that they were at this point driving back and forth.)

The current manager of the casino kindly followed up my inquiry about the weekday opening hours for the club at that time and, with the help of some long-standing members, I was able to ascertain that they were between 2 p.m. and 4 a.m. daily.[15] However, Nizam claims that he and Arthur were there in 'the early part of the evening', when in fact they must have left no later than 4 p.m. to have been seen in Wimbledon at 4.40 p.m. Considering that sunset was at 4.59 p.m. that day, and Nizam even then was incapable of accuracy, let alone honesty, that is not enough reason to dismiss the possibility.

As for the other claims – the disturbed bed in Hafeeza's room and the garment found in it (which does not tally with the clothes that Muriel was wearing when she was abducted) – these were more likely relics of the visit to the farm by the two nurses, Hazrah and Margaret, on 18 December, since Margaret slept alone in either Hafeeza's or Rudi's bedroom that night, having barricaded herself in to avoid the prowling Nizamodeen.[16]

Freida confirms that the house was in a mess when they returned from Germany after Christmas and that it looked as though there had been 'some sort of fight'. Cautiously, this gives some credence to Nizam's current claims that Muriel was held prisoner in one of the bedrooms in the farm, rather than in the outbuildings. However, his claim to Elsa that the prison governor had advised him not to reveal what happened to Muriel is absurd, and a typical example of the Hoseins' bizarre strain of invention and blame-shifting.

At the end of his 1971 book on the case, Norman Lucas reported that Tom Mangold was told by Elsa that when she visited Nizamodeen, she had asked him about the involvement of a third party, and he had replied, 'Arthur says that we must never talk about that because if we do, the children will be in great danger. There would be reprisals.'[17] It is, again, a typical example of Nizam shifting blame and casting himself as the considerate one. Mangold told me that he has absolutely no knowledge of this conversation, and stressed that 'Nizam, like Arthur, is incapable of telling the truth'.[18] More than anything else, let us remember that during his conversations with Ian McKay, M3 claimed that because he was trying to help the family, his wife and children were now 'in danger' – Nizamodeen, as ever, learning his lines from Arthur.[19]

A number of files on the McKay case remain firmly closed until 2062. This ruling is because Section 38(1)(a) of the Freedom of Information Act (FOI) 2000 exempts information that, if it was released, would endanger the physical or mental health of an individual.

I engaged in lengthy FOI negotiations when beginning work on this project, and was partially successful, but regarding those files which I was refused access to, was told:

> These files concern the murder, kidnap, false imprisonment and blackmail concerning Mrs Muriel McKay and include references to events leading up to the kidnap and detail the blackmail that the McKay family were subjected to. This level of detail will not be available in the public domain.
>
> Release would endanger the mental health of the victim's remaining family members and also the family of the defendants. Release of this material after such a prolonged period of time would be likely to have the same endangering effect on the mental health of the witnesses in this case as releasing it for the first time.[20]

The outcome of a public interest test was:

> The families of Mrs McKay and the Hoseins would not have knowledge that these details would be put in the public domain after such a significant amount of time.

The Crown Prosecution Service is satisfied that Section 38 is engaged and that the public interest in not endangering the mental health of Mrs McKay's relatives or the relatives of the Hoseins substantially outweighs the public interest in the disclosure of this information.

There is a profound public interest in not endangering the mental health of the remaining family members of both the victim and the defendants.

The response also observed that certain information within the records is covered by Section 40(2) of the FOI, which exempts personal information about a 'third party' if revealing it would break the terms of data protection legislation and be unfair or at odds with the reason why it was collected, or where the subject had officially served notice that releasing it would cause them damage or distress:

In this case, the exemption applies because the record contains the personal and the sensitive personal information of a number of identified individuals assumed still to be living. These individuals have a reasonable expectation of privacy which would not include the release of this information into the public domain by the National Archives during their lifetime. To do so would be likely to cause damage and/or distress and would be a breach of the first data protection principle, which is concerned with the fair, lawful and transparent processing of information of this kind.

Although the McKay family themselves continue to battle for access to these files, the law allows no exemptions in the matter. If a file is opened, it is always opened to the wider public rather than to selected individuals. Despite the McKays themselves simply wanting answers and declaring that they have imagined every possibility in their minds already, the protection of the Hosein children is clearly the primary concern here. The date of 2062 is telling, as the FOI assessors consider that 100 years from birth, a person is presumed to be dead.

I very much doubt that these files contain any information that would drastically change what is believed about the case. Tom Mangold told me that having worked so closely with the police and having enviable access to the case papers when making *Worse Than Murder*, he is unaware of any other key information, except for one theory of Bill Smith's about where Muriel's body might be, which I will cover shortly. Aubrey Rose, who would also have had access to the complete case papers, is similarly unaware of anything significant that may be contained within them.

My own FOI applications allowed for a considerable amount of information to be made public for the first time, some of which has subsequently been redacted, some files even being wholly closed again. Most of that new information concerned Arthur Hosein's sexual behaviour. What I suspect will be contained within these files, since they are notably absent from the ones I have seen, are more extensive statements from Elsa Hosein concerning the abuse that she suffered during her marriage, hoaxes and blackmail attempts, statements from David Coote and details of Nizamodeen Hosein's suicide attempts while in custody. However, there is a substantial amount of paper being withheld here, so quite what else can be written on it remains a mystery, probably for another three decades at least.

★★★

I have tried to build up the most thorough and exploratory account of this case on record and have had the benefit of more resources than any previous writer. My investigation into the death of Muriel McKay is almost over. I will now present my conclusions.

Arthur's mind was obviously darkening at a faster and faster pace throughout the autumn of 1969. One sees an increasingly deluded, reckless and rapaciousness man on a path towards the committing of a dreadful crime. He had been trying to buy a shotgun for some time, without success. The television interview with Rupert Murdoch flashed before his eyes and lured him over the edge into the abyss of criminality. Shortly after that, acquiring the shotgun at the Old Rectory auction was a further step on that journey. He continued in his usual lifestyle of overspending, forcing himself on women and boasting of becoming a millionaire as the idea for the crime took shape in his head. By the end of October, he had colluded with Nizam to ensure that Elsa and the children would be away for Christmas, while they would remain behind. He was aware that Nizam's visitor permit was soon to expire and was offering him the means to remain in Britain rather than to return to his feared father and to his family home, where he was unwanted.

Even before Elsa and the children had left England, Arthur was behaving like a man devoid of responsibilities and well above the law. He and Nizam had arranged for two schoolgirls to be at the farm to prey upon when they returned, drunk, from seeing Elsa safely out of sight, and Arthur continued in his predatory behaviour with increasing aggression and violence over the Christmas period.

When the Hoseins took the shotgun to the Strubes to be repaired the week before Elsa left, the barrels had not been sawn down, and the gun was still in the farmhouse on Wednesday, 17 December, as Mrs Hunt saw it on the sideboard when she came back in from being assaulted by Arthur. She said that she did not mention the assault to her husband immediately 'because on the sideboard there was a shotgun and I was frightened, but I told him on the way home'.[21]

However, within twenty-four hours, that shotgun had been transferred to the Volvo, since the following night the Hoseins lured the two nurses back to the farm, and when Margaret sat in the back of the Volvo with Nizam she found that she was 'sitting on something hard and uncomfortable. It was covered in brown paper, and I somehow formed the opinion that it was a shotgun.'[22] Presumably, it still hadn't been sawn down at this point, as Ernest Woollard said in his statement that he felt that it was 'sometime after Christmas' that he loaned Nizam the hacksaw.[23]

They returned the nurses to London on Friday, 19 December, by now still trying to discover Rupert Murdoch's address. That afternoon, they drove to the GLC offices, again without success. They cannot have successfully followed the Rolls-Royce that afternoon because Murdoch himself was still using it that day. They must have followed it to Arthur Road on Monday, 22 December, the first day that Alick used it, because the following morning Arthur took the car in to a garage at Hoddesdon, getting a cab back to Stocking Pelham in a nervous state. The driver of the cab remembered Arthur talking incessantly about how he did not get on with the locals and had nothing to do with them, forming 'the impression that he was very agitated. From the time he got in the car he wanted a drink and appeared to want to talk to someone.'[24] The car being taken to a garage was presumably to ensure it was match-fit for the forthcoming operation – there is an echo of this in Nizam having the tyres checked at Gates garage while awaiting the suitcases – and Arthur's agitation was presumably because he was now about to carry out his appalling plan.*

The brothers cannot have followed the car the following day, Christmas Eve, because Alick was home by mid-afternoon, at which time the Hoseins were drinking in the Raven at Berden and collecting their Christmas turkey from Sleepy Hollow.

---

* If the brothers did carry out the attack on Wilfred Lane, it may have been a practice for the kidnapping or to test Nizam's commitment.

Since the shotgun was already in the car, albeit possibly in its unmutilated form, a week before Christmas, it is reasonable to assume that the Elastoplast, billhook and bailing twine were transferred there at some point before 29 December too, perhaps to be on hand whenever the chance might strike, as time was running short before Elsa and the children returned, the Hoseins having lost over a week between her leaving and them locating what they thought was Murdoch's address.

Now in possession of an address, the Hoseins must have realised, as the kidnap plot became a real possibility, that to keep a hostage for any length of time, she would need to be sedated. They may have asked Hazrah, Arthur's second cousin, whom he shared a bed with on 18 December, for some sedatives, but without success, which would explain why they then persistently harassed Liley over Christmas to come and cook for them at the farm. She finally agreed to come over on Boxing Day, only for Arthur to attempt to rape her.

Arthur later told the police that the tablets came from 'Nizam's girlfriend' and were to help him sleep, since he did not trust doctors. Liley had possibly never met Arthur before and only knew Nizam slightly, but I asked the opinion of an NHS worker on how easy it was and how significant it was for an NHS worker at that time to take away some prescription-only drugs. He told me that, unlike today, when every pharmaceutical item is electronically tagged, back then withdrawals and breakages were simply written in a book. He said, 'If one of them had simply said to her, "Can you bring something to help my brother sleep?" it would have been much less of a big deal.'[25] Also, although they were 'prescription-only', neither of those drugs was restricted by the Dangerous Drugs Act.

The Hoseins had to sit out the rest of Christmas, which was a long holiday that year, with most companies not reopening their offices until Monday, 29 December. It is a measure of how powerful Arthur's arrogance and greed must have been by now that even the police presence at the farm on 28 and 29 December did not deter him. In fact, on the eve of the kidnapping, Arthur was so arrogant and obsessed as to drop Murdoch's name in the Plough at Great Munden. As Barry Hudson QC later said, when reflecting on this aspect of the case, 'These people … are incredible.'[26]

We will never know where Arthur and the Volvo were on the morning of 29 December, when PC Felton called at the farm and spoke to Nizam, but the brothers remained unaccounted for until they were seen in Wimbledon at 4.40 p.m., and Arthur made no visits to any tailors that day. Since they made no attempts to be witnessed anywhere in the early part of the day behaving as normal, I am tempted to think that they were not completely intent on carrying out the kidnapping that day. (In court, Liley confirmed that when she was invited to the farm at Christmas, no limit was made on how long she might stay.)

I am persuaded by the idea of them going drinking in the afternoon, to calm their nerves if nothing else. They then drove to Wimbledon, perhaps partly to have another look at the house and make a study of the routines of the household. They were noticed driving slowly back and forth along Parkside at 4.40 p.m., deep in conversation, Arthur having already been seen in Arthur Road on foot. Both were spotted on foot walking up Arthur Road at 5.45 p.m., Arthur wearing dark glasses. They would have needed to pass the house on foot several times to grasp the logistics of gaining entry, since driving past in a car, however slowly, they would only have snatched the briefest view of the doorway. They presumably were able to have a better look at the house while Muriel was dropping Mrs Nightingale home, after which they parked up at the spot 50 yards up the road, from where they could see Muriel return and had ascertained that no one else had come home in the meantime.

Although they had no guarantee that Alick would not be returning at any moment, Arthur then decided, fortified by drink, that this was their chance, and after waiting for ten minutes, during which time Muriel would have garaged her car, taken off her overcoat and settled with her cup of tea, they drove up to St Mary House. (Alick said that it was unusual for her to leave the overcoat untidily over the kitchen chair, but she had perhaps decided to wait until she had another reason for going upstairs to take it up there, if that was its home.) She must have been indoors for some time before her abduction, due to the evidence of the newspaper and the unguarded fire in the den, and the empty cup and saucer in the kitchen.

We now come to the question that was raised on the very first page: how did the Hoseins negotiate that outer door? Essentially, there are only two possibilities. One is that Muriel simply forgot to put the chain on it, on this occasion. This seems unlikely, given how scrupulous she was about it. The only other way that the chain could have been off is by her having lifted it off herself, but why would she have done that? She would not have lifted it off to let in a stranger, so therefore, if she did lift it off, it must have been for another reason, namely, to go back outside, for which she would have again put on her driving shoes.

The fact that Muriel's driving shoes were missing does not necessarily mean that she was wearing them when the Hoseins arrived. Although her formal shoes were on the stairs, the driving shoes may have been in the porchway or in the hall and so were equally close to hand. However, the other possibility is that she was wearing them at the time.*

After many months of puzzling over this, one new explanation occurred to me. Muriel had settled in the den, with her cup of tea, reading the *Evening News* and awaiting the television news. The dog was by her feet. According to Mrs Nightingale, the dog 'used to bark his head off'[27] when the doorbell rang and Muriel tended to tuck him under her arm when she answered it, rather than shut him in the den, which was where he was found. Also, Alick insisted that she would never leave the dog in front of an unguarded fire for any significant length of time. Therefore, if the Hoseins did not ring the doorbell, how was Muriel alerted to their presence on the driveway? From the den, one cannot hear or see any vehicle coming up the drive.

The significant clue, for me, is the used cup and saucer that Alick saw in the kitchen when he returned home. We know that it was not used by Mrs Nightingale, because she was clear that she washed and put hers away before she left. We also know that Muriel was 'an exceptionally tidy person'.[28] I believe that Muriel finished her cup of tea (the cup that she told Mrs Nightingale that she would have when she got back from dropping her off) and then, having seen the headlines, returned the used cup and saucer to the kitchen, closing the door of the den behind her to keep the dog and the heat in. At that point, the Volvo drew up in the drive. From the kitchen, she could have heard the engine and the tyres on the gravel, and even seen the flash of the headlights on the front windows.

No one is anticipating kidnapping, and anyone fearful of burglary would not be expecting burglars to drive up to the front door. She may well have thought that it was Alick arriving home, and so put the cup and saucer down and went to the porch to let him in. Having opened the front door (she would not have been able to see through the outer door's frosted glass), she then lifted the chain on the outer door, opened it and saw the unfamiliar car. The Hoseins

---

* It occurred to me that she may have been returning from garaging her car when she was accosted, but I would have thought she would be wearing her coat to do that, and it is more likely that she garaged the car when returning from dropping off Mrs Nightingale than that she went inside, settled in the den, then went out into the cold again.

would have then immediately rushed at her, one discarding the sheets of newspaper that the shotgun was wrapped in, which would explain how they came to be found on the driveaway by Alick when he arrived home.

Muriel, in terror, fled back into the house. The outer door of the porchway opened outwards, so she would not have been able to shut it behind her and rechain it without fatally slowing herself down. She would have slammed the front door and made for the telephone. The Hoseins then frantically forced their way through the inner door in time to wrest the telephone from her before she had managed to dial 999.

With this possibility in mind, without leading him, I asked Nizamodeen Hosein several times how they gained entry to the house. After initially claiming that they simply opened the door, then that had tricked Muriel into opening it by saying that he was in need of help, he said, when pressed further, 'She came back out of the house.'[29] There is little value in anything he says, but this was an interesting admission.

The second brother, most likely Nizam, who was probably driving, must have then entered the hallway too, probably wielding the billhook and discarding its wrapping, which would explain why more sheets of newspaper were found in the hallway.

Their first objective once they had got Muriel away from the telephone would have been to silence her screams. If they already had strips of Elastoplast prepared, these cannot have been stuck to the insides of their coats, since no fibres were found on the two strips left on the hall table. Either way, their first attempt to gag her went wrong, probably because she was putting up a considerable fight. They probably had her pinned against the table, which is why those two strips that had self-adhered were found on it. The billhook was probably placed on the bureau because they both were needed to restrain her, and the one who had been holding the billhook now had to tear off another strip of Elastoplast.

Once she was silenced, the next action was probably for Nizam to check that there was no one else in the house, and probably his circuit around the ground floor was the point at which the photograph fell from his pocket. Although he told me that Muriel told them where the jewellery was and that she fetched it, she cannot have told them after she had been gagged, which would have been their first priority. Instead, Arthur must have ordered her to lead him to it and, once upstairs, she removed it from her drawer herself, which would explain why the drawer was not rummaged through. While she was in the bedroom, she would have been told to take a coat. (I cannot believe that if either brother had taken the jewellery by themselves, he would have bothered while he was in the bedroom to find her a coat too.)

Reassembling in the hallway and collecting the telephone disc bearing the number, they would then have needed to get her into the car, and so cut some of the bailing twine on the sharp edge of the billhook, resting the billhook on the table while tying her hands. She cannot have been blindfolded immediately, because she must have been able to see her way to the bedroom, though she may have been blindfolded with the Elastoplast when she was returned to the hall. She was then taken out and put into the back or the boot of the Volvo.

The Hoseins had left behind the billhook, the rest of the bailing twine and the photograph, but not any instructions about not calling the police. In the 21 January call to Ian McKay, M3 said that they 'had the note delayed, but it so happened that your mum, you know, she was a bit upset'.

It is horrific to contemplate Muriel being imprisoned, gagged and in that car boot for two hours, during which time there would be a serious risk of her vomiting and, due to the gag, choking. Whether the Hoseins contemplated these risks is unlikely, but how likely is it that Muriel really did travel to Rooks Farm in the back seat with Nizamodeen? It is probable that Nizam was doing the driving on the way to Wimbledon, since the witness Alfred Anderson said that the passenger was 'a head shorter than the driver'.[30] Arthur was probably too drunk, so it is reasonable to assume that Nizam also drove back to Rooks Farm.

If Muriel was in the back seat of the car, they could have been reasonably sure that she would not have been able to open the door because she would have been tied up by now, but she would have to be kept on the floor of the vehicle or other motorists would have noticed her gag and blindfold. (Nizam did tell me that she was gagged, but this was after having told me that it was in the car on the way to the farm that they learned from her that she was not Anna Murdoch.) However, if she was gagged and blindfolded on the floor of the Volvo, why did the Hoseins not simply put her in the boot? Possibly because there was more risk of a passer-by noticing this happening and being alerted than if she were bundled directly from the door into the back seat of the car, and also perhaps because they were aware that putting her in the boot was extremely dangerous. We will never know. When trying to understand the motivations of the brothers for anything, we must always remember that concerns for Muriel would have been much less of a priority for them than concerns for themselves.

They must have arrived back at the farm sometime after 8 p.m. Nizam must have left the farm again an hour later, by which time the brothers had secured Muriel in such a way that she could be left alone with just one of them. They must have gleaned by now her true identity too, because Nizam knew it before he made the first M3 call (although it is possible that he telephoned Arthur later, before making that call).

It seemed obvious to me that Muriel was imprisoned in one of the outbuildings at the farm, despite Nizam's claims that she was kept inside the farmhouse, with her escape barred by the guard dogs, which were on extendable chains and could therefore cover both the front and back doors. (This was after him having claimed, ridiculously, that Muriel had befriended the guard dogs.)*

However, there is some corroboration regarding the dogs. Liley said that when she arrived on Boxing Day, the dogs were chained up in the shed outside the kitchen door[31] and one of the regular visitors to the farm, Harold Prime, said:

> Normally the two Alsatians were locked away when I called, but on the last two occasions in early January, the dogs were on chains so that I couldn't get to the door of the house and walk in as I used to do, so I sat outside in the car and waited for someone to come out.[32]

Gerald Gordon, arriving at the farm early in the morning on New Year's Eve, said that he would not walk round the back of the farm, as the dogs were 'too near the back door for my liking',[33] and although he says nothing about the front door, it is clear that the dogs were certainly effective at keeping visitors from approaching the house at all, whether or not a hostage within the house could potentially escape out via the front door without alerting them.

If Muriel was kept in one of the outbuildings, and not where they could see her, then despite the freezing conditions, one of them must have kept a constant guard on her, or else they were confident that she was secure enough to be left unattended, either because she was under lock and key, heavily sedated or because the dogs were guarding her. However, if they were able to leave

---

* Much as Muriel adored dogs, apparently, she would never have been comfortable around fierce Alsatians.

her unattended, they would surely have used the opportunity to be seen elsewhere by people and create alibis for themselves?

Muriel stated in two separate letters that she was cold, but that does not rule out her having been inside the farmhouse. Leonard Smith's wife noticed when visiting the farm for dinner in October that 'the house seemed to be very cold'.[34] Muriel does say, however, 'only blankets', which gives an impression of somewhere much more spartan than the bedroom she was given in Nizam's account, and the fact the Hoseins took the trouble to ensure that she brought a coat with her suggests that she was going to be kept somewhere other than in the farmhouse.

Unfortunately, I also cannot give any credence to Nizam's claims that she was well treated during her captivity. If Muriel had been well treated, she would have mentioned it in her letters, knowing that her family were frantic with worry and desperate for reassurance. Instead, she said, 'What have I done to deserve this treatment?' Although Nizam denied that Arthur mistreated Muriel during her captivity, he is not qualified to give an absolute assurance on the matter, because an hour after the brothers arrived back at Rooks Farm with her, he drove back to London, leaving Arthur alone with her for five hours.

We have no record of the Hoseins' movements during the daytime on 30 December, except for the posting of the first letter in Tottenham, late in the afternoon, and the second M3 call, made at 4.45 p.m. However, there is the odd possibility that they visited the Patemans' farm in the afternoon to buy the calf. Nizam said that Muriel was never left at the farm unattended and I cannot believe that if the Hoseins had felt able to leave her unattended, they would not have acquired a more effective alibi. I think it much more likely that the calf was bought on 31 December, just before the brothers drove to Liley's in London, part of a frantic need to appear normal in the wake of whatever awful events had happened in the previous twenty-four hours.

The only other certain event of that day was that the brothers watched the 8.50 p.m. *BBC News*. Muriel said in her letter that she 'heard it' but that may have been dictated to her by the Hoseins, especially since she thanked Dianne for 'looking after Daddy', something that the broadcast did not really imply, and the word 'Daddy' is reminiscent of Arthur's words to Dianne on New Year's Day, 'I wanted to speak to your daddy'.

As I detailed in Chapter 6, four hours before this broadcast, the Hoseins had no idea of the police involvement in the case. I am convinced that their shock at realising that they were now the targets of a colossal manhunt and Arthur's anger at being described as someone 'who doesn't know anything about money', along with his realisation that the McKays were unlikely to be the source of his long-dreamed-of £1 million, and the massive publicity the case had attracted (which they cannot have been expecting as they had not inspected any newspapers that day) were what led to Muriel's death.

Too many factors stand against the possibility that Muriel died of natural causes. First, as the courts recognised, the brothers had made repeated threats to kill her. Secondly, they entered St Mary House armed with lethal weapons, so had no compunction about the risk of, at the very least, a fatal accident. Also, the kidnapping and extortion were intended to be achieved in a very short timeframe, a maximum of forty-eight hours from first contact to pay-off, at the end of which, it was made clear, Muriel would be killed if the money was not handed over. Such a determined, desperate scenario would have meant that murder was one of the accepted outcomes from the very beginning.

Considering Liley's arrival at the farm on New Year's Eve, if Muriel had died other than at the hands of the Hoseins, she must have died by some other means within thirty-six hours of her abduction, which, unless it was due to an accident when trying to escape, is highly improbable. And the Hoseins having forced her to write four further letters immediately before her death makes the idea of her death being unplanned increasingly implausible.

And finally, if she had died of natural causes, why did the brothers refuse to confess this and avoid a charge of murder? Why did they refuse to reveal the location of her body if it could have proved that she died of natural causes? It is beyond all reasonable doubt that Muriel McKay was murdered.

Initially, the brothers may have contemplated letting her go, and she may have been in earshot, since a later letter contains the line 'Tonight I thought I see you, But it seems hopeless', adding, in a line clearly dictated by an enraged Arthur, 'You betrayed me by going to the Police and not cooperating with the M3 Gang'. I believe it was then decided to murder her, although whether there would ever have been a realistic chance of her being released if the extortion had been successful seems highly unlikely. Elsa's return was imminent, the Hoseins had gone to Wimbledon armed with lethal weapons, and also, no mention was ever made in those early letters or telephone calls of promises of release if the ransom was paid, only threats to kill if it was not paid.

The brothers would have made her write the final letters which, unlike the first letter – written to show that she was alive – were written to maintain the illusion that she was still alive. She was then perhaps sedated again, portions of her clothing were cut off and she was murdered, surely with a shot fired from the left barrel of the shotgun, either at the back of the farm or after her having been driven to wherever they planned to dispose of her.

Interestingly, Nizam denied to me that the shotgun was used because 'the squire would have heard it'.[35] I asked whether he was referring to Captain Barclay, and he confirmed this. While Pelham Hall was nearly 2 miles away, it hinted that there might have been some discussion between him and Arthur about whether a shot fired at the farm might alert someone.

They disposed of her body over the night of 30 December, and the following morning, after the visit of Gerald Gordon, removed any remaining traces of her from the farm. It is important to remember that almost every item of evidence found at Rooks Farm that connected the Hoseins with the kidnapping was an item related to events *after* her death, such as the paper flowers, and the paper containing indentations of the letters sent to the *News of the World* and the family in January. All items connected to Muriel herself had long since been removed in what had obviously been an unusually thorough clean-up by the brothers.

Two deliveries were made to the farm on New Year's Eve. Margaret Shepherd, the butcher's rounds lady, left the meat order in the porch between 9.30 a.m. and 10.30 a.m., while Bernard Law, the bread man, called between 1 p.m. and 1.30 p.m., leaving the bread also in the front porch.

Farmer Leonard Smith claimed that Arthur telephoned him on either 30 or 31 December, saying that his car had broken down and that he needed a tow. Smith was unable to help him, but noted that, 'He almost begged me to go over there and was pleading with me to go, but I just couldn't do it. He seemed to be rather upset and agitated, but I did not go over.' While this may have been a desperate attempt at an alibi, it could also have been the case that the car had indeed broken down at a crucial time, causing Arthur's blatant panic. When the Volvo was impounded following Arthur's arrest, the nearside light defect was found to be due to a missing fuse, which was possibly swapped out to restore the car at the end of December and not replaced.

After covering their tracks at Rooks Farm, the brothers must then have driven to the Patemans', taken the calf back to the farm, then driven to London in the hope of persuading Liley to return to Stocking Pelham with them. Nizam had not returned her call on the 29th or honoured his plan to spend the day with her in London on New Year's Eve, and the Hoseins must have been frantic to have resorted to inviting her back to the farm after her experience there on Boxing Night. Once there, her unwitting role was to be their posthumous alibi, able to say that neither brother was behaving unusually nor that they went out at all. (The supposedly sensitive Nizam, having been a party to murder within the previous twenty-four hours, displayed no signs of concern at all, instead bleating that he was homesick on his first Christmas away from Trinidad.)

The events of New Year's Day will forever remain a mystery. Where did Nizam go in the afternoon that made him leave Liley alone with Arthur, despite promising otherwise? It is unlikely that he went to the pub, since no witness could be produced to corroborate this, and the pub would have closed at 3 p.m. He was still insisting to me that he went to Bishop's Stortford to buy some medication (not that Liley saw any evidence of this) and claimed to me, typically idiotically, that the reason he went alone was because 'I was in a hurry and didn't want her telling me to stop here and stop there'.[36] Also, the judge pointed out during the trial that if he had simply needed some fresh air, as he claimed, he would not have needed to leave the farm, since there were 14 acres of land to walk around.

Nizam's disappearance on New Year's Day may have been a delayed reaction to the events of the previous twenty-four hours, perhaps nausea or shock, which prompted him to escape the farm and Liley for a while, but as he appeared to show no emotional unease at all during her visit there, this seems unlikely. Perhaps something concerning the disposal of the body needed attending to which had been overlooked.

As for the two M3 calls made that evening, despite Liley saying that Arthur did not go out that evening, either Liley must have forgotten or Arthur managed to slip out without her noticing, especially likely considering that she was there simply to provide them both with alibis. (At the trial, Nizam said that he did not take the car when he went out on New Year's Day as it would have been heard, suggesting that he was deliberately being circumspect and was conscious of what Liley might witness.)[37]

The long silence from M3 that followed was probably a combination of lack of opportunity after Elsa's return, confusion and uncertainty about what the next move should be and panic about the level of publicity the case was attracting. After over a week, with Arthur confident enough that Muriel's body would not be discovered and the police would not track him down, and in possession of four more letters from Muriel and samples of her clothing, the temptation to resume the blackmail demands must have overwhelmed him.

The further facts in the case are mostly well established.

***

We must now, lastly, turn to the most familiar question associated with this dreadful affair: where was Muriel buried? Bill Smith told the BBC in 1970 that he believed Muriel was murdered and 'somewhere up there she is buried, in or around the farm'.[38] This is an important remark, showing that Smith held the belief even after such intensive searching of the area, aware that the results of any search at the time, however rigorous, could never be indisputable.

In June 1968, Arthur employed a labourer, George Duncan, to cut the grass at the front of the farm, which was by now 'two or three feet tall, mixed up with nettles and thistles',[39] but Duncan had to abandon the job when a chair that had been dumped in the undergrowth got caught in the cutter bar. He tried to break it up with a billhook, which he then mislaid. At the trial, there was a casual remark by Elsa that she had found a billhook similar to the one found at Arthur Road 'in the garden the other day'.[40] Presumably, this was the one that Duncan lost, and perhaps this demonstrates the fallibility of searches conducted with the limited resources of 1970.

However, on the question of Muriel being buried at Rooks Farm, although many killers show a curious lack of intelligence in disposing of their victims – and the Hoseins were certainly unimaginative and careless enough to have conceivably buried her so close to home – it should be noted that the brothers made a very thorough job of removing all other traces of Muriel from Rooks Farm. It therefore seems odd that they would make so little effort concerning her burial.

As I have said before, all through the remaining weeks of the ransom demands, and throughout their arrest, remand, custody and trial, they showed absolutely no concern that she would be found, despite being aware of the colossal search operation that was underway. I am reminded constantly of Arthur's apparent claim in prison that he was confident of acquittal because the police had not found the body and that they were looking in the wrong place. I remain disbelieving of Nizamodeen's unlikely account of burying Muriel on the farm, of him digging a deep hole in the frozen ground, or of lines of police officers missing a recently dug grave several feet deep.

At the end of 1979, the tenth anniversary of the crime, the *Birmingham Post* ran a piece on the case, stating that every time a body was found in that part of Hertfordshire, it had to be eliminated from this inquiry. The last time had been five years earlier, when a skeleton was found not far from Rooks Farm, although dental and other checks unfortunately proved that it was not the final piece of the jigsaw. Bill Smith stated that he had visited Arthur in prison a few years previously and found that 'he had been able to shut the case right out of his mind and was totally unaffected by the memory of what he had done'.[41]

The article also aired for the first time Smith's specific theory about what happened to Muriel's body, and not simply that she was buried 'in or around the farm'.[42] He stated that, at the time of the murder, 'huge North Sea Gas pipes were being laid near the farm and ... it was more likely that her body was encased in the cement used as the foundations for them'. Smith repeated this theory again in his last interview in 2001, reflecting on 'what an ideal place it would be to hide a body'.[43]

However, the story does not quite end there. When I interviewed Tom Mangold about his 1971 film on the case, he clarified:

At that time, North Sea Gas were laying the first trench from East Anglia to London, which I believe passed fairly close to the farm. The trench was dug but couldn't be filled in because it was bitterly cold, so it was left open for a time. The theory was that the Hoseins put the body into the trench and covered it with a little bit of earth, and then when work resumed it was filled in.[44]

He then added an extraordinary final detail:

Several years later, Alick McKay was asked by the Home Office whether he wanted them to try to find the body by digging up 2 or 3 miles of the trench. I think that by then he had remarried, and he took the view that if her body was there, he would rather that she was left in peace.

Recruitment adverts from North Sea Gas for production drillers in the area can be found in the *Herts and Essex Observer* from June 1969. That local pipeline work was completed at the end of 1971. What cannot be located is any kind of paper trail relating to this case. Why the Home Office were in a position to commission an excavation of the pipes some years later but not at the time of the initial inquiry, we will never know, but the fact that they contacted Alick about it means that there must have been a document at the time recording the theory, which perhaps resides in one of the closed files – and with a fairly specific location in mind. While there was probably nothing to connect the Hoseins to the trench in question, one imagines that Bill Smith probably passed the course of the pipeline on his regular visits to Rooks Farm and that the idea gradually firmed up in his mind.

Nothing could ever realistically be done now to investigate this theory, but it is tantalising to consider that if, by the time of their arrest, the brothers were aware that the pipes were now covered, it could explain their complete confidence that the body would not be found. However, I am not sold on the idea of them deciding to kill Muriel (or, for the sake of argument, discovering her dead) and then landing upon this convenient solution so readily. How did they know in advance that the trench had been dug and temporarily abandoned? Perhaps they tried the site as a first option and, once there, saw their opportunity, but considering how close it must have been to Stocking Pelham, and considering how much intensive work would be continuing there in the near future, I am unconvinced. I have always believed that the Hoseins' success at hiding Muriel's body was more due to luck than skill. This scenario feels rather too clever for them.

In January 2022, a former resident of Furneaux Pelham contacted the McKays after reading of Nizamodeen's supposed confession. Her story was that over the New Year of 1969–70, late one night she saw a car crawl very slowly past her house with no lights on. She and a neighbour watched the car proceed up the Causeway and stop at the entrance to a disused field that had once been a refuse tip.* She told me that the neighbour identified the car as belonging to the Hoseins, and she watched the two occupants open the boot, at which point the inner light came on. They pulled a rolled-up carpet out of the rear of the car, rested it on the gate and then disappeared into the field for about fifteen minutes, returning without it and then driving away. The witness told me that she reported the incident to the desk sergeant at Bishop's Stortford Police Station at the time and mentioned it again some time later when visiting the police on a separate matter, but that nothing was done about it.

---

* The 1½-acre site was used as a refuse tip by Braughing Rural Council between 1947 and 1962 (*Herts and Essex Observer*, 18 March 1982, p. 7).

It sounded an exciting lead, but sadly, on close examination, there was little to connect the incident to the case. The witness was adamant that the car was a hatchback, hence the inner light coming on when the boot was opened and the carpet being pulled out rather than lifted. She was unshakeable on this, so therefore was identifying the wrong vehicle, because the Volvo saloon that Arthur owned did not have a fold-down back seat and was not a hatchback.

As well as describing the wrong car, she also said that although the driver had Arthur's build, she could not positively identify either man. Also, strangely, she said that it was likely to be the Hoseins because 'they had a sideline dealing in carpets, you used to see a roll of carpet on the roof rack of their van', when in fact they owned no van, and I can find no mention anywhere in the thousands of documents relating to the case of any dealings in carpets. Arthur was being sued at the time over the outstanding debt for his living-room carpet, a debt that he would have been less likely to have run up if he had a carpet business of his own.

Furthermore, although the witness had an extremely low opinion of the police, every other scrap of information presented to them at the time about any suspicious activity in the vicinity of Rooks Farm was strenuously acted on, with excavations all around Furneaux Pelham, Much Hadham and Sleepy Hollow. Therefore, it stretches credulity that any officer would ignore a piece of information as potentially vital as this while every lead, no matter how slight, was being followed up.

Serial killers are curiously careless about disposing of their victims, whereas those who kill not because of compulsion but to cover up their crime are generally more careful. The Hoseins' motive for murder was to avoid detection, so therefore it is logical that they would make their victim as hard as possible to find. While it is impossible to put oneself precisely in the mindset of men such as the Hoseins, my feeling is that they would have had two priorities in disposing of their victim. They would want to take her to a place as far away as possible from anywhere that they could be connected to (Rooks Farm), while also making sure that it was somewhere that they knew well enough to be confident that she would not be discovered.

When I embarked on this project, rather idealistically, I was convinced that while witnesses remained alive, while Nizamodeen Hosein remained alive and while police files were being opened, there was hope of some light being shed on this appalling matter. A naive hope persisted that I would find some tiny clue, some undiscovered morsel of information, that I could present to the McKay family and which could finally offer up an answer to the question they need an answer to above all others: where is Muriel's body?

To my astonishment, that hope may not have been in vain.

20

LAST RESORT

Hope you are all well and happy, including Carl! Will be home Wed, about 5, I think. Best regards to you all. See you soon.

Muriel McKay, Mallorca, 19 September 1969.

Journeying back one last time to Stocking Pelham and its surroundings, having built up such a vivid picture of village life there in 1969, it is disorientating to be reminded that today this is not a land of farmers in remote pubs doing lunchtime deals over cattle, but wealthy commuters living in what were once the modest homes of agricultural workers and artisans. Today one must have that £1 million to live here; it is not enough simply to crave it.

Sleepy Hollow, immortalised in those bleak, blue newsreel images of treacherous frozen ponds, is today a bright, pretty spot, and like so much of rural England, better manicured now, compared with the scruffy, bleak countryside of the past. In the churchyard at Brent Pelham, just along from the Black Horse, one of the few pubs from the case that still trades, and which still proudly exhibits the souvenirs of the Puckeridge Hunt, lies Captain Charles Barclay. Above his grave an English flag flies boldly. Even in death, he remains a symbol of everything that Arthur Hosein coveted and yet resented.

The Raven has long since vanished from Berden, although the red call box which became a subject for Court Number 1 at the Old Bailey, as the box from where Arthur was suspected of making his final M3 call, still stands 100 yards opposite. The Cock at Stocking Pelham was destroyed by fire in 2008, although its shell has been rebuilt and petitions for it to reopen persist. These were pubs that belonged to a world long since gone away. Local people still talk sweetly of them, as they do of other quirky taverns of that time, such as the 'Crazy' pub at Hunsdon* and the Plough at Great Munden, complete with cinema organ, where Arthur and Nizam drank on the eve of the kidnapping.

This was once a land of affordable cottages and farmhouses and cheap and colourful pubs. The picture of south Hertfordshire that has built up before me, even allowing for my own childhood nostalgia, seems decidedly appealing, especially in an age of chain pubs, pub closures and extortionate property prices. This was, in many ways, a happy land. If only it could have been enough for the Hoseins.

Unfortunately, it was in other ways that Arthur Hosein thrived in those times. The 1960s were a time of astounding vision but, depressingly, a dreadful number of blind eyes were still being turned. When detailing the relentless sexual assaults that Arthur committed on local women (one dreads to think of how many other victims there were before he moved to Stocking Pelham), one is shocked by how the victims clearly felt unable or disinclined to report such behaviour. It is an appalling measure of the era that on 23 December 1969, the *Sun* ran a feature entitled 'Is There Such a Thing as Rape?', in which Elizabeth Prosser asked, 'Can a woman be the victim of rape if she has a history of promiscuity? Or can only the virgin honestly say she has been raped?'[1] This was located a few pages away from a pull-out songbook of Christmas carols.

Many have been led to the wrong Rooks Farm when poking around the district in recent years. There is another Rooks Farm at Berden, which even the local newspaper misidentified in a recent piece about the case. Arthur Hosein's former home, even today, remains hidden from the public gaze, and even though the feared Alsatians are no longer in residence, eerily, as one approaches, one is dissuaded from approaching by what prove to be rather malevolent wooden sculptures of large dogs on each side of the driveway. A footpath runs along the perimeter of the estate, from which one can glimpse that, compared with the shabby, grim, haunted site that it was in 1970, today it is a bright, immaculate place, its white walls glistening in the sunshine and its lawns neatly trimmed. The only thing that persists from its past is its secrecy. Once again contemplating how far it is separated from the rest of the world by the snaking drive, and how concealed it is, I cannot believe that

---

* The delightful 'Crazy' pub was officially the Unique Turkey Cock. Ten miles south of Stocking Pelham, it was a roadside fun palace crammed with novelties, gewgaws and bric-a-brac, all presided over by landlord Burleigh Dixon. It closed in 1985.

Arthur's move here was not at least in part because already something of his crime was forming in his mind, that he was following some strange calling for seclusion.

The parade of pylons trooping across the landscape from the Stocking Pelham substation, with its links to the North Sea Gas pipeline, are a constant reminder of Bill Smith's theory about where Muriel may be. A motif of the British landscape, unnoticed and then suddenly inescapable, as I gaze at them, I wonder whether the answer to this mystery is right before my eyes, hiding in plain sight.

For some unknown reason, this vast, quiet landscape has never given up its secrets regarding the burial place of Muriel McKay. Perhaps it does not hold such secrets. Perhaps the answer lies not in Stocking Pelham, but somewhere quite different.

I might just have unearthed the answer – not in the countryside of south Hertfordshire but among a sheaf of neglected papers in a box in southwest London.

There are three boxes of files, separate from the other existing files on the case and therefore easy to overlook. They were closed until 2011 but have surely never been comprehensively examined because, if they had been, the information they contain would have already been investigated.

Unlike the other files, these are not Metropolitan Police, Central Criminal Court or Director of Public Prosecutions files, but Court of Criminal Appeal files. At first glance, they appear to be of little value, mostly comprised of duplicate copies of all fourteen books of the trial transcript, together with a copy of the Court of Appeal's judgement on the Hoseins' failed attempt to appeal their verdicts and sentences. However, at the bottom of the third box, after one has waded through sundry papers relating to the preparation, failure and administrative costs of the brothers' appeals, are a clutch of letters which, as far as I can tell, have never been seen by the police, or any other interested parties.

It will be remembered that in March 1971, the brothers' attempts at appeal ended in failure. Nizamodeen made no further attempts to appeal, Douglas Draycott QC never having considered there were any realistic grounds even when acting for him. However, Arthur Hosein refused to accept his punishment. When reporting on the appeals in Chapter 17, I added that he made a further attempt to appeal in 1972 and that I would examine this matter in the final chapter.

In 1972, Arthur was serving his sentence at HMP Wakefield. At the end of October, he wrote a letter to the Court of Appeal:

Dear Sir,

Since I has been given permission from the Home Office authorities to seek for legal aid in obtaining a solicitor to act upon my behalf upon this wrongful conviction which I am at present shouldering. I very much seek your assistance with respect to this matter in granting me legal aid, for the purpose of solicitor making searches for additional evidence to substantiate my innocence, however, you will like to learn that I has given my assets to my then wife whom has divorced me, and re-married to a German husband, now residing in Germany.

I sincerely hope that you will consider my request upon this matter.

I thank you in advance, and I await hearing from you.

I remain,

Yours sincerely, Arthur Hosein[2]

A month later, the assistant registrar replied, telling Arthur that the registrar was 'not able to grant you legal aid for the purpose you indicate'.[3] Legal aid is only granted to pay for legal advice, family mediation and court or tribunal representation. However, Arthur had already approached a new solicitor to act for him, a Mr George E. Brown, of George Brown and Co. Solicitors, Birmingham, and three days later, Brown replied to the Court of Appeal's letter on Arthur's behalf.

The letter, which has never been made public before, might just be the most important piece of paper in existence regarding the whereabouts of Muriel McKay, because in this letter, Arthur's new solicitor not only reveals that Arthur has told him where Muriel is buried, but actually reveals the location:

Dear Sir,

Re: A. Hosein, No. 081065

HM Prison, Love Lane, Wakefield

The above tells me that he has applied to you for Legal Aid to enable him to be advised by me on an appeal. He has asked me to pay him a visit. This I am prepared to do to see whether there is any merit in this man's allegations.

I have received information that the body of Mrs McKay, who was the alleged victim in this case, was buried at Jaywick Sands, a fact which I have communicated to the local police.

It may be that there is some merit in what this man says, but of course if he has no further funds with which to investigate the matter further – and he assures me that all the matrimonial property has been disposed of and his ex-wife has taken off to Germany – I cannot see how one can help him under the Legal Aid Scheme. That is to say there is no provision for me to go to Wakefield and charge the Legal Aid fund for that. I could only charge for advice under the Legal Aid and Advice Act.

However, if he was granted a Legal Aid certificate by you for further investigations for the prospects of success regarding his proposed appeal, I could investigate the matter and report. If I thought there was no possibility of success I should tell him so. Nonetheless, I do feel that in the circumstances and in view of the fact that this man is pressing me, some measure of help should be given to him and I would greatly appreciate your assistance if you could advise me as to what could be done in these peculiar circumstances.

Yours Faithfully,

George Brown[4]

'These peculiar circumstances' is certainly an apt phrase. In fact, it is something of an understatement. This is an extraordinary exchange. I showed the correspondence to Roger Street, who agreed how extremely odd it is for a solicitor to make such a statement, since 'by doing so, he is indicating that his client has made admissions which suggest that he was culpable in some way'.[5] Furthermore, no competent lawyer would publicly ask for money for a client who has not yet been proven to be telling the truth, but would visit the client first.

A week later, George Brown and Co. received a reply:

Dear Sirs,

Regina v. Arthur Hosein

In reply to your letter dated 24th November 1972, the Registrar has no power to grant legal aid in connection with matters not current in the Court of Appeal (Criminal Division).

I observe that you have received certain information from Mr Hosein which you have communicated to the police. They will no doubt investigate it, and if those investigations lead the Secretary of State to refer Mr Hosein's case to the Court under the provisions of S.17, Criminal Appeal Act 1968, the question of legal aid can of course be considered then.

Yours Faithfully,

Assistant Registrar[6]

The rest is silence. The paper trail ends there. The only further items in the box are Arthur's limp attempts in 1980 to appeal to the European Court of Human Rights, for which he made a request for a transcript of his trial, only to cancel it a few days later.

Although Brown's letter does not identify the source of his information, the reply from the assistant registrar confirms that source to have been Arthur Hosein. This makes the document the only piece of paper, of all the thousands of pages of available evidence in this case, that actually names a location for where Muriel's body may be, if one disregards jailhouse gossip and the like. Furthermore, that information has come from Arthur Hosein, making this the only time on record that he ever volunteered any information on the matter.

Let us consider the letters piece by piece. Brown had not visited Arthur at this point but was requesting funds to do so. Therefore, the information that Arthur presented to him must have been in writing. He describes Arthur's information as 'allegations'. There is reference to Arthur 'pressing' him and a detectable note of concern, as if whatever narrative Arthur's revelation about the location formed a part of, George Brown felt it worthy of investigation.

It is unclear how locating Muriel's body could have helped Arthur in any way, other than by improving his prospects of parole many years in the future. However, two words within the letters are important. One is 'appeal', meaning that this information is intended to attempt to correct or add to the facts established at the trial. The other is the word 'allegations', which points towards this being some new story dreamed up by Arthur, perhaps along the lines of his failed Robert Maxwell yarn.

Let us suppose then that he had concocted a story that would somehow allow him to reveal the location of Muriel's body while blaming her death on others. An obvious question then arises: how would revealing the location of Muriel's body help him, unless that location proved to be genuine? Whether or not Arthur's plan had any hope of success, how could a false claim possibly help him? Or would finding her body help his appeal by proving that she had died of natural causes?

The Solicitors Regulation Authority (SRA) informed me that the firm of George Brown and Co. merged to become George Brown, Philip Baker & Co., and closed in 1991. It was then acquired by Talbots, which closed in 1999. It is common for documents relating to wills and probate records to be retained after a firm of solicitors closes and for someone to act as a point of contact on them, though there is less chance of the correspondence in this matter having survived, especially since it never officially became an active case for the firm.

There was a note on the SRA's records from 2014 naming the current custodian of the surviving files, but sadly, he was unable to assist. He told me that it is 'highly unlikely that George Brown is still alive, as I am not at all sure that he was in 1992, and Talbots would almost certainly not have acquired any paperwork of that nature'.[7] He also added that the SRA's records were incorrect and that he had no access to any papers himself.

He also doubted that any former partners of Talbots were still practising, and recalled:

George Brown, Philip Baker & Co. were intervened by the Law Society, Talbots stepping in to clear up the mess.[*] I was not a partner at that time, but I do recall an absolute shambles which required sorting out. I have never met nor had any information concerning George Brown.[8]

Since this had led nowhere, instead I pursued the final key point in the letters. Brown claimed that he had communicated the information concerning the whereabouts of Muriel's body 'to the local police'. It is impossible to determine whether this would be the police local to George Brown in Birmingham, to Arthur, in Wakefield, or to the burial site, which would have been Essex Police, but whoever, if anybody, George Brown might have told, there is absolutely no trace of any such information ever having been received by any police force.

We can immediately dismiss the possibility that information relating to this matter lies in the closed files, as those files run no later than 1971. We have seen that in the two decades following the crime, there were countless messages sent to the police about possible burial sites, many of which came via different regional police forces. Without fail, each message that is now in the

---

*   The firm were fined £500.

files, however eccentric, was acknowledged and referred to either Bill Smith or, after his retirement, to a serving officer who had worked on the inquiry. Some were referred to Roger Street, but neither he nor Peter Rimmer have any knowledge whatsoever of this affair.

Peter and I spoke again a few days after I showed him the correspondence:

I've given some thought to this, and this is a mystery. Lots of the team were still in Wimbledon in 1972, and it would not have been at all difficult for Arthur to have been seen again by one of us going up to Wakefield. I'm frustrated as hell about that letter. You know, years later, whenever some of the officers from that team met up, it was always in the back of your mind, someone would say, 'Remember McKay, that still frustrates me that we never ever found her', and I still feel that way, especially for the family. It was always there, with all of us. Any of us would have longed to have got involved in trying to find her.[9]

Since I could find no record of the police having received the information, and as there is no record of any of the files on the case having been called up again in the period immediately following these letters, I tried instead to discover whether either George Brown or a police officer had visited Arthur as a result of this disclosure. This meant attempting to locate the prison visitors' books for HMP Wakefield in 1972. Brian Roberts, a former Met detective, explains:

There are two ways for a police officer to visit a serving prisoner. The first is as an invited visitor. You would write to the prisoner, and if he agreed to see you, he would write to invite you. That would then be recorded in the prison visitors' book. The other way is to go on a legal visit, where the prisoner is only told on the day that you arrive that you are there to see him. He can then decide whether to see you; he may refuse to leave his cell. [This was the sequence of events when Bill Smith, while at HMP Parkhurst in 1975, asked whether Nizamodeen would agree to see him, which he did.]

Whether that sort of visit went into the visitors' book would depend on that particular prison's regime. There were different ways of logging it. If a trustee was logging it, they didn't tend to list them as they didn't want the other prisoners finding out that a police officer was visiting a prisoner. It could kick off if they suspected he was informing. However, if it was maintained by a civilian employee, it would be more likely to have been recorded.

The easiest way to judge is to look at the first few pages of the book and see if there are generally police officers listed in the book.[10]

HMP Wakefield no longer holds the relevant visitors' books, but they have survived in a local archive, which the prison kindly allowed to action my request. The books are restricted records, as they contain potentially sensitive information about living individuals, but if I could prove that the individuals concerned were deceased, any record they have of them having paid a visit to Arthur could be shared with me.

Frustratingly, in the 1970s, visitors to the prison signed their names but did not typically list which inmate they were visiting and why, or enter their own occupation, so it would not be possible to confirm whether someone was definitely visiting Arthur Hosein. However, it would still be possible to tell whether any of the names that I provided visited that prison over the relevant period. I provided them with proof of deaths for Bill Smith, John Minors and George Brown, and specimen signatures from each of them for comparison with the entries in the book. As a result, the archivist confirmed that the book did not appear to have the signatures of any of those men in it.[11] This is not necessarily conclusive, as there is a possibility that the only names being listed in this book were those of the prison's board of visitors rather than visitors to inmates.[12]

However, it is clear from the correspondence that George Brown was not prepared to visit Arthur without funding, and there is nothing to suggest that Bill Smith ever knew anything about this matter, since his notes after visiting Nizamodeen three years later, and his correspondence with serving officers in later years, following other communications, make no mention of it. I was satisfied that the information which Arthur had imparted to George Brown had never been shared with the police, perhaps because, despite his claim, Brown chose not to inform them. The only place left to go was the location itself.

Jaywick is an hour's drive from Stocking Pelham and, significantly, lies on the nearest stretch of coastline to it. The landscape changes quite dramatically on the journey, from the quaintness of rural Essex to the bleakness of barren fens as the coast slides into view. A seaside town in winter can be a forlorn place, and at neighbouring Clacton-on-Sea, any summer crowds that might still gather have long since scattered. The seaside is fantasy land, offering the adrenalin of the rollercoaster and the make-believe of the ghost train. Surveying the amusement arcades, and pondering the gambles that people take in the hope of become rich – gambles that almost always fail – I am reminded of a moment in the Hoseins' trial, when a reference was made to gambling, and the judge said, 'That does not matter. Gambling has nothing to do with this case.'

I think that gambling had a great deal to do with this case. Arthur was a mad and stupid gambler. Whether he really was in a gambling club on the afternoon of the kidnapping, whether Nizam is correct to call him 'a gambler', in some perverse way, his appalling crime was a colossal gamble for an ill-deserved jackpot.

I visited Jaywick with former Detective Chief Superintendent Paul Dockley. Built on salt marshes and fields unsuitable for agriculture because of their risk of flooding, Jaywick was created in the 1930s specifically as a cheap holiday resort for Londoners, and for thirty years achieved its aim, as historic postcards will testify. Although the houses were never intended as permanent residences, today, forty years after the closure of its Butlin's Holiday Camp, this is one of the poorest places in Britain. Much to the frustration of many in what is a strong local community, to the outside world Jaywick is notorious for its high rates of drug use and low rates of employment, having been assessed to be one of England's most deprived area.

However, in 1969, Jaywick was still primarily a holiday resort. If Arthur and Nizamodeen Hosein did drive here on the night of 30 December 1969, they would have been confident of privacy. If Muriel was buried on Jaywick Sands, it would have been a great deal easier to dig a grave here than in frozen clay.

Paul and I parked by the Martello tower and strolled along the silvery shoreline, which is breathtakingly beautiful in the sharp winter sun, all the while considering, if the Hoseins did bury her here, where a likely place might have been. Since it is impossible to dig into wet sand without it instantly filling up again, an area beyond the normal reach of the tide would have been the only option. They also could only have chosen a place a short distance from wherever the car could be parked.

We both agreed that the most obvious places would be among the clusters of dunes or the small area of scrub between the beach and the road, both of which are masked from the town by the sea wall. Also, it is a minor point, but as far as I am aware, no spade was ever found at the farm, so if one was used to bury Muriel, it must have been disposed of after burying the body. If it bore nothing but traces of the soil around Rooks Farm, there would be little need to remove it, but if it bore traces of sand, that would be a different matter.

I said before that, if I were Arthur Hosein, I would have been searching my mind for a burial place as far away from anywhere that could be connected with me as possible, but also one that I could be reasonably confident would not be disturbed. If one then adds to this the reality of how hard the earth would have been that winter, the softer ground of the coast surely becomes a possibility.

Day trip destinations and holiday resorts provide that balance of being far from home and yet familiar. I asked Freida whether the family ever had day trips to the seaside. She said that they did, although she could not remember any place names. All the same, we know from the letter that the name 'Jaywick Sands' was known at least to Arthur. Back in London, I compared the location today with the largest-scale Ordnance Survey maps from the period, which confirmed that the relevant area has remained unchanged since 1969 and no nearby areas have been developed since then.

I consulted Professor Patricia Wiltshire, a remarkable forensic ecologist, botanist and palynologist, who has worked on nearly 300 criminal cases as an expert witness since Paul first used her to help detect a murder in the 1990s. She explained that the fetch – the distance travelled by the waves, which determines the ferocity with which the coast is battered and sands are disturbed and redistributed – in theory could be relatively small here, as the waves are only coming off the short span of the English Channel, compared with those crashing on to the Atlantic shoreline, and that from the photographs I had taken of the site, 'one might think that there was a fairly reasonable chance that human remains might still be there'.[13]

However, despite the gentle fetch, the coastline here has been subject to dramatic developments since 1969. Coastal erosion over the years washed away much of the beach sand, leaving a muddy strata. To provide additional protection from the sea, in the mid-1980s a successful operation began to bring heavy rock boulders from Norway to create large fish-tail groynes. Huge quantities of sand were also pumped ashore from further along the coast. The project was extended from the tower near the golf course, at the opposite end of the beach, all the way to the neighbouring town of St Osyth. Because of this work, and the effects of wind and tide, in many places the beach level has increased considerably.[14]

Whether Arthur's last resort, his desperate attempt to escape his punishment, was to tell something of the truth, with lies having failed him all the way, we cannot yet say. I have passed all my research to the McKay family, who remain committed to finding the truth – and to finding Muriel. Despite what they have had to live with all these years, Muriel's children are now in their eighties. It is heart-breaking to consider that, given their longevity, Muriel would probably have lived to a similar age, had it not been for the Hoseins. They probably denied her three decades of life.

The winter sun is setting. Christmas is returning once more. Other families are preparing to gather together again. Maybe Muriel McKay is here. Maybe she is at Rooks Farm. Maybe she is somewhere that remains unknown. But whichever sorrowful place she may rest in and might still one day be recovered from, wherever else she is, she remains in the hearts and minds of those who mourn her, a life lived kindly, and ended unforgivably.

AFTERWORD

This is the Parliament. This is the last. Thought you'd like it.
Muriel McKay, The Hague, 15 November 1969.

On 4 November 2020, the Prisoners (Disclosure of Information About Victims) Act, received Royal Assent. It was christened 'Helen's law', after Helen McCourt, who vanished in 1998 and whose body has never been found. Her mother, Marie McCourt, spent many years campaigning for the legislation, but Helen's killer, Ian Simms, who had been convicted on DNA evidence, was released on licence several months before the law was enacted.

The first person to have been denied parole as a result of the law was Glyn Razzell, serving a life sentence for the murder of his estranged wife, Linda, who disappeared in 2002. The Parole Board ruled that he could remain in an open prison but would not, for now, be released, stating:

> Continued withholding of such important information suggested a need to retain a perception of himself and maintain self-preservation through keeping control of the narrative. This and a marked lack of empathy for those involved in the case were seen to bear on the panel's risk assessment.[1]

However, the law is still flexible in this area, human rights laws preventing a simple 'no body, no parole' rule. If the Parole Board deem a prisoner to be no longer a risk to the public, even if that prisoner refuses to disclose the whereabouts of a victim, they can still be considered for release, despite the withholding of such information usually revealing a lack of empathy or remorse.

As long as our race survives, families will continue to suffer the horror of losing a loved one through the actions of evil men. No longer should any family's pain be compounded by the additional suffering that the McKays continue to endure.

REFERENCES

A Note on Money

1. '50p at 50: How Britons' Living Costs Have Changed Since 1969', *Guardian*, 14 September 2019.

Chapter 1: Home

1. Witness statement of Mona Lillian, 5 January 1970, Metropolitan Police (MEPO) 26/33.
2. Author interview with Peter Rimmer, 13 September 2021.
3. Visit to St Mary House, 27 June 2021, and email from Ewen and Nicky Gilmour, 22 June 2021.
4. *The Observer*, Adelaide, 1 January 1927, p. 16.
5. *Ibid.*, 8 September 1928, p. 59.
6. *The Register News-Pictorial*, 30 June 1930, p. 24.
7. M3 telephone call, 19 January 1970.
8. Dianne McKay interview, *Times*, 26 August 2021.
9. Lady Jodi Cudlipp, interviewed on *Manhunt: The Press Baron's Wife*, ITV, 27 November 2001.
10. *The News*, Adelaide, 17 June 1935, p. 3.
11. *Kangaroo Island Courier*, 9 April 1932, p. 2.
12. Author interview with Dianne McKay, 2 May 2022.
13. Author interview with Jennifer McKay, 15 May 2022.
14. *Ibid.*
15. *Banner Headlines* by Stafford Somerfield (Scan, 1979), p. 203.
16. Witness statement of Margery Nightingale, 6 January 1970, MEPO 26/30.
17. *Have You Seen This Woman?* by Michael O' Flaherty (Corgi, 1971), p. 24.
18. *Ibid.*, p. 23.

19. Author interview with Aubrey Rose, 11 November 2021.
20. *Wimbledon News and Advertiser*, 31 October 1969, p. 1.
21. Dr Tadeus Markowicz, 17 September 1970, J82/1578 *Regina vs Hosein*, trial transcript, Vol. 4, pp. 42–6.
22. Witness statement of Dr Tadeus Markowicz, 14 April 1970.
23. Witness statement of Ellen Maud Richards, 8 January 1970, MEPO 26/30.
24. Witness statement of Dianne Muriel Dyer née McKay, 14 January 1970, MEPO 26/30.
25. Witness statement of Alick Benson McKay, 30 December 1969, MEPO 26/30.
26. Witness statement of Margery Nightingale, 6 January 1970, MEPO 26/30.
27. Witness statement of Dr Tadeus Markowicz, 5 January 1970, MEPO 26/30.
28. Alick McKay, 15 September 1970, J82/1578, *Regina vs Hosein*, trial transcript, Vol. 2, p. 20.
29. Witness statement of Margery Nightingale, 6 January 1970, MEPO 26/30.
30. Witness statement of Gloria Pugh, 31 December 1969, MEPO 26/30.
31. Witness statement of Ellen Maud Richards, 8 January 1970, MEPO 26/30.
32. Lady Jodi Cudlipp, interviewed on *Manhunt: The Press Baron's Wife*, ITV, 27 November 2001.

Chapter 2: Paper Tigers

1. 'Rupert Murdoch Slashes Value of the Sun Newspaper to Zero', *Daily Telegraph*, 12 June 2021.
2. Stead, quoted in *The Rise and Fall of the Political Press*, Vol. 1: 'The Nineteenth Century', (University of North Carolina Press, 1981), p. 342.
3. *City of Dreadful Delight: Narratives of Sexual Danger in Late-Victorian London* by Judith R. Walkowitz (Virago, 1992), p. 84.
4. *Pall Mall Gazette*, 17 August 1887, p. 12.
5. *Saint or Sensationalist? The Story of W.T. Stead* by Victor Pierce Jones (Gooday, 1988), p. 11.
6. *Pall Mall Gazette*, 6 July 1885, p. 6.
7. *Daily Mirror*, 30 July 1949, p. 1.
8. Unattributed quote in *Fall: The Mystery of Robert Maxwell* by John Preston (Penguin, 2021), p. 66.
9. *Banner Headlines* by Stafford Somerfield (Scan, 1979), p. 153.
10. *News of the World*, 20 October 1968, p. 2.
11. *Murdoch* by William Shawcross (Chatto and Windus, 1993), p. 137.
12. *Banner Headlines* by Stafford Somerfield (Scan, 1979), p. 169.
13. *The Newspaper Reading Public of Tomorrow* by Dr Mark Abrams (Odhams Press Ltd, 1964) p. 57.
14. *Waterhouse on Newspaper Style* by Keith Waterhouse (Viking, 1989), p. 43.
15. Cecil Harmsworth King, speaking on *World in Action: The Sun*, Granada/ITV, 15 September 1964.
16. *The Sun*, 15 September 1964, p. 1.

17. *The Newspaper Reading Public of Tomorrow* by Dr Mark Abrams (Odhams Press Ltd, 1964), p. 73.
18. *Waterhouse on Newspaper Style* by Keith Waterhouse (Viking, 1989), p. 43.
19. *Press Gang: How Newspapers Make Profits from Propaganda* by Roy Greenslade (Macmillan, 2003), p. 216.
20. *News of the World*, 26 October 1969, p. 1.
21. *Ibid.*, 2nd November 1969, p. 1.
22. *The Sun*, 15 November 1969, p. 1.
23. *News of the World*, 28 September 1969, p. 1.
24. *UK Press Gazette*, 20 October 1969, 769:11.
25. *Daily Mirror*, 4 October 1969, p. 4.
26. *Reading Evening Post*, 6 October 1969, p. 2.

Chapter 3: Desperation

1. *Madame Tussauds and the History of Waxworks* by Pamela Pilbeam (Hambledon & London, 2003), p. 212.
2. Author interview with Aubrey Rose, 11 November 2021.
3. *24 Hours: Worse Than Murder*, 21 April 1971, BBC1.
4. Psychiatric Report on Arthur Hosein by Dr H. Terry, Senior Medical Officer, HM Prison Brixton, 4 August 1970, CRIM 1/5395/3.
5. Author interview with Freida Hosein, 5 April 2022.
6. Author interview with Aubrey Rose, 11 November 2021.
7. *The Murder of Muriel McKay* by Norman Lucas (Mayflower, 1971), pp. 25–6.
8. *24 Hours: Worse Than Murder*, 21 April 1971, BBC1.
9. *The Murder of Muriel McKay*, by Norman Lucas (Mayflower ,1971) p. 27.
10. *24 Hours: Worse Than Murder*, 21 April 1971, BBC1.
11. Independent Psychiatric Report on Arthur Hosein by Dr Philip Connell of the Maudsley Hospital, 3 September 1970, CRIM 1/5395/3.
12. *The Murder of Muriel McKay* by Norman Lucas (Mayflower ,1971), p. 25.
13. HMS *Hilary* Passenger Lists, October 1955, Incoming Passenger Lists, 1878–1960, Immigration Department.
14. *Wimbledon News and Advertiser*, 10 October 1969, p. 1.
15. Independent Psychiatric Report on Arthur Hosein by Dr Philip Connell of the Maudsley Hospital, 3 September 1970, CRIM 1/5395/3.
16. Witness statement of Robert Augustine Cullen, 11 February 1970.
17. Author interview with Aubrey Rose, 11 November 2021.
18. *Psychology* by Douglas Bernstein, Louis A. Penner, Alison Clarke-Stewart and Edward Roy, 2nd edition (Houghton Mifflin, 1991), p. 613.
19. Interview with Elisabeth Hosein, conducted by DCS Ron Harvey, 9 February 1970, MEPO 26/29.
20. Independent Psychiatric Report on Arthur Hosein by Dr Philip Connell of the Maudsley Hospital, 3 September 1970, CRIM 1/5395/3.
21. *Daily Mirror*, 7 October 1970, p. 15.

22. Independent Psychiatric Report on Arthur Hosein by Dr Philip Connell of the Maudsley Hospital, 3 September 1970, CRIM 1/5395/3. This diagnosis was disputed in psychiatric assessments prepared before the trial.
23. Witness statement of Adam Hosein, 12 February 1970, MEPO 26/29.
24. *Ibid.*
25. Interview with Elisabeth Hosein, conducted by DCS Ron Harvey, 9 February 1970, MEPO 26/29.
26. Author interview with Freida Hosein, 5 April 2022
27. Witness statement of William Harold White, 20 February 1970, MEPO 26/31.
28. Witness statement of Elsie Footit, 16 February 1970, MEPO 26/31.
29. Witness statement of Leonard Harry Welham, 16 February 1970, MEPO 26/31.
30. Letter from Arthur Hosein to HM Passport Office, 24 June 1967.
31. 'The Poet and the Cheese' in *A Miscellany of Men* by G.K. Chesterton (Methuen & Co. Ltd, 1912).
32. *Fact, Fiction and Foul Deeds: The History of a Hertfordshire Village* by David D. Bailey (Stocking Pelham Millennium Committee, 2000).
33. *Herts &and Bucks (Penguin Guide)* edited by L. Russell Muirhead (Penguin, 1949), pp. 29–30.
34. Author interview with Peter Miller, 22 November 2021.
35. Interview with Elisabeth Hosein, conducted by DCS Ron Harvey, 9 February 1970, MEPO 26/29.
36. Author interview with Yasmin Strube, 27 August 2021.
37. Witness statement of Joyce Agnes Bunkall, 15 February 1970, MEPO 26/31.
38. Witness statement of Robert Cecil Lionel Bunkall, 15 February 1970, MEPO 26/31.
39. Witness statement of Abraham Eckhardt, 10 February 1970, MEPO 26/33.
40. *Daily Mirror*, 7 October 1970, p. 16.
41. Author interview with Jill Murray, 4 May 2022.
42. Witness statement of Jon Nicholas Finch, 26 February 1970, MEPO 26/31.
43. Notes of various conversations between Elisabeth Hosein and DCS Ron Harvey, MEPO 26/29.
44. Witness statement of Michael Griffith Davies, 23 February 1970, MEPO 26/29.
45. *Have You Seen This Woman?* by Michael O' Flaherty (Corgi, 1971), p. 185.
46. Witness statement of Frederick James Cecil Capel Butler, 14 February 1970, MEPO 26/29.
47. Witness statement of Ernest Walter Woollard, 9 February 1970, MEPO 26/33.
48. Witness statement of Joyce Adele Smith, 17 February 1970, MEPO 26/31.
49. Witness statement of William Franklyn George Baker, 13 February 1970, MEPO 26/31.
50. Witness statement of Herbert Clement Mardell, 11 February 1970, MEPO 26/33.
51. Witness statement of Alice May Spelling, 19 February 1970, MEPO 26/31.
52. Witness statement of Frederick Harold Westlake, 18 February 1970, MEPO 26/33.

53. *Daily Mirror*, 7 October 1970, p. 16.
54. *Have You Seen This Woman?* by Michael O' Flaherty (Corgi, 1971), p. 187.
55. Elsa Hosein, 22 September 1970, J82/1578 *Regina vs Hosein*, trial transcript, Vol. 9, p. 9.
56. Witness statements of Maurice Herman, 19 February 1970, and Morris Sunshine, 20 February 1970, MEPO 26/31.
57. Author interview with Freida Hosein, 5 April 2022.
58. Witness statement of Elsie May Brown, 18 February 1970, MEPO 26/31.
59. Witness statement of Eric Jackson, 16 February 1970.
60. Witness statement of Eileen Green, 16 February 1970, MEPO 26/31.
61. Witness statement of Jack Fletcher, 17 February 1970, MEPO 26/31.
62. Author interview with Sharly Hughes, 19 January 2022.
63. Author interview with Aubrey Rose, 11 November 2021.
64. Psychiatric Report on Nizamodeen Hosein by Dr H. Terry, Senior Medical Officer, HM Prison Brixton, 4 August 1970, CRIM 1/5395/3.
65. Independent Psychiatric Report on Nizamodeen Hosein by Dr Philip Connell of the Maudsley Hospital, 3 September 1970, CRIM 1/5395/3.
66. Previous Convictions Report on Nizamodeen Hosein, MEPO 26/29.
67. Witness statement of Joyce Agnes Bunkall, 15 February 1970, MEPO 26/31.
68. Witness statement of Adam Hosein, 12 February 1970, MEPO 26/29.
69. Witness statement of Shauffie Ali, 21 February 1970, MEPO 26/33.
70. Witness statement of Rahim Mohammed, 21 February 1970, MEPO 26/33.
71. *Ibid.*
72. Adam Hosein, 24 September 1970, J82/1578 *Regina vs Hosein*, trial transcript, Vol. 9, p. 19.
73. Letter from Nizamodeen Hosein to the Immigration/Nationality Department, Home Office, 25 September 1969, MEPO 26/33.
74. *The Murder of Muriel McKay* by Norman Lucas (Mayflower, 1971), p. 29.
75. Interview with Elisabeth Hosein, conducted by DCS Ron Harvey, 9 February 1970, MEPO 26/29.
76. Witness statement of Harold George Prince, 17 February 1970, MEPO 26/31.
77. Witness statement of Alfred Noel Bardwell, 18 February 1970, MEPO 26/31.
78. Witness statement of Joyce Agnes Bunkall, 15 February 1970, MEPO 26/31.
79. *Murder in the Fourth Estate* by Peter Deeley and Christopher Walker (Victor Gollancz, 1971), p. 42.
80. Author interview with Tom Pateman, 11 December 2021.
81. Witness statement of Frederick James Cecil Capel Butler, 14 February 1970, MEPO 26/29.
82. Witness statement of Audrey Strube, 9 February 1970, MEPO 26/30.
83. Author interview with Yasmin Strube, 27 August 2021.
84. Author interview with Sharly Hughes, 19 January 2022.
85. Interview with Elisabeth Hosein, conducted by DCS Ron Harvey, 9 February 1970, MEPO 26/29.
86. Witness statement of Joyce Adele Smith, 17 February 1970, MEPO 26/31.

87. Witness statement of Adam Hosein, 12 February 1970, MEPO 26/33.
88. *Herts and Essex Observer*, 3 October 1969, p. 23.
89. Witness statement of Joyce Adele Smith, 17 February 1970, MEPO 26/31.

Chapter 4: Advent

1. Witness statement of Herbert Clement Mardell, 11 February 1970, MEPO 26/33.
2. Witness statement of Charles Geoffrey Edward Barclay, 11 February 1970, MEPO 26/31.
3. Obituary, Captain Charlie Barclay, *Daily Telegraph*, 27 July 2002.
4. *Murder in the Fourth Estate* by Peter Deeley and Christopher Walker (Victor Gollancz, 1971), p. 44.
5. Witness statement of Charles Geoffrey Edward Barclay, 11 February 1970, MEPO 26/31.
6. *Murder in the Fourth Estate* by Peter Deeley and Christopher Walker (Victor Gollancz, 1971), p. 44.
7. Witness statement of Charles Geoffrey Edward Barclay, 11 February 1970, MEPO 26/31.
8. Letter from Arthur Hosein to Captain Charles Barclay, quoted in *Murder in the Fourth Estate* by Peter Deeley and Christopher Walker (Victor Gollancz, 1971), p. 44.
9. *Herts and Essex Observer*, 21 November 1969, p. 7.
10. Witness statement of Abraham Eckhardt, 10 February 1970, MEPO 26/33.
11. Witness statement of Steve Kutner, 16 February 1970, MEPO 26/31.
12. Witness statement of Audrey Strube, 9 February 1970, MEPO 26/30.
13. Witness statement of Yasmin Elizabeth Strube, 13 February 1970.
14. Author interview with Yasmin Strube, 27 August 2021.
15. Witness statement of Audrey Strube, 9 February 1970, MEPO 26/30.
16. Witness statement of Yasmin Elizabeth Strube, 13 February 1970.
17. Author interview with Yasmin Strube, 27 August 2021.
18. Witness statement of Wilfred Roy Hunt, 19 February 1970, MEPO 26/29.
19. Witness statement of Sylvia Millicent Hunt, 19 February 1970, MEPO 26/29.
20. Witness statement of Margaret Ramdye Ramkalawan, 6 March 1970, MEPO 26/31.
21. *Ibid.*
22. Witness statement of Hazrah Mohammed, 6 March 1970, MEPO 26/31.
23. Witness statement of Maureen Dorothy Callanan, 20 February 1970, MEPO 26/29.
24. Witness statement of Wilfred John Lane, 27 December 1969, MEPO 26/31.
25. *Ibid.*, 1 January 1970, MEPO 26/31.
26. Witness statement of James McGowan Eggenton, 10 February 1970, MEPO 26/33.
27. *Herts and Essex Observer*, 26 December 1969, p. 12.

28. Witness statement of Mubarak Khartoun Liley Mohammed, 11 February 1970, MEPO 26/33.
29. *Ibid.*
30. *Ibid.*, 8 February 1970, MEPO 26/33.
31. Witness statement of Joyce Adele Smith, 17 March 1970, MEPO 26/33.
32. Witness statement of DS Gerald Summerville, 25 February 1970, MEPO 26/31.
33. Witness statement of DC Carl Gray, 25 February 1970, MEPO 26/31.
34. Supplementary Crime Report for Chief Constable, Stevenage, 5 January 1970, MEPO 26/31.
35. Witness statement of Malcolm Stephenson Reid, 20 February 1970, MEPO 26/31.
36. Witness statement of Gerald Carrington, 24 February 1970.
37. Witness statement of Sylvia Millicent Hunt, 19 February 1970.
38. Witness statement of John Robert Bailey, 30 June 1970, MEPO 26/29.
39. Witness statement of PC Richard J. Felton, 28 February 1970, MEPO 26/33.
40. Witness statement of Ernest Walter Woollard, 9 February 1970, MEPO 26/33.

Chapter 5: Trespasses

1. Witness statement of Margery Nightingale, 6 January 1970, MEPO 26/30.
2. Witness statement of Dr Tadeus Markowicz, 14 April 1970.
3. 'Life After the Death Sentence' by Henry Russell Douglas, *Sun*, 29 December 1969, p. 2.
4. Witness statement of Margery Nightingale, 30 December 1969, MEPO 26/30.
5. *Ibid.*, 6 January 1970, MEPO 26/30.
6. Witness statement of Dianne Muriel Dyer née McKay, 14 January 1970, MEPO 26/30.
7. *The Murder of Muriel McKay* by Norman Lucas (Mayflower, 1971), p. 35.
8. Witness statement of Alfred Anderson, 19 April 1970, MEPO 26/33.
9. *Regina. vs Hosein*, Court of Appeal, p. 5, J82/1578.
10. Witness statement of Jaunsz Zarzycki, 4 January 1970, MEPO 26/33.
11. *Ibid.*, 9 February 1970, MEPO 26/33.
12. Witness statement of George Cecil Rhodes List, 6 February 1970, MEPO 26/30.
13. Witness statement of Mona Lillian, 5 January 1970, MEPO 26/33.
14. Witness statement of Jack Harvey, 10 January 1970, MEPO 26/30.
15. Witness statement of Alick Benson McKay, 18 March 1970, MEPO 26/29..
16. *Ibid.*
17. Witness statement of Paul Edward Stafford, 6 January 1970, MEPO 26/30.
18. Witness statement of Inspector William Anderson, 16 March 1970, MEPO 26/29.
19. *24 Hours: Worse Than Murder*, 21 April 1971, BBC1.
20. Witness statement of Inspector William Anderson, 18 January 1970, MEPO 26/29.
21. DS Graham Birch, interviewed on *Manhunt: The Press Baron's Wife*, ITV, 27 November 2001.

22. Email to author from Jeff Edwards, 24 September 2021.
23. DS Graham Birch, interviewed on *Manhunt: The Press Baron's Wife*, ITV, 27 November 2001.
24. *Murder in the Fourth Estate* by Peter Deeley and Christopher Walker (Victor Gollancz, 1971), p. 54.
25. 'Detective's Casebook' by J. Plimmer, *Police Review*, 6 March 1988, p. 28.
26. *Daily Mirror*, 30 December 1969, p. 1.
27. Witness statement of David Randolph Dyer, 14 January 1970, MEPO 26/30.
28. *Murder in the Fourth Estate* by Peter Deeley and Christopher Walker (Victor Gollancz, 1971), p. 57.
29. Witness statement of Zaneefa Mohammed, 3 July 1970, MEPO 26/33.
30. Brief from Wilfred Smith to Assistant Commissioner, C Department, 2 April 1970, CRIM 1/5395.
31. Interview with Elisabeth Hosein, conducted by DCS Ron Harvey, 9 February 1970, MEPO 26/29.
32. Transcript of BBC Radio 1 *News Summary*, 1 a.m., 30 December 1969.
33. Terence Underwood, interviewed on *Manhunt: The Press Baron's Wife*, ITV, 27 November 2021.
34. Witness statement of Terence Underwood, 30 December 1969, MEPO 26/29.
35. Brief from Wilfred Smith to Assistant Commissioner, C Department, 2 April 1970, pp.127–28, CRIM 1/5395.
36. *Ibid.*, p. 116.
37. Witness statement of Joyce Agnes Bunkhall, 20 February 1970, MEPO 26/31.

Chapter 6: Ruins

1. Witness statement of DS Walter Whyte, 31 December 1969, MEPO 26/29.
2. Author interview with Walter Whyte, 10 March 2019.
3. Witness statement of Alfred Noel Bardwell, 18 February 1970, MEPO 26/31.
4. Witness statement of Eileen Molly Butler, 23 February 1970, MEPO 26/33.
5. Witness statement of Michael Griffith Davies, 23 February 1970, MEPO 26/29.
6. Witness statement of Elsie May Brown, 16 February 1970, MEPO 26/31.
7. Alick McKay, 15 September 1970, J82/1578, *Regina vs Hosein*, trial transcript, Vol. 2, p. 15.
8. Witness statement of Margery Nightingale, 6 January 1970, MEPO 26/30.
9. Author interview with Peter Rimmer, 13 September 2021.
10. Lady Jodi Cudlipp, interviewed on *Manhunt: The Press Baron's Wife*, ITV, 27 November 2001.
11. Author interview with Roger Street, 2 July 2021.
12. Author interview with Peter Rimmer, 13 September 2021.
13. Author interview with Aubrey Rose, 11 November 2021.
14. Author interview with Roger Street, 2 July 2021.
15. DCS Bill Smith, interviewed on *Manhunt: The Press Baron's Wife*, ITV, 27 November 2001.
16. Author interview with Walter Whyte, 10 March 2019.

17. Author interview with Peter Rimmer, 13 September 2021.
18. Author interview with Roger Street, 2 July 2021.
19. Author interview with Jennifer McKay, 15 May 2022.
20. Jim Parker, interview on *Manhunt: The Press Baron's Wife*, ITV, 27 November 2021
21. *Daily Express*, 31 December 1969, p. 1.
22. *Daily Mail*, 31 December 1969, p. 1.
23. *Sun*, 2 January 1970, p. 3.
24. *Daily Mirror*, 1 January 1970, p. 20.
25. Charles Pateman, 23 September 1970, J82/1578, *Regina vs Hosein*, trial transcript, Vol. 8, p. 30.
26. *Evening News*, 30 December 1969, p. 1.
27. *Murder in the Fourth Estate* by Peter Deeley and Christopher Walker (Victor Gollancz, 1971), p. 52.
28. *Evening News*, 30 December 1969, p. 1.
29. David Dyer, 16 September 1970, J82/1578, *Regina vs Hosein*, trial transcript, Vol. 3, p. 3.
30. Transcript of *BBC Evening News* report by Richard Whitmore, 8.50 p.m., 30 December 1969.
31. Witness statement of Ernest Walter Woollard, 9 February 1970, MEPO 26/33.
32. Gerald Gordon, 23 September 1970, J82/1578, *Regina vs Hosein*, trial transcript, Vol. 8, p. 45.
33. *Ibid.*

Chapter 7: Voices

1. Preliminary report by Charles Frederick Maxwell Fryd, Principal Scientific Officer, 6 January 1970, MEPO 26/33.
2. Author interview with Roger Street, 2 July 2021.
3. Arthur Brine, 16 September 1970, J82/1578, *Regina vs Hosein*, trial transcript, Vol. 5, p. 19.
4. Witness statement of Mubarak Khartoun Liley Mohammed, 1 March 1970, MEPO 26/33.
5. Witness statement of Harold George Prime, 17 February 1970, MEPO 26/31.
6. Witness statement of Mubarak Khartoun Liley Mohammed, 1 March 1970, MEPO 26/33.
7. Transcript of ITN *News at Ten* report by Michael Brunson ITV, 31 December 1969, MEPO 26/29.
8. *BBC News* report by Martin Bell, 1 January 1970.
9. Witness statement of Mubarak Khartoun Liley Mohammed, 14 April 1970.
10. *Evening Standard*, 1 January 1970, p. 32.
11. Brief from Wilfred Smith to Assistant Commissioner, C Department, 2 April 1970, p. 26, CRIM 1/5395.
12. Witness statement of Mubarak Khartoun Liley Mohammed, 14 April 1970.
13. *Daily Mail*, 2 January 1970, p. 1.

Chapter 8: Whispers

1. *BBC News* report, 2 January 1970.
2. Witness statement of Dr Tadeus Markowicz, 14 April 1970.
3. Bill Smith, interviewed on *Manhunt: The Press Baron's Wife*, ITV, 27 November 2001.
4. *Ibid.*
5. *Shall We Ever Know?* by William Cooper (Hutchison & Co., 1971), p. 33.
6. 'Plot to Kidnap Clore Probed', *Sun*, Tuesday, 23 December 1969, p. 2.
7. *Daily Mail*, 1 January 1970, p. 1.
8. *Evening Standard*, 2 January 1970, p. 1.
9. Bill Smith, interviewed on *Manhunt: The Press Baron's Wife*, ITV, 27 November 2001.
10. Witness statement of Anne Owen, 15 January 1970, MEPO 26/30.
11. *Sun*, 3 January 1970, p. 1.
12. *West Essex Gazette and Guardian (Epping, Ongar and Villages)*, 9 January 1970, p. 1.
13. Author interview with Aubrey Rose, 11 November 2021.
14. *The Murder of Muriel McKay* by Norman Lucas (Mayflower, 1971), p. 62.
15. Author interview with Roger Street, 2 July 2021.
16. Undated commendation recommendation by Bill Smith, MEPO 26/29.
17. *Ibid.*
18. John Minors, interviewed on *Manhunt: The Press Baron's Wife*, ITV, 27 November 2001.
19. *Evening Standard*, 24 February 1970, p. 13.
20. *Daily Mirror*, 3 January 1970, p. 1.
21. *Evening Standard*, 24 February 1970, p. 13.
22. *Ibid.*, 20 February 1970, p. 12.
23. *Manhunt: The Press Baron's Wife*, ITV, 27 November 2001.
24. Author interview with Jennifer McKay, 15 May 2022.
25. *Evening News*, 2 January 1970, p. 1.
26. Author interview with Roger Street, 2 July 2021.
27. Bill Smith, interviewed on *Manhunt: The Press Baron's Wife*, ITV, 27 November 2001.
28. Michael O'Flaherty, interviewed on *Manhunt: The Press Baron's Wife*.
29. *Murder in the Fourth Estate* by Peter Deeley and Christopher Walker (Victor Gollancz, 1971), pp. 113–14.
30. Author interview with Peter Rimmer, 13 September 2021.
31. *News of the World*, 4 January 1970, p. 1.
32. *Ibid.*, p. 2.
33. *Ibid.*
34. Undated commendation recommendation by Bill Smith, MEPO 26/29.
35. Email to author from Chloe Baveystock, 1 July 2021.
36. Bill Smith, interviewed on *24 Hours: Worse Than Murder*, 21 April 1971, BBC1.
37. Author interview with Peter Rimmer, 13 September 2021.

38. *Sun*, 5 January 1970, p. 1.
39. Author interview with Peter Rimmer, 13 September 2021.
40. 'Detective's Casebook: The Metropolitan Police Investigation into the Kidnap of Muriel McKay in 1969', John Plimmer, *Police Review*, 6 March 1998, p. 28.
41. Witness statement of Ian Francis Burgess, 4 January 1970, MEPO 26/30.
42. Bill Smith, interviewed on *Manhunt: The Press Baron's Wife*, ITV, 27 November 2001.

Chapter 9: Silence

1. Bertha Cellini, 22 September 1970, J82/1578, *Regina vs Hosein*, trial transcript, Vol. 8, pp. 50–1.
2. Witness statement of Sergeant Roy Herridge, 9 February 1970, MEPO 26/30.
3. Author interview with Roy Herridge, 30 November 2021.
4. Author interview with Freida Hosein, 5 April 2022.
5. *24 Hours: Worse Than Murder*, 21 April 1971, BBC1.
6. Witness statement of DS Gerald Summerville, 25 February 1970, MEPO 26/31.
7. Witness statement of DC David McEnhill, 9 February 1970, MEPO 26/30.
8. Witness statement of Savvas Michael, 13 April 1970, MEPO 26/29.
9. *Daily Express*, 8 January 1970, p. 1.
10. *Daily Mirror*, 9 January 1970, p. 6.
11. Witness statement of Albert Edward Tietjen, 9 January 1970, MEPO 26/30.
12. *Evening Standard*, 9 January 1970, p. 40.
13. Transcript of *BBC Evening News* report by Richard Whitmore, 8.50 p.m., 9 January 1970, MEPO 26/29.
14. *Ibid.*
15. *Evening Standard*, 9 January 1970, p. 40.
16. *Daily Express*, 10 January 1970, p. 1.
17. *Ibid.*, 12 January 1970, p. 1.
18. Witness statement of Rose Young, 25 February 1970, MEPO 26/31.
19. Witness statement of Alexander Brunton, 12 February 1970, MEPO 26/31.
20. Witness statement of Stafford William Somerfield, 17 January 1970, MEPO 26/29.

Chapter 10: Epiphany

1. Author interview with Peter Rimmer, 13 September 2021.
2. *Times*, 16 January 1970, p. 5.
3. Author interview with Freida Hosein, 5 April 2022.
4. Bill Smith, interviewed on *24 Hours: Worse Than Murder*, 21 April 1971, BBC1.
5. Bill Smith, interviewed on *Manhunt: The Press Baron's Wife*, ITV, 27 November 2001.

6. *Murder in the Fourth Estate* by Peter Deeley and Christopher Walker (Victor Gollancz, 1971), p. 115.
7. Ian McKay, interviewed on *24 Hours: Worse Than Murder*, 21 April 1971, BBC1.
8. *Murder in the Fourth Estate* by Peter Deeley and Christopher Walker (Victor Gollancz, 1971), p. 115.
9. Letter from Arthur Hosein to Dennis Saunders, 23 January 1970, MEPO 26/33.
10. Witness statement of Audrey Strube, 9 February 1970, MEPO 26/30.
11. Letter from Nizamodeen Hosein to Dolly Premchand, 30 January 1970, MEPO 26/33.

Chapter 11: Paper Flowers

1. Author interview with Roger Street, 2 July 2021.
2. *Ibid.*
3. Kenneth Rextrew, interviewed on *Manhunt: The Press Baron's Wife*, ITV, 27 November 2001.
4. Roger Street, interviewed on *Manhunt: The Press Baron's Wife*.
5. Kenneth Rextrew, interviewed on *Manhunt: The Press Baron's Wife*.
6. Bill Smith, interviewed on *Manhunt: The Press Baron's Wife*.
7. Author interview with Aubrey Rose, 11 November 2021.
8. *Daily Mirror*, 3 February 1970, p. 2.
9. *West Essex Gazette*, 6 February 1970, p. 1.
10. Witness statement of Bernard Charles Law, 23 March 1970, MEPO 26/29.

Chapter 12: Paper Chase

1. *Times*, 7 October 1970, p. 2.
2. *Daily Express*, 7 October 1970, p. 8.
3. John Bland, interviewed on *24 Hours: Worse Than Murder*, 21 April 1971, BBC1.
4. Joyce Armitage, interviewed on *24 Hours: Worse Than Murder*.
5. Witness statement of Frederick James Cecil Capel Butler, 14 February 1970, MEPO 26/29.
6. John Minors, interviewed on *24 Hours: Worse Than Murder*.
7. John Bland, interviewed on *24 Hours: Worse Than Murder*.
8. Robert Kelly, interviewed on *24 Hours: Worse Than Murder*.
9. Witness statement of WDC Joyce Armitage, Flying Squad, 3 March 1970, MEPO 26/29.
10. Witness statement of DS Nicholas Birch, Flying Squad, 24 February 1970, MEPO 26/29.
11. John Bland, interviewed on *24 Hours: Worse Than Murder*.
12. Call log, Bishop's Stortford Police, 6 February 1970, MEPO 26/29.
13. Witness statement of Michael Griffith Davies, 23 February 1970, MEPO 26/29.
14. Witness statement of Beverley Marilyn Grice, 9 February 1970, MEPO 26/29.

15. Witness statement of Frederick James Cecil Capel Butler, 14 February 1970, MEPO 26/29.
16. Alan Smith, interviewed on *Manhunt: The Press Baron's Wife*, ITV, 27 November 2001.
17. Author interview with Jennifer McKay, 15 May 2022.

Chapter 13: Disconnect

1. Witness statement of DCS Bill Smith, 3 March 1970, MEPO 26/29.
2. Witness statement of James Parker, 21 March 1970, MEPO 26/29.
3. Witness statement of DCS Bill Smith, 3 March 1970, MEPO 26/29.
4. Author interview with Peter Rimmer, 13 September 2021.
5. Witness statement of DCS Bill Smith, 3 March 1970, MEPO 26/29.
6. *Ibid.*
7. Witness statement of Dr Maxwell Muller, 11 March 1970, MEPO 26/33.
8. Author interview with Roger Street, 2 July 2021.
9. Diary of Ian Burgess, 9 February 1970.
10. Nizamodeen Hosein, interviewed on *The Wimbledon Kidnapping*, Sky/Caravan, 21 August 2021.
11. Author interview with Aubrey Rose, 11 November 2021.

Chapter 14: Midwinter

1. *Herts and Essex Observer*, 13 February 1970, p. 2.
2. *Ibid.*, 20 February 1970, p. 1.
3. Author interview with Freida Hosein, 5 April 2022.
4. Author interview with Yasmin Strube, 27 August 2021.
5. Ronald Harvey, 17 September 1970, J82/1578 *Regina vs Hosein*, trial transcript, Vol. 4, p. 41.
6. Author interview with Des Hillier, 19 November 2021.
7. DCI Cyril Thomas, interviewed on ITN *News at Ten*, ITV, 9 February 1970.
8. Author interview with Sharly Hughes, 19 January 2022.
9. Author interview with Roger Street, 2 July 2021.
10. Peter Hardy, interviewed on *The Wimbledon Kidnapping*, Sky/Caravan, 21 August 2021.
11. Witness statement of Leonard John Smith, MEPO 26/31.
12. Witness statement of Stephen Walter Burgess, 2 March 1970, MEPO 26/31.
13. Author interview with Peter Miller, 22 November 2021.
14. Author interview with Peter Rimmer, 13 September 2021.
15. *The Rainbow Never Ends* by Aubrey Rose (Lennard, 2006), p. 94.
16. Author interview with Des Hillier, 19 November 2021.
17. Author interview with Peter Miller, 22 November 2021.
18. Interview with Elisabeth Hosein, conducted by DCS Ron Harvey, 9 February 1970, MEPO 26/29.

19. Author interview with Freida Hosein, 5 April 2022.
20. Witness statement of Adam Hosein, 12 February 1970, MEPO 26/29.
21. *Evening News*, 13 February 1970, p. 1.
22. Witness statement of William John Bell, 22 February 1970, MEPO 26/31.
23. Witness statement of John McCafferty, Senior Experimental Officer, Metropolitan Police Forensic Science Laboratory, Holborn, 5 March 1970, MEPO 26/29.
24. Witness statement of John Vincent Jackson, Senior Experimental Officer, 15 April 1970, MEPO 26/29.
25. Witness statement of Leonard John Smith, 19 March 1970, MEPO 26/30.
26. Undated letter from Nizamodeen Hosein to Liley Mohammed, MEPO 26/33.
27. Witness statement of Michael Patrick Kelleher, 20 March 1970, MEPO 26/29.
28. *Herts and Essex Observer*, 6 March, p. 2.
29. Witness statement of Michael Patrick Kelleher, 20 March 1970, MEPO 26/29.
30. Author interview with Des Hillier, 19 November 2021.

Chapter 15: Evidence

1. *Evening Standard*, 26 February 1970, p. 1.
2. Witness statement of Alick Benson McKay, 18 March 1970, MEPO 26/29.
3. Witness statement of DCI Arthur Brine, 24 March 1970, MEPO 26/29.
4. Bill Smith, interviewed on *Manhunt: The Press Baron's Wife*, ITV, 27 November 2001.
5. Email to author from Andrew Wood, 9 December 2021.
6. Email to author from Chloe Baveystock, 1 July 2021.
7. Correspondence between A.J. Richards, Anne Kerr MP and the Home Office, MEPO 26/32.
8. Author interview with Aubrey Rose, 11 November 2021.
9. *Close Encounters of a Legal Kind* by Aubrey Rose (Lennard, 1997), p. 66.
10. Author interview with Aubrey Rose, 11 November 2021.
11. Letter from DI John Minors to Commander, C2, 10 July 1970, MEPO 26/29.
12. Author interview with Tom Pateman, 11 December 2021.
13. Undated witness statement of DCS Wilfred Smith, MEPO 26/29.
14. Witness statement of DCS Wilfred Smith, 19 August 1970, MEPO 26/29.
15. Committal memo, 16 June 1970, MEPO 26/29.
16. Author interview with Peter Rimmer, 13 September 2021.
17. Ronald Harvey, 17 September 1970, J82/1578 *Regina vs Hosein*, trial transcript, Vol. 4, p. 38.
18. Email to author from David Ryan, 10 August 2022.
19. Arthur Hosein, application for legal aid, 16 June 1970, MEPO 26/29.
20. Arthur Hosein, statement of means, 18 February 1970, CRIM 1/5395/1.
21. Arthur Hosein, application for legal aid, 16 June 1970, MEPO 26/29.
22. Nizamodeen Hosein, application for legal aid, 16 June 1970, MEPO 26/29.

23. Notice of particulars of alibi on behalf of Nizamodeen Hosein, from Aubrey Rose to solicitor, New Scotland Yard, 22 June 1970, MEPO 26/29.
24. Witness statement of John Robert Bailey, 30 June 1970, MEPO 26/29.
25. Witness statement of Adam Hosein, 8 July 1970, MEPO 26/29.
26. Letter from David Coote to Governor, HMP Brixton, 17 July 1970, MEPO 26/29.
27. Author interview with Freida Hosein, 5 April 2022.
28. Elsa Hosein, expenses claim, 8 September 1970, CRIM 1/5395/3.
29. Author interview with Peter Rimmer, 13 September 2021.

Chapter 16: Judgement

1. *Shall We Ever Know?* by William Cooper (Hutchison & Co., 1971), p. 126.
2. *Times*, 7 October 1970, p. 2.
3. Author interview with Aubrey Rose, 11 November 2021.
4. John Robert Bailey, 24 September 1970, J82/1578 *Regina vs Hosein*, trial transcript, Vol. 9, p. 13.
5. *Shall We Ever Know?* by William Cooper (Hutchison & Co., 1971), p. 16.
6. *Ibid.*, p. 43.
7. Author interview with Aubrey Rose, 11 November 2021.
8. Barry Hudson QC, 15 September 1970, J82/1578 *Regina vs Hosein*, trial transcript, Vol. 2, p. 7.
9. Mr Justice Shaw, 15 September 1970, J82/1578 *Regina vs Hosein*, trial transcript, Vol. 2, p. 13.
10. *Shall We Ever Know?* by William Cooper, (Hutchison & Co., 1971), p. 47.
11. Arthur Rosenthal, 16 September 1970, J82/1578 *Regina vs Hosein*, trial transcript, Vol. 3, p. 28.
12. Mr Justice Shaw, 16 September 1970, J82/1578 *Regina vs Hosein*, trial transcript, Vol. 3, p. 30.
13. Arthur Rosenthal, 16 September 1970, J82/1578 *Regina vs Hosein*, trial transcript, Vol. 3, pp.32–3.
14. Mr Justice Shaw, 18 September 1970, J82/1578 *Regina vs Hosein*, trial transcript, Vol. 5, p. 28.
15. Ibid., p. 40.
16. *All England Law Reports*, 1, 1955, p. 247.
17. Barry Hudson QC, 21 September 1970, J82/1578 *Regina vs Hosein*, trial transcript, Vol. 6, p. 51.
18. Arthur Hosein, 22 September 1970, J82/1578 *Regina vs Hosein*, trial transcript, Vol. 7, p. 1.
19. *Ibid.*
20. *Ibid.*, p. 2.
21. *Ibid.*
22. Witness statement of William Franklyn George Baker, 13 February 1970, MEPO 26/31.

23. Arthur Hosein, 22 September 1970, J82/1578 *Regina vs Hosein*, trial transcript, Vol. 7, p. 3.
24. *Ibid.*, p. 4.
25. *Ibid.*, p. 5.
26. *Ibid.*, p. 9.
27. *Ibid.*, p. 20.
28. *Ibid.*, p. 22.
29. *Ibid.*, p. 24.
30. *Ibid.*, p. 26.
31. *Ibid.*, p. 37.
32. *Ibid.*
33. Witness statement of Robert Maxwell, 23 September 1970, MEPO 26/29.
34. Author interview with Aubrey Rose, 11 November 2021.
35. Arthur Hosein, 22 September 1970, J82/1578 *Regina vs Hosein*, trial transcript, Vol. 7, p. 45.
36. Sir Peter Rawlinson, 22 September 1970, J82/1578 *Regina vs Hosein*, trial transcript, Vol. 7, p. 48.
37. Mr Justice Shaw, 22 September 1970, J82/1578 *Regina vs Hosein*, trial transcript, Vol. 7, p. 49.
38. Arthur Hosein, 22 September 1970, J82/1578 *Regina vs Hosein*, trial transcript, Vol. 7, p. 50.
39. Independent Psychiatric Report on Arthur Hosein by Dr Philip Connell of the Maudsley Hospital, 3 September 1970, CRIM 1/5395/3.
40. Mr Justice Shaw, 23 September 1970, J82/1578 *Regina vs Hosein*, trial transcript, Vol. 7, p. 52.
41. Arthur Hosein, 23 September 1970, J82/1578 *Regina vs Hosein*, trial transcript, Vol. 8, p. 9.
42. *Ibid.*, p. 5.
43. *Ibid.*, p. 26.
44. *Ibid.*, p. 29.
45. *Shall We Ever Know?* by William Cooper (Hutchison & Co., 1971), p. 118.
46. Charles Pateman, 23 September 1970, J82/1578 *Regina vs Hosein*, trial transcript, Vol. 8, p. 30.
47. Gerald Gordon, 23 September 1970, J82/1578 *Regina vs Hosein*, trial transcript, Vol. 8, p. 41.
48. Elsa Hosein, 23 September 1970, J82/1578 *Regina vs Hosein*, trial transcript, Vol. 8, p. 52.
49. *Ibid.*, p. 54.
50. *Ibid.*, p. 59.
51. Arthur Hosein, 23 September 1970, J82/1578 *Regina vs Hosein*, trial transcript, Vol. 8, p. 59.
52. *Shall We Ever Know?* by William Cooper (Hutchison & Co., 1971), p. 130.
53. Author interview with Peter Rimmer, 13 September 2021.
54. Dr Julius Grant, 24 September 1970, J82/1578 *Regina vs Hosein*, trial transcript, Vol. 9, p. 56.

55. Author interview with Aubrey Rose, 11 November 2021.
56. Dr Julius Grant, 25 September 1970, J82/1578 *Regina vs Hosein*, trial transcript, Vol. 10, p. 2.
57. Author interview with Peter Rimmer, 13 September 2021.
58. Nizamodeen Hosein, 25 September 1970, J82/1578 *Regina vs Hosein*, trial transcript, Vol. 10, p. 24.
59. Douglas Draycott QC, 25 September 1970, J82/1578 *Regina vs Hosein*, trial transcript, Vol. 10, p. 54.
60. Nizamodeen Hosein, 28 September 1970, J82/1578 *Regina vs Hosein*, trial transcript, Vol. 11, p. 1.
61. *Ibid.*, p. 7.
62. *Ibid.*, p. 10.
63. Nizamodeen Hosein, 29 September 1970, J82/1578 *Regina vs Hosein*, trial transcript, Vol. 12, p. 6.
64. Mr Justice Shaw, 29 October 1970, J82/1578 *Regina vs Hosein*, trial transcript, Vol. 12, p. 22.
65. *Shall We Ever Know?* by William Cooper (Hutchison & Co., 1971), p. 168.
66. *Ibid.*, p. 151.
67. *Evening Standard*, 30 September 1970, p. 9.
68. *Times*, 1 October 1970, p. 2.
69. Mr Justice Shaw, 5 October, J82/1578 *Regina vs Hosein*, trial transcript, Vol. 14, p. 32.
70. *Ibid.*
71. Arthur Hosein, 6 October, J82/1578 *Regina vs Hosein*, trial transcript, Vol. 14, p. 35.
72. Mr Justice Shaw, 6 October, J82/1578 *Regina vs Hosein*, trial transcript, Vol. 14, p. 36.
73. Sebag Shaw, quoted in letter from Inspector Alan Grant, X Division, to Commander, V Division, 8 October 1970, MEPO 26/29.
74. *Daily Sketch*, 7 October 1970, p. 1.
75. Elsa Hosein, interviewed on *24 Hours: Worse Than Murder*, 21 April 1971, BBC1.
76. *Daily Mirror*, 7 October 1970, p. 5.
77. *Daily Sketch*, 7 October 1970, p. 13.
78. Arthur Hosein, 23 September 1970, J82/1578 *Regina vs Hosein*, trial transcript, Vol. 8, p. 23.
79. *Daily Sketch*, 7 October 1970, p. 13.
80. *Evening Standard*, 7 October 1970, p. 9.
81. *Daily Mirror*, 7 October 1970, p. 5.
82. Alick McKay, interviewed on *24 Hours: Worse Than Murder*, 21 April 1971, BBC1.
83. *Sun*, 8 October 1970, p. 1.

Chapter 17: Echoes

1. *Times*, 7 October 1970, p. 2.
2. *Sunday Times*, 8 October 1970, p. 9.
3. Postscript to commendation nominations by Commander Garrett, V Division, 13 November 1970, MEPO 26/29.
4. Letter from Aubrey Rose to Commander Guiver, 8 October 1970, MEPO 26/29.
5. Author interview with Aubrey Rose, 11 November 2021.
6. Letter from Sir Peter Rawlinson to the Commissioner, 7 October 1970, MEPO 26/29.
7. Author interview with Peter Rimmer, 13 September 2021.
8. Bill Smith, interviewed on *24 Hours: Worse Than Murder*, 21 April 1971, BBC1.
9. *Herts and Essex Observer*, 20 November 1970, p. 2.
10. *Daily Telegraph*, 3 December 1970.
11. *Herts and Essex Observer*, 4 December 1970, p. 2.
12. Letter from registrar, Court of Appeal, to Arthur Hosein, 14 December 1970, J82/1578.
13. Letter from Arthur Hosein to registrar, 5 January 1971, J82/1578.
14. Summary of grounds for appeal, 8 March 1971, J82/1578.
15. Nizamodeen Hosein, statement of grounds for appeal, 31 October 1970, J82/1578.
16. *Shall We Ever Know?* by William Cooper (Hutchison & Co., 1971), p. 220.
17. Lord Justice Edmund Davies, J82/1578 *Regina vs Hosein*, Court of Appeal hearing transcript, p. 1.
18. *Ibid.*, p. 3.
19. *Ibid.*, p. 4.
20. *Ibid.*, p. 25.
21. *Ibid.*, p. 27.
22. Undated correspondence between the Commissioner and the Assistant Commissioner (Crime), MEPO 28/8.
23. Letter from Eric Wright, head of BBC News, to Scotland Yard Press Office, 18 June 1971, MEPO 28/8.
24. Undated draft reply from Scotland Yard press secretary for House of Commons oral question asked by Arthur Lewis, MP for West Ham North, on 6 May 1971 (*Hansard*, Commons, 6/5/71, cols. 423–4).
25. Author interview with Tom Mangold, 9 May 2022.
26. *The Listener*, 3 February 1972, Vol. 87, Issue 2236, p. 136.
27. *24 Hours: Worse Than Murder*, 21 April 1971, BBC1.
28. *Daily Telegraph*, television review, 22 April 1971.
29. *Daily Express*, television review, 22 April 1971.
30. *Times*, television review, 22 April 1971.
31. Letter from David Keddie to Sir John Waldron, 23 April 1971, MEPO 28/8.

32. *Murder in the Fourth Estate* by Peter Deeley and Christopher Walker (Victor Gollancz, 1971), p. 45.
33. *Fact, Fiction amd Foul Deeds: The History of a Hertfordshire Village* by David D. Bailey (Stocking Pelham Millennium Committee, 2000), p. 61.
34. Author interview with Freida Hosein, 5 April 2022.
35. *Daily Mail*, 28 July 1971, p. 12.
36. Letter from Chief Inspector A.P. Roberts, Gwynedd Constabulary, Abergele, to Chief Superintendent, Llandudno, 17 December 1971, MEPO 26/29.
37. *Daily Mirror*, 19 October 1971, p. 5.
38. *Herts and Essex Observer*, 8 October 1971, p. 4.
39. *Ibid.*, 9 March 1973, p. 1.
40. Statement of Anthony John Wyatt, J 267/122.
41. Psychiatric report by B.L.M. Turner, Senior Medical Officer, HMP Brixton, 16 November 1972, J 267/122.
42. *Daily Mail*, 8 January 1973, p. 11.
43. *The Hate Factory: Thirty Years Inside with the UK's Most Notorious Villains* by David Leslie (Mainstream, 2010), Ch. 16.
44. *A View of Epping Forest* by Nicholas Hagger (O Books, 2012).
45. Letter from DCS Wilfred Smith to Commander, C2, 23 September 1975, MEPO 26/29.
46. *Ibid.*, 19 May 1976, MEPO 26/29.
47. Letter from Nizamodeen Hosein to David McNee, Metropolitan Police Commissioner, 9 February 1979, CRIM 1/5395.
48. Letter from Commander Williams to Commander Lampard, 9 April 1979, CRIM 1/5395.
49. Author interview with Freida Hosein, 5 April 2022.
50. Letter from Arthur Hosein to the registrar, Court of Appeal, Criminal Division, 15 July 1980, J 82/1578.
51. Author interview with Dianne McKay, 2 May 2022.
52. Letter from Douglas Batten to the Commissioner, Metropolitan Police, 31 March 1981, MEPO 26/29.
53. Letter from DS Rose, M Division, to Chief Superintendent, M Division, 8 June 1981, MEPO 26/29.
54. *Sunday Express*, 2 February 1981.
55. Anonymous letter to New Scotland Yard, postmarked 6 July 1981, MEPO 26/29.
56. Witness statement of Anne Maria Stout, 6 August 1987, Thames Valley Police, MEPO 26/29.
57. Letter from DI Fitzgerald to Commander, Organised Crime Group, 13 November 1996, MEPO 26/29.
58. Ed Devereaux, interviewed in *Daily Mail*, 17 October 1992, p. 32.
59. Author interview with Roger Street, 2 July 2021.
60. *Sunday Mirror*, 12 March 1995, p. 9.

61. Death certificate for Arthur Hosein, B62D/ 531/1B/125, County of Hertfordshire, 6 March 2007.
62. Death certificate for Mubarak K. Liley Mohammed, B61/ 2551B/ 58, London Borough of Waltham Forest, May 2001.
63. Author interview with Aubrey Rose, 11 November 2021.
64. Author interview with Freida Hosein, 5 April 2022.
65. *Daily Sketch*, 7 October 1970, p. 13.
66. Arthur Hosein, 23 September 1970, J82/1578 *Regina vs Hosein*, trial transcript, Vol. 8, p. 3.
67. *Shall We Ever Know?* by William Cooper (Hutchison & Co., 1971), p. 151.
68. Dianne McKay, interviewed on *Woman's Hour*, BBC Radio 4, 19 January 2022.

Chapter 18: Legacy

1. 'I Want Answers to Mum's Kidnap and Death', *Times*, 26 August 2021.
2. *Sun*, 2 January 1970, p. 3.
3. 'Muriel McKay's Kidnap Killer Reveals Burial Place After 51 Years', *Times*, 18 December 2021.
4. *Trinidad and Tobago Guardian*, 16 January 2022.
5. *Ibid*.
6. Author interview with Norie Miles, 18 May 2022.
7. Letter from Cressida Dick to Dianne McKay, 2 February 2022.
8. Witness statement of Detective Chief Superintendent Bill Smith, 3 March 1970, MEPO 26/29.
9. Author interview with Nizamodeen Hosein, 14 May 2022.

Chapter 19: Conclusions

1. Author interview with Roger Street, 2 July 2021.
2. Author interview with Paul Bickley, 7 July 2021.
3. Witness statement of Adam Hosein, 12 February 1970, MEPO 26/29.
4. *Ibid*.
5. Email to author from Clive Stafford Smith, 10 May 2022.
6. *Telegraph India*, 15 October 2004.
7. *Shall We Ever Know?* by William Cooper (Hutchison & Co., 1971), p. 129.
8. Author interview with Aubrey Rose, 11 November 2021.
9. Letter from DCS Wilfred Smith to Commander, C2, 19 May 1976, MEPO 26/29.
10. Author interview with Dr Dominic Watt, 4 February 2022.
11. Author interview with Freida Hosein, 5 April 2022.
12. *The Rise and Fall of the Murdoch Empire* by John Lisners, (John Blake, 2012), p. 122.
13. *Ibid*., p. 126.

14. Interview with Elisabeth Hosein, conducted by DCS Ron Harvey, 9 February 1970.
15. Email to author from Austin Graham, general manager, London Victoria Casino, 15 December 2021.
16. Witness statement of Margaret Ramdye Ramkalawan, 6 March 1970, MEPO 26/31.
17. *The Murder of Muriel McKay* by Norman Lucas (Mayflower, 1971), p. 175.
18. Author interview with Tom Mangold, 9 May 2022.
19. M3 call to Ian McKay, 3 February 1970, terminating at 1.30 p.m.
20. Email to author from Freedom of Information assessor, 7 March 2021.
21. Witness statement of Sylvia Millicent Hunt, 19 February 1970, MEPO 26/29.
22. Witness statement of Margaret Ramdye Ramkalawan, 6 March 1970, MEPO 26/31.
23. Witness statement of Ernest Walter Woollard, 9 February 1970, MEPO 26/33.
24. Witness statement of James McGowan Eggenton, 10 February 1970, MEPO 26/33.
25. Author interview with NHS worker (anonymous), 18 May 2022.
26. 'R. v Hosein and Hosein' by Barry Hudson QC, *Medico-Legal Journal*, Vol. 40, p. 130.
27. Witness statement of Margery Nightingale, 6 January 1970, MEPO 26/30.
28. *24 Hours: Worse Than Murder*, 21 April 1971, BBC1.
29. Author interview with Nizamodeen Hosein, 14 May 2022.
30. Witness statement of Alfred Anderson, 19 April 1970, MEPO 26/33.
31. Witness statement of Mubarak Khartoun Liley Mohammed, 1 March 1970, MEPO 26/33.
32. Witness statement of Harold George Prime, 17 February 1970, MEPO 26/31.
33. Gerald Gordon, 23 September 1970, J82/1578, *Regina vs Hosein*, trial transcript, Vol. 8, p. 45.
34. Witness statement of Joyce Adele Smith, 17 February 1970, MEPO 26/31.
35. Author interview with Nizamodeen Hosein, 14 May 2022.
36. *Ibid*.
37. Nizamodeen Hosein, 28 September 1970, J82/1578 *Regina vs Hosein*, trial transcript, Vol. 11, p. 9.
38. Bill Smith, interviewed on *24 Hours: Worse Than Murder*, 21 April 1971, BBC1.
39. Witness statement of George Rattray Duncan, 13 February, MEPO 26/31.
40. Elsa Hosein, 23 September 1970, J82/1578 *Regina vs Hosein*, trial transcript, Vol. 8, p. 53.
41. *Birmingham Post*, 28 December 1979, p. 4.
42. Bill Smith, interviewed on *24 Hours: Worse Than Murder*, 21 April 1971, BBC1.
43. Bill Smith, interviewed on *Manhunt: The Press Baron's Wife*, ITV, 27 November 2001.
44. Author interview with Tom Mangold, 9 May 2022.

Chapter 20: Last Resort

1. *Sun*, 23 December 1969, p. 21.
2. Letter from Arthur Hosein to the Court of Appeal, 30 October 1972, J82/1578.
3. Letter from assistant registrar, Court of Appeal, to Arthur Hosein, 21 November 1972, J82/1578.
4. Letter from George Brown to assistant registrar, Court of Appeal, 24 November 1972, J82/1578.
5. Email to author from Roger Street, 6 September 2021.
6. Letter from assistant registrar, Court of Appeal, to George Brown, 30 November 1972, J82/1578.
7. Email to author from Colin Parker, 15 October 2021.
8. *Ibid.*, 18 October 2021.
9. Author interview with Peter Rimmer, 13 September 2021.
10. Author interview with Brian Roberts, 1 November 2021.
11. HMP Wakefield Visitors' Book, November 1972–January 1973, West Yorkshire Archives, C118/A/Box4.
12. Email to author from Abbi Leckebusch, archivist, West Yorkshire History Centre, 8 November 2021.
13. Email to author from Professor Patricia Wiltshire, 11 November 2021.
14. Email to author from Williams Stevens, Jaywick Local History Society, 27 July 2022

Afterword

1. *Guardian*, 27 October 2021.

INDEX

Numbers in *italic* refer to images in the text; *fn* refers to a page's footnote.

The History Press
The destination for history
www.thehistorypress.co.uk